Maqām
and
Liturgy

Raphael Patai Series in Jewish Folklore and Anthropology

A complete listing of the books in this series can be found online at wsupress.wayne.edu

Maqām and Liturgy

Ritual, Music, and Aesthetics of Syrian Jews in Brooklyn

Mark L. Kligman

Wayne State University Press
Detroit

Manufactured in the United States of America.

13 12 11 10 09 5 4 3 2 1

Library of Congress Cataloging-in-Publication Data

Kligman, Mark L., 1962–
Maqām and liturgy : ritual, music, and aesthetics of Syrian Jews in Brooklyn / Mark L. Kligman.
p. cm. — (Raphael Patai series in Jewish folklore and anthropology)
Includes bibliographical references and index.
ISBN 978-0-8143-3216-0 (cloth : alk. paper)
1. Jews, Syrian—New York (State)—New York—Music—History and criticism. 2. Jews, Syrian—New York (State)—New York—Identity. 3. Maqām—New York (State)—New York. 4. Arabs—Syria—Music—History and criticism. 5. Sabbath—Liturgy. 6. Shaharit. I. Title.

ML3195.K55 2009
296.4'50899275691074723—dc22
2008020369

∞

Publication of this book was made possible through the generosity of the Bertha M. and Hyman Herman Endowed Memorial Fund.

Designed and typeset by Anna Oler
Composed in Minion and Present

To my parents, Leonard and Sandra Kligman,
and my parents-in-law, Herbert and Sonia Abrams:
your enduring love and support is timeless.

Contents

Illustrations

PHOTOGRAPHS

FIGURES

CHARTS

Musical Examples

Tables

Acknowledgments

THIS BOOK BEGAN as doctoral research and would not have been possible without the assistance of many people at various stages of the process. First, a big thanks to Kay Kaufman Shelemay who led me to the Syrian liturgical tradition as an outgrowth of her own work. I am forever grateful for her guidance in opening new doors to study Jewish music. She oversaw the writing of my dissertation and has continued to be supportive. Her warmth and encouragement aided the course of this study and stand as a model for me to carry in the future.

A special thanks to the many members of the Syrian community for sharing their liturgical tradition with me. Cantors Moses and David Tawil and Isaac Cabasso unselfishly provided me with their expertise and love of Syrian liturgy. They have been supportive of my work for many years. I hope this study will add to the legacy. I would also like to express my appreciation to the many members of Congregation Beth Torah for welcoming me to the synagogue. Joe Bijou, Isaac Ades, and Rabbi Ralph Tawil enlightened me with their life experiences. Rabbi Zevulun Lieberman graciously answered my questions concerning Beth Torah's history and the Syrian community. My thanks to the members of the Pizmonim class 1991–92 for making me feel welcome and for answering my many inquiries. Ted Bush of the Sephardic Community Center aided my access to recordings in the Sephardic archives. Hakki Obadia, my 'ud teacher helped me learn Arabic music; I am most appreciative of his assistance with transcription of Arabic songs used in this study.

A special thanks to Sheila Schweky, daughter of Moses Tawil, who has helped with the completion of this book in a caring and supportive manner. She assisted me in obtaining photographs and in countless ways with many final details.

Funding for this project was made possible through grants from the Memorial Foundation for Jewish Culture, for the years 1992–93 and 1993–94, and the National Foundation for Jewish Culture, for the academic year 1992–93.

To the administration and faculty of Hebrew Union College—Jewish Institute of Religion, especially Dr. Norman Cohen, Cantor Israel Goldstein, and Cantor Dr. Bruce Ruben, my heartfelt appreciation for their flexibility in allowing me the needed time to complete this study and for financial support for my ongoing research.

My understanding of Judaic sources was broadened with the help of Dr. Moshe Sokol and Rabbis David Barnett, David Levine, and Fyvel Schuster. Professors Rosalie Kamelhar and Stanley Nash reviewed my translations of Hebrew texts used in this study.

Many assisted with useful and informative comments after reading earlier drafts: Professors Eliyahu Schleifer, Edwin Seroussi, and Rolf Groesbeck, as well as my colleagues Judah Cohen and Marion Jacobson. Professor Walter Zenner, of blessed memory, provided access to his studies of the Syrian community by furnishing me with copies of his articles. Many of our conversations helped form my ideas in this research. Mason Resnick assisted me in the formatting the photographs contained in this book.

A special thanks to the talented and professional team at Wayne State University Press that helped make this publication possible—Kristin Harpster Lawrence, Anna Vitale, and Kathryn Wildfong.

Support and encouragement were provided by many friends: Sara and Bernie Weinstein, Deena and Chet Edelman, David Barnet, Zev Mydlarz, Michael Rabin, Howie Sherman, and my siblings (Yocheved, Elissa, and Larry). My family's ongoing reassurance was a source of strength; my parents, Leonard and Sandra, and my in-laws, Herbert and Sonia Abrams, your love and support is a gift. To my children, Yonina Rachel and Shmuel Nissim: thank you for understanding my many busy times at home.

Last, and by no means least, to my wife, Jessica: thank you for your multifaceted assistance with editing earlier drafts, translating Hebrew texts, and transcribing recordings. You provided words of encouragement when I needed them, and always helped to put things into perspective. Most of all, your care, concern, and love have been a constant source of inspiration. Without your help this book would not have been possible.

Introduction

The Spontaneity of Prayer

On a Saturday morning in Brooklyn in the fall of 1991, during my initial fieldwork on this topic, a non-Syrian guest joined a member of a Syrian synagogue for the morning service. I sat behind these two men and listened intently as the Syrian man described the service to his friend. His comments focused on the various events of the service; he pointed out when in the service the congregation sings and when they listen, when they sit and when they stand. I found these comments particularly insightful since they provided some order to what otherwise might have seemed chaotic. Before the *ḥazzan* (cantor) began the main part of the morning service (Shaḥarit), our unintentional guide said of the music, "There is this excitement with what comes next, because *it* is not the same from week to week." Like the non-Syrian guest, I paid particular attention to these comments. At first I thought the "it" in his description referred to the melodies the *ḥazzan* sings; the Syrian man went on to describe to his friend that the congregation was never sure what melody the *ḥazzan* was going to sing until it happened. Later I discovered that the dynamic nature of the Syrian cantor's musical rendering of the service goes well beyond singing different melodies. I set out to study the nature of Syrian prayers, to learn the rules that cantors must follow in their rendering of the service, and to understand the role of music in the worship experience.

My knowledge of Syrian liturgy grew rapidly through my many encounters with Syrian cantors. I learned that the *maqāmāt* (Arab modal system; sing., *maqām*) play a crucial role in organizing the music in the liturgy, that Arab music serves as the source for music in the liturgy, and, most important, that a cantor needs to deliver the liturgical text sweetly, to assist and inspire others in their prayers. Moses Tawil, my main informant, is a Syrian cantor who has lived and served the community for decades. He was born in Brooklyn, made his living as a businessman, and is now retired. In addition to his ongoing fundraising efforts for synagogues and educational institutions in the community, Cantor Tawil is actively engaged in perpetuating the Syrian cantorial tradition. Tawil's father was born in Aleppo and immigrated to America in early 1913. The Tawil family is dedicated to Jewish tradition in religious practices, learning, and the singing of music. Tawil is considered by members of the community to be a leading figure in Syrian *ḥazzanut* (cantorial artistry); he is responsible for training Syrian cantors in Brooklyn. He started a cantorial school in Brooklyn to perpetuate the Syrian cantorial tradition.

During my first meeting with Tawil on August 21, 1991, and every one thereafter, I noted his pride in the Syrian tradition. In each of our conversations Tawil discussed the *maqāmāt.* The *maqāmāt* play a central role in organizing and structuring Syrian liturgy. In fact, the *maqāmāt* are so significant that Tawil singled them out when distinguishing Syrian liturgy from Ashkenazic and other Sephardic traditions, saying, "Our minhagim are unique in the way in which we use *maqām* [in the prayers]. . . . It's mind-boggling. When I spoke to some Ashkenazim [Ashkenazic Jews] recently, they said, 'Aren't you afraid you will lose some of your beautiful minhagim, this your beautiful traditions that you have?' and I told them we're not because so long as we are adhering to the *maqām* we only gain and we don't lose. In other words, we are not giving up anything" (M. Tawil, interview, June 6, 1993).

The interactive relationship between music and text in the liturgy stood out in my conversations with Syrian cantors. The cantor's goal is to express musically the meaning of the liturgical text. The characteristics of a *maqām,* such as its "flavor" and unique scalar qualities, are incorporated into Syrian liturgy in a complex manner. Ḥazzan David Tawil, Moses Tawil's younger brother and a respected cantor and teacher in the Syrian community, comments: "*Yitgadal v'Yitkadash* [extol and sanctify] . . . we bless Him with or praise Him with the most grandiose ways possible.[1] So we use melodic systems that are long and so on: very expressive, very differentiating, extensive in octave. It's not only a [single] chord, a tetrachord that we use.[2] You'll find that we'll jump from one to two and sometimes even to a third tetrachord to give the expression of the music. Because of the grandiose [nature] of God's blessing at this point" (D. Tawil, interview, July 29, 1992). Praising and extolling God is done through elaborate musical means. Musical characteristics associated with a *maqām,* such as moving between the tetrachords of a *maqām,* convey the meaning of the text. *Maqām* plays a central role in defining, organizing, and expressing Syrian liturgy.

Providing both spontaneity in the service and expression of the liturgical text through a *maqām* remain the central challenges for Syrian cantors. The cantor's particular manner of melodic expression applied to designated sections within the morning liturgy makes this Jewish liturgy uniquely Syrian. The music is informed by melodies, performance practices, and theoretical concerns of Arab provenance. In contrast, the text of the liturgy follows the broader Jewish tradition. Arab music and the Jewish text inform one another in multiple dimensions. The process of synthesis between music and text, informed by Arab and Jewish elements, is at the heart of this study.

Syrian Sabbath Morning Service

THE SYRIAN JEWS in Brooklyn, New York, number more than forty thousand and constitute the largest single group of Jews from Syria in the world.[3] Members of the Syrian community have emigrated from two centers in Syria—Aleppo and Damascus—beginning shortly after the turn of the twentieth century and continuing to the present. Both groups maintain a common tradition, yet they see themselves as different from each other. For example, the two groups maintain separate synagogues within close proximity to each other in Brooklyn. Most Syrian Jews seek to maintain their particular identity through their religious institutions (synagogues and schools) and social affiliations with other members of the Syrian community. There are fifteen Syrian synagogues in the Flatbush section of Brooklyn, thirteen follow the Aleppo tradition and two follow the Damascus tradition (D. Tawil, interview, July 29, 1992). The Jews from Aleppo are the focus of this study. That is, in denoting Syrian Jews in Brooklyn, I refer to members of the Jewish religion who are immigrants from Aleppo and their descendants.

The Sabbath morning service for Aleppo Syrian Jews is more musically elaborate than both the Friday evening (Arvit) and Saturday afternoon (Minḥa) services. The Sabbath morning service includes the prayers for Shaḥarit, Musaf, and four other liturgical sections (Birkhot ha-Shaḥar, Zemirot, Torah reading, and the sermon, an optional spoken section). Each section of the Sabbath morning service is unique in terms of the type of musical or verbal delivery, and Shaḥarit, containing mandated ritual components, is the service's main liturgical section. Several musical rendering styles are used in Sabbath morning liturgy—reciting of melodic formulas, singing melodies, and improvisation of *maqāmāt*—depending on the needs of the various liturgical sections. The influence of Arab music in the liturgy can be seen in melodies, extramusical associations, performance practices, and aesthetics. That is, Syrian liturgy is revealing of Arab musical use in a Jewish context, and the result is a Judeo-Arab synthesis.

A Note on Research Process and Method

I BECAME INTERESTED in studying Syrian liturgy for several reasons. As an ethnomusicologist I wanted to carry out fieldwork in Jewish liturgical music where I could be, in some form, the "other." Since I am an Ashkenazic Jew who is observant in a traditional fashion, a topic centered on Sephardic music would situate me as a partial outsider.[4] On a personal level, I have always been interested in the role of music and religion, and I wanted to explore this topic in a reflexive manner, not only as an observer, but, more important, as a participant. I entered the New York University doctoral program the year after the conclusion of a team research project of the Syrian *pizmon* (paraliturgical songs sung in the synagogue and at life cycle events). My advisor, Kay Kaufman Shelemay, and the students participating in the project carved a path for a broader liturgical study.

I first attended a Syrian Sabbath service in the spring of 1990 and was immediately struck by the enthusiasm of the members of the congregation during the service, as well as the manner in which the music was an intrinsic part of worship. As I discovered how Syrians pray, I learned about individuals and their love of Jewish life, in addition to their knowledge of music and religion. This also allowed me the opportunity to reflect on my own religious tradition. Similar experiences are described by other insiders who studied Jewish culture (see Heilman 1976 and 1982 for studies of synagogue life; Kugelmass 1988 for a collection of ethnographic essays; Summit 2000 on contemporary Jewish worship; and Koskoff 2001 on Lubavitch Hassidim).

This study is based primarily on ethnographic materials gathered through participant observation at Sabbath services, interviews with cantors and other members of the community, and private *ūd* lessons. Beginning in August 1991, I studied the liturgical tradition with respected lay cantors. I conducted multiple interviews with Cantors Moses Tawil, David Tawil, and Isaac Cabasso. Our meetings focused on the cantor's responsibilities for Sabbath morning prayers, and Moses Tawil taught through example. He sang portions of the liturgy; I subsequently tried to replicate what he taught me. I recorded each session, and portions of the transcript of our interactions appear in the text of this study. David Tawil recommended that I study the *ūd*, stating that learning the *ūd* was essential to acquire an understanding of the *maqāmāt*. Additionally, he recommended a specific teacher, Hakki Obadia, who has ongoing contact with the Syrian community.[5] I also attended and participated in cantorial classes that trained young men, ages twenty through forty, in *pizmon* melodies and their application to the liturgy. These classes were taught by Ḥazzan Isaac Cabasso from November 1991 through March 1992. The discussions in the class allowed me to witness how the Syrian liturgical tradition is acquired, transmitted, and maintained. Additionally, I made use of liturgical recordings available at the Sephardic Archives of the Sephardic Center in Brooklyn.[6] The initial phase of this research culminated in my doctoral dissertation (Kligman 1997). Since then I have continued working with members of the community, including service as a research consultant for a video taping of the community for the Milken Family Foundation on October 6, 1999 (a weekday evening where recording was permissible). The Sabbath morning service and Rosh ha-Shanah prayers were also recorded, and material from these tapes is included in this study. I have also published several articles and chapters focusing on general aspects of Jewish life in Brooklyn (Zenner and Kligman 2000), the *maqāmāt* (2001), psalm chanting (2003), organization of the Sabbath ritual (2005), and the Judeo-Arab synthesis (2005–2006).

To more fully understand the complexity of the Syrian Sabbath service I chose to attend weekly Sabbath morning services for a full liturgical Jewish year. I participated in Sabbath services at Congregation Beth Torah, as well other holidays and occasionally weekday services, from September 1991 through September 1992. I also attended services at many of the other Syrian synagogues.

Located at 1061 Ocean Parkway, Beth Torah was established in 1958. Services were first held at a social club half a block from the site of the current building, which was completed in 1969. The majority of the founding members of Beth Torah are of Aleppo descent and longtime residents of other nearby sections of Brooklyn. Other members of the synagogue include Sephardic Jews and their descendants from such diverse locales as Israel, Iraq, Iran, Greece, Morocco, and Tunisia. While Syrian members of the congregation explicitly state that Beth Torah is open to any Jew, the synagogue's careful adherence to the customs of Aleppo particularly attracts those of Syrian descent. Rabbi Zevulun Lieberman and Ḥazzan Isaac Cabasso began their positions at the inception of the synagogue and were Beth Torah's religious leaders for over three decades; Rabbi Lieberman retired in 1998. The rabbi's position is paid. Ḥazzan Cabasso is also a businessman in the garment district of New York City. Since 1990 Beth Torah employed a second *ḥazzan*, Yeḥezkiel Zion, who grew up in Israel and was retrained in the Brooklyn Syrian liturgical practices. Other Syrian rabbis and learned lay people in the community involve themselves with Beth Torah, including David Tawil, who instructs men in recitation of prayer, reading of the Torah, and studying rabbinic texts.[7] I occasionally attended these classes.

Present-day ethnographers are self-conscious both about their role as researchers and the relationships they build with the individuals they study, including the manner in which both are represented in their scholarly writings (see Clifford 1988; Seeger 1988; Turino 1993; Barz and Cooley 1997). Ethnographers use the term "participant observation" to describe interaction in fieldwork. The fact that I am a Jewish male who is religiously observant in the Ashkenazic tradition was important for this study. Both my gender and traditional observance of Judaism provided access to Syrian services and traditions. My gender enabled me to observe and participate in the Sabbath services; women sit in a separate section in Syrian synagogues and cannot be religious officiants. My status as an observant Jew facilitated my efforts to gain the congregants' and leaders' respect and ensured some degree of acceptance—although this came about only after they tested my Jewish and musical knowledge. I was often informally quizzed on my understanding of Arab music, particularly in regard to knowledge of the *maqām* system. During the six-month period of the *pizmonim* class after Sabbath morning services, members of the class often gathered to discuss the *ḥazzan*'s performance of Shaḥarit. I was asked on several occasions if I could identify the melodies employed during the service and the change in the *maqāmāt* throughout the service. Ironically, my degree of acceptance among Syrians was due in large part to my traditional status as an Ashkenazic Jew. I came to this study with Jewish liturgical experience, so cantors did not have to provide me with liturgical textual knowledge.[8] I was continually reminded by virtually all research associates that I was Ashkenazic. Moses Tawil would take great pride in his Aleppo heritage and would frequently say, "You Ashkenazim do . . ." to show his clear preference for his own tradition in opposition to my own.

A useful characterization of my status is expressed by Lila Abu-Lughod's use of the term "halfie," people whose national or cultural identity is mixed by virtue of migration, overseas education, or parentage (1991, 146). I was accepted as a Jew but not given the same status as a Syrian Jew. Just as Jeffrey A. Summit viewed his role as a "guest observer and a participant" and reflects on the careful treading as an insider (2000, 5–8), I was of the same religious heritage as the Syrians but not the same ethnic heritage. The relationships that emerged between members of the community and myself were all influenced by my status as an observant Jew, reminding me of the importance of negotiating a relationship between the scholar and those who are studied (Daniel 1984, 43; see also Barz and Cooley 1997). As a result, there were some questions regarding religious observance and the historical background of prayers that I felt I could not pose to individuals in the Syrian community. On occasions when I did inquire, I was often met with the expectation that I already knew the answers to these questions and told that they were not capable of answering them for me. (Perhaps, if I were not a religious male I would have received answers.) As a result, many of my remarks on religious observance are taken from my observations rather than collected from interview information. Additionally, since I am not Syrian and not studying to be a cantor, I occasionally met with some resistance whereby information was not furnished to me. Nevertheless, through forging a relationship with cantors who did willingly give of their time and experiences, I was able to draw from their insights and experiences to gather material for this study.

Recent ethnographic studies call for researchers to convey the research experience more fully and allow insiders to speak for themselves (Clifford and Marcus 1986; Clifford 1988). I have chosen to include my experiences through observations and quotations, including extended excerpts from interviews in order to better represent the people with whom I studied. The questions I asked are often included in the text to document my interaction with members of the Syrian community, rendering the ethnographic process part of the written record of this study.

Fieldworkers customarily make use of audio or visual recordings in addition to writing notes that are later expanded. On some occasions I was unable to follow these common documentary practices and had to devise other solutions. To wit, audio recordings on the Sabbath are prohibited by Jewish law. The Syrians, who strictly adhere to religious precepts for the Sabbath, would not allow recordings of the liturgy at that time; likewise, my own practice precludes recording and taking notes on the Sabbath. Furthermore, it is difficult to convey the "actual" experience since the ritual activity involves interaction between the cantor and the congregation.[9] To circumvent these problems I requested that the cantors record material for me outside the context of a service and then I would place these recordings in context with my many observations of Sabbath morning services. At the beginning, I found it difficult to remember many specific events from the three-hour morning service. However, after repeated attendance at Beth Torah I became familiar with the liturgy and was able to concentrate on specific sections of the service. During the period of fieldwork, I wrote down my observations after sundown on Saturday night. In a sense, I lived with my fieldwork for an entire day each week, making it part of my personal routine. My attendance at Sabbath service was not just to observe but also to participate. I prayed and sang with the congregation. This role as participant-observer helped to forge relationships with members of the community and to deepen my understanding of their liturgy. At first it seemed as if the music and the liturgy were a mysterious puzzle. Many of the complexities still remain in my thinking about the Syrian tradition, but the spontaneous nature of the service and intense joy that I encounter praying in Syrian services was an important part of my experience. This book is an effort to document my experience with Syrian cantors and their liturgy. Although I have become accustomed to knowing "what comes next" when attending Syrian liturgy, the excitement for me will always remain "because *it* is not the same from week to week."

Organization of the Book

THE CHAPTERS OF this book are organized to trace a Judeo-Arab cultural synthesis in the Syrian liturgy by focusing on the interaction of music and text. Part 1 provides background on my approach to the research. In chapter 1 the theoretical framework of cultures in contact through music serves as a foundation for the investigation. Chapter 2 establishes a historical and social context for Jewish and Arab culture contact before focusing on the current community's setting in Brooklyn. Background on Jewish liturgy appears in chapter 3, which elucidates the textual features of liturgy and relevant textual processes for paraliturgical purposes. Part 2 describes the Sabbath morning ritual. Chapter 4 focuses on the music life of Syrian Jews in Brooklyn and particularly emphasizes their practice of the *maqāmāt* system. A detailed discussion of the interaction of music and text in the Sabbath morning liturgy is set forth in chapters 5–9 with musical components illustrated by specific examples. Part 3 depicts the Judeo-Arab synthesis in Syrian liturgy. Chapter 10 focuses especially on the *maqām* and biblical reading associations that organize the use of the *maqāmāt* in the liturgy. Chapter 11 is a discussion of broader aesthetic elements and the maintenance of the tradition. The effectiveness of this interaction within the service, and other parts of Syrian religious life, is contextualized within a larger cultural framework of a Jewish and Arab synthesis, which is offered as a conclusion.

Part One

Background

1

Cultures in Contact through Music

ETHNOMUSICOLOGISTS VIEW RITUAL in its performative sense to show parallels with other cultural domains, including aesthetics (Feld 1982 [1990]), social relationships (Seeger 1988), beliefs (Titon 1988), and healing practices (Roseman 1991). With a focus on process or enactment of ritual, I endeavor to explore the interconnection between ritual, music, and culture and to provide a descriptive account not only of Syrian Sabbath liturgy but of how the music in the liturgy functions as a cultural system. The following questions guide this study: Since Syrian Jews in Brooklyn are primarily descendants of immigrants, why do they persist to pray in a decidedly Middle Eastern fashion? Does the retention of Arab music and aesthetics merely reflect a perpetuation of the past, or does it shape their particular Jewish identity and religious, cultural experience? To what extent can the religion and culture of Syrian Jews be separated, both historically and in the present?

The aesthetic synthesis of Arab music in a Jewish liturgical context is a reflection of Syrian Jewish identity. The musical rendering of the ritual provides a forum in which Syrian Jews may act out their identity as a people who historically lived in an Arab land and now live in America. My focus in this study is the musical process of prayer: how prayer is rendered and how it reveals Arab musical aesthetics deeply embedded in Syrian Jewish life in Brooklyn.

Previous studies of the Syrian liturgical tradition have not considered the Sabbath service in detail (e.g., Idelsohn 1923a, 1923b; Nulman 1977–78).[1] Paraliturgical aspects of the Syrian tradition have been considered with regard to two song genres, *bakkashot* (supplicatory poetry sung before prayers) (e.g., Katz 1968; G. Goldberg 1988; Yayama 2003) and *pizmonim* (e.g., Shelemay

1988, 1994, 1998). Kay Kaufman Shelemay's book *Let Jasmine Rain Down* explores the merging of Arab and Jewish traditions in this repertory and its multiple signification in Syrian Jewish life in Brooklyn. Other scholarly inquiries concerning the life and history of this community have been limited (e.g., Zenner 1965, 328–64; Zenner 1983; M. Sanua 1990; Zenner and Kligman 2000).[2] Joseph A. D. Sutton's studies portray the history and life of Aleppo Jews in Aleppo and Brooklyn and is written from his perspective as a member of the community (1979, 1988).

Studies of Sephardic liturgical music, although not plentiful, do document various Jewish Middle Eastern traditions. Abraham Zvi Idelsohn discusses the role of *maqām* in various Sephardic liturgical traditions, including Syrian (1923a, 20–120; 1923b, 43–120; 1929, 24–71). Amnon Shiloah also discusses the use of *maqām* in liturgical and paraliturgical traditions (1992, 125–26, 151). Edwin Seroussi looks at the practice of *maqām* among Jews in Turkey (1990b) and the life of a Turkish Sephardic cantor (1989); elsewhere he discusses contemporary studies of Sephardic liturgical tradition in Israel and other countries (1993b, 62–65). Ezra Barnea looks at the practice of Yerushalmi Sephardim, Middle Eastern cantors in Israel, and stresses the significant influence of cantors from Aleppo (1996–97). Mark Slobin only briefly considers the Sephardic cantorate in his study of the American cantorate (1989, 206–8). Drawing on these studies, I show how the liturgical tradition is situated in the Jewish tradition.

Investigations of Middle Eastern Jewish musical practices, beyond the liturgical context, are few. Idelsohn comments on Middle Eastern practices, labeling them as "Oriental." Volume 4 of his *Hebräish-orientalisher Melodienschatz* (Thesaurus of Hebrew and Oriental melodies; 1923a, 1923b) discusses the music of Syrian Jews, and his seminal study *Jewish Music in Its Historical Development* (1929) also includes Syrian Jewish liturgical comments. While Idelsohn considers Arab musical elements, a fuller treatment is found in Robert Lachman's *Jewish Cantillation and Song in the Isle of Djerba* (1940). Seroussi's studies on North African and Ottoman liturgical music document a range of musical activity (1985, 1989, 1990b, 1999, 2000; see also Shiloah and Cohen 1983). Middle Eastern Jews from the Levant had shared musical practices and under Ottoman rule were influenced by their surroundings. Prior to the twentieth century active social interaction among Jews, Christians, and Muslims shows deep intimate contact in linguistic sharing and musical practices, including liturgical (Quataert 2000, 179). In the twentieth century Jews from the Levant integrated their liturgical customs and became known as Yerushalmi Sephardim. In terms of musical practices of the liturgy, the Aleppo tradition had a significant influence. Ezra Barnea, *ḥazzan* and educator of Middle Eastern cantorial practices, explains:

> The great turning point occurred (to my humble opinion) at the beginning of the century with the *aliyah* [arrival in Israel] of those from Aleppo and Aram Zoba [biblical name for Aleppo] who, among other things, are known as followers of tradition in song and piyyut. The melody of the *bakkashot* that they brought with them, was continued in the old city. The melody of the *bakkashot* attracted *hazzanim* and scholars of Torah and it was pleasant to hear these new melodies. The new melodies were absorbed into sections of the prayer as was the Sephardic song which had been dominant in the synagogue. Only a minority continued with the previous tradition. (1996–97, 22)

Barnea also states that melodies and practices from Aleppo significantly changed the practices of Persian and Bukaharian immigrants (23). Thus the Aleppo tradition in Israel was a significant force (see also Shelemay 1998, 83). The subject of musical interaction and change of Middle Eastern Israeli Jews is found in Amnon Shiloah and Eric Cohen's 1983 study. Israel is certainly the major source for twentieth-century Middle Eastern Jewry and has had a significant influence on Brooklyn Syrian Jews with the arrival of Israeli cantors (Shelemay 1998, 83–84). While Israel is an important center, Brooklyn Syrian Jews maintain their own Syrian style that is substantially similar to the practice of Yerushalmi Sephardim but slightly different. While I focus on the practice of Brooklyn Syrians, I do comment on some differences found in Israel.

Music and Ritual Process

MY APPROACH IS informed by recent ethnographic investigations that emphasize the "process," the manner of performance, of a cultural event rather than just text or music. Seminal studies following this approach include the investigation of ritual by anthropologists (Turner 1969; Ortner 1978; Rappaport 1979; Tambiah 1979) and the treatment of verbal performance by linguistic anthropologists (Bauman 1977; Briggs 1988; Bauman and Briggs 1990).[3] These studies focus on the nature of the performance of an event, the "how," to derive a process. Ethnomusicologists closely follow this performative approach to uncover a musical process; these studies use the term "ethnography of musical performance" (Herndon and McLeod 1980; Blacking 1981; Béhague 1984; Qureshi 1987; Seeger 1988; Wolf 2001). As Bruno Nettl explains, "If ethnomusicological research of the 1980s is distinct from what went before, it is distinguished chiefly by an increased interest in the study of processes, and of music as process rather than simply as product. Perhaps one can say that there is now more interest in how things happen than in how things are" (1992, 381). The musical performance of an event, the process, rather than the music itself, becomes the focus of study. An emphasis on "how things happen" allows not only for an inquiry of the various elements that constitute performance of the music but also an understanding of the creation and structure of music and ritual. Ethnomusicological perspectives are increasingly social, linking the structure and practice of musical performances and styles with music's deep embeddedness in local and translocal forms of social imagination, activity, and experience (Feld and Fox 1994, 25). Reaching beyond the music promotes further consideration of the role of music in culture. This allows the explanation of such issues as conceptualization of self, meaning, and worldview, all of which are at the center of investigation in recent ethnomusicological studies.

Ritual provides a context for investigating the use of music as a process and reflects some unique aspect of culture. In the case of Syrian Jews, their Judeo-Arab synthesis is an activity expressed "only in ritual" (Rappaport 1979, 173) and allows one to "experience what thought cannot frame" (Wagner 1984, 145). When looking at both the Arab and Jewish elements in the Sabbath morning service, the synthesis expresses and communicates the essential nature of the ritual, making the experience of prayer more meaningful. Arab music is the vehicle. Other aspects of Syrian life combine Arab and Jewish characteristics, but the Sabbath service, as an example of liturgy, holds a special place. Walter Paul Zenner's brief comment concerning music in the liturgy highlights this relationship: "The most Arab of cultural forms for Syrian Jews in Brooklyn is paradoxically one of the most Jewish" (2002, 166). In the Sabbath morning ritual, the Arab component of the ritual is located in the music, and the Jewish component is context.

The multidimensional interaction of music and text is at the core of this study. I will explore how the various means of musical expression match up with the ritual structure, how the text informs the music, and how the music conveys the meaning of the text (Feld and Fox 1994). In addition to the descriptive features revealed in the interaction of music and language, the functional aspects of music in the context of a ritual are also significant. Charles Lafayette Boilès states, "It is possible to recognize to what degree the music itself is operative in the act. Is the power in the music itself and therefore, *concomitant* to the occasion? Or is the music an appropriate but non-essential aspect, merely *concurrent* for the purposes of the occasion?" (1978, 15). The function of music in Syrian liturgy is both concomitant and concurrent with the ritual occasion. It depends on the specific religious requirements or the desired goal of the liturgical section. In some instances, music serves as the primary conveyor of the needed emotion; at other times, musical formulas serve as the vehicle to recite the text. Different melodic styles are used for different parts of the service. The music is concurrent at the beginning and ending of the service, but concomitant in the middle. Shaḥarit is the highlight, since music in this section focuses on deeply conveying the meaning of the liturgy. This section led by the *ḥazzan* is the most elaborate. In Syrian liturgy, textual style and ritual function determine music's role, an idea that is explained further in chapter 9.

Musical Concerns That Inform the Ritual

THE ORDERLY USE of Arab melodies is the main musical process in the liturgy.[4] The *maqāmāt* organize the Arab melodies in the liturgy and integrate them into the service. The *maqām* system, as the primary organizational tool, provides a point of entry into a consideration of the Syrian liturgy and aesthetics. In fact, explication of Syrian liturgy through the use of *maqāmāt* is the only theoretically justifiable lens. A *maqām* not only describes the liturgy in musical terms but, perhaps more important, it aids in understanding the liturgy from the perspective of Syrian cantors. Cantors think in terms of adhering to a *maqām* while rendering prayers.

The music of the Syrian liturgy goes beyond the recycling of known melodies. Arab performance practices and aesthetics are also incorporated. For example, the recitation of the Qur'an and the singing of Arab songs both require interaction between the reader or singer and the listener. Likewise, Syrian cantors follow a set of rules for using melodies that facilitate congregational participation at specific points of the liturgy. Additionally, the presence of extramusical associations such as affective elements of the *maqāmāt* are a common feature.[5] Syrian Jews select a *maqām* according to extramusical associations of that mode in connection with the weekly biblical reading (see discussion in chapter 10). An investigation of Arab performance practices, musical aesthetics, and musical forms (such as the *waṣlah,* or suite) is an intrinsic part of considering the nature of Syrian prayers. The music of Syrian worship transforms Arab melodies in a new context. The use of both Arab musical elements and extramusical associations provides an opportunity to investigate the synthesis of Arab aesthetics in a Jewish religious context.

To consider Syrian Sabbath liturgy within the context of contemporary practice of Arab music, I draw upon the following areas of study: contemporary Arab usage of *maqāmāt* (Shiloah 1979, 1981; S. Marcus 1989, 1992); aesthetics of performance practice (Racy 1991a); improvisation (Touma 1976; al-Faruqi 1978); stylistic features related to Qur'anic recitation (Nelson 1982, 1985; al-Faruqi 1987); and adaptation of Arab musical genres (al-Faruqi 1981; Racy 1983; Danielson 1997).

The recycling of preexisting music in Syrian liturgy, the primary manner of musical acquisition, has numerous precedents in music history, and it is a well-researched topic in musical scholarship. This type of musical process, found in both Western and non-Western cultures, is often referred to as "borrowing." In musicological literature, the terms *contrafactum* and *parody* are used to describe this phenomenon in Western music (Schrade 1955; Lockwood 1966; Meyer 1967 [1994]; Burkholder 1995).

The term most often used by musicologists is *contrafactum,* the practice of composing new texts to older melodies (Falck 1980, 700). In the plainchant repertory, text for new feasts were "routinely adapted to older melodies" (ibid.). The source of the existing melody could be secular or sacred:

> As the term is used in the modern sense, no precise limits have been observed in the designation of a song or composition as contrafactum. There is no general agreement as to whether the term should be restricted to sacred adaptations of secular melodies, or the degree of correspondence necessary before a contrafactum becomes a free adaptation, or when conscious adaptation becomes coincidental similarity. In the strictest sense, a contrafactum would not only employ the melody, rhymes and metric scheme of the model, but would also be in some sense an adaptation of the meaning of the original poem. (Ibid.)

Strict usage of contrafactum by employing melody, rhyme, and metric scheme of the original does not happen often (ibid.).[6] Contrafactum is not used as regularly in contemporary Western music because of a focus on compositional uniqueness and originality.

The term *parody,* on the other hand, denotes the use of previously used but reworked music: "In Renaissance music the borrowing of material from one composition as the basis of another was commonplace. The essential feature of parody technique is that not merely a single part is appropriated to form a cantus firmus in the derived work, but the whole substance of the source—its themes, rhythms, chords and chord progressions—is absorbed into the new piece and subjected to free variation in such a way that a fusion of old and new elements is achieved" (Tilmouth 1980, 238). Although contrafactum and parody are similar phenomena in that they both refashion older material, the exact boundaries of the two are unclear (Picker 1980, 701).

In his aesthetic considerations of music in the twentieth century, Leonard Meyer lists four ways in which "art of other epochs has been used in the present: paraphrase, borrowing, simulation, and modeling" (1967 [1994], 195). Meyer is sensitive to the specific uses of recycled music in a new context and states that these four ways of alluding to the past overlap (195): they can "come together . . . within the oeuvre of a single artist and even within a single work of art" (209). While paraphrase and borrowing make use of specific existing material, simulation and modeling seek to adapt and reshape the old into a new context. Therefore, Meyer's four processes can be understood as a topology where one can situate a recycled work of music along a continuum from an exact use to a reworking of the material, surprisingly similar to the basic distinction between contrafactum and parody. Since his primary concern is music written in the twentieth century, Meyer's focus is on the final musical product and not the manner of performance. Additionally, he investigates uses of the past for new works in a modern idiom. However, his four categories of reusing music contain subtleties of context rather than just labeling all reuses as borrowing. J. Peter Burkholder follows a similar approach in his study of the music of Charles Ives as he seeks to uncover the "distinctive relationship between the source and the new composition" (1995, 4).

Syrian prayers provide an opportunity to investigate popular Arab music refashioned into a sacred context. In Syrian liturgy, paraphrasing and borrowing occurs with Arab melodies. The simulating and modeling of Arab performance practices, aesthetics, and musical genres are evidence of the reuse of other Arab musical elements. Meyer's categories provide useful parameters to investigate the manner in which recycled materials are used by determining what is maintained and what is varied in the new context. Because Syrian liturgy recycles more than just Arab melodies, this study extends Meyer's categories beyond the use of music to also include the consideration of performance practices, aesthetics, and musical genres.

The term *adaptation* is another useful designation for the process of recycling music. Most important for appreciating Syrian liturgy is understanding how this process is viewed by the cantors themselves, uncovering how they conceive this process of adaptation and its organization in the service. The adaptation of melodies used in the Syrian *pizmonim* (Shelemay 1998) and Sabbath liturgy is not unique to this Jewish community. It is a musical process found in other Jewish cultural settings: the ballad in the Judeo-Spanish tradition (Seroussi and Weich-Shahak 1990–91); popular music of Oriental Jews in Israel (Shiloah and Cohen 1983, Cohen and Shiloah 1985); contemporary nigunim among Hasidic Jews in America (Koskoff 1978, 2001); and contemporary worship (Summit 2000). Interestingly, Arab music in the twentieth century is also formed by adaptation of past Arab melodies, forms, and styles. In addition, Western musical influences have shaped Arab music (Racy 1981). Commenting on contemporary Arab music, Virginia Danielson notes, "Innovation has frequently yielded hybrid musics, drawn from a variety of styles and genres, indigenous and foreign" (1988, 142).

A mere identification of the borrowed music reveals little; context and specifics of adaptation show how it is done. Similarly, Roy A. Rappaport justifies looking at how a ritual operates: "Liturgical orders bind together disparate entities and processes, and it is this binding together rather than what is bound together that is peculiar to them" (1979, 206). Syrian liturgy binds together musical and textual entities by adaptation of indigenous and foreign elements.

Cultural Considerations

STUDIES OF JEWISH and Arab cultural syntheses in other geographic locales and periods of time are plentiful and provide a foundation for the present study of Syrian liturgy.[7] For Jews, the formative period of the Judeo-Arab synthesis was during the tenth to twelfth centuries in Spain during its golden age. At this time, when many aspects of Jewish culture were influenced by Arab culture, traditional areas of Jewish scholarship were developed and innovative forms of expression created.[8] The most notable of these were philosophy, biblical commentary, Jewish law, and poetry.

A Judeo-Arab synthesis is also a dynamic part of Middle Eastern Jewish life in the present.[9] Israeli Jews in modern times are involved in "remaking Levantine culture" (Alcalay 1993; see also Goitein 1955, 10, 216–17). Although the majority of Jews who lived in Arab lands until the first half of the twentieth century currently reside in Israel, studies on the life of Jews from Arab lands outside of Israel show the continuation and further development of the interaction between Jewish and Arab cultures.[10] In his study of *mimuna,* Harvey E. Goldberg shows the similarities between this Jewish celebration and a Muslim rite. Particularly noteworthy is his approach, which does not favor one over the other but, rather, shows the contact as an effective way to understand *mimuna.* He writes, "I find it useful to set aside an *a priori* judgment as to what is internal (Jewish) and what is external (Moslem). . . . [T]he same mechanisms are involved in both the internal development (transformation) and in the borrowing of symbolic forms" (1978, 76). Rather than looking at cultural contact in terms of internal and external factors I prefer to note spheres of interactions. For example, the following excerpt from Amnon Shamosh (b. 1929), an Aleppo-born novelist who emigrated to Israel in 1938, illustrates cultural interaction when he writes of his personal experiences in his book *My Sister the Bride* (1979):

> Halab, otherwise known as Aleppo or Aram Zova, was the meeting point of three cultures. This was expressed not only in the three names by which we called our city, but also and especially in the languages we spoke. It was Arab at home, French in society and on the street, and Hebrew in synagogue. Of the fourth element, the Sephardi one, I was not aware (until my arrival in Eretz Israel that is, where I was immediately downgraded to the status of *sfaradi*). Ladino, the Spanish-Jewish dialect, had been cast aside; nobody spoke it. Several generations before, it is true, waves of Ladino-speaking Jews had migrated to our city from all the Mediterranean countries, especially the north. But the immigrants had been completely absorbed into the eastern society and in my generation there was no distinguishing them. (5)

Although Shamosh specifically refers to linguistic elements, he comments that beginning at the age of five his varied singing repertoire included songs by Muḥammed ʿAbd al-Wahhāb (an Arab composer and singer), Maurice Chevalier, and Jewish liturgical settings (6). Shamosh's childhood world, with the confluence of elements, is similar to that of Syrian Jews born and raised in Brooklyn.[11] The pointed statement he makes about immigrant acculturation into Eastern society that "there was no distinguishing them" reflects a syncretic rather than a hegemonic view of neighboring cultures.

The interaction between cultures is seemingly inevitable with groups that are in close proximity. James Clifford details the variety of terms used to "name" cultural synthesis: "An unruly crowd of descriptive/interpretive terms now jostle and converse in an effort to characterize the contact zones of nations, cultures and regions: terms such as *border, travel, creolization, transculturation, hybridity,* and *diaspora*" (1994, 303). Hybrid traditions are a given in late-twentieth-century musical life. In assessing musical processes that display this contact, ethnomusicological approaches vary. In the past they have focused on the interaction of Western influences upon a non-Western music culture. Margaret J. Kartomi writes, "Most references to musical contact between cultures were made with regards to the colonial European empires in Asia and Africa and the internal colonial system of the Americas" (1981, 227). The approach of detecting Western influence is followed, for example, in the studies of Bruno Nettl (1978, 1983, 1985). Now it is recognized that "intercultural musical synthesis is not the exception but the rule" (Kartomi 1981, 230).

Recent ethnomusicological studies have focused on the contact of music cultures in a variety of contexts, including religious ceremonies, festivals, films, and recordings; much of this contact results from changes in technology (see Kartomi and Blum 1994). Kartomi provides the following description of culture contact:

> The effects of contact range from the making of minor adjustments within existing musical styles, such as the small-scale transfer of discrete musical traits from one music into another, to the creative transformation of whole styles and of the ideological and music-organizing principles on which they are based. Creative transformation, which may be termed syncretism, synthesis or transculturation, normally occurs as a result of convergence between cultures over a prolonged period of contact.[12] Such convergence may result in an influx of new musical ideas, organizing principles and repertoires. They may result in a greater level of individual and corporate creativity than before. . . . Thus it is that whole styles, repertoires, genres, pedagogical methods, extra-musical meanings commonly attached to music, the manner of theorizing about music, and even the way a group dresses or behaves at musical events may change as a result of convergence in contact situations. (Kartomi and Blum 1994, ix)

Syrian liturgy is the result of "creative transformation" of a musical style and the "ideological and music-organizing principles on which they are based," the extreme end of Kartomi's continuum.

Kartomi has grouped the product of music cultures in contact into five categories: virtual rejection of an impinging music, transfer of discrete musical traits, pluralistic coexistence of musics, nativistic musical revival, musical abandonment, and musical impoverishment (1981, 235–39).[13] Syrian liturgy presents a unique situation from which to view culture contact. Rather than the interaction of two music cultures, the liturgy combines Arab music and Jewish ritual practices. Syrian liturgy combines Kartomi's second and third categories—the transfer of musical traits in the adaptation of Arab music to Jewish texts and pluralistic coexistence in the desire of Syrian Jews to partake of Arab aesthetics. The pluralistic coexistence represents the intertwining of cultural and religious meaning, the result of the social conditions of Syrian Jewry stemming both from Aleppo and earlier historical models. Thus, adaptation and synthesis provide useful parameters to view the liturgy in order to determine "where 'borrowing' ends [and] creative musical change begins" (Kartomi 1981, 229). Consideration of a composite tradition reflecting culture contact through the interaction of music and text is more informative than simply labeling certain elements of the liturgy "Arab" and others "Jewish."[14] This study stresses the practices and explanations of cantors to show the Judeo-Arab synthesis through individual decision making (Herndon 1987, 456) and views the liturgy through the practice of individual cantors who inform and shape the tradition, since Arab and Jewish elements are negotiated by participants within the service.

The deep interconnection of Arab practices within Brooklyn Syrian Jewish life is at the center of other recent studies. Community and religion are not perceived as distinct realms for Middle Eastern Jews, so changes and new orientations are not ruptures from the past (Goldberg 1987, 28–29). Viewing cultural practices needs to go beyond the surface and obvious features (such as dress; see Stillman 1996, 69). Full contextualization into the components of these practices uncovers varying levels of cultural interaction. Just as in other cultural realms, such as occupations (Zenner 2000, 128), foods (Zenner 2002, 164–66) and literature (Zenner and Kligman 2000, 172–74), the Arab-Jewish hybrid in religious life retains the insular and cohesive structure with Syrian day schools, rabbinic authority, and specific minhagim.[15] In her study of the paraliturgical musical practices of this community, Shelemay concludes: "Indeed, it may be suggested that perpetuation of the Ḥalabi [Aleppo] musical culture, especially given the ubiquitous presence of musical activity in social and religious life, serves as a surrogate for Arabic language use and provides the main venue through which the community maintains continuity with its Middle Eastern past while keeping its equilibrium in an ever-changing American setting" (1998, 224). Walter Paul Zenner expresses this "equilibrium" as "ethnic persistence." For Zenner Syrian cultural accommodations are unique since they are an ethnic enclave that has survived not out of poverty (2000, 175–76) but persisted cohesively somewhere between that of Hasidic Jews and Jews that are assimilated (189). Retaining various Arab practices expresses not only Syrian culture contact but also how they maintain and perpetuate their identity.

Liturgy is a performative event residing at the center of Syrian Jews' religious lives. Music and liturgy in the synagogue reflect and can be compared to other realms of Syrian culture. While previous studies view the Syrian community in relation to Jews of other Jewish traditions, I maintain that a consideration of Syrian liturgy needs to grow out of its Judeo-Arab heritage and not solely out of its Jewish heritage.[16] Amnon Shiloah claims that inquiries into Jewish musical practices influenced by Arab culture have resulted in studies focusing more on thought and theory, particularly in the past, rather than the music itself (1982, 36; see also 1993 for a collection of his historically focused articles). This study follows Shiloah's approach by looking at the music itself and situates Syrian liturgy in the present while acknowledging musical practices informed and influenced by the past.

2

History of the Syrian Jewish Community in Brooklyn

The scarcity of in-depth historical studies of Jews from Syria is largely because of limited past scholarship; only recently have scholars focused on the history of Jews from the Middle East. Walter Zenner and Harvey Goldberg, anthropologists who delve into Jewish history for their work with Middle Eastern communities, suggest that this neglect stems from historians of the past seeing Middle Eastern Jews as "less civilized" and as people who did not produce significant contributions—religiously, intellectually, culturally—to Judaism (Goldberg 1978, 75; Zenner 1980, 379). Studies of Middle Eastern Jewish history mention Jews in the Levant (e.g., Cohen 1973; Stillman 1979, 1991). Zenner specifically focuses on the nineteenth- and twentieth-century history of Syrian Jews (1965, 30–98; 1982a; 1982b; 2000). To provide a thorough history of Syrian Jews' aesthetic preference, cultural, and religious background, I draw from studies of Jewish communities in the Levant (Zenner 1965, 1968, 1980, 1982a, 1982b, 1983, 1988, 1990, 2000; Cohen 1972; Stillman 1979, 1991, 1996) and Ottoman Empire (Shaw 1991) and place recent developments within the broad Levantine history of this period (Hournai 1991), including immigration to America (Naff 1983, 1994).[1]

General History of Syrian Jews

Biblical and Early Events

Syrian Jews in Brooklyn take great pride in their heritage. The Bible mentions Aleppo and Damascus by their Hebrew names—Aram-Tsoba and Aram-

Damasek, respectively.[2] The name Ḥalab, the exact origin of which is unclear, refers to Aleppo: "Tradition among Aleppo's Jews is that Ḥalab received its name when the patriarch, Abraham, upon arriving in the city after leaving Ḥaran some eighty miles to the east, 'milked his cows' there ('Ḥalab' means 'milked' in Aramaic, Hebrew, and Arabic)" (Sutton 1979, 155).[3] Subsequently Italian merchants used the name Aleppo in the fourteenth and fifteenth centuries (Sutton 1979, 199n1). An early Jewish community in Aleppo likely dates back fifteen hundred years, since a synagogue was constructed there in the fifth century (Baron 1957, 3:104–5).[4]

Arab rule over the city of Aleppo began in the seventh century. Aleppo became a hub of commerce and culture after 1450 when trade with India increased. The city was an important center of Jewish learning from the twelfth century onward. Several Aleppo rabbis were in contact with prominent rabbis in Palestine and Baghdad, including the famous Rabbi Moses Maimonides. Although several periods of unrest included attacks upon Jews, many Jews prospered as wealthy merchants, officials, craftsmen, and outstanding rabbinic scholars (Cohen 1972, 562).

Events within the Ottoman Milieu

In 1517 Ottoman Turks conquered Greater Syria and Egypt. Syria was under Ottoman control until 1921, save for the years 1832–40, when the khedive of Egypt, Mohammed Ali, conquered the territory. Syria was governed by the French from 1921 to 1945, whereupon Syria gained its independence. President Afez al-Assad assumed power in 1971 and ruled until he died in 2000. His son Bashar al-Assad continued as president.

Under Ottoman rule Jewish life developed with Arab influence. Historian Stanford Shaw divides the population of Jews in the Ottoman Empire into four groups: Romaniote, Sephardic, Mizraḥim (Oriental or eastern Jews), and European (1991, 1, 44–45). The Romaniote were Greek-speaking Jews surviving persecution of late Roman and Byzantine times. Sephardic, or Ladino-speaking Jews, were driven from Iberian Peninsula in the fifteenth century and from lands where they most immediately took refuge—Italy and North Africa.[5] These Jews were businessman and leading intellectuals and never experienced the isolation of a ghetto. They mixed with Muslims and Christians as they had previously in Spain. Mizraḥim were Arabic-speaking Jews, also known as Musta'rab, or Arabized Jews (ibid.). The Europeans, from west-central and northern Europe, fled Christian persecution. Though each of the four groups had separate religious customs, they did share some religious practices.

Syrian Jews consider themselves Mizraḥim influenced by Sephardic Jewish traditions. Sephardic Jews interacted with the indigenous Jews that existed prior to their arrival in Syria. Particularly, Sephardic Jews brought their experiences of interaction with non-Jewish authorities and worldliness; thus a new period of financial opportunities emerged for Jews in Syria. In the late fifteenth to early sixteenth centuries, Jews who were expelled from Spain settled in Greece, Turkey, Egypt, and Syria. Initially, the Jews in Aleppo and Damascus were divided between these refugees from Spain and southern Italy and the indigenous community (Zenner 1965, 32). The immigration of Jews to Syria continued in the seventeenth century with the arrival of Frankish Jews from Italy and France.[6] These repeated migrations had an effect on liturgical traditions and religious authority within the community. As a result, Aleppo became known as a religious center with many important rabbis.[7] Syrian Jews are not only proud of their historical lineage from antiquity but they also view themselves as bearers of the rich Sephardic cultural and religious tradition.

Life for Jews in Syria, and throughout the Ottoman Empire, from the sixteenth to the nineteenth centuries varied. The sixteenth and seventeenth centuries are known as the golden age of the Ottoman Empire: territory was expanded, economic opportunities were plentiful, and culture flourished. Like all inhabitants of the region, the Jews prospered. The end of the seventeenth century saw a decline in the Ottoman Empire's prominence in the world economy (Hournai 1991, 259). Consequently, the Jewish communities suffered decreasing financial opportunities (Stillman 1979, 90–91). An increase of western European financial assistance in the eighteenth century stabilized the region. Western influence continued in the nineteenth century and resulted in new economic opportunities, challenges, and influences and renewed cultural aspirations and ideals. The Jews in Syria maintained their existence in the region, but diminished financial resources and social pressure forced them to seek opportunity elsewhere.

Aleppo in the Eighteenth and Nineteenth Centuries

In the eighteenth and nineteenth centuries, Aleppo was a cosmopolitan city, with trade and commercial activity connecting it with Europe and other parts of the Near East (Zenner 1965, 36). Yet the Jews in Arab lands were viewed as a distinct group with their own customs and characteristics (Stillman 1979, 4; A. Marcus 1989, 39). Throughout most of this period, Jews had autonomy and could worship freely. Their freedom resulted from their *dhimmī* status:

> The Muslim government obliges itself to protect the life and the property of the non-Muslims (*dhimmīs*), exempts them from military service, and guarantees them religious freedom, although with certain restrictions. The *dhimmīs,* on their part, are obliged to pay the poll tax (*jizya*), not to insult Islam, not to convert Muslims to their religions, not to build new churches or synagogues, and not to betray the Muslim government by conspiring with the enemy, e.g., hiding its spies. (Ashtor 1972, 1604)

Although Jews lived in separate sections of the city, they did not remain isolated from Aleppo's rich cultural life but took part in and contributed to it. Zenner writes:

> The different religious communities maintained their distinct identities, set of rules, and boundaries. Each group had its own laws governing marriage, divorce, and inheritance. The patterns of prayer, meditation, and scriptural reading in the houses of worship of the different sects were also distinctive, as were dietary regulations and the use of music. For instance, the emotional meaning of a particular *maqām* (melody type) used in local music might be different among Jews among Muslims. *Ma'amul,* a semolina cookie eaten at Purim (a Spring Jewish festival), was an Easter sweet for Christians. (Zenner 2000, 36)

The rich cultural interaction of Muslim and Christians during the premodern era continued into the twentieth century (see Shamosh 1979, 5).

Abraham Marcus's study on Aleppo in the eighteenth century effectively describes the fruitful mixture of cultural and religious interests. Because of the increased influence of European financial opportunities in the Levant, religion was important but not the only influence in Aleppo: "In this eclectic milieu the oral, the illiterate, the popular, and the nonreligious occupied an important place, and ought not to be dismissed or belittled in favor of the written, the literate, the high and the religious. The various elements actually fed on each other, and tend to illuminate the culture best when seen as parts of a whole rather than as self-contained spheres" (1989, 219–20). Marcus highlights the role of religion in Aleppo, which sought to combine the spiritual and worldly, one significantly influencing the other, as reflective of Middle Eastern culture.

The vast majority of the society was Muslim; Christians were the minority, with a comparatively small Jewish population. Religious devotion was seen as a way of life interwoven into daily practices. There was no single type of religious experience in Aleppo, as religious adherence varied from devout followers to casual adherents. The debates did not center on the level of belief but on religious intensity. Religion was represented in sacred acts. Marcus explains, "For the majority, the religious experience tended to be expressed in acts of worship more than in intellectual reflection. . . . [O]bservance was expected, unquestioned and the norm" (1989, 223). Education meant religious learning, and separate Muslim, Christian, and Jewish schools were maintained (ibid., 222–34).

The surrounding culture's religious propensity affected Jewish tradition. Mysticism figured prominently in everyday Aleppo Jewish life (Zenner 1980, 386–88). Superstition replaced science; amulets, charms, and magical formulas were used to heal wounds (Shaw 1991, 132). Stemming from the growth of kabbalistic learning in Safed from the sixteenth century and onward, the tenor of mysticism characterized Aleppo culture generally and manifested itself prominently into Jewish life in the eighteenth century and onward.[8]

Sacred and secular influences of Muslim culture on Judaism were balanced by distinct residential locations and religious practices. The Jews lived in a separate quarter from Muslims and Christians but regularly interacted with members of the surrounding culture. Though Arab culture became the primary cultural influence for the Jewish community, religion provided a deep boundary between communities. Each religion had its own laws governing marriage, divorce, inheritance, and prayer.

At times, the Jews in Aleppo during premodernity enjoyed a prosperous life. Interaction with the surrounding culture was in limited yet important spheres such as business and socializing at coffeehouses. Differences that remained were religiously defined. The blurring of boundaries between sacred and secular domains allowed for groups to influence one another. Aleppo Jews were, on one hand, set apart from Muslim society because of their religion, yet Jews maintained the same culture preferences as Muslims, and did not live in isolation. All residents shared Arab culture and adapted to meet the needs of what was religiously acceptable.

Changes in Nineteenth-Century Immigration to America

The need for European financial support in the Ottoman Empire increased during the nineteenth century, and so did European influence. In 1854 a railway was established that expanded trade within the Levant; Syria likewise built its own railway. But the most significant factor in economic dynamics was the opening of the Suez Canal in 1869. European factory products were shipped into the region causing great hardships to handicraft centers; textile weaving and other established industries suffered with competition of European goods. In some cases, people were forced to adjust and expand their opportunities—others had greater difficulties (Hournai 1991, 277).

The nineteenth century was a period of challenges and changes. The new ruling Arab elites, fueled by nineteenth-century Arab nationalism, favored merchant trade with Europe, thus shifting economic wealth and power in the region. Unrest generated from Islamic perceptions that they were threatened by the outside world; consequently, non-Muslims were endangered in Arab nations (Hournai 1991, 277; Zenner 2000, 49). The economic decline contributed to antisemitism. Although the blame for poverty throughout Syria in the early nineteenth century was directed initially at Christians, European antisemitism gradually spread to Muslims from the French traders and missionaries in the region (Stillman 1979, 104). Christians and later Muslims jointly blamed the Jews as the source of their economic problems.

In 1840 what became known as the Damascus Affair began a long period of tension for Jews in the region. Local Christians, wanting to gain support from Arabs in pursuit of a common enemy (Cohen 1973, 43), accused Jews of the murder of an Italian friar. Seven Jewish members of the community were arrested and tortured. Other reprisals against Jews spread throughout Syria and the Levant region, extending to Palestine and Egypt (Stillman 1979, 105). The unrest continued into the late nineteenth and early twentieth centuries with the rise of Zionism (Cohen 1973, 15; Stillman 1979, 107).

Despite these tensions, nineteenth-century modernity brought several benefits in education, literacy, and cultural influences. European and American organizations set up schools in the region, including universities and some educational opportunities for women. The Alliance Israélite Universelle established schools throughout the Ottoman Empire, from Morocco to Iraq. These schools prepared students for foreign trade and taught French, English, Hebrew, and Arab. Increased literacy and education in the region, although not enjoyed by all, gave rise to translated French and English studies into Arab (Hournai 1991, 304). Printing presses first appeared in the Levant in the late sixteenth century in Safed. Most significantly, the rediscovery of Arab classical poetry influenced renewed interest in creating new poetry and literature (ibid., 305). Likewise, Arab music built on traditional genres, now termed "classical," supplanted Turkish or Ottoman music.

Economic and social changes led Jews to seek fortunes elsewhere. In the twentieth century Jews, along with Syrian Christians who were later marginalized by Muslim nationalism, left the region. Although some Syrian Jews did settle in Israel, most chose to go elsewhere. In the 1920s, Syrian Jews, like compatriots of other religions, emigrated to Egypt and later to the Americas.

Emigration in search of better financial opportunities began in the 1880s. Syrian Jews left for other locales, including Egypt, present-day Lebanon, Palestine (now Israel), Latin America, North America, and England (Zenner 1965, 330; 2000, 177–79). At the same time, Syrian Christians and Sephardic Jews from the dissolving Ottoman Empire arrived in the United States.

The two major periods of Arab immigration to the United States include a predominantly Arab-Christian period from the 1870s to the 1940s and a post–World War II Palestinian or Muslim period. The vast majority of Arab Americans in the early period were from Syria and the surrounding areas of Lebanon and Jordan (Naff 1983, 9). Christians arriving in the United States in the 1870s hoped to stay for a few years before returning with added financial resources to aid their families (Naff 1994, 23). However, the continued decline of the Syrian economy in the late 1800s and early 1900s made living in the United States more desirable (Saliba 1983, 34). Many were peddlers, since this occupation took little training, skill, or knowledge of English. Most sold small goods such as jewelry, dry goods, bed linens, silk, and cloth (Naff 1983, 16).

By 1910 Arab immigrants settled across the United States. The immigration of Sephardic Jews to the United States and their settlement follows some of the trends of Arab Americans and also diverges. For Arab Americans, assimilation developed over time but post–World War II politics in the Middle East changed Arab identity. First- and second-generation Arab American immigrants assimilated, while recent immigrants are more vigilant in adhering to Arab language, culture, and, consequently, identity because of more recent political developments. Syrian Jews have a slightly different history in their resettlement. The large wave of Jewish immigrants to the United States, starting in the 1880s, included a few thousand Sephardic Jews (Papo 1992, 270). This represented a small fraction compared to the 2.5 million eastern European Jewish immigrants.[9] Since the 1880s there have been several waves of immigration from the Middle East. Although most Sephardic Jews settled in New York City, they have also established communities in Rochester (New York), Atlanta, Birmingham, Indianapolis, Los Angeles, San Francisco, Portland, and Seattle (Elazar 1989, 164).

Immigrants usually drew themselves together into groups according to their cities and townships of origin, like the Ashkenazic *lansmanshaftn*. Where Ashkenazic Jews had Yiddish as a unified language, Sephardic Jews did not; they spoke Ladino, Greek, Arabic, and Turkish. Each group exhibited its own unique traits in the institutions it built during the early period of immigration and the goals it sought in America.

Many cite the Syrian community in Brooklyn as an exception to other Sephardic communities. Zenner writes that "the Syrian Jewish community in Brooklyn has long been seen as one of the most cohesive Jewish comminutes outside of Ḥasidim in the diaspora" (2000, 127). The Arabic-speaking Syrians stressed family unity and a thorough religious education early on in the United States. Greek-speaking Sephardic Jews maintained their individualism (Papo 1992, 271). The Judeo-Spanish–speaking Jews "by far the largest of the three groups, were spurred on by a desire to regain their historic status and assert their equality with Ashkenazi Jewry" (ibid., 272). Zenner sees "out-of-towners," those not living in populated Syrian centers like Brooklyn, Los Angeles, or Chicago, as more likely to intermarry and be less involved in Jewish culture and religious practices; in this regard they are like other Sephardim in America (Zenner 2000, 147–49). Syrian Jews mostly reside in the same location (Brooklyn) and have their own synagogues and religious institutions, whereas Sephardic Jews in other locations attend Ashkenazic schools. Socializing for Syrian Jews is almost exclusively with their own group. They prefer to support their own family and social ties.

Immigration to the United States was ongoing. The first immigrants, during the early part of the twentieth century, established institutions and businesses that have endured to the present. The next major period of emigration from Syria began in the late 1940s and early 1950s, just after Israel became an independent state, thus following the immigration trend of Arab Americans. In April of 1992 it was estimated that four thousand Jews were left in Syria, most of them in Damascus, with a few in Aleppo and outlying areas. It is estimated that more than three thousand individuals have arrived in Brooklyn since President Assad of Syria lifted travel restriction in May 1992. The new immigrants are being actively absorbed into the Brooklyn Syrian community (Yellin 1995, 17; Zenner 2000, 56–61).

The Syrian Community in Brooklyn

UNLIKE ARAB AMERICAN Christians, Syrian Jews are not scattered throughout the United States. The building of synagogues and Jewish religious schools is a distinguishing feature that has curbed assimilation. Likewise, social insularity is a mainstay of the community, in contrast to Arab Americans and most other Sephardic Jews, who do not marry within their own communities. Another characteristic of the Syrian community is its strong desire to retain some form of Arab culture, particularly in manner, attitude, and tastes (culinary and musical). Strong cultural preferences promote communal cohesion maintained through proximity in residence and economic ties (Zenner and Kligman 2000, 175–76).

Similar to many of their European coreligionists, Syrian Jewish immigrants to America first arrived in New York City and settled in the Lower East Side of Manhattan. As merchants, they followed the occupations they had practiced in Aleppo (Sutton 1979, 13). The goal of the early immigrants was to establish a stable line of work and to send money to support their families in Syria. After 1910, businesses developed, most prominently in the retail and wholesale clothing industry (ibid., 11–12; Zenner 2000, 129). Money was sent to family members who had remained in Syria for their passage to New York City, and as a result, the presence of families increased significantly around World War I (Sutton 1979, 18, 24). Some Syrian businessmen, merchants, bankers, and manufacturers developed well-established businesses that are today still operated by their descendants. Only in the past twenty years or so have more Syrians chosen professional careers.

Syrians had business contacts with Ashkenazic Jews on the Lower East Side, though they differed in way of life, language, and cultural sensibilities. According to Joseph Sutton, Ashkenazic Jews considered themselves superior and viewed Syrian and Ladino-speaking Sephardic Jews as "uncouth," since they did not speak Yiddish or English (1979, 21). As a result, Syrians considered themselves a minority within a minority: both as Jews within the U.S. population and as Syrians among the more populous Ashkenazic Jewish mainstream (Zenner 1965, 354–55; 1983, 186–88; 2000, 138–41). This self-identification through two levels of difference continues to be expressed by Syrian Jews and is the defining framework in the construction of their separate identity.

The Syrian synagogues in Manhattan and early-twentieth-century Brooklyn were initially organized and led by lay leaders. As Alixa Naff has stated with regard to the early immigration of Syrian Christians, religious institutions were set up as a sign of permanence for the community once established religious leaders were brought in from Syria. The first official rabbi of the Syrian community, appointed in 1934, was Rabbi Jacob Saul Kassin (1900–1994), a descendant of a long and distinguished line of Aleppo rabbis (Sutton 1979, 24, 40, 84).[10] Moses Ashear (1877–1940), a cantor who emigrated from Aleppo in 1912, was an important transmitter of liturgical and paraliturgical musical practices from Aleppo.[11] Ashear established, maintained, and developed Aleppo traditions in Brooklyn. Both Rabbi Kassin and Ḥazzan Ashear served at the Magen David Congregation (Sutton 1979, 40). Rabbi Kassin later moved with the community to its new location in Flatbush, Brooklyn, and had a significant influence on maintaining Aleppo religious traditions in Brooklyn.

With increased financial resources, families in the community first moved to the present site in Flatbush beginning in the early 1940s. The first residential area was established along Avenues S and T, adjacent to Ocean Parkway. Congregation Shaarei Zion, the largest Syrian synagogue, was built at this location in 1963. In the 1950s, people moved to an area near Avenue J, where Congregation Beth Torah was established. Today the Syrian community is spread out along and adjacent to a 1.5-mile stretch of Ocean Parkway, where various other synagogues have been built (see figure 1). Due to the traditional prohibition against driving on the Sabbath, Syrians live within walking distance of their synagogues. Thus, the majority of the community members dwell in residences a few blocks east or west of Ocean Parkway (Zenner and Kligman 2000, 156–58).

The community supports over forty institutions, including fifteen synagogues, fifteen schools, and other social and communal organizations. In addition to the fifteen synagogues, there is one Egyptian synagogue and two Lebanese synagogues; these non-Syrian synagogues do have Syrian members in addition to Egyptian and Lebanese members, some of whom emigrated from Syria prior to residing in Egypt and Lebanon. Syrian, Egyptian, and Lebanese Jews share liturgical and cultural traditions (Sanua 1977, 284–85; Sutton 1988, 81) yet are distinct from Iraqi, Iranian, and Yemenite Jews who live nearby but maintain separate synagogues.

Religious observance of Syrians varies. Zenner designates the range of religious observance, based on his fieldwork in Brooklyn in the late 1950s and early 1960s as follows: atheists and rebels (who do not affiliate), indifferent or casual, conscientiously Orthodox, or ultra-Orthodox. This categorization may also be used to describe the present level of religious observance. The ultra-Orthodox, largely young Syrian rabbis trained at Ashkenazic yeshivot are not part of the mainstream. Instead, Sutton describes normative religious practice as "middle-of-the-road Orthodoxy" (1988, 98). Several ultra-Orthodox organizations try to move the "normative" community religious practices to a stricter level. The present chief rabbi of the community, Rabbi Saul Kassin, seeks to maintain a balance in the community in favor of a middle of the road approach to unify the community (Yellin 1995, 17). This categorization and religious observance is equally descriptive of the community in the 1990s (Zenner and Kligman 2000, 167). For some, the initial purpose of synagogue attendance is an opportunity to socialize, as it was for early immigrants (Chira 1994, 67). In recent years a more substantial religious desire has motivated many younger members of the community to attend and participate in synagogue services. Daniel Elazar notes that the Syrian community is the most religious of the Sephardic communities in America (1989, 171).

Zenner states that Syrian synagogues in Brooklyn have acquired many

Figure 1. *Syrian synagogues in Brooklyn*

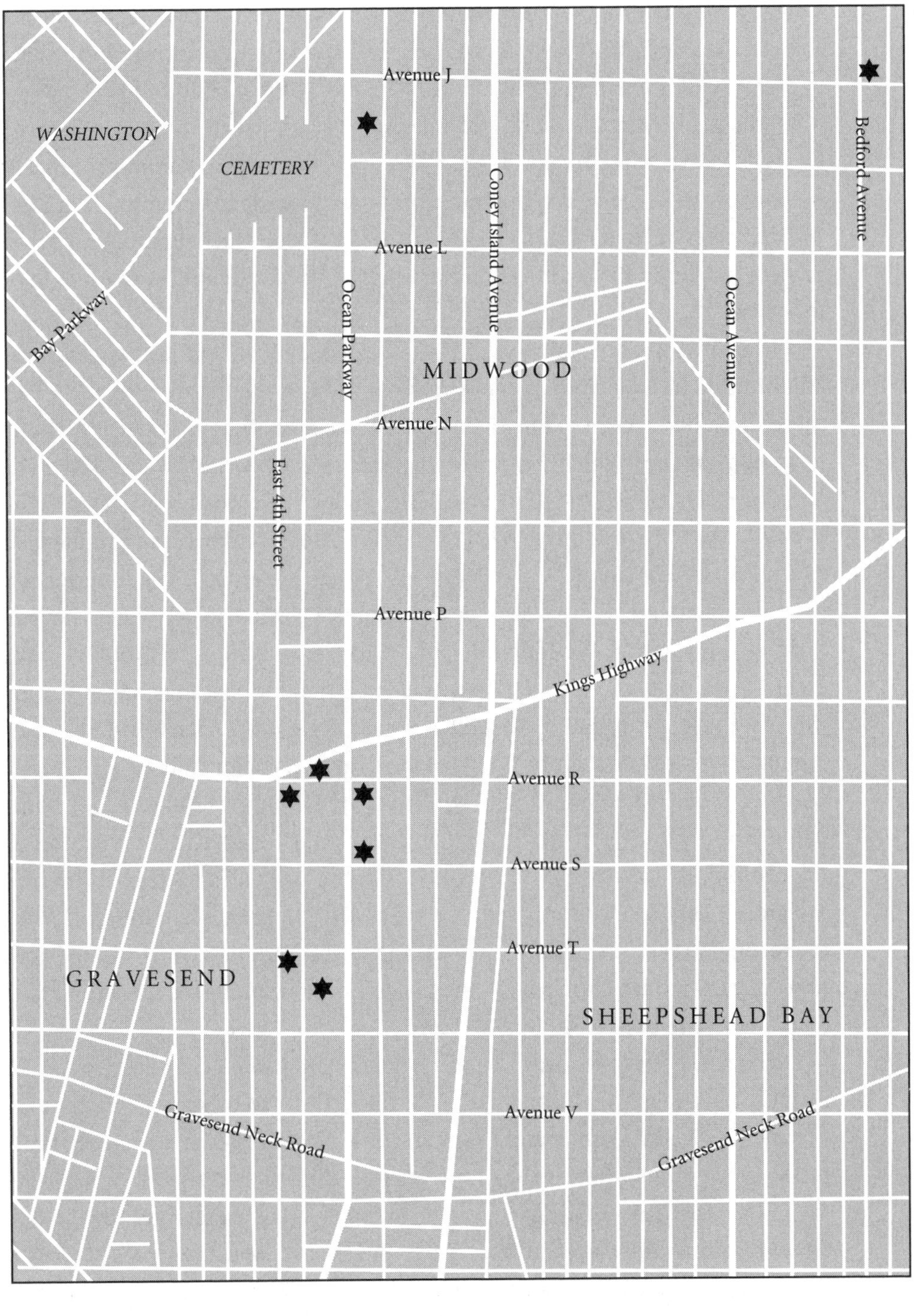

characteristics common to U.S. synagogues (1983, 183). The following traits are indicative of American synagogue, or Ashkenazic, influence on Syrian synagogues: professionalization of the positions of the religious leaders rather than leadership, which is lay-driven; formality and organization of the synagogue service, including the wearing of a robe by the cantor and reading of a prepared sermon by the rabbi; and wearing of black hats by rabbis, influenced by Ashkenazic religious observers.[12] One practice of the community that is not American influenced is the tradition of magic and medicine, or what Zenner describes as "folk religion" (1983, 182–83). These practices include special prayers for ill family members and amulets from saintly rabbis that are used for cures.

Syrian Jews maintain a strong sense of solidarity that emphasizes ties to the community. In Israel Syrians have many options as Sephardim; in the 1990s there was a resurgence of interest in Syrian heritage, seen in Tel Aviv with the formation of the World Center for the Heritage of Aram Tzova. While the *ḥaredi*-secular divide is wide in Israel, Aleppo Jews remained committed to the State of Israel; there is an increasing trend of Aleppo rabbis being influenced by Ashkenazi *ḥaredim* (Zenner 2000, 97). Aleppo Jews in Latin America, on the other hand, are not as free to be a part of the general society since they are not Spanish Catholics or Indians (ibid., 125). Thus, Syrians in Brooklyn have greater freedoms, and it is perhaps even more striking that they have retained their heritage. They prefer to affiliate with their own social and religious organizations rather than to participate in Ashkenazic or non-Jewish groups (Zenner 1965, 341). Zenner, who studied Syrian identification in Israel, compared that community with Syrians in Brooklyn; he claims that Syrian ties to the community are stronger in Brooklyn: "In the United States [Brooklyn], the Syrian Jews are a sub-group within a religious minority, while in Israel, they are recognized as part of the religio-ethnic Jewish minority. In Israel, they are more stimulated to participate in the general organizations than in the United States, where it 'pays' to be Syrian" (1965, 344).

Ashkenazic Jews remain the main external reference group for Syrians in Brooklyn, although they have had little formal involvement with each other (Zenner 1965, 359; Zenner and Kligman 2000, 139–40).[13] Interestingly, Syrians reside in locations where Ashkenazic Jewish religious institutions also thrive: the Lower East Side, Bensonhurst, and Flatbush. Other Sephardim live in different sections: Yemenites in Boro Park, Bukharians and Iranians in Queens. Syrians maintain limited contact with Ashkenazic Jews (Sanua 1977, 284) and tend to marry other Syrians (Sutton 1979, 35; Chira 1994, 65). Marriage to Ashkenazic Jews is not uncommon, but marriage to non-Jews is rare.[14] Syrian Jewish marriage practices are today similar to those of Syrian-Christians of earlier generations: in-group marriages lead to cohesion, a passionate goal of Syrian rabbis.

Insularity is an apt characterization of Syrian Jewish social patterns. For the Syrians, particularly compared to other Sephardic Jews, relationships with non-Jews are minimal. Although Syrian Jews are in businesses similar to those operated by Syrian Christians, they keep their distance; the two groups have even settled in different sections of Brooklyn. Syrian Christians reside in Bay Ridge and still operate their groceries and stores along Atlantic Avenue; for Syrian Jews living in Bensonhurst and Flatbush, Kings Highway is the location of numerous groceries and restaurants. Zenner even suggests that there is probably less contact in Brooklyn between Syrian Jews and Christians than there was in Aleppo (1983, 187). However, one activity where there is contact with Syrian Christians is music: Arab Americans frequently serve as musicians for parties and other celebrations (Shelemay 1998, 113, 132; Zenner and Kligman 2000, 167).

These strong, insular social ties affect many aspects of Syrian Jewish life (Shelemay 1998, 65). The majority of children in the community attend private Syrian religious schools (Zenner and Kligman 2000, 167). Many members of the Syrian community vacation in the same locations and have summer homes in Bradley Beach and Deal, New Jersey. The community uses distinctive terminology to refer to themselves, including "Ḥalabi" (one from Ḥalab), "Syrians," "SY," and "Sephardim." Conversely, Ashkenazic Jews are often referred to in an oppositional manner as "Yiddish," "Itchies" (referring to the beards of religious Ashkenazic men), "Jay-Dub" (Jewish or Yiddish speaker), and "Ashkenazim" (Zenner 1965, 355; Sutton 1979, 151; Zenner and Kligman 2000, 136).

Syrian Jews' Cultural Preferences

OTHER AREAS OF culture mix of Arab and American influences. Wedding ceremonies follow the Sephardic rite, and the celebrations mix elegant New York style catering with Middle Eastern Jewish customs (Zenner 1983, 182; Shelemay 1998, 139); some include Ashkenazic style hors-d'oeuvres and food (Zenner 1983, 182; Zenner and Kligman 2000, 156). Entertainment for the community in the past consisted of attending nightclubs and participation in social dancing, such as ballroom dancing, in New York City as well as frequenting the plentiful Arab and Turkish coffeehouses; the latter were an important point of gathering for Syrians on the Lower East Side (Sanua 1977, 282; Elazar 1989, 171; Shelemay 1998, 67).[15] Many of these coffeehouses are no longer in operation. Middle Eastern–style restaurants in the New York area offering

Arab entertainment are frequented by Syrian Jews, as evidenced by the advertisements in these establishments of the availability of Kosher food. However, some Syrian Jews have become increasingly more uncomfortable socializing in non-Jewish Arab milieu because of tense political tensions between Arabs and Jews in Israel. At times musical performances may transcend these tensions (Shelemay 1998, 228).

Despite these influences, Syrians are still more religious and insular than other Sephardic Jews. The close proximity and limited contact with religious Ashkenazic Jews has also had an effect on their desire to remain distinct and to maintain their proud Jewish traditions. Zenner explains, "The Ashkenazim had preempted the term *Jew* for themselves. Jewish as a language means Yiddish and 'Jewish food' is East European in origin. The Syrian Jews were probably soon aware of the negative, anti-Semitic stereotypes that Christian Americans held of the East European Jews and they may have preferred to identify as other than Jewish for public purposes. Syrians were a less important target as scapegoats than were Jews" (1983, 187). Hence, there is a desire to maintain their cultural preferences since in Brooklyn it "pays to be Syrian" rather than to identify with the Ashkenazic Jewish majority.

The historical conditions of Syrian Jews living in an Arab society in Syria placed them on a secondary status (*dhimmī*) but allowed them to practice Judaism. In America, their insularity is a choice, not something forced upon them by the ruling majority. Today, Arab cultural preferences, like their identity, is also a choice but deemed to have value that goes back ultimately to an older more pristine time:

> Their conceptualizations of their distant past; the manner in which aspects of their various identities as Syrian/Arab/Jewish diaspora/Sephardic community still shape their outlook; the various routes they traveled to arrive at their late-twentieth-century locations; and the manner in which their community remains one in continual motion, linked through kinship, marriage, travel, and communications within a transnational grid. (Shelemay 1998, 68)

Rabbinic restrictions pertain only to religious behavior, not to culture. Music is a reflection of Syrian Arab predilections and desire to maintain their past. This is more then simply singing their favorite music. Perpetuating their musical and Middle Eastern heritage is intrinsic to their way of being.

3

Syrian Liturgy and Prayer Books

The Siddur

THE CANONIZATION OF the text in Jewish liturgy was a process that developed between the eighth and the eleventh centuries (Hoffman 1979, 8–9). The earliest compilation of prayer, known as *Seder Rav Amram,* dates to the ninth century and includes biblical (particularly psalmodic), rabbinic, and poetic texts. The liturgy consists of distinct textual types dating from different periods of time and contrasting literary forms. These include biblical texts from the Hebrew Bible; rabbinic literature from the Mishnah and Babylonian Talmud, compiled from the first century to as late as the seventh century; and liturgical poetry (piyyutim) composed after the seventh century (ibid.). Each of the three textual types employs different styles of Hebrew language, meter, and rhyme.

Passages drawn from the Bible and rabbinical prayers encompass the core of Jewish liturgy. Neither of these textual types make extensive use of meter or rhyme. Some textual passages in the liturgy consist of liturgical poetry, which do make use of meter and rhyme. Two portions of the morning service, the Shema and the Amidah, and the prayers of their environs, serve as examples.[1] The inclusion of the Shema and the Amidah in the service is mandatory according to Jewish law.[2] The Shema is the creed affirming the unity of one God, taken from three biblical passages (Dueteronomy 6:4–9 and 11:13–21 and Numbers 15:37–41). The Amidah is said in place of daily sacrifices once performed in the Temple; this text evolved slowly and was defined as it is known today in the seventh century (Heinemann 1972, 840). In the morning liturgy the Shema appears first, framed by postbiblical passages and blessings, and then is followed by the Amidah. By the tenth century, the extended intervening textual passage between the Shema and the Amidah was canonized in the form known today. The late date is most noticeable in the use of rhymed passages and an alphabetic acrostic of one intervening liturgical poem, Kel Adon (Elbogen 1913 [1993], 17–18). Additionally, Kel Adon follows a medieval Hebrew poetic model; it contains the same number of words in each line. The culling of phrases or passages from other Jewish texts characterizes the liturgy. The Shema, Amidah, and the various framing texts constitute the core liturgical section of the Sabbath morning service; thus, they are referred to specifically as Shaḥarit. Within Shaḥarit only a brief portion makes use of rhymed phrases; most portions are unrhymed biblical or rabbinic prose, which predominates the entire Sabbath morning service.

In general, two rites divide the history of Jewish liturgy: Ashkenazic and Sephardic.[3] The major distinguishing features between the two rites entail small changes in the order of the prayers and in the inclusion or exclusion of psalms and various liturgical poems (Goldschmidt 1972, 398). The statutory prayers of the two major rites are the same, with slight differences in wording. The Sephardic rite, a development originally from Spain, influenced the local rites of those European and Middle Eastern communities that received an influx of Spanish Jews after the expulsion from Spain in the sixteenth century.

The liturgical and religious custom of Aleppo is known as minhag aram-tsoba; the earliest compilation is *maḥzor aram-tsoba,* published in Venice (1523–27), a prayer book for the High Holidays of Rosh ha-Shanah and Yom Kippur (portions of the texts appear in Idelsohn 1923b, 33–38). Since the sixteenth century the liturgy of Aleppo was significantly influenced by the Spanish Jewish exiles' rite (Zenner 1965, 32; Goldschmidt 1972, 400). Today the liturgical rite for Aleppo Syrians in Brooklyn is close to the Spanish and Portuguese rite with some local modifications.[4] The liturgical text of the Sabbath morning service is, for present purposes, synonymous with the Sephardic rite. Additionally, there is more variation and use of local custom with High Holiday liturgy than there is with the Sabbath morning liturgy.

Prayer Books

RITES MAY BE viewed as an expression of a community's identity rather than merely an indicator of a specific textual influence (Hoffman 1987, 55–59, 69). Specifically, Lawrence Hoffman writes, "The differences among rites reflect different ways that worshipping communities see themselves vis-à-vis others" (ibid., 55). Focusing on the reasons for the formulation of a rite, Hoffman considers issues that go "beyond the text," in particular noting two European historical examples in which ideological change accompanied liturgical change: the Hasidic movement in the seventeenth century and the German Reform movement of the eighteenth century (54, 57). In both instances, liturgical change was a marker of self-definition. Similarly, Sephardic Jews in America today use a Sephardic prayer book at least in part to affirm their Sephardic heritage.

The printing of prayer books in the Brooklyn Syrian community is a recent phenomenon.[5] Sam Catton, an American-born member of the community, is the founder of the Sephardic Heritage Foundation, which publishes prayer books in the Brooklyn community. The prayer books appear in two forms: a siddur (lit., "order") for weekday, Sabbath, and holiday prayers (*Siddur kol ya'akov,* 1985, 1990, 1995) and a *maḥzor* (lit., "cycle"), a special volume for holidays (*Maḥzor shelom yerushalayim,* 1989, 1990, 1991, 1994).[6] Catton explains that several prayer books were published by companies for use in Sephardic communities, but these prayer books do not follow the specific customs of Aleppo (Catton, interview, November 22, 1991).[7] Other editions were made by members of the community.[8] *Siddur kol ya'akov* is considered superior for its accuracy and the quality of its printing, binding, and paper (ibid.). The authority of this prayer book rests upon the role that rabbinic and lay authorities of the Brooklyn community played in its preparation (ibid.) and the clarity of its organization (M. Tawil, interview, August 21, 1991).

Hoffman delineates three areas of liturgical expression that are affected by a prayer book: content, structure, and potential choreography (1987, 70–71). The content is the actual text of the prayer book, which, in the case of the Syrians, essentially follows Sephardic practice. The structure of a prayer book is the layout, design, organization, and language of instruction (70). Choreography refers to the way the service is conducted (71), which is often indicated by instructions. In many instances, instructions are not given and one must rely on familiarity with the style of the service in order to follow it in the text.

In the Syrian prayer books he published, Catton innovatively sought to provide a layout that was easy for the congregant to follow. The instructions—indications for when to respond, stand, or sit—are in both Hebrew and English. Most other Sephardic prayer books include only Hebrew instructions and the liturgical text is also only in Hebrew. Catton recently published a prayer book with the entire text of the liturgy in both Hebrew and English as well as bilingual instructions (*Siddur kol ya'akov* 1985). Thus, the content of the prayer book reflects the needs of the community. Other prayer books, such as *Siddur kol sassoon* (1995), include a linear English translation of each Hebrew line; this follows similar new prayer books printed in Brooklyn in the Ashkenazic community.[9]

The newly printed Syrian prayer books provide an example of how the structure of the prayer book intersects with the performance of the service. I extend Hoffman's description of choreography from "the way the service is conducted" to liturgical performance. The Sabbath morning service is rendered according to the Syrian liturgical performance tradition. The *ḥazzan* begins with the liturgical text Nishmat Kol Ḥai; certain sections are highlighted by a song initiated by the cantor and other portions are melodically improvised.[10] Figure 2 compares the Nishmat Kol Ḥai text as published in two editions by other publishers (2a, 2b) and in two editions by the Sephardic Heritage Foundation (2c, 2d).[11] This liturgical portion consists of a text in several paragraphs of which three passages are highlighted by the cantor; these are marked by numbers in circles in figure 2 (each sample is read upper-right to upper-left, then lower-right to lower-left). The first passage occurs at the beginning of the section and is easy to locate in all four texts. The second passage begins a new sentence in the middle of the textual portion, which is not clearly reflected in figures 2a and 2b but is placed at the start of a new paragraph in figures 2c and 2d. The third passage is the concluding phrase of the liturgical portion, which is only clearly conveyed by the text layout in figure 2d, being set-off, like the second passage, by three asterisks. This is a deliberate attempt by Catton, the editor, to convey visually the performance practice or melodic rendering of the service.[12] Catton explains that this layout is used to make the services easier to follow and to facilitate prayer (interview, November 22, 1991).[13] In effect, oral practice is represented visually to aid liturgical performance. The new prayer books are textual representations that reflect the process of learning and understanding the ritual experience.

Editor Catton is most proud of the High Holiday prayer books and recounts that "it got a lot of credit and praise from top experts" (ibid.). Like the siddur, these High Holiday prayer books are distinguished by publishing quality, including the bond of paper used, the gilded pages, the layout of the text on the page, and the artful style of the Hebrew typeface. Syrians and, in some cases, other Sephardic Jews throughout the world use these prayer books (ibid). In the introduction to the Rosh ha-Shanah and Yom Kippur prayer books Catton writes, "Since the year 1527, no prayer book of the liturgy of *'Aram Soba* [*sic*] was published. This deeply venerated and most sacred tradition, preserved and transmitted orally over the generations has now been painstakingly and faithfully reproduced in this edition, entitled *Shelom Yerushalayim*" ([5]).

The printing of prayer books in the Syrian community is a salient example of

Figure 2a. *Excerpt from* Sidur tefilat yeshurun: ke-minhag kehilot ha-kodesh shel ha-yehudism ha sephardim be-artzot ha-mizraḥ me-kodemet moshvoteihem. *New York: Hebrew Publishing Company, [1935].*

מתפללים כל סדר התפלה עד ובכן ישתבח ואחר כך מתחילין כאן:

נשמת כל חי תברך את שמך יהוה אלהינו ורוח כל בשר תפאר ותרומם זכרך מלכנו תמיד. מן העולם ועד העולם אתה אל. ומבלעדיך אין לנו מלך גואל ומושיע פודה ומציל. ועונה ומרחם. בכל עת צרה וצוקה. אין לנו מלך עוזר וסומך אלא אתה:

אלהי הראשונים והאחרונים אלוה כל בריות. אדון כל תולדות. המהלל בכל התשבחות. המנהג עולמו בחסד ובריותיו ברחמים. ויהוה ער. לא ינום ולא יישן. המעורר ישנים והמקיץ נרדמים. מחיה מתים ורופא חולים. פוקח עורים וזוקף כפופים. המשיח אלמים והמפענח נעלמים. ולך לבדך אנחנו מודים:

ואלו פינו מלא שירה כים. ולשוננו רנה כהמון גליו. ושפתותינו שבח כמרחבי רקיע. ועינינו מאירות כשמש וכירח. וידינו פרושות כנשרי שמים. ורגלינו קלות כאילות. אין אנו מספיקין להודות לך יהוה אלהינו. ולברך את שמך מלכנו. על אחת מאלף אלפי אלפים. ורוב רבי רבבות. פעמים הטובות. נסים ונפלאות שעשית עמנו ועם אבותינו מלפנים: ממצרים גאלתנו יהוה אלהינו. מבית עבדים פדיתנו. ברעב זנתנו. ובשבע כלכלתנו. מחרב הצלתנו. ומדבר מלטתנו. ומחלאים רעים ורבים דליתנו. עד הנה עזרונו רחמיך ולא עזבונו חסדיך. על כן אברים שפלגת בנו. ורוח ונשמה שנפחת באפנו. ולשון אשר שמת בפינו. הן הם יודו. ויברכו. וישבחו. ויפארו. וישוררו את שמך מלכנו תמיד. כי כל פה לך יודה. וכל לשון לך תשבח. וכל עין לך תצפה. וכל ברך לך תכרע. וכל קומה לפניך תשתחוה. והלבבות ייראוך. וכל קרב וכליות יזמרו לשמך. כדבר שנאמר כל עצמותי תאמרנה יהוה מי כמוך:

מציל עני מחזק ממנו ועני ואביון מגוזלו:

שועת עניים אתה תשמע. צעקת הדל תקשיב ותושיע. וכתוב רננו צדיקים ביהוה לישרים נאוה תהלה. בפי ישרים תתרומם. ובשפתי צדיקים תתברך. ובלשון חסידים תתקדש. ובקרב קדושים תתהלל:

במקהלות רבבות עמך בית ישראל. שכן חובת כל היצורים. לפניך יהוה אלהינו ואלהי אבותינו להודות. להלל. לשבח. לפאר. לרומם. להדר ולנצח. על כל דברי שירות ותשבחות דוד בן ישי עבדך משיחך:

ובכן ישתבח שמך לעד מלכנו האל המלך הגדול והקדוש בשמים ובארץ. כי לך נאה יהוה אלהינו ואלהי אבותינו לעולם ועד. שיר ושבחה. הלל וזמרה. עז וממשלה נצח. גדלה. וגבורה. תהלה ותפארת. קדשה ומלכות ברכות והודאות לשמך הגדול והקדוש ומעולם ועד עולם אתה אל:

ברוך אתה יהוה מלך גדול ומהלל בתשבחות אל ההודאות אדון הנפלאות בורא כל הנשמות רבון כל המעשים הבוחר בשירי זמרה מלך אל חי העולמים. אמן: ח"ק

חזן ברכו את יהוה המברך:

ועונין בקול רם:

ברוך יהוה המבורך לעולם ועד:

ברוך אתה יהוה אלהינו מלך העולם יוצר אור ובורא חשך. עשה שלום ובורא את הכל.

Figure 2b. *Excerpt from* Siddur bet yosef ve-ohel avraham: ke-minhag aram tsoba le-edot ha-sephardism be-kol mekomoteihem. *Jerusalem: Aleppian Publication Society, 1980.*

יאהדונהי עד־יעבר עם־זו קנית: תבאמו ותטעמו בהר נחלתך מכון לשבתך פעלת יהוה יאהדונהי מקדש אדני כוננו ידיך: יהוה יאהדונהי ימלך לעלם ועד: יהוה יאהדונהי ימלך לעלם ועד: יהוה יאהדונהי מלכותיה קאים לעלם ולעלמי עלמיא: כי בא סוס פרעה ברכבו ובפרשיו בים וישב יהוה יאהדונהי עלהם את־מי הים ובני ישראל הלכו ביבשה בתוך הים:

כי ליהוה יאהדונהי המלוכה. ומושל בגוים: ועלו מושעים בהר ציון לשפט את־הר עשו. והיתה ליהוה יאהדונהי המלוכה: והיה יהוה יאהדונהי למלך על־כל־הארץ. ביום ההוא יהיה יהוה יאהדונהי אחד ושמו אחד:

נשמת כל חי תברך את שמך יהוה יאהדונהי אלהינו ורוח כל־בשר תפאר ותרומם זכרך מלכנו תמיד. מן־העולם ועד־העולם אתה אל. ומבלעדיך אין לנו (מלך) גואל ומושיע. פודה ומציל. ועונה ומרחם. בכל־עת צרה וצוקה. אין לנו מלך עוזר וסומך אלא אתה:

אלהי הראשונים והאחרונים. אלוה כל בריות. אדון כל־תולדות. המהלל בכל־התשבחות. המנהג עולמו בחסד ובריותיו ברחמים. ויהוה יאהדונהי אלהים אמת לא ינום ולא יישן. המעורר ישנים והמקיץ נרדמים. מחיה מתים. ורופא חולים. פוקח עורים. וזוקף כפופים. המשיח אלמים. והמפענח נעלמים. ולך לבדך אנחנו מודים: ואלו פינו מלא שירה כים. ולשוננו רנה כהמון גליו. ושפתותינו שבח כמרחבי רקיע. ועינינו מאירות כשמש וכירח. וידינו פרושות כנשרי שמים. ורגלינו קלות כאילות. אין אנחנו מספיקין להודות לך יהוה יאהדונהי אלהינו. ולברך את־שמך מלכנו. על אחת מאלף אלפי אלפים ורוב רבי רבבות פעמים. הטובות נסים ונפלאות שעשית עמנו ועם אבותינו. מלפנים ממצרים גאלתנו יהוה יאהדונהי אלהינו. מבית עבדים פדיתנו. ברעב זנתנו. ובשבע כלכלתנו. מחרב הצלתנו. מדבר מלטתנו. ומחלאים רעים ורבים דליתנו. עד הנה עזרונו רחמיך ולא עזבונו חסדיך. על כן אברים שפלגת בנו. ורוח ונשמה שנפחת באפינו. ולשון אשר שמת בפינו. הן הם. יודו ויברכו. וישבחו.

ויפארו. וישוררו. את־שמך מלכנו תמיד. כי כל־פה לך יודה. וכל־לשון לך תשבח. וכל־עין לך תצפה. וכל־ברך לך תכרע. וכל־קומה לפניך תשתחוה. והלבבות ייראוך והקרב והכליות יזמרו לשמך. כדבר שנאמר א) כל עצמתי | תאמרנה יהוה יאהדונהי מי כמוך מציל עני מחזק ממנו. ועני ואביון מגזלו: שועת עניים אתה תשמע. צעקת הדל תקשיב ותושיע. וכתוב ב) רננו צדיקים ביהוה יאהדונהי. לישרים נאוה תהלה:

בפי י שרים תת ר ומם:
ובשפתי צ דיקים תת ב רך:
ובלשון ח סידים תת ק דש:
ובקרב ק דושים תת ה לל:

במקהלות רבבות עמך בית ישראל. שכן חובת כל היצורים לפניך יהוה יאהדונהי אלהינו ואלהי אבותינו. להלל. לשבח. לפאר. לרומם. להדר. ולנצח. על כל דברי שירות ותשבחות דוד בן ישי עבדך משיחך: ובכן **ישתבח** שמך לעד מלכנו האל המלך הגדול והקדוש בשמים ובארץ כי־לך נאה

יהוה יאהדונהי אלהינו ואלהי אבותינו לעולם ועד. א שיר. ב ושבחה. ג הלל. ד וזמרה. ה עז. ו וממשלה. ז נצח. ח גדולה. ט גבורה. י תהלה. יא ותפארת. יב קדשה יג ומלכות. ברכות והודאות לשמך הגדול והקדוש. ומעולם ועד עולם אתה אל. ברוך אתה יהוה יאהדונהי מלך גדול ומהלל בתשבחות. אל ההודאות. אדון הנפלאות. בורא כל הנשמות. רבון כל המעשים. הבוחר בשירי זמרה מלך אל חי העולמים אמן:

בשבת תשובה יאמר

א) שיר המעלות. ממעמקים קראתיך יהוה יאהדונהי: אדני שמעה בקולי תהיינה אזניך קשבות. לקול תחנוני: אם־עונות תשמר־יה. אדני מי יעמד: כי־עמך הסליחה. למען תורא: קויתי יהוה יאהדונהי קותה נפשי. ולדברו הוחלתי: נפשי לאדני. משמרים לבקר שמרים לבקר: יחל ישראל אל־יהוה יאהדונהי כי־עם־יהוה יאהדונהי החסד. והרבה עמו פדות: והוא יפדה את־ישראל. מכל עונותיו: ע״כ. ואומר החזן חצי קדיש

יתגדל ויתקדש שמה רבא. אמן בעלמא די ברא כרעותיה. וימליך מלכותיה. ויצמח פורקניה. ויקרב משיחיה. אמן בחייכון וביומיכון ובחיי דכל בית ישראל בעגלא ובזמן קריב ואמרו אמן. אמן יהא שמיה רבא מברך. לעלם ולעלמי עלמיא יתברך. וישתבח. ויתפאר. ויתרומם. ויתנשא. ויתהדר. ויתעלה.

Figure 2c. *Excerpt from* Siddur kol ya'akov: ke-minhag aram tsoba ha-shalem. *New York: Separdic Heritage Foundation, 1985.*

אֶל־נְוֵה קָדְשֶׁךָ: שָׁמְעוּ עַמִּים יִרְגָּזוּן חִיל אָחַז יֹשְׁבֵי פְּלָשֶׁת: אָז נִבְהֲלוּ אַלּוּפֵי אֱדוֹם אֵילֵי מוֹאָב יֹאחֲזֵמוֹ רָעַד נָמֹגוּ כֹּל יֹשְׁבֵי כְנָעַן: תִּפֹּל עֲלֵיהֶם אֵימָתָה וָפַחַד בִּגְדֹל זְרוֹעֲךָ יִדְּמוּ כָּאָבֶן עַד־יַעֲבֹר עַמְּךָ יְהֹוָה עַד־יַעֲבֹר עַם־זוּ קָנִיתָ:

תְּבִאֵמוֹ וְתִטָּעֵמוֹ בְּהַר נַחֲלָתְךָ מָכוֹן לְשִׁבְתְּךָ פָּעַלְתָּ יְהֹוָה מִקְּדָשׁ אֲדֹנָי כּוֹנְנוּ יָדֶיךָ: יְהֹוָה ׀ יִמְלֹךְ לְעֹלָם וָעֶד: יְהֹוָה ׀ יִמְלֹךְ לְעֹלָם וָעֶד: יְהֹוָה מַלְכוּתֵהּ קָאִים לְעָלַם וּלְעָלְמֵי עָלְמַיָּא: כִּי בָא סוּס פַּרְעֹה בְּרִכְבּוֹ וּבְפָרָשָׁיו בַּיָּם וַיָּשֶׁב יְהֹוָה עֲלֵהֶם אֶת־מֵי הַיָּם וּבְנֵי יִשְׂרָאֵל הָלְכוּ בַיַּבָּשָׁה בְּתוֹךְ הַיָּם:

כִּי לַיהֹוָה הַמְּלוּכָה, וּמֹשֵׁל בַּגּוֹיִם: וְעָלוּ מוֹשִׁעִים בְּהַר צִיּוֹן, לִשְׁפֹּט אֶת־הַר עֵשָׂו, וְהָיְתָה לַיהֹוָה הַמְּלוּכָה: וְהָיָה יְהֹוָה לְמֶלֶךְ עַל־כָּל הָאָרֶץ, בַּיּוֹם הַהוּא יִהְיֶה יְהֹוָה אֶחָד וּשְׁמוֹ אֶחָד:

נִשְׁמַת כָּל־חַי, תְּבָרֵךְ אֶת־שִׁמְךָ יְהֹוָה אֱלֹהֵינוּ, וְרוּחַ כָּל־בָּשָׂר, תְּפָאֵר וּתְרוֹמֵם זִכְרְךָ מַלְכֵּנוּ תָּמִיד: מִן־הָעוֹלָם וְעַד־הָעוֹלָם אַתָּה אֵל. וּמִבַּלְעָדֶיךָ אֵין לָנוּ מֶלֶךְ גּוֹאֵל וּמוֹשִׁיעַ. פּוֹדֶה וּמַצִּיל, וְעוֹנֶה וּמְרַחֵם, בְּכָל־עֵת צָרָה וְצוּקָה. אֵין לָנוּ מֶלֶךְ עוֹזֵר וְסוֹמֵךְ אֶלָּא אָתָּה: אֱלֹהֵי הָרִאשׁוֹנִים וְהָאַחֲרוֹנִים, אֱלוֹהַּ כָּל־בְּרִיּוֹת, אֲדוֹן כָּל־תּוֹלָדוֹת, הַמְּהֻלָּל בְּכָל־הַתִּשְׁבָּחוֹת, הַמְנַהֵג עוֹלָמוֹ בְּחֶסֶד, וּבְרִיּוֹתָיו בְּרַחֲמִים: וַיהֹוָה אֱלֹהִים אֱמֶת לֹא־יָנוּם וְלֹא־יִישָׁן. הַמְעוֹרֵר יְשֵׁנִים, וְהַמֵּקִיץ נִרְדָּמִים, מְחַיֶּה מֵתִים. וְרוֹפֵא חוֹלִים, פּוֹקֵחַ עִוְרִים, וְזוֹקֵף כְּפוּפִים, הַמֵּשִׂיחַ אִלְּמִים, וְהַמְפַעֲנֵחַ נֶעֱלָמִים, וּלְךָ לְבַדְּךָ אֲנַחְנוּ מוֹדִים:

וְאִלּוּ פִינוּ מָלֵא שִׁירָה כַּיָּם, וּלְשׁוֹנֵנוּ רִנָּה כַּהֲמוֹן גַּלָּיו, וְשִׂפְתוֹתֵינוּ שֶׁבַח כְּמֶרְחֲבֵי רָקִיעַ, וְעֵינֵינוּ מְאִירוֹת כַּשֶּׁמֶשׁ וְכַיָּרֵחַ, וְיָדֵינוּ פְרוּשׂוֹת כְּנִשְׁרֵי שָׁמָיִם, וְרַגְלֵינוּ קַלּוֹת כָּאַיָּלוֹת. אֵין אֲנַחְנוּ מַסְפִּיקִין לְהוֹדוֹת לְךָ יְהֹוָה אֱלֹהֵינוּ, וּלְבָרֵךְ אֶת־שִׁמְךָ מַלְכֵּנוּ, עַל־אַחַת מֵאֶלֶף אַלְפֵי אֲלָפִים, וְרֹב רִבֵּי רְבָבוֹת, פְּעָמִים הַטּוֹבוֹת, נִסִּים וְנִפְלָאוֹת שֶׁעָשִׂיתָ עִמָּנוּ, וְעִם אֲבוֹתֵינוּ. מִלְּפָנִים מִמִּצְרַיִם גְּאַלְתָּנוּ יְהֹוָה אֱלֹהֵינוּ, מִבֵּית עֲבָדִים פְּדִיתָנוּ, בְּרָעָב זַנְתָּנוּ, וּבְשָׂבָע כִּלְכַּלְתָּנוּ. מֵחֶרֶב הִצַּלְתָּנוּ, מִדֶּבֶר מִלַּטְתָּנוּ, וּמֵחֳלָיִם רָעִים וְרַבִּים דִּלִּיתָנוּ: עַד הֵנָּה עֲזָרוּנוּ רַחֲמֶיךָ, וְלֹא עֲזָבוּנוּ חֲסָדֶיךָ: עַל כֵּן אֵבָרִים שֶׁפִּלַּגְתָּ בָּנוּ, וְרוּחַ וּנְשָׁמָה שֶׁנָּפַחְתָּ בְּאַפֵּינוּ, וְלָשׁוֹן אֲשֶׁר שַׂמְתָּ בְּפִינוּ. הֵן הֵם. יוֹדוּ וִיבָרְכוּ, וִישַׁבְּחוּ, וִיפָאֲרוּ, וִישׁוֹרְרוּ אֶת־שִׁמְךָ מַלְכֵּנוּ תָּמִיד: כִּי כָל־פֶּה לְךָ יוֹדֶה, וְכָל־לָשׁוֹן לְךָ תְשַׁבֵּחַ, וְכָל־עַיִן לְךָ תְצַפֶּה, וְכָל־בֶּרֶךְ לְךָ תִכְרַע, וְכָל־קוֹמָה לְפָנֶיךָ תִשְׁתַּחֲוֶה: וְהַלְּבָבוֹת יִירָאוּךָ. וְכָל קֶרֶב וּכְלָיוֹת יְזַמְּרוּ לִשְׁמֶךָ: כַּדָּבָר שֶׁנֶּאֱמַר. כָּל עַצְמוֹתַי תֹּאמַרְנָה, יְהֹוָה מִי כָמוֹךָ: מַצִּיל עָנִי מֵחָזָק מִמֶּנּוּ. וְעָנִי וְאֶבְיוֹן מִגֹּזְלוֹ:

שַׁוְעַת עֲנִיִּים אַתָּה תִשְׁמַע, צַעֲקַת הַדַּל תַּקְשִׁיב וְתוֹשִׁיעַ: וְכָתוּב, רַנְּנוּ צַדִּיקִים בַּיהֹוָה, לַיְשָׁרִים נָאוָה תְהִלָּה:

בְּפִי **יְ**שָׁרִים תִּתְ**רוֹ**מָם :
וּבְשִׂפְתֵי **צַ**דִּיקִים תִּתְ**בָּ**רַךְ :
וּבִלְשׁוֹן **חֲ**סִידִים תִּתְ**קַ**דָּשׁ :
וּבְקֶרֶב **קְ**דוֹשִׁים תִּתְ**הַ**לָּל :

בְּמִקְהֲלוֹת רִבְבוֹת עַמְּךָ בֵּית יִשְׂרָאֵל. שֶׁכֵּן חוֹבַת כָּל־הַיְצוּרִים לְפָנֶיךָ, יְהֹוָה אֱלֹהֵינוּ וֵאלֹהֵי אֲבוֹתֵינוּ, לְהוֹדוֹת לְהַלֵּל, לְשַׁבֵּחַ לְפָאֵר, לְרוֹמֵם לְהַדֵּר וּלְנַצֵּחַ, עַל כָּל דִּבְרֵי שִׁירוֹת וְתִשְׁבְּחוֹת דָּוִד בֶּן יִשַׁי, עַבְדְּךָ מְשִׁיחֶךָ:

וּבְכֵן יִשְׁתַּבַּח שִׁמְךָ, לָעַד, מַלְכֵּנוּ, הָאֵל הַמֶּלֶךְ הַגָּדוֹל וְהַקָּדוֹשׁ, בַּשָּׁמַיִם וּבָאָרֶץ: כִּי־לְךָ נָאֶה יְהֹוָה אֱלֹהֵינוּ וֵאלֹהֵי אֲבוֹתֵינוּ, לְעוֹלָם וָעֶד. שִׁיר וּשְׁבָחָה, הַלֵּל וְזִמְרָה, עֹז וּמֶמְשָׁלָה, נֶצַח, גְּדוּלָּה, גְּבוּרָה, תְּהִלָּה וְתִפְאֶרֶת, קְדֻשָּׁה וּמַלְכוּת, בְּרָכוֹת וְהוֹדָאוֹת, לְשִׁמְךָ הַגָּדוֹל וְהַקָּדוֹשׁ, וּמֵעוֹלָם וְעַד עוֹלָם אַתָּה אֵל: בָּרוּךְ אַתָּה יְהֹוָה, מֶלֶךְ גָּדוֹל וּמְהֻלָּל בַּתִּשְׁבָּחוֹת: אֵל הַהוֹדָאוֹת, אֲדוֹן הַנִּפְלָאוֹת, בּוֹרֵא כָל הַנְּשָׁמוֹת, רִבּוֹן כָּל הַמַּעֲשִׂים, הַבּוֹחֵר בְּשִׁירֵי זִמְרָה, מֶלֶךְ אֵל חַי הָעוֹלָמִים, אָמֵן:

Figure 2d. *Excerpt from* Maḥzor shelom yerushalayim, ḥlek shelishi: seder tefilot le-kavod ḥag ha-sukkot ke-minhag ha-sefardim ve-edot ha-mizraḥ be-kol-mekomot moshvoteihem ha-shem aleihem yeḥyu. *New York: Sephardic Heritage Foundation, 1990.*

כִּי לַיהוה הַמְּלוּכָה, וּמשֵׁל בַּגּוֹיִם:
וְעָלוּ מוֹשִׁעִים בְּהַר צִיּוֹן, לִשְׁפֹּט אֶת־הַר עֵשָׂו
וְהָיְתָה לַיהוה הַמְּלוּכָה:
וְהָיָה יהוה לְמֶלֶךְ עַל־כָּל־הָאָרֶץ
בַּיּוֹם הַהוּא יִהְיֶה יהוה אֶחָד וּשְׁמוֹ אֶחָד:

נִשְׁמַת כָּל־חַי
תְּבָרֵךְ אֶת־שִׁמְךָ
יהוה אֱלֹהֵינוּ:
וְרוּחַ כָּל־בָּשָׂר
תְּפָאֵר וּתְרוֹמֵם
זִכְרְךָ מַלְכֵּנוּ תָּמִיד:
מִן־הָעוֹלָם
וְעַד־הָעוֹלָם
אַתָּה אֵל:

וּמִבַּלְעָדֶיךָ, אֵין לָנוּ מֶלֶךְ גּוֹאֵל וּמוֹשִׁיעַ, פּוֹדֶה וּמַצִּיל, וְעוֹנֶה וּמְרַחֵם, בְּכָל־עֵת צָרָה וְצוּקָה, אֵין לָנוּ מֶלֶךְ עוֹזֵר וְסוֹמֵךְ, אֶלָּא אָתָּה:

אֱלֹהֵי הָרִאשׁוֹנִים וְהָאַחֲרוֹנִים, אֱלוֹהַּ כָּל־בְּרִיּוֹת, אֲדוֹן כָּל־תּוֹלָדוֹת, הַמְּהֻלָּל בְּכָל־הַתִּשְׁבָּחוֹת, הַמְנַהֵג עוֹלָמוֹ בְּחֶסֶד, וּבְרִיּוֹתָיו בְּרַחֲמִים:

כִּי כָל־פֶּה לְךָ יוֹדֶה, וְכָל־לָשׁוֹן לְךָ תְשַׁבֵּחַ, וְכָל־עַיִן לְךָ תְצַפֶּה, וְכָל־בֶּרֶךְ לְךָ תִכְרַע, וְכָל־קוֹמָה לְפָנֶיךָ תִשְׁתַּחֲוֶה:

וְהַלְּבָבוֹת יִירָאוּךָ, וְהַקֶּרֶב וְהַכְּלָיוֹת יְזַמְּרוּ לִשְׁמֶךָ: כַּדָּבָר שֶׁנֶּאֱמַר. כָּל עַצְמֹתַי תֹּאמַרְנָה, יהוה מִי כָמוֹךָ: מַצִּיל עָנִי מֵחָזָק מִמֶּנּוּ, וְעָנִי וְאֶבְיוֹן מִגֹּזְלוֹ:

* * *

שַׁוְעַת עֲנִיִּים אַתָּה תִשְׁמַע
צַעֲקַת הַדַּל תַּקְשִׁיב וְתוֹשִׁיעַ:
וְכָתוּב, רַנְּנוּ צַדִּיקִים בַּיהוה
לַיְשָׁרִים נָאוָה תְהִלָּה:

בְּפִי יְשָׁרִים תִּתְרוֹמָם
וּבְשִׂפְתֵי צַדִּיקִים תִּתְבָּרַךְ
וּבִלְשׁוֹן חֲסִידִים תִּתְקַדָּשׁ
וּבְקֶרֶב קְדוֹשִׁים תִּתְהַלָּל:

בְּמִקְהֲלוֹת רִבְבוֹת עַמְּךָ בֵּית יִשְׂרָאֵל. שֶׁכֵּן חוֹבַת כָּל־הַיְצוּרִים, לְפָנֶיךָ, יהוה אֱלֹהֵינוּ וֵאלֹהֵי אֲבוֹתֵינוּ. לְהוֹדוֹת, לְהַלֵּל, לְשַׁבֵּחַ, לְפָאֵר, לְרוֹמֵם, לְהַדֵּר וּלְנַצֵּחַ. עַל כָּל־דִּבְרֵי שִׁירוֹת וְתִשְׁבְּחוֹת דָּוִד בֶּן יִשַׁי, עַבְדְּךָ מְשִׁיחֶךָ:

וַיהוה אֱלֹהִים אֱמֶת, לֹא־יָנוּם וְלֹא־יִישָׁן. הַמְעוֹרֵר יְשֵׁנִים, וְהַמֵּקִיץ נִרְדָּמִים. מְחַיֵּה מֵתִים, וְרוֹפֵא חוֹלִים. פּוֹקֵחַ עִוְרִים, וְזוֹקֵף כְּפוּפִים. הַמֵּשִׂיחַ אִלְּמִים, וְהַמְפַעֲנֵחַ נֶעֱלָמִים. וּלְךָ לְבַדְּךָ אֲנַחְנוּ מוֹדִים:

וְאִלּוּ פִינוּ מָלֵא שִׁירָה כַּיָּם, וּלְשׁוֹנֵנוּ רִנָּה כַּהֲמוֹן גַּלָּיו, וְשִׂפְתוֹתֵינוּ שֶׁבַח כְּמֶרְחֲבֵי רָקִיעַ, וְעֵינֵינוּ מְאִירוֹת כַּשֶּׁמֶשׁ וְכַיָּרֵחַ, וְיָדֵינוּ פְרוּשׂוֹת כְּנִשְׁרֵי שָׁמַיִם, וְרַגְלֵינוּ קַלּוֹת כָּאַיָּלוֹת:

אֵין אֲנַחְנוּ מַסְפִּיקִים, לְהוֹדוֹת לְךָ יהוה אֱלֹהֵינוּ, וּלְבָרֵךְ אֶת־שִׁמְךָ מַלְכֵּנוּ, עַל אַחַת מֵאֶלֶף אַלְפֵי אֲלָפִים, וְרֹב רִבֵּי רְבָבוֹת פְּעָמִים, הַטּוֹבוֹת, נִסִּים וְנִפְלָאוֹת, שֶׁעָשִׂיתָ עִמָּנוּ, וְעִם אֲבוֹתֵינוּ מִלְּפָנִים:

מִמִּצְרַיִם גְּאַלְתָּנוּ יהוה אֱלֹהֵינוּ, מִבֵּית עֲבָדִים פְּדִיתָנוּ, בְּרָעָב זַנְתָּנוּ, וּבְשָׂבָע כִּלְכַּלְתָּנוּ. מֵחֶרֶב הִצַּלְתָּנוּ, וּמִדֶּבֶר מִלַּטְתָּנוּ. וּמֵחֳלָיִם רָעִים וְרַבִּים דִּלִּיתָנוּ:

עַד־הֵנָּה עֲזָרוּנוּ רַחֲמֶיךָ, וְלֹא עֲזָבוּנוּ חֲסָדֶיךָ. עַל כֵּן אֵבָרִים שֶׁפִּלַּגְתָּ בָּנוּ, וְרוּחַ וּנְשָׁמָה שֶׁנָּפַחְתָּ בְּאַפֵּינוּ, וְלָשׁוֹן אֲשֶׁר שַׂמְתָּ בְּפִינוּ: הֵן הֵם יוֹדוּ, וִיבָרְכוּ, וִישַׁבְּחוּ, וִיפָאֲרוּ, וִישׁוֹרְרוּ, אֶת־שִׁמְךָ מַלְכֵּנוּ תָּמִיד:

וּבְכֵן, יִשְׁתַּבַּח שִׁמְךָ, לָעַד מַלְכֵּנוּ, הָאֵל הַמֶּלֶךְ הַגָּדוֹל וְהַקָּדוֹשׁ, בַּשָּׁמַיִם וּבָאָרֶץ: כִּי לְךָ נָאֶה יהוה אֱלֹהֵינוּ וֵאלֹהֵי אֲבוֹתֵינוּ, לְעוֹלָם וָעֶד. שִׁיר וּשְׁבָחָה, הַלֵּל וְזִמְרָה, עֹז וּמֶמְשָׁלָה, נֶצַח, גְּדֻלָּה, גְּבוּרָה, תְּהִלָּה וְתִפְאֶרֶת, קְדֻשָּׁה וּמַלְכוּת, בְּרָכוֹת וְהוֹדָאוֹת, לְשִׁמְךָ הַגָּדוֹל וְהַקָּדוֹשׁ, וּמֵעוֹלָם וְעַד עוֹלָם אַתָּה אֵל:
בָּרוּךְ אַתָּה יהוה, מֶלֶךְ גָּדוֹל וּמְהֻלָּל בַּתִּשְׁבָּחוֹת:

* * *

אֵל הַהוֹדָאוֹת
אֲדוֹן הַנִּפְלָאוֹת
בּוֹרֵא כָּל־הַנְּשָׁמוֹת
רִבּוֹן כָּל־הַמַּעֲשִׂים
הַבּוֹחֵר בְּשִׁירֵי זִמְרָה
מֶלֶךְ אֵל חַי הָעוֹלָמִים
אָמֵן:

שִׁיר הַמַּעֲלוֹת מִמַּעֲמַקִּים קְרָאתִיךָ יהוה: אֲדֹנָי שִׁמְעָה בְקוֹלִי תִּהְיֶינָה אָזְנֶיךָ קַשֻּׁבוֹת לְקוֹל תַּחֲנוּנָי: אִם־עֲוֹנוֹת תִּשְׁמָר־יָהּ אֲדֹנָי מִי יַעֲמֹד: כִּי־עִמְּךָ הַסְּלִיחָה לְמַעַן תִּוָּרֵא: קִוִּיתִי יהוה קִוְּתָה נַפְשִׁי וְלִדְבָרוֹ הוֹחָלְתִּי: נַפְשִׁי לַאדֹנָי מִשֹּׁמְרִים לַבֹּקֶר שֹׁמְרִים לַבֹּקֶר: יַחֵל יִשְׂרָאֵל אֶל־יהוה כִּי־עִם־יהוה הַחֶסֶד וְהַרְבֵּה עִמּוֹ פְדוּת: וְהוּא יִפְדֶּה אֶת־יִשְׂרָאֵל מִכֹּל עֲוֹנוֹתָיו:

Hoffman's claim that a community expresses its identity particularly reflecting the way they "see themselves vis-à-vis others" (1987, 55). Before the printings of prayer books in the Syrian community in the 1980s, other Sephardic prayer books were used. The recently printed prayer books by Syrians express their identity while faithfully maintaining their time-honored past traditions, allowing, as Catton explained above, the community to "painstakingly and faithfully reproduce" their past.[14] This is significant especially because the Aleppo liturgical textual tradition is not fundamentally distinct from general Sephardic practice. During the 1980s and 1990s Sephardic communities have sought to restore their ancient traditions and proudly rededicate themselves to these customs.

Paraliturgical Texts

Background

Piyyutim—the genre of Hebrew liturgical texts that embellish obligatory prayers—were composed from the first century through the eighteenth century (Fleischer 1972a, 573). In some communities the tradition of creating new texts continues today (Shiloah 1992, 122). Historically, the texts were composed for specific sections within the liturgy and were typically used to elaborate the liturgy for major holidays or a specific religious theme for a regular Sabbath. In certain Middle Eastern communities piyyutim were written to mark a life cycle occasion such as a circumcision, bar mitzvah, or wedding (Fleischer 1972, 573–74). Some of the well-known piyyutim were incorporated into the liturgy during the canonization period, from the eighth to the tenth centuries.

The fixing of the liturgical text in Judaism was a slow process that developed over time, changing the role of the *ḥazzan* as a result. The function of the *ḥazzan* during the first millennium was to create and sing religious poetry (Schirmann 1954, 239; Werner 1976, 10; Slobin 1989, 6; Shiloah 1992, 67–68).[15] The *ḥazzan* elaborated designated religious themes into his poetry by creating newly composed texts (Carmi 1981, 14). There was some resistance to the writing of the prayers (Schirmann 1953–54, 134), but as certain piyyutim became known, these texts were incorporated into the liturgy. This process of standardization continued with the printing of prayer books (Elbogen 1913 [1993], 226); consequently, the function of the piyyut changed. Amnon Shiloah explains:

> In olden times the *paytan* [cantor, poet] performed a three-fold task: he wrote the text, adapted the words to the melody, and per-

> formed the work as part of the prayers or other religious rites. Once a body of *piyyutim* had acquired an accepted place within the regular prayers, fewer and fewer new poetic works were absorbed into the liturgy. This limited the function of the *paytan* to aspects of musical adaptation and performance. At the same time, the writing of *piyyutim* continued to flourish outside the framework of prayer and ritual worship, *piyyutim* being sung with the Sabbath Psalms, the lamentations, the penitential prayers and supplications, as well as at paraliturgical events such as circumcisions, weddings, and so on (1992, 122).[16]

The role of the cantor as textual composer is replaced today by the cantor as melodic improviser. Syrian cantors' musical expertise for prayers is wedded with a facility with texts. Although there are few creators of piyyutim in the Syrian community today, cantors are proficient with the *bakkashot* and *pizmonim* texts used in the community. Their role as textual expert and facilitator has been redefined.

Paraliturgical Texts of the Syrian Community

The piyyut tradition has been kept alive in the Syrian community. Many poems—in the form of *bakkashot* and *pizmonim*—composed in Aleppo in the nineteenth century are still sung in Israel and the Syrian Diaspora, while new texts have been written in Brooklyn in the twentieth century (see Yayama 2003).[17]

The *bakkashot* and the *pizmonim* serve different functions in Syrian liturgical and daily life. The *bakkashot* texts are usually sung before Sabbath morning prayers, a practice still extant among a small number of Syrian Jews in Brooklyn.[18] The *pizmonim* singing occurs on a more regular basis in a variety of contexts; in the synagogue they sing while the Torah scrolls parade around the synagogue during the Sabbath morning service procession and between readings of the Torah. Outside the synagogue, *pizmonim* are sung during Sabbath meals, during the *sebet* (an informal gathering at home in the Sabbath afternoon), and at the Brit Milah. The melodies of the *pizmonim,* and to a lesser extent those of the *bakkashot,* are set to various portions of the liturgy during worship. These two genres thus comprise the primary basis of liturgical melodies in the Syrian Jewish community. Since 1980 there has been renewed interest in the singing of *pizmonim* in Brooklyn, with the teaching of this practice in day schools and community-sponsored classes and concerts (Shelemay 1988, 381; 1998, 34–37). The continued publication of new editions of *Shir ush'vaḥa, hallel v'zimrah* (*SUHV*) has played an important part in the rejuvenation of the *pizmonim* (Cabasso, interview, May 29, 1992), although before the first edition of this publication other books were available, mainly private collections in the possession of a few members of the community. *SUHV* contains the texts of *bakkashot* and *pizmonim* composed within the last fifty to one hundred years (Shelemay 1998, 138–43); some of the *bakkashot* are older piyyutim written by poets of the golden age of Spain.[19]

SUHV is dedicated to two Syrian poets, as a translation of the title page indicates:

> To commemorate the memory of the famous *paytanim* [poets] for praise and blessing, the first in holiness, Rabbi Raphael Antebi Taboush, who should be remembered with a blessing, and the next in line, the pleasant singer of Israel, Rabbi Moshe Ashkar HaCohen, who should be remembered with a blessing, who was privileged to compose in their spirit of holiness holy songs, sweet as honey and great in vision. They broadened the borders of song by raising students, cantors and singers. May their memory be a blessing forever.[20]

A number of *pizmonim* in this publication were written by Taboush and Ashear. Born in Aleppo, both men were rabbis, poets, and cantors. In many ways they resemble the poet-cantor of a thousand years earlier; the first line of the dedication uses the Hebrew word *paytanim,* thus equating Taboush's and Asher's efforts with their medieval predecessors. Taboush, who immigrated to Israel prior to his death in Egypt, was the teacher and Ashear his beloved student (Shelemay 1998, 29–33). The pupil was appointed the official *ḥazzan* and Torah reader of Aleppo in 1903 (Ashear 1985, 11–13) and immigrated in 1912 to America, where he settled in Brooklyn. The *pizmonim* of both Taboush and Ashear are still sung today; many of them were written by the latter in honor of various members of the Brooklyn community for such occasions as bar mitzvahs and weddings. *Ḥazzanim* wrote *pizmonim* for specific occasions and family members sing these texts to remember individuals (Shelemay 1998, 46). The *bakkashot* are considered to be older texts and melodies (Cabasso, *pizmonim* class, November 18, 1991). Few texts have been added in recent years (Shelemay 1998, 185–87).

The *bakkashot* and *pizmonim* are poetic texts that follow models of other forms of poetry and adapt a variety of influences, culling from other Hebrew texts and poetic models, for example. Both textual genres closely follow the poetic construction of the piyyut in terms of the rhyme scheme pattern and use of an acrostic (ibid., 45). Textual styles do vary since there is no one poetic model to follow. Indeed, some *pizmonim* follow the free poetic format of modern Hebrew poetry. Additionally, the *pizmonim* draw from the originating Arabic song text as a model for poetic construction, meaning, and use of assonance and cognates.[21] The *pizmonim* in particular offer a textual process of adaptation that bases the poetry on both Hebrew models and the source Arabic text. Kay Kaufman Shelemay sees this practice as an effective combination of the past and the present: "The texts initiate and sustain a dialogue between the present occasion and others of its kind, as well as with the different domains of Jewish thought, oral tradition, and written discourse. . . . [T]he repeated singing of a pizmon serves to recall specific occasions in the individual life cycle and to bind that event to others of its kind, thereby enhancing its meaning" (1998, 215). This presents a model of synthesis through textual adaptation that includes poetic style, structure, and meaning. The musical adaptation of these melodies in the liturgy continues the process. However, the tightly constructed textual patterns of the *bakkashot* and *pizmonim* are not found in the liturgy. The music accommodates the demands of the liturgical text and function, and the melodies accommodate the new textual context. The musical examples in chapter 7 continue this discussion.

Pizmonim and the Interaction of Music and Text

THE MELODIES OF these poetic texts are themselves taken from preexisting melodies, the vast majority from Arab music (Cabasso, *pizmonim* class, December 9, 1991, November 18, 1992; D. Tawil, interview, July 29. 1992).[22] The melody used for a *pizmon* is usually indicated in *SUHV* along with the name of its author, a practice common in Sephardic and Mizraḥi communities for several centuries (Seroussi 1990a, 1990b). The Taboush *pizmonim* originate from Arab melodies popular in Middle Eastern communities during the late nineteenth century, while Ashear set popular melodies of the first third of the twentieth century. Syrian *ḥazzanim* adapt both vocal and instrumental compositions (see Shelemay and Weiss 1985; Shelemay 1998, 17) and the newly composed Hebrew words closely model the preexisting melody. One typical example is the *pizmon* Go'alekh, go'alekh (You redeem, You redeem; *SUHV* #373). The original Arabic melody carried the Arabic text Gemalekh, gemalekh (Beauty, beauty).

Non-Arabic melodies are also used for *pizmonim,* but they comprise only a small part of the repertoire (D. Tawil, interview, July 29, 1992). Some *pizmonim* by Taboush have the melodic designation of "*muzikah,*" which is said to be an indication of a non-Arab melody that may be either Turkish or European (ibid.).[23] It was not uncommon for Ashear to make use of European melodies, as seen in Malakhei marom (*SUHV* #189), which has the designation "German music" (Cabasso, *pizmonim* class, November 18, 1991).[24] Many of the melodies designated "*muzikah*" are from songs no longer known by members of the community. The process of adapting melodies from the surrounding environment for use in *pizmonim* continues in the United States (Shelemay and Weiss 1985). For example, "God Bless America," is used for Shiru shirah ḥadashah (*SUHV* #202), composed in 1951 for the opening of Congregation Aḥi Ezer in Brooklyn. "O Tannenbaum" surprisingly provides the source melody for Mif'alot elokim (*SUHV* #189), which has the indication "sixty-two" for Public School 62—the melody was used as a school anthem, with the words "Oh Sixty-two" replacing "O Tannenbaum." The melody of "Fiddler on the Roof," carrying the text Ashir na shir tikvah (*SUHV* #509b) was composed for a bar mitzvah (see Shelemay 1998, 183–98). However interesting these examples are of the community's adaptation of American melodies, they are not nearly as common as the hundreds of Arabic melodies that make up the mainstay of the *pizmonim* repertoire and liturgical melodies.

Part Two

Sabbath Morning Service

4

Syrian Musical Life

The Maqām *System as Practiced in Brooklyn*

THE MUSICAL TASTES of Syrians in Brooklyn incorporate a diverse range of styles, including Arab, popular American, opera, and other ethnic musics. In a sense, their musical preferences are an appropriate reflection of their cultural life: steeped in various forms of American culture with a marked preference for Arab culture. First and second generation immigrants favor Arab music, evidently nurtured by an exposure to Arab music from their premigratory days or from immigrant parents. A major component to the perpetuation of the music in the liturgy is their practice of *maqām.* The adaptation of Arab music is central to not only the acquisition of melodies but aesthetics and genres.

Musical Life

THE MUSICAL REPERTOIRE for Syrian Jews has changed with the times. Music in Aleppo was made up of both local music and general Middle Eastern music, including repertoires that spanned folk, popular, and art music (A. Marcus 1989, 233). Arab American immigrants from Aleppo at the turn of the twentieth century drew from a variety of musical sources, including *qaṣā'id,* a vocal responsorial varied form; *muwwashshaḥāt,* a vocal classical form of strophic poetry; and *bashārīf,* a contemporary instrumental prelude (Rasmussen 1991, 72).[1] Aleppo residents, both Jewish and non-Jewish, were always known for the finest of tastes in music (M. Tawil, interview, August 21, 1991; see also Shelemay 1998, 105). As one recent Jewish immigrant stated, "Aleppo's people are known to have very developed taste, in music, in their clothes, their architecture; all of them, Muslims, Jews, and Christians; especially in music, they are world-renowned. It is said that every Arab musician, if he has won the approval of the people of Ḥálab [*sic*], he has carte blanche to audiences everywhere" (Sutton 1988, 228).[2] Middle Eastern music radically changed in the late nineteenth and early twentieth century. Turkish culture waned in favor of a desire for national forms of music. The Western presence in the region influenced many cultural developments, including language, fashion, food, and music (Hournai 1991, 304–8).[3] Syrian musical repertoire kept pace with these changes. Recent printings of *SUHV* include the repertoire known and currently practiced in the community (Catton, interview, November 22, 1991; Cabasso, interview, May 29, 1992). The discontinued, or oldest, *pizmonim* were based on Turkish music; the newer melodies, adapted between the 1920s and the 1940s, with many currently in use, come from Arab music (D. Tawil, interview, July 29, 1992; Shelemay 1998, 199–205). The change in preferred melodies of Arab origin reflect the aesthetic desires of the community.

The Judeo-Arab musical tradition of Syrians in Brooklyn is covered thoroughly in Kay Kaufman Shelemay's *Let Jasmine Rain Down: Song and Remembrance among Syrian Jews*. Shelemay bases her study on a broad and thorough investigation of the *pizmonim* repertoire by examining daily and religious life, identity, and the ongoing construction of an idealized past. In her consideration of the Judeo-Arab synthesis she continually notes that technology plays an important role.[4] Arab music is kept alive through the vast recordings (Racy 1978), which are readily available in Brooklyn at Arab music stores along Atlantic Avenue (Rashid 2002). Several members of the community take great pride in their collections of 78 RPM recordings and the recent reissues of these older recordings on CD. Shelemay also documents the vivid memories that many members of the communities express about the role of music in their homes. Arab singers such as Muḥammad 'Abd al-Wahhāb (c. 1910–92), Umm Kulthūm (1899–1975), Sayyid Darwīsh (1892–1923), Zakarīyā Aḥmad (1896–1961), Farīd al-Aṭrash (1915–1974), Fairouz (1935–), and Warda (1940–) (Shelemay 1998, 109–15) are well known to singers and members in the community. Muḥammad 'Abd al-Wahhāb and Umm Kulthūm in particular are held in high regard for their significant musical achievements in Arab music.[5]

Shelemay also discusses the contexts of musical awareness and acquisition (1998, 67). In the early part of the twentieth century, coffeehouses and cafes provided important meeting grounds for Arab musical awareness prior to the proliferation of recordings (Sanua 1977, 282; Elazar 1989, 171). As might be expected, when recordings became more readily available coffeehouses declined in importance. Shelemay adds that some attend concerts of Arab musicians in New York City but parties and life cycle events (bar mitzvahs and weddings) are the primary ongoing occasions for the performance of Arab music.[6]

The singing of *pizmonim* is an important opportunity for cultural perpetuation and a link to Arab music. Shelemay suggests that *pizmonim* have replaced the Judeo-Arab language as a vestige of the past (1998, 224). She reflects on the extent to which Arab music permeates Syrian Jewish life:

> Today the Judeo-Islamic symbiosis in Syrian-Jewish musical life remains powerful. . . . Many Syrian Jews may be said without hyperbole to inhabit a sound world of Arab music, ranging from the businessman who keeps Arab music cassettes in his office so that while he is working he can listen to them "all day," to the elderly woman who listens to tapes of Umm Kulthūm and ʿAbd al-Wahhāb before going to bed at night. (229)

In order to situate the musical practices of Syrian Jews in Brooklyn, I draw from Anne Katharine Rasmussen's work on Arab Americans (1991). During the 1930s to the 1970s music for Arab Americans developed and there was a need for professional musicians. These musicians played at *ḥaflāt* and *mahrajānāt,* private and public parties, which were new contexts that grew out of traditional Arab life.[7] These important musical pioneers modeled their music after luminary figures such as Muḥammad ʿAbd al-Wahhāb and Umm Kulthūm (1991, 80–88). Just as for Syrian Jews, the recordings were an important source for Arab Americans for keeping pace with Arab music developments while living in the Diaspora. In the 1960s and 1970s, musical innovation was the goal. The context of music making changed from parties to nightclubs (ibid., 88–89). New musical innovators made the music more palatable and intriguing for Western audiences.[8] In the 1980s and 1990s, the nightclub musical innovations decreased in favor of a pan-Arab folk style (ibid., 96).

The musical practices of first generation Arab Americans were more homogeneous than the musical repertoire of recent immigrants from the twenty-two nations of the Arab world, which is shaped by the musical tastes of various regional immigrant groups (ibid., 97). Rasmussen does note one exception to the present heterogeneity of Arab American music styles: Aleppo and Damascus Arab Americans in the Blackstone Valley of southern Massachusetts established a Syrian American community at the turn of the century (ibid., 99). They have been recognized as more appreciative, responsive, and sophisticated listeners compared with other Arab Americans. She further describes the musical tastes of this community as incubators of residual culture where "ancient principles of music appreciation, and performer/audience dynamics are retained" (ibid.). The Syrian Arab Americans in Blackstone parallel the musical tastes of Syrian Jews in Brooklyn; both are insular groups that prefer to retain a vestige of the past rather than embrace the latest musical innovations.

Music making by Syrian Jews in Brooklyn exists largely on an amateur level, consisting primarily of the singing of *pizmonim* at community and domestic events as well as at life cycle rituals. While there are few instrumental musicians in the community, Syrians are avid listeners and devotees of Arab music, with an impressive knowledge of the music and lives of well-known Arab performers. It is not uncommon for Syrian Jews to hire a group of professional Arab musicians for private parties. Yet many in the present generation are not engaged solely with Arab music. Today the music for Syrian weddings may include both an Arab and an American band. For religious functions, however, the preference is for Arab music.

Syrian cantors are particularly immersed in the world of Arab music. Moses Tawil, a retired businessman, was previously lay cantor at Congregation Shaarei Zion and spends part of his time training younger cantors. David Tawil is actively involved in the religious life of Congregation Beth Torah, participating as a part-time cantor and teacher. The brothers remember hearing and singing Arab music as children and frequently had parties in their home. Isaac Cabasso is the senior cantor at Beth Torah and is actively involved in perpetuating the liturgical tradition. Cabasso's teacher was Eliyahu Menaged (1890–1964) (Shelemay 1998, 34). The younger generation cantors are Israeli-born, and trained in Brooklyn as "Aleppo-style" cantors (ibid., 83–84). The younger cantor at Congregation Beth Torah is Yeḥezkiel Zion; he is Israeli-born and grew up in Jerusalem, where he worshipped at the Aleppo synagogue Beit Kenneset Ades. Zion has been in Brooklyn since the late 1980s and trained with Moses Tawil and Isaac Cabasso. David Shiro has been *ḥazzan* of congregation Shaarei Zion since the late 1990s and is a student of Moses Tawil.

Moses and David Tawil come from a musical family and are important transmitters of the Syrian Aleppo tradition. They are the youngest of six brothers and a sister. Their father was born in Aleppo and then moved to Israel, where he married his wife and they had their first four children. In 1913 the family moved to the United States. Moses was born in 1915, then David in 1921. David explains the musical world he was born into:

> I was born here on Sixty-sixth Street in Bensonhurst. I have spent practically all of my life here in Brooklyn. I grew up with the insti-

1. (far left) Hazzan Isaac J. Cabasso (photo by Jack Schweky)
2. (left) Hazzan Moses Tawil (photo by Jack Schweky)

> tution they had, the Talmud Torah, until I was fifteen. And I was attracted to the awesome sessions they had of the synagogue during prayer time especially Saturday afternoons when the head cantor, alav hashalom, Moshe Ashkar, would gather fourteen, sixteen, eighteen students or disciples. He would have them sit on stage with him and for about forty or forty-five minutes render so many *pizmonim*. They were absolutely beautiful. (interview, October 6, 1999)

Moshe Ashkar (or Ashear) was a prominent progenitor of the Syrian Aleppo cantorial tradition and a contemporary of Moses and David Tawil's father. Their older brothers learned from Ashkar and Naphtali, who is considered Ashkar's chief disciple (ibid.; see *SUHV,* 16). Moses's three primary influences were his father, his oldest brother, Ezra, and Naphtali (interview, October 6, 1999).

The Tawils credit their father as creating both a model of communal involvement and a love for music. He was the first president of the Magen David Congregation, established in Bensonhurst in 1923. Moses has served as the vice president of the Magen David Yeshiva and the chairman of the education department. He has also been involved with congregations in Bradely Beach, New Jersey, and North Miami Beach, Florida. David is an active teacher of rabbinic texts at Congregation Beth Torah. Moses recalls:

> At the age of seven we went to Mexico City, my parents, from here. My first love was Spanish music from the ages of seven to about

3. *Hakham David A. Tawil (photo by author)*

> thirteen. From thirteen onward I became enamored with Arabic music; really I was very influenced by particularly the talent of ʻAbd al-Wahhāb. Although in my house there was music all the time I was very familiar with all of the older artists in the Arabic world . . . that music was always played and used in our homes. In the back of my mind it was always there. And I grew with it. But then when I really fell in love with Arabic music nothing could replace it. Because it's a very broad music. Based on the *maqāmāt,* it's just so broad. (interview, October 6, 1999)

Dedication to the community involvement with music in their Jewish life within the Arab realm defines the life of the Tawils and typifies the Syrian Jews.

The *Maqām* System as Defined and Practiced in Brooklyn

THE MAQĀM SYSTEM as practiced by Syrians in Brooklyn permeates many levels of the liturgy. In general,

> *Maqām* can refer to either a simple or a very complex set of phenomena. In its simplest form, it may refer to a specific scale. Defined in greater depth, *maqām* may refer to a specific scale with a tonic,

alternative directional notes, accidentals, a specific ambitus, a specific tetrachordal structure with alternative tetrachordal structures, one or more prominent notes besides the tonic, starting notes, specific path for performance, melodic motives, specifics of intonation, and extra-musical associations. (S. Marcus 1992, 191n1)

I offer an overview of this musical system as understood and practiced by the community. It will be contextualized within the present-day practice among Arab musicians.

Syrian cantors focus on *maqām* as a mode comprised, typically, of two tetrachords.[9] Ḥakham David Tawil, a recognized authority in the Syrian Jewish community on the community's liturgical tradition and music, states, "There are a basic set of eight primary *maqāmāt,* variations or other *maqāmāt* are derived from these eight; tetrachordal composition determines the *maqām;* the designation of the *maqām* of a given musical performance is determined by its concluding phrase" (interview, July 29, 1992). His observations are consistent with Arab musical practice as found in the modern period.

The eight basic *maqāmāt* that Tawil discusses are defined in a chart that he prepared for pedagogical purposes (reproduced as table 1).[10] Table 1 maps the distinct pitches of each *maqām* and the pitch from which each *maqām* originates. The arrangement is not arbitrary since it conveniently displays the relationship of the *maqāmāt* to starting pitches: *rast* and *nahawand* both start on the pitch C; *bayat, saba, kurdy,* and *hijaz* start on the pitch D; *ajam* and *seyga* start on B flat and E quarter flat, respectively. Note that *rast, bayat,* and *seyga* contain the same pitches, but each starts on a different pitch. The unique feature of a *maqām* is the lower tetrachord; the structure of this tetrachord determines the *maqām.* Changes are made to the upper tetrachord, which then produces a variant.

Table 1. *Eight Basic Maqāmāt*

Ajam	B♭	C	D	E♭	F	G	A	B♭			
Rast		C	D	E𝄳[1]	F	G	A	B𝄳	C		
Nahawand		C	D	E♭	F	G	A♭	B♭	C		
Bayat			D	E𝄳	F	G	A	B𝄳	C	D	
Saba			D	E𝄳	F	G♭	A	B𝄳	C	D	
Kurdy			D	E♭	F	G	A	B♭	C	D	
Hijaz			D	E♭	F♯	G	A	B♭	C	D	
Seyga				E𝄳	F	G	A	B𝄳	C	D	E𝄳

1. The 𝄳 indicates a quarter flat note, which is three-quarters of the distance between the adjacent notes of the scale. For example, the note designated as 𝄳E is three-quarters of the distance above the note D and three-quarters below the note F.

The layout of table 1 shows the relationship of the *maqāmāt* and their clear similarities and differences and proved to be a useful aid for me during my many discussions with David Tawil. For example, he pointed out that the difference between the lower tetrachords of *rast* and *nahawand* is very slight, consisting of only one pitch; the third pitch of *rast* is an E quarter flat, whereas the respective pitch in *nahawand* is an E flat. The intervallic values of adjacent pitches of the eight basic *maqāmāt* are illustrated in a second chart prepared by Tawil, which displays the name of each *maqām* with its ascending scale on a staff, with the name of each note indicated below. The intervallic value of adjacent notes is also provided in whole numbers and fractions (in table 2, only the intervallic content has been reproduced).

Table 2. *Intervallic Value of Adjacent Notes in Eight Basic Maqāmāt*

	1st		2nd		3rd		4th		5th		6th		7th		8th
Ajam		1		1		½		1		1		1		½	
Rast		1		¾		¾		1		1		¾		¾	
Nahawand (natural)		1		½		1		1		½		1		1	
Bayat		¾		¾		1		1		¾		¾		1	
Saba		¾		¾		½		1½		¾		¾		1	
Kurdy		½		1		1		1		½		1		1	
Hijaz		½		1½		½		1		½		1		1	
Seyga		¾		1		1		¾		¾		1		¾	

The ability to recognize the unique tetrachord that defines the upper and lower halves of a *maqām* is important for determining a *maqām* and its variants: each of the eight basic *maqāmāt* contain a unique lower tetrachord. Tetrachord content is illustrated in table 3, taken from a third chart by Tawil.[11] Seven of the eight tetrachords (1–6 and 8) are defined by only three notes, or two resulting intervals.[12] The one exception is *maqām saba* (number 7 in table 3), which is defined by four notes, or three intervals. The characteristic element of this *maqām* is the half-step between the third and fourth notes. The first two intervals of *maqām saba,* two three-quarter intervals, are identical to lower trichord of *maqām bayat* (number 4).

Tawil emphasizes that the important elements are the resulting intervallic relationships between the pitches, since any *maqām* can be created by starting on any pitch. The notes given in table 3 are the customary note designations of the *maqāmāt.* Tawil's parenthetical indication of "major" and "minor" for *maqāmāt ajam* and *nahawand,* respectively, in table 3 illustrates his bimusicality and familiarity with Western music.

Table 3. *Lower Tetrachord Definition*

Notes and intervals	Name of *Maqām* used	Traditional key final note	Arabic name of note
B♭ C D 1 1	*Ajam* (major)	B♭	*Ajam*
C D E𝄳 1 ¾	*Rast*	C	*Rast*
C D E♭ 1 ½	*Nahawand* (minor)	C	*Rast*
D E𝄳 F ¾ ¾	*Bayat*	D	*Dogah*
D E𝄳 F Gb ¾ ¾ ½	*Saba*	D	*Dogah*
D E♭ F ½ 1	*Kurdy*	D	*Dogah*
D E♭ F# ½ 1½	*Hijaz*	D	*Dogah*
E𝄳 F G ¾ 1	*Seyga*	E𝄳	*Seyga*

Maqām as Defined by Modern Arab Theorists

TAWIL'S FUNCTIONAL DESCRIPTION of the *maqāmāt* is consistent with the practice of Arab musicians in the modern period on virtually every level. The most comprehensive scholarly treatment of *maqāmāt* is found in Scott Marcus's doctoral dissertation, "Arab Music Theory in the Modern Period" (1989), for which Marcus consulted over forty-five sources (334). Marcus confirms that the number of *maqāmāt* is not limited to a fixed number, such as eight, but is conceptualized by musicians as an "open system" within which one can create new *maqāmāt* (330–31).[13] Establishing the number of *maqāmāt* depends upon the criteria used and the level of specificity; the number of *maqāmāt* mentioned in written Arab musical sources ranges from about a dozen to slightly over one hundred. In actual practice today, Arab theorists and practitioners recognize a dozen *maqāmāt* as making up the core of performance practice (334).

Since the 1932 congress in Cairo—which aimed to systematize Arab music (Racy 1991b)—most contemporary Arab music theorists have recognized a concept known as the "principal *maqāmāt*" (S. Marcus 1989, 333), a system of relationships whereby the principal *maqāmāt* are varied in recognized patterns. The term *fasịlah* denotes the genus or family of a *maqām* (see ibid., 377–96). Therefore, the *rast fasịlah,* as defined by Tawil (and more broadly in pan-"eastern-Arab" usage), refers to a family of *maqāmāt* that share the same initial *rast* tetrachord but have different upper tetrachords. For example, *maqām māhūr* contains the same lower tetrachord as *maqām rast,* yet has a different upper tetrachord, as follows:

Rast:	C	D	E𝄳	F	G	A	B𝄳	C
Māhūr:	C	D	E𝄳	F	G	A	B	C

The difference is the second-to-last pitch (a B instead of a B quarter flat). *Rast* is the name of both the *maqām* and the tetrachord that defines the *rast faṣīlah,* and *maqām māhūr* is a recognized variant in the *rast faṣīlah.* Marcus claims that there are between seven and fifteen *faṣā'il*; nine or eleven are most often discussed by modern Arab music teachers and performers.[14]

Although not called *faṣā'il,* Tawil's eight *maqāmāt* are identical to eight of the nine standard *faṣā'il* defined by Marcus. Marcus adds the *nawa anthar faṣīlah.* He notes that Muḥammad Ṣalāḥ al-Dīn, a mid-twentieth-century theorist, listed only eight *faṣā'il* by including *nawa anthar* in the *nahawand faṣīlah* (1989, 381). Therefore, in contextualizing the Syrian community's use of *maqāmāt,* the precise articulated number is not the primary issue. The differences in the number of *maqāmāt* is a question of different methods of conceptualization. David Tawil's discussion of the *maqāmāt* is thus consistent with modern Arab musical practice.

The Syrian community itself uses more than one description of the *maqāmāt* and their derivative *maqām* families. Moses Tawil asserts seven major *maqāmāt* (M. Tawil, interviews, October 22, 1991, and June 6, 1993) omitting *kurdy* as a *faṣīlah* and subsuming it under *bayat.* The importance of describing the Syrian praxis of the *maqāmāt* lies in the fact that not only is their definition of specific *maqāmāt* consistent with the practice of modern Arab music but the manner in which they talk about the *maqāmāt* is shaped by it as well. With this in mind, I will examine how both David Tawil and Moses Tawil view the variants of the *faṣā'il.*

As previously mentioned, a *maqām* has two tetrachords—one lower and one upper. Identifying the lower tetrachord determines the *faṣīlah;* the upper tetrachord determines the exact variant. *Maqām rast* consists of two *rast* tetrachords:

Rast: C D E𝄳 F G A B𝄳C
1 ¾ ¾ 1 1 ¾ ¾
rast *rast*

Rast is the name of a *faṣīlah,* and consequently the name of a *maqām* and a tetrachord. *Maqām māhūr* contains a *rast* and an *ajam* tetrachord:

Māhūr: C D E𝄳 F G A B C
1 ¾ ¾ 1 1 1 ½
rast *ajam*

Again, this is part of the *rast faṣīlah* because *maqām māhūr*'s lower tetrachord is in *rast.* However, the upper tetrachord is not in *rast;* this is a variant that appears regularly, and *māhūr* is its unique name. As David Tawil explains:

> There is variation in the second tetrachord [of a *maqām*]. . . . [T]he flavor of the music . . . is going to be in the upper tetrachord. . . . Now Umm Kulthūm has a lot of very famous pieces in *iraq,* and the essence of her themes revolve around *bayat,* which is the upper tetrachord—which is [a] very effective kind of thing.[15] And this is the marvel of the difference in the scales of European music and . . . Arabic music. . . . The rest of it is a question of the upper tetrachord, [which] is where you get variations. They crisscross each other. You can have *bayat* with the upper part being in *nahawand,* or the upper part could be in *rast.* (interview, July 29, 1992)

Tawil is knowledgeable of the many variants of *maqām* and is able to describe and demonstrate the differences skillfully; several of our discussions focused upon *maqāmāt,* and we talked about the issue of *maqām* variants at great length. However, he is one of very few members of the community who possesses the knowledge and vocabulary concerning the interrelations of the *maqāmāt* and *faṣā'il.* Most Syrian cantors demonstrate a practical knowledge of the *maqām* system. The major emphasis in learning and understanding the *maqām* system is the eight basic *maqāmāt.* The following extended excerpt from a discussion with Moses Tawil supports this assessment:

> Moses Tawil: *Nawa anthar* [*nawa anthar*], now I challenge anyone who does not play an instrument to tell the difference with *nawa anthar* and *nahawand.*[16]
>
> Mark Kligman: The difference is that the sharp note, here it has a little bit of the *hijaz* flavor almost, right?[17]
>
> MT: Yeah. So now you have to play an instrument to really be able to denote that. But to a person just singing, you can't.

. . . When you look at the note itself, it is practically identical. . . . *Bastanikār, bastanikār* is not a *maqām*. . . . I told you the most proficient people separating the *maqāmāt* are the Turks. Some people say they have two or three hundred names [for the *maqāmāt*]. Now, because it [*bastanikār*] starts in the *saba* and finishes in the *seyga*—you end in the *seyga*. It doesn't mean that the song has to end that way. You understand? You are singing *saba* [he sings the first few notes of a *maqām*]—I started in *saba*, and I wound up in *seyga*. So they have a name to that *maqām: bastanikār. Hijaz,* which you know; *hijaz-kar* [*hijazkar*], there's another *maqām*—they call it a *maqām*. It's only one way of just going down a little bit lower then when you started *hijaz* itself to make it a *hijaz-kar. Saba* ʿ*ushāq, sūznāk* are names adopted from the Turks.

MK: Isn't *sūznāk* a form of *rast* in a way?

MT: Yeah, it's close. *Nagreez* [*nakrīz*] is not a *maqām;* I mean, it's just a little flavor, but yet it's called *nagreez* [he sings an example]. To compose and make a whole composition of that, it really [is] quite limited. And *zingerān*, again you are singing *ajam* and you wind up down in *hijaz*. Really, actually you have to find it as *hijaz-kar* even for it to be *zingerān*.

Within this excerpt he mentions five *faṣā'il* (*nahawand, hijaz, saba, seyga,* and *ajam*) and five variants (*nawa anthar, nakrīz, bastanikār, hijaz-kar,* and *zingerān*). But, he states repeatedly, the variants are an additional flavor, one pitch comprising the difference from the originating *faṣīlah*. This can be limiting—as in the case of *nakrīz*—if an entire composition is based on one of the variants. In short, neither David Tawil nor Moses Tawil see the variants as entities that must be understood fully by their students. They feel the proficient *ḥazzan* will develop his understanding of the variants over time with experience. The Tawils' chief concern is the basic *maqāmāt;* as one becomes skilled he adds flavor in an idiosyncratic manner.

The Practice of the *Maqām* System

THE ORGANIZATION OF the *pizmonim* and the *bakkashot* in *SUHV* sheds some light on the question of how the theory of the *maqāmāt* is put into practice.[18] The arrangement of the *pizmonim* is according to their *maqāmāt,* while the *bakkashot* are grouped together but not categorized by *maqām.*[19] Table 4 illustrates the order of the *maqāmāt* as they appear in *SUHV*.[20] Moses Tawil estimates that less than half of the melodies for the 625 texts listed in *SUHV* are known by members of the community (interview, October 22, 1991).[21]

Table 4. Maqāmāt *used in* Shir ush'vaḥa, hallel v'zimrah

All *maqāmāt* used

	Pizmonim	*Bakkashot*	Total	Percentage
rast	69	8	77	12
mahur	31	0	31	5
sazkar	3	2	5	1
ajam	54	1	55	9
nahawand	54	8	62	10
lami	1	0	1	0
bayat	100	8	108	17
muḥayyar bayat	15	8	23	4
ḥuseini	26	8	34	5
asiran	2	0	2	0
rahaw nawa	20	0	20	3
saba	64	9	73	12
awj	2	0	2	0
seyga	54	13	67	11
iraq	0	3	3	0
hijaz	62	0	62	10
Total	**557**	**68**	**625**	

Regrouped by *faṣā'il*

	Pizmonim	*Bakkashot*	Total	Percentage
rast	100	8	108	17
ajam	57	3	60	10
nahawand	74	8	82	13
bayat	143	24	167	27
saba	64	9	73	12
seyga	54	16	70	11
hijaz	62	0	62	10
Total	**554**	**68**	**622**	

Only seven *faṣā'il* are listed in table 4; *maqām kurdy,* usually referred as *kurd* or *kurdī* by Arab musicians, is not found in the liturgy. David Tawil's listing of *kurdy* as one of the eight basic *maqāmāt* demonstrates his general knowledge of Arab music, extending beyond the specific practices of the Syrian community. He also states that *kurdy* is the weakest *maqām* and little used (Shelemay

1998, 247n28, 247n30). Although nineteenth- and twentieth-century Arab treatises include this *maqām* and Lois Ibsen al-Faruqi claims that *kurdy* is a contemporary melodic mode (1981, 150), melodies in *kurdy* were not a source for the Syrian liturgy or *pizmonim* up to the 1940s. Since *kurdy* is used in modern Arab music, it provides an interesting gauge for assessing the music of Syrian Jews. Moses Tawil does not include *kurdy* as one of the basic *maqāmāt*, as stated earlier. This suggests that knowledge of the *maqāmāt* system is shaped significantly by the community than by general contemporary Arab musical practices.

The seven *faṣā'il*, ranked in order of the greatest to least number of *pizmonim* and *bakkashot* melodies in *SUHV* and in active transmission, are as follows (see Shelemay 1998, 201):

	Pizmonim in SUHV		*Pizmonim* in active transmission	
	number	percent	number	percent
bayat	167	27	26	16
rast	108	17	34	21
nahawand[22]	82	13	27	17
saba	73	12	19	12
seyga	70	11	21	13
hijaz	62	10	17	11
ajam	58	9	16	10

The total number of *maqāmāt* is seventeen (see table 4). *Bayat, rast,* and *nahawand* constitute over 50 percent of the number of *pizmonim* in *SUHV* and in active transmission. If the *maqāmāt* that contain three or fewer texts are eliminated (*sāzkār, lami, 'ushayrān, awj,* and *iraq*), eleven remain. These eleven *maqāmāt* make up the core of the Syrian community's musical practice, particularly in their liturgy. Table 5 lists the eleven *maqāmāt* grouped by *faṣīlah* and defines their customary pitch content in the Syrian community in Brooklyn. These eleven comprise the *maqāmāt* in the liturgy and will be discussed through this study, they are: *ajam, rast, mahur, nahawand, rahaw nawa, bayat, muḥayyar, ḥuseini, saba, hijaz,* and *seyga.* The practice of using eleven *maqāmāt* derived from seven *faṣā'il* is supported by the application of the *maqāmāt* within the Sabbath morning liturgy. Three separate charts at the end of *SUHV,* titled "Seder nigun nishmat ve-yotzer ve-khu[le]" ("Order of [the] melodies [for] *nishmat* and *yotzer,* etc."), list the specific liturgical sections to be sung and the melodies that may be used in these sections.[23]

Table 5. Maqāmāt *used by Syrian Jews in Brooklyn*

ajam	B♭	C	D	E♭	F	G	A	B♭			
rast		C	D	E𝄳	F	G	A	B𝄳	C		
mahur[1]		C	D	E𝄳	F	G	A	B	C		
nahawand		C	D	E♭	F	G	A♭	B♭	C		
rahaw nawa		G	A	B♭	C	D	E♭	F	G		
bayat			D	E𝄳	F	G	A	B𝄳[2]	C	D	
muḥayyar[3]			D	E𝄳	F	G	A	B𝄳	C	D	
ḥuseini[4]			D	E𝄳	F	G	A	B𝄳	C	D	
saba			D	E𝄳	F	G♭	A	B♭	C	D	
hijaz			D	E♭	F♯	G	A	B♭	C	D	
seyga				E𝄳	F	G	A	B𝄳	C	D	E𝄳

1. Starts on C of upper octave.
2. The most common upper tetrachord has a B quarter flat; B flat is occasionally used.
3. Starts on upper D and focuses on upper tetrachord.
4. Starts on A.

Comparison of the *maqām* practice of the Syrian Jewish community and that of eastern Arab tradition reveals that the Syrian Jewish usage is not out of the ordinary. Marcus states that Arab folk musicians make use of seven or eight *maqāmāt* in their music (1989, 334). The vocal repertoire of "mainstream," or "popular," singers, such as Umm Kulthūm, 'Abd al-Ḥalīm Ḥāfiz, Fairouz and Wardah make use, most commonly, of about a dozen or more *maqāmāt* (ibid., 334–35). *Rast, bayātī,* and *nahāwand* account for almost 45 percent of the singers' repertoire, while *huzām* and *kurdy* are also common (Danielson 1991, 381; 1997, 145). These last two *maqāmāt* are not employed by the Syrians in their liturgy, while over 50 percent of the *pizmonim* melodies are in the three most common *maqāmāt.* The Syrian Jewish practice is thus largely compatible with modern Arab practice since their liturgical melodies are adapted from the songs of well-known singers. By adopting Arab musical practice as the source for music in the community, they adopt the theory behind the practice of this music as well. Arab songs adapted for Syrian Jewish liturgical melodies derive from both vocal and instrumental repertories. Vocal genres represented include *muwashashaḥ, mawwāl, qaṣīdah, dawr, ṭaqṭūqah,* and occasionally a *layālī.* Instrumental genres are primarily from *bashraf* or *samāī. Bakkashot* are original composed texts and music, while *pizmonim* are original Hebrew texts set to known Arab melodies; both are sung in an Arab musical style.

Syrians acquire proficiency of *maqām* in a practical manner. Learning a *pizmon* provides the basis for knowing a *maqām* (Cabasso, *pizmonim* class, November 18, 1991; Shelemay 1998, 122–23). Ḥazzan Gabriel Shrem described this means of acquisition as learning a tune in a *maqām,* which then "becomes your measuring stick" (interview, January 9, 1986). After learning a song in each *maqām,* one applies the "measuring stick" to new melodies. In the *pizmonim* classes I attended, the teacher, Isaac Cabasso, stated that our goal was to learn *pizmonim.* In actuality he taught us more than that; he constantly used as an example the process by which a *ḥazzan* renders the Sabbath service. In the first session he explained that if one does not know a *maqām* well and is about to pray, the individual can sing a *pizmon* and use that melody to "get into" the *maqām.* When Cabasso taught a *pizmon* he would often comment on where this melody would appropriately fit within the liturgy. The presentation of the material in class went beyond simply knowing a *pizmon* to learning how to apply its melody to the liturgy, all the while learning the *maqāmāt. Pizmonim* (and *bakkashot*), liturgy, the role of the *ḥazzan,* and the *maqāmāt* are all closely interrelated and dependent upon one another.

The singing of *pizmonim* is used not only to teach *maqāmāt* but also to demonstrate their characteristics. Cabasso describes the quarter-flat difference between *maqām rast* and *maqām ajam* as "very small" and says that to get the feeling for *maqām rast* one has to sing the note of *seyga* (*pizmonim class,* November 18, 1991, November 25, 1991), the Arab name of the note E quarter flat.[24] Cabasso sang *pizmonim* melodies in order to illustrate this difference. He uses *rast* to relate to other *maqāmāt;* it was the first *maqām* discussed in the *pizmonim* class. Likewise, Arab theorists view *rast* as the first *maqām.* Certain *pizmonim* are considered difficult to sing—for instance, Yaḥid ram (*SUHV* #238)—because of a high range or the use of several related *maqāmāt,* as in Renanot shiru (*SUHV* #212). In order to learn *maqām nahawand*—equivalent intervallically to the Western minor scale—Cabasso told us that he thought of the popular Latin American love song "*Besa me mucho*" ("Kiss me a lot").

The *maqāmāt* become the prism through which to view all music, providing a framework for understanding melody as well as a method for its acquisition. This demonstrates the assimilation of Arab and American culture. Since the 1980s, there has been renewed interest in learning the *maqāmāt* among younger members of the Syrian community. Benjamin Zalta, a young man born in Damascus, Syria, immigrated to New York in 1987 to study medicine. He acknowledged that it has become "stylish to learn the *maqāmāt,* something to be proud of" (interview, March 16, 1990). The Israeli-trained cantors who are employed at several Syrian synagogues in Brooklyn are seen by members of the Syrian community as experts in the *maqāmāt.* Their ability to move in and out of the *maqāmāt* with great ease has been likened to an athletic skill (Cabasso, *pizmonim* class March 23, 1992). Learning the *maqāmāt* is an important skill, necessary for a *ḥazzan* to be respected and proficient.

In summary, the Syrian community makes use of seven basic *maqām* families, or *faṣā'il,* using only the primary *maqām* and four *faṣā'il,* and using one or two variants in the three other *faṣā'il,* resulting, for the most part, in the use of eleven *maqāmāt.* These *maqāmāt* make up the repertoire of the melodies used in the Syrian Jewish liturgical practice. The *maqāmāt* that are used and the manner by which they are explained by members of the community are, with the exception of *rahaw nawa,* consistent with modern Arab musical practices. *Ḥazzanim* are not limited to these eleven *maqāmāt;* the more proficient cantors know, and make use of, other variants. These variants are considered to provide additional flavor, elaborations, and variants within the seven *faṣā'il.*

Responses to the Use of Preexisting Melodies

THE USE OF non-Jewish melodies adapted for Jewish purposes is not new in the history of Jewish music. In the case of Syrian liturgy, the *maqām* of a melody becomes the conduit to make this process possible, the subject of chapter 10. Rabbinical response to the adaptation of music has varied in Jewish history and in different cultural contexts. The appropriateness of using non-Jewish melodies for liturgical and paraliturgical purposes and the question of whether Jews should even listen to non-Jewish music has been discussed in rabbinic literature for almost one thousand years.[25] Several musicological studies have focused on these issues (see, e.g., Adler 1966; Adler 1975; Seroussi 1990a; Shelemay 1994; Shelemay 1998, 27–28, 206). Past and present rabbinic opinions on the use of non-Jewish melodies for liturgical and paraliturgical purposes range from complete prohibition to acceptance. The prohibition stems from the fear that the use of non-Jewish melodies will adversely affect Jewish spirituality. The most common reason used to sanction utilization of such melodies is the Hasidic response, which states that the non-Jewish melody is elevated and sanctified since it is used for holy purposes (Koskoff 1978; Shiloah 1992, 71, 76–77).[26]

Pertinent for present purposes is the rationale of Aleppo rabbis and rabbis that Syrian Jews respect. A survey of extant sources shows acceptance and rejection of the use of Arab melodies on moral, aesthetic, and religious grounds. Written accounts are found in rabbinic *responsa* literature and the introductions in the collections of *bakkashot* and *pizmonim.*[27] Israel Najara (c. 1555–1625) resided in Damascus and is credited with establishing "the basis for what later became standard poetic and music practice among Ottoman Jews" (Seroussi 1990b, 51), piyyutim based on Arab, Spanish, Turkish, and Greek songs. Najara's music and textual adaptations in the sixteenth and seventeenth centuries testify to the historic basis of this practice.

A. Antebi, a nineteenth-century rabbi (died ca. 1850) from Aleppo, disapproved of listening to Arab and Turkish songs; however, he wrote, "Hymns to God, even if written to the music of Arab or Turkish love songs, were praiseworthy, but the songs on which they were based were deplored by the moralists."[28] Changing the text was the only acceptable vehicle for rabbinic approval for the singing of Arab and Turkish songs.

Mordecai Abbadi agrees, but for different reasons. In his *Divre Mordekai* (Aleppo, 1873), a collection of *bakkashot* texts, he states: "By the singing of (foreign) tunes you cause God to take account of the nation whose song is sung, for having persecuted you. Consequently the ancient and contemporary poets borrowed the tunes of foreign (=Arabic) songs and composed for them holy words" (folio 27b, found in Fenton 1982, 125n6). Use of Arab music takes on significance because it is utilized for more than just pleasure. Arab songs are imbued with religious meaning; employing them in a Jewish context is not only justified but holy, as long as words are changed.

The introductions to the Syrian community's publications of *bakkashot* and *pizmonim* in *SUHV* offer some insight into the opinions of Brooklyn Syrian rabbis and cantors on this subject. Abbadi's attitude is acknowledged and discussed by the compilers and contributors of *SUHV*, in both its present publication and earlier renditions (Goldberg 1988, 11–12).[29] In his introduction to *Hallel ve-zimrah* (1928), Moses Ashear approaches the use of non-Jewish melodies in a somewhat defensive manner.[30] He equates the process of writing new texts in order to create songs with providing "ḥidushei Torah" (new religious insights). He suggests that the content of the new poetic text contains important religious ideas. The *pizmon*, therefore, is a rabbinic work and not viewed as a musical creation. "Hearing" the new rabbinic insight is synonymous with hearing the music.

Contemporary *responsa* by prominent Sephardic rabbis discuss the process of using non-Jewish melodies. Two treatments of this subject are offered by Ḥakham Ovadiah Yosef (b. 1920), former Sephardic chief rabbi of Israel, a widely recognized rabbinic authority among both Ashkenazic and Sephardic Jews, and a spiritual leader particularly to the Jews of Middle Eastern communities. In the Syrian community, Ḥakham Yosef's opinions are treated with the utmost respect and are well known to the leaders and members of the community. In the first response, *Sefer she'eilot u-teshuvot yabi'a omer* (1976, #6, 18–21), Yosef permits the use of non-Jewish melodies even if they originate from "idolatrous practices." He regards music as intangible and thus usable for liturgical and paraliturgical purposes if the intention is holy (also discussed in Shiloah 1992, 83–84). This perspective on music is of particular interest since physical manifestations of idolatry, such as a building—or house—of worship, cannot be used for Jewish purposes. Physical objects cannot be transformed, but intangible items, such as music, can be transformed, presumably because they are "made anew" each time the melody is sung. This opinion is not divergent from the Hasidic approach but is reasoned differently.[31] It is also significant that this subject is treated in a serious manner by a major rabbinic figure.

The second response, *Sefer she'eilot u-teshuvot yehaveh da'at* (1978, vol. 2, #5, 24–28), deals with the application of love song melodies to liturgical passages during prayer.[32] The response is remarkable both for its content and the style of writing. Rabbi Yosef lists the collections of *bakkashot* and *pizmonim* by nineteenth-century Aleppo poets, such as Avraham Antebi, Mordecai Levaton, and Mordecai Abbadi. He states:

> Their *bakkashot* and *pizmonim* are composed to melodies of [Arab] love songs. Similarly, in our generation we are privileged to hear from the holy mouths of the cantors—who are wise men, righteous, and upright—who have pleasant voices that pray in a sweet Eastern style, and compose melodies like the love songs that [are applied to] certain portions of the prayers in the Kaddish and the Kedushah. They take the melodies of the land [Israel] and set it to song for God, Blessed is He, who "chooses songs of praise," with pleasant "words of the counsel of the holy seraphs (angels)."[33] The heart of the community follows after them [the cantors] in compassion and mercy, with joy and generous thanks, and in the voice of song. "Praiseworthy is the people for whom this is so" (Psalm 145: 15) (ibid., 25).

Yosef concludes that "when the law is unclear, go out and see what the community does, and do as such."[34] In other words, it is permissible to use love songs since "God-fearing," or respectable, communities do so and, in this case, the law should follow the practice. Since the congregation is moved by the cantor's use of love songs and the "sweet Eastern style" of singing, it should be not only permitted but also praised. Yosef's only word of caution is that such music should be sung for holy purposes and in a manner that the words are not forced to accommodate the music, that is, the music should complement the words (ibid., 27–28). Absorbed into Yosef's approach is the generalized acceptance of mysticism, a feature of Syrian and Mizraḥi Jewry prior to their arrival in America (see chapter 2). Some recent prayer books include sources of mystical writings in their commentary to the siddur.[35]

Ḥakham Yosef's style of writing is encyclopedic in nature; he cites and quotes numerous sources.[36] In addition, he injects commonly known passages from the liturgy, as in the excerpt quoted earlier. In many ways this is analogous to the process of creating poetry in which passages are culled from various sources to create a new text. Similarly, biblical and liturgical phrases, as well as names, are embedded into the texts of *pizmonim* (see Shelemay 1994, 45–46; Shelemay 1998, 174–76). Therefore, liturgical, paraliturgical, and rabbinic texts make use of a similar process, that of textual adaptation.

5

Sabbath Morning Service

THE SABBATH MORNING service of the Syrian Jews in Brooklyn consists of six distinct sections.[1] Each section makes use of a variety of musical performance styles, including recitation, song (both fixed and improvisatory forms), and spoken discourse. The performance style depends on the nature of the liturgical text and its liturgical importance. Each section consists of a unique combination of textual styles, and, hence, the musical performance practice varies.

An important characteristic of Syrian liturgical performance practice is the unison delivery of the Hebrew liturgical text through the participation of many people praying aloud together.[2] Variety in the service is part of the design: as different leaders sing the prayers, one *maqām* is prominent in each section through reciting, singing, and improvising (see figure 3). The text determines the *maqām* and its varied rendering styles.

The following description is based on observation at Beth Torah during participation in Sabbath morning worship services and materials drawn from focused interviews with several cantors. The description of the Sabbath morning service is not taken from one specific service. Rather, it is based on my overall experiences as a participant-observer. Occasionally, relevant information will be incorporated regarding Sabbath morning liturgical practice at other Syrian synagogues in Brooklyn.[3] Although each synagogue has its own character that reflects how the service is created, Syrian liturgy is based on a series of shared rules. My approach in this descriptive account of the Syrian Sabbath morning service is a composite.[4]

Figure 3. *Liturgical sections for the Syrian Sabbath morning service*

Liturgical sections	Leader	*Maqām*	Length
Birkhot ha-Shaḥar (introductory morning blessings)	none	mainly *seyga*	15 minutes
Zemirot (psalms)	two congregants	*seyga* contrasting *maqām*	30 minutes
Shaḥarit (morning prayers)	*ḥazzan*	*maqām* of the day	45 minutes
Torah reading	Torah reader	*seyga*	60–75 minutes
Sermon	rabbi		15 minutes
Musaf (additional service)	*ḥazzan* or skilled congregant	varies *seyga*	15 minutes

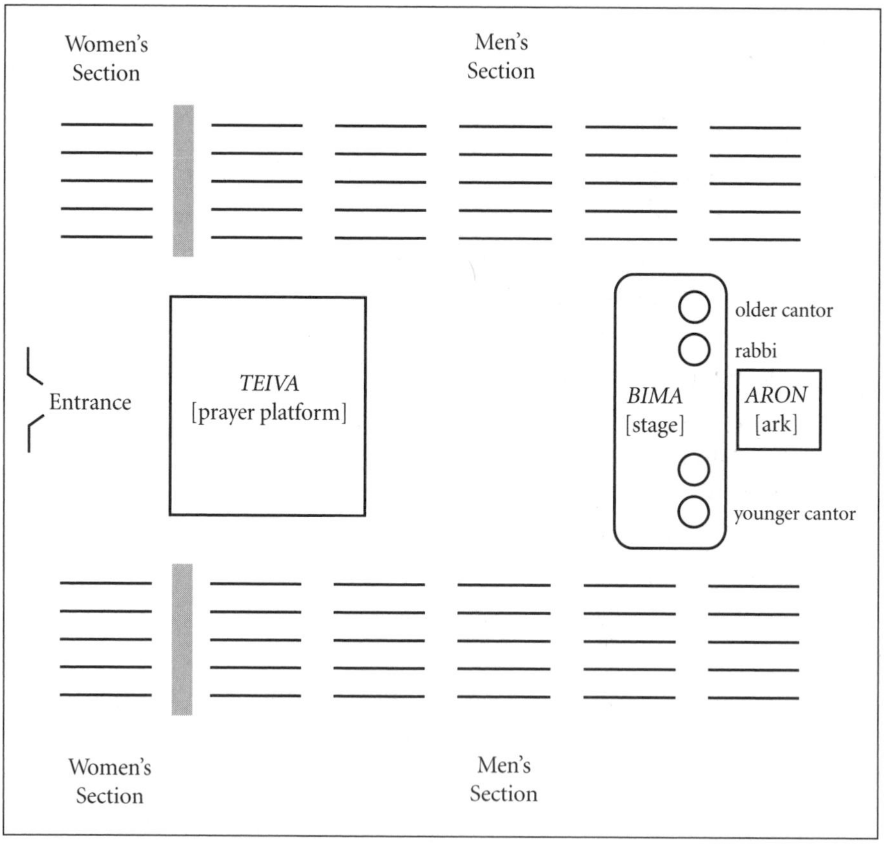

The six sections of the morning service are Birkhot ha-Shaḥar (morning blessings), Zemirot (songs), Shaḥarit (morning prayers), the Torah reading, the rabbi's sermon, and Musaf (addition service).[5] Shaḥarit is the centerpiece, framed by two liturgical sections: Zemirot and the rabbi's sermon. The Zemirot section, which immediately precedes Shaḥarit, is textually fixed, with recitation formulas mainly set in *maqām seyga*. Recitation of the Torah reading is also in *maqām seyga* but varies textually from week to week. The weekly reading determines the *maqām* used during Shaḥarit based on a system of extra-musical associations of its subject matter (see chapter 10), but that *maqām* is not used for the recitation of the Torah itself. This provides an interesting relationship between Shaḥarit and the Torah reading: what is textually fixed (the liturgical text of Shaḥarit) varies melodically, and what varies textually (the Torah reading) is fixed melodically. This arrangement, together with the *maqām* associations with the weekly reading, provides several levels of fixity and flexibility. Music and text interact according to liturgical necessity and the aesthetics of worship.

Other studies have also applied fixity and flexibility to understand the relationship between music and culture (Wade 1976) and to view music's role in ritual (Boilès 1978; Sweet 1983). I will highlight the various elements that together constitute each liturgical section: the nature of the text and its liturgical function; the role of the leader in each section, including the *ḥazzan* and others who participate; the *maqām* that is used; and the type of vocal style.

Approaches to Rendering Styles

ETHNOMUSICOLOGICAL APPROACHES TO performance draw from linguistic anthropology and performance studies (Béhague 1984, 4). Case studies explore the modes of vocal styles in various cultures (see Feld 1982 [1990];Seeger 1988; Titon 1988; Roseman 1991). Mary Bateson's linguistic approach to texture rather than structure in ritual (1974) provides a useful method to apply to Syrian liturgy. Bateson looks into what she describes as "modes of action." She investigates the constituent elements that characterize a liturgical section through each section's density of specific activity in order to determine higher levels of meaning; her method consists of comparing and contrasting various sections (1974, 151–53). The resulting process, considering the overall ritual in relation to its constituent parts, is termed *ritualization*.[6] Bateson argues that texture analysis provides "single segmentation of sequenced units at different levels" in contradistinction to structural segmentation, which looks at "multilevel hierarchy of sequenced units in many modalities at each level" (159). She applies texture analysis to a tongues-speaking prayer group in order to show how textural changes create fusion. Fusion occurs when a large number of words express a small amount of meaningful utterances (159–60). She further states that there are different degrees of fusion in every ritual (162). Therefore, various textures produce meaningful moments throughout the ritual.

Table 6. *Liturgical sections of the Syrian Sabbath morning service*

Liturgical section	Page(s)[1]	Leader	*Maqām*	Type	Fixed or flexible
1. Birkhot ha-Shaḥar	1–59	none	*seyga*	recitation	fixed
Kaddish de-Rabbanan	59–61	congregant	*seyga*	recitation	fixed
2. Zemirot	61–69, 443–87				
2.1. Hodu la-Shem Kir'u bi-Shemo	61	congregation	*seyga*	song	fixed
Va-Ya'amideha le-Ya'akov le-Ḥok	63–65	congregant	*seyga*	recitation	fixed
2.2. Kel Nekamot Ha-Shem	65–67	congregant	*seyga*	recitation	fixed
2.3. Aromimkha Ha-Shem	67–69	congregant	*seyga*	recitation	fixed
2.4. Ha-Shem Melekh*	69	*ḥazzan*: congregation[2]	*maqām* of day	song	flexible
2.5. Lamnatse'aḥ Mizmor le-David	443–45	2 congregants	*seyga*	formula	fixed
2.6. Rannenu Tsaddikim	445–47	2 congregants	*seyga*	formula	fixed
2.7. Le-David, be-Shannoto et Tamo	447–49	2 congregants	*seyga*	formula	fixed
2.8. Tefillah le-Moshe	449–51	2 congregants	*seyga*	formula	fixed
2.9. Yoshev be-Seter Elyon	451–453	2 congregants	*seyga*	formula	fixed
2.10. Mizmor, Shiru la-Shem	453–55	2 congregants	*seyga*	formula	fixed
2.11. Shir la-Ma'alot, Essa Einai	455	2 congregants	*seyga*	formula	fixed
2.12. Shir ha-Ma'alot le-David, Samaḥti	455–57	2 congregants	*seyga*	formula	fixed
2.13. Shir ha-Ma'alot, Elekha	457	2 congregants	*seyga*	formula	fixed
2.14. Shir ha-Ma'alot le-David, Lulei	457	2 congregants	*seyga*	formula	fixed
2.15. Halleluyah, Hallelu et Shem	459–61	2 congregants	*seyga*	formula	fixed
2.16. Hodu la-Shem Ki Tov	461–63	2 congregants	*seyga*	formula	fixed
2.17. Barukh she-Amar	465	congregation	*nahawand*	song	fixed
Blessing [continuation]*	465	*ḥazzan*	varies	improvisation	flexible
2.18. Mizmor Shir le-Yom ha-Shabbat*	465–67	*ḥazzan*	varies	improvisation	flexible
2.19. Ha-Shem Malakh Ge'ut Lavesh*	467–69	*ḥazzan*	varies	improvisation	flexible

2.20. Yehi Khavod	469–71	2 congregants	usually *seyga*[3]	formula	fixed
2.21. Ashrei Yoshvei	471–73	2 congregants	usually *seyga*	formula	fixed
2.22. Halleluyah, Halleli Nafshi	473	2 congregants	usually *seyga*	formula	fixed
2.23. Halleluyah, Ki Tov Zamrah	475–77	2 congregants	usually *seyga*	formula	fixed
2.24. Halleluyah, Hallelu et Ha-Shem	477	2 congregants	usually *seyga*	formula	fixed
2.25. Halleluyah, Shiru la-Shem	479	2 congregants	usually *seyga*	formula	fixed
2.26. Halleluyah, Hallelu Kel be-Kadsho*	479	*ḥazzan* and congregation[4]	varies	song	flexible
2.27. Barukh Ha-Shem le-Olam	479–83	2 congregants	*seyga*	formula	fixed
2.28. Az Yashir Moshe (Shirat ha-Yam)	483–87	2 congregants	*seyga*	formula	fixed
3. Shaḥarit	487–539				
[introduction] Ki la-Shem ha-Melukhah	487	*ḥazzan*	*maqām* of day	improvisation	flexible
3.1. Nishmat Kol Ḥai	487–93	*ḥazzan*			
3.1.1. Nishmat Kol Ḥai*	487	*ḥazzan*	*maqām* of day	song	flexible
3.1.2. U-mi-Bal'adekha Ein Lanu	487–89	*ḥazzan*	*maqām* of day	improvisation	flexible
3.1.3. Ve-Illu Finu	489–91	*ḥazzan*	*maqām* of day	improvisation	flexible
3.1.4. Shav'at Aniyyim* Be-Fi Yesharim[5]	491	*ḥazzan* and congregation	*maqām* of day	song	flexible
3.1.5. Be-Mikehalot Rivevot Amkha	491	*ḥazzan*	*maqām* of day	improvisation	flexible
3.1.6. U-ve-khen Yishtabaḥ	491–93	*ḥazzan*	*maqām* of day	improvisation	flexible
3.1.7. Kel ha-Hodaot*	493	*ḥazzan* and congregation	*maqām* of day	song	flexible
3.2. Kaddish*	495	*ḥazzan*	*maqām* of day	song	flexible
3.3. Bar'khu and pre-Shema blessings	495–505				
3.3.1. Bar'khu and congregational responses	495	*ḥazzan* and congregation	*maqām* of day	improvisation	flexible
3.3.2. Baruk . . . Yotser	495–97	*ḥazzan* and congregation	*maqām* of day	improvisation	flexible
3.3.3. Kel Adon	497–99	*ḥazzan* and congregation	*maqām* of day	improvisation	flexible

3.3.4. Semeḥim be-Tseitam*	499	*ḥazzan* and congregation	*maqām* of day	song	flexible
3.3.5. La-Kel Asher Shavat	499–501	*ḥazzan*[6]	*maqām* of day	improvisation	flexible
3.3.6. Titbarakh la-Netsaḥ	501–3	*ḥazzan*[7]	*maqām* of day	improvisation	flexible
3.3.7. La-Kel Barukh	503	*ḥazzan*	*maqām* of day	improvisation	flexible
3.3.8. Ahavat Olam	503–5	*ḥazzan*	*maqām* of day	improvisation	flexible
3.4. Shema	507–9	*ḥazzan* and congregation	*seyga*	formula	fixed
3.5. Post-Shema blessing	511–15	*ḥazzan*	*maqām* of day	improvisation	flexible
3.5.1. Ve-Yatsiv	511	*ḥazzan*	*maqām* of day	improvisation	flexible
3.5.2. Ezrat Avoteinu	511–13	*ḥazzan*	*maqām* of day	improvisation	flexible
3.5.3. Mi-mits'rayim Gealtanu*	513	*ḥazzan* and congregation	*maqām* of day	song	flexible
3.5.4. Ve-Natnu Yedidim Zemirot	513–15	*ḥazzan*	*maqām* of day	improvisation	flexible
3.6. Amidah[8]	515–39		[silently by congregation; repeated aloud by *ḥazzan*]		
3.6.1. Opening blessings	515–17	*ḥazzan*	*maqām* of day	improvisation	flexible
3.6.2. Nak'dishakh*	519	*ḥazzan*: congregation	*maqām* of day	song	flexible
3.6.3. Yismaḥ Moshe	519–25	*ḥazzan*	*maqām* of day	improvisation	flexible
3.6.4. Modim	525	*ḥazzan* and congregation[9]			
3.6.5. Birkat Kohanim	531	*ḥazzan* and *kohanim*	*maqām* of day	improvisation	flexible
3.6.6. Concluding blessing	531–35	*ḥazzan*	*maqām* of day	improvisation	flexible
3.7. Kaddish	537–39	*ḥazzan*	variable	formula	fixed
4. Torah service	541–47				
4.1. Taking out the Torah scrolls					
4.1.1. Atah Har'eita	541	*ḥazzan* and congregation		song	fixed
[Blessing for the State of Israel][10]	823–824	rabbi		[read]	

[a member of the congregation is given the honor of taking the Torah out of the ark]

4.1.2. Ashrei ha-Am	542	*ḥazzan*: congregation	*ajam*	song	fixed
4.1.3. Romemu	542	congregation	*ajam*	song	fixed
4.1.4. Singing of pizmon		congregation	*maqām* of day	song	flexible
[the congregant holding the Torah walks around the sanctuary while the congregation sings]					
4.2. Torah reading		Torah reader	*seyga*	formula	melody fixed; text variable
4.3. Prophetic reading					
4.3.1. Blessing before reading	544	congregant		formula	fixed
4.3.2. Prophetic reading				formula	melody fixed; text variable
4.3.3. Blessings after reading	544–46	congregant		formula	fixed
[4.4. Blessing for new month if the Sabbath precedes a new month]	549–50	rabbi		read	
4.5. Ashrei Yoshvei	551–53	*ḥazzan*	*seyga*	formula	fixed
4.6. Returning of the Torah to the ark	555–57				
4.6.1. Yimlokh Ha-Shem le-Olam	555	congregation	*ajam*	song	fixed
4.6.2. Mizmor le-David: Havu . . .	557	congregation		song	fixed
5. Rabbi's sermon					
6. Musaf	557–94				
6.1. Kaddish	557–59	*ḥazzan*	*seyga*	formula	fixed
6.2. Amidah[11]	559–83		[silently by congregation; repeated aloud by *ḥazzan*]		
6.2.1. Opening blessings	559–61	*ḥazzan*	varies	improvisation	flexible
6.2.2. Keter*	561–63	*ḥazzan*: congregation	varies	song	flexible
6.2.3. Tikkanta Shabbat	565–73	*ḥazzan*	varies	improvisation	flexible
6.2.4. Modim	573	*ḥazzan* and congregation[12]			
6.2.5. Birkhat Kohanim	577–79	*ḥazzan* and kohanim	varies	improvisation	flexible
6.2.6. Concluding blessing	581–83	*ḥazzan*	varies	improvisation	flexible
6.3. Kaddish	583–85	*ḥazzan*	*seyga*	formula	fixed
6.4. Kol Yisrael	585	*ḥazzan* or congregant	*seyga*	formula	fixed
6.5. Kaddish	585–91	*ḥazzan* or congregant	*seyga*	formula	fixed

6.6. Bar'khu and congregational responses	591–92	*ḥazzan* and congregation	*seyga*	formula	fixed
6.7. Aleinu	592–94	*ḥazzan* and congregaion	*seyga*	formula	fixed

Note: An asterisk (*) indicates liturgical sections discussed in chapter 7.

1. The page numbers refer to a recent prayer book published by the Syrian community; *Siddur kol ya'akov ha-shalem ke-minhag aram tsoba*, English title also given, *Daily prayer Book According to the Minhag [custom] of Aleppo (Aram Ṣoba)* [*sic*], 1990.

2. "*Ḥazzan*: congregation": responsorial singing; first *ḥazzan*, then congregation.

3. LSS 2.20–2.25 may continue the *maqām* established in LSS 2.18 and 2.19.

4. "*Ḥazzan* and congregation": *ḥazzan* and congregation sing together (initiated by *ḥazzan*).

5. Shav'at Aniyyim consists of two lines of text, and Be-Fi Yesharim consists of four lines of text. They are listed separately because they may have separate melodies; in most instances the melody used for Shav'at Aniyyim is continued in Be-Fi Yesharim.

6. Congregational response within the section Mizmor Shir le-Yom ha-Shabbat (A psalm, a song for the Sabbath day); this is the title of Psalm 92, which refers to the Sabbath—it is a part of the Zemirot section of the liturgy (LS 2.18). After the praise of God in the previous section, the present liturgical passage—recited by the *ḥazzan*—states that God rested from His work and sat on His throne. The section continues, claiming that the seventh day is a day of rest, and praise is given to God. The *ḥazzan* sets up the congregational response with the words "And the seventh day gives praise saying"; the congregation responds, "A psalm, a song for the Sabbath day"; and the *ḥazzan* continues, "It is good to thank God."

7. Two congregational responses are contained in this section—both are biblically prophetic passages: "Kadosh, Kadosh, Kadosh Ha-Shem Tseva'ot, melo khol ha-arets kevodo" ("Holy, holy, holy! The Lord of Hosts! His presence fills all the earth!" [Isaiah 6:3]); "Barukh Kevod Ha-Shem Mi-mekomo" ("Blessed is the Presence of the Lord, in His place" [Ezekiel 3:12]).

8. The Amidah for the Sabbath is comprised of seven blessings. The first three and last three blessings are the same as in the weekday Amidah. The fourth, or middle, blessing is special for the Sabbath. The liturgical passages in this section are not explicated by their liturgical function. The five subsections listed delineate the different types of musical interaction between the *ḥazzan* and the congregation.

9. The *ḥazzan* and the congregation recite different texts at the same time.

10. At Congregation Bet Torah, the prayer for the State of Israel, read by the rabbi, takes place at this point. Other congregations may recite this prayer after the Torah reading.

11. The Amidah for Musaf has a similar construction to the Amidah of Shaḥarit (LS 3.6).

12. The *ḥazzan* and the congregation recite different texts at the same time.

The interaction of music and text in Syrian liturgy necessitates a consideration of both structure and texture. Bateson's suggestion of using texture to identify "sequenced units at different levels" is useful but must be associated with structure. Rather than separating out structure and texture, I consider how they are combined. I see structure as the function of the text within the liturgy; each liturgical section has a unique function and purpose. Thus, texture reflects the type of textual delivery. Determining the relationship between structure and texture in Syrian liturgy shows where music propels the recitation of the liturgy or highlights the meaning of the text, derived from Charles Boilès terms *concurrent* and *concomitant*, respectively (1978, 15). As a result, multiple possibilities emerge—different textures serve different structures.

Music propels and highlights the text in each of the liturgical sections. Every liturgical section is unique in how it is done. This approach, facilitated through ritualization, enables the identification of multiple approaches to the interaction of structure and texture, or text and music.

The five musical sections of the Syrian Sabbath morning service contain four types of vocal performance: recitation, formulaic singing, the singing of songs, and vocal improvisation (see table 6). Recitation and formulaic singing follow the rhythmic pattern determined by the text. Recitation is the closest to speech, with occasional melodic interjections, and differs slightly from formulaic singing, which makes use of opening and closing formulas applied to the text. These two styles differ from the singing of songs and vocal improvisation. A wider range of vocal possibilities result from singing and improvising since the melody is chosen by the cantor. Furthermore, the music, not the text, determines the rhythmic pace of song singing. Attention to the relationship between the structure of the text and the texture of the music sheds light on the very nature of Syrian liturgy. The dynamic relationship of music and text in Syrian liturgy provides a rich source for the exploration of music's role in a ritual, as well as for the adaptability of Arabic music, performance practices, and aesthetics.

Six Sections of the Liturgy

THE THIRD AND sixth sections of the service—Shaḥarit and Musaf—make use of the alternation of singing and reciting of texts. The other four sections differ. The first, second, and fourth sections (Birkhot ha-Shaḥar, Zemirot, and the Torah reading) make use of recitation formulas. The fifth section is the rabbi's spoken sermon. Except for the sermon, which is given in English, all sections are melodic renderings of Hebrew texts.[7] In addition, a different person or group leads the performance of the liturgy. Some congregants may lead a section of the service, each week it may be a different person. These events take place in different locations in the sanctuary.

A diagram of Congregation Beth Torah's layout is found in figure 3. Men and women sit separately along the two sides of the sanctuary. The prayer leader or leaders, stand at the *teivah* (a raised platform), and the rabbi delivers his sermon from a lectern on the *bimah* (stage). Both the rabbi and the two cantors of Beth Torah sit on the *bimah,* facing the congregation.

Services begin at 8:15 A.M. and last approximately three hours. A handful of men recite Birkhot ha-Shaḥar; they alternate reciting the prayers from their seats. This proceeds for about fifteen minutes.

4. Exterior of Congregation Beth Torah (photo by author); 5. Interior of Congregation Beth Torah (photo by author)

For the second section, Zemirot, two members of the congregation lead. They stand at the *teivah.* During Zemirot, these two men recite several psalms to a recitation formula in *maqām seyga.* Interspersed the congregation sings three textual portions; the *ḥazzan* recites a textual portion in the middle of this section in a contrasting *maqām.*

The cantor leads Shaḥarit, the third section, from the *teivah.* Shaḥarit, recited in the *maqām* of the day, is the most dynamic section musically. The cantor initiates seven sung sections within Shaḥarit. The liturgy surrounding and between these seven portions is melodically improvised by the cantor in the *maqām* of the day and other *maqāmāt.*

The fourth section, the Torah reading, follows. This reading employs recitation formulas in *maqām seyga,* but it differs from the Zemirot *seyga* formula. The delivery of Torah cantillation requires careful enunciation. The scrolls are taken out of the *aron* (ark), where they are returned after the reading. The Torah procession consists of several men with the rabbi and *ḥazzan* parading from the *bimah* to the *teivah.* During this procession the congregation sings several songs. Often, the *ḥazzan* or a skilled congregant begins the singing of a *pizmon;* this most often occurs between readings of the Torah. The choice of melody varies from songs associated with a celebrated life cycle event to melodies that congregants enjoy singing where there is no association for its use. Similarly, the congregation sings for the recession of the Torah back to the *bimah* when the Torah is returned to the *aron.*

The rabbi's sermon, delivered from a lectern on the *bimah,* addresses a variety of concerns. Typically, the rabbi explains an aspect of the Torah reading and applies it to contemporary life. The Musaf section, led by the *ḥazzan* or a skilled congregant, concludes the service. Together, the congregation sings a liturgical passage to a melody initiated by the cantor; this melody can be in one of several *maqāmāt.* Musaf is considerably shorter and more informal than the other sections of the service.[8]

6

Birkhot ha-Shaḥar and Zemirot

Birkhot ha-Shaḥar

BIRKHOT HA-SHAḤAR IS an introductory liturgical section consisting of blessings, scriptural readings, and rabbinic texts.[1] It was the last liturgical section to become codified (Hoffman 1979, 128) and was initially recited at home prior to coming to the synagogue (Elbogen 1913 [1993], 76); now it is part of the morning service. This section, recited every day of the week, has nothing added for the Sabbath. Likewise, the manner of recitation of Birkhot ha-Shaḥar follows the weekday method: recitation in *maqām seyga*. The text is declaimed with a slight melodic intonation, a style of recitation close to speech (see musical example 1). The melodic range is narrow. The leader recites many words on one note, and only at the end of this portion of the text does the rhythm become clear and defined.

At Beth Torah, about a dozen men are present when services begin. Most others arrive by the beginning of Shaḥarit, but the peak of attendance is during the Torah reading. There is no designated leader during Birkhot ha-Shaḥar. A congregant begins by reciting the first text from his seat. Then others alternate in reciting the remaining texts of the Birkhot ha-Shaḥar liturgical section. A handful of men participate from week to week, but others choose not to recite a textual portion. Occasionally, two men will begin the next prayer at the same time. When this happens, one man will gesture to the other to take over. In some synagogues, including Beth Torah, the same person recites certain passages from week to week.

Example 1. *Birkhot ha-Shaḥar* seyga *formula applied to Eloheinu ve-elokei avoteinu. Sung by David Tawil, July 28, 1995.*

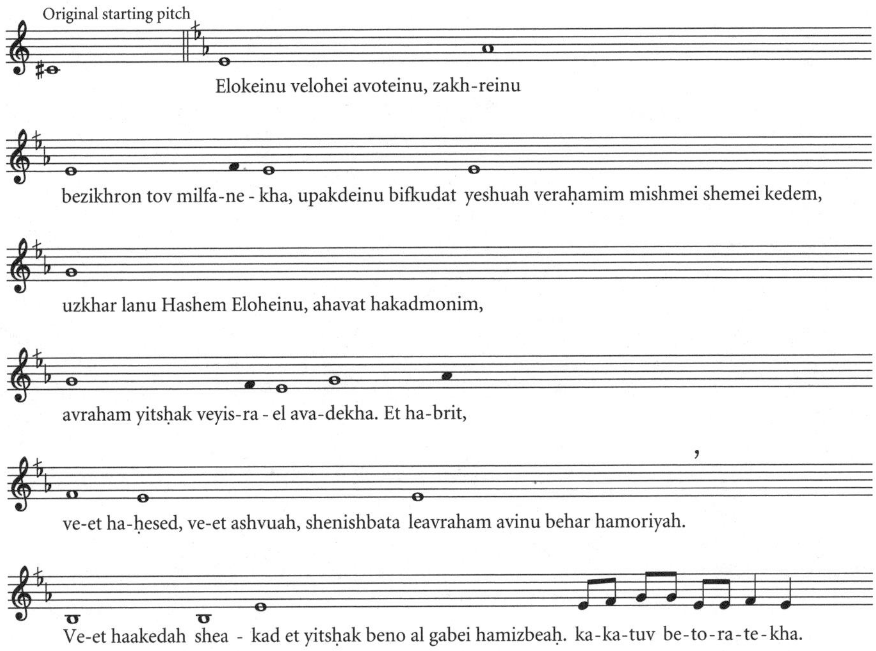
Original starting pitch
Elokeinu velohei avoteinu, zakh-reinu
bezikhron tov milfa-ne - kha, upakdeinu bifkudat yeshuah veraḥamim mishmei shemei kedem,
uzkhar lanu Hashem Eloheinu, ahavat hakadmonim,
avraham yitsḥak veyis-ra - el ava-dekha. Et ha-brit,
ve-et ha-ḥesed, ve-et ashvuah, shenishbata leavraham avinu behar hamoriyah.
Ve-et haakedah shea - kad et yitsḥak beno al gabei hamizbeaḥ. ka-ka-tuv be-to-ra-te-kha.

The Birkhot ha-Shaḥar section ends with the recitation of the Kaddish; this important text is an affirmation of the sanctity and perpetual essence of God.[2] At the conclusion of Birkhot ha-Shaḥar, mourners in the congregation recite the Kaddish de-Rabbanan (the rabbi's Kaddish).[3] Again, no leader is designated; mourners rise and recite the text together. The congregation responds at various points with certain phrases or the word *amen*. This concludes the Birkhot ha-Shaḥar section.

Zemirot

CONTRASTING TO THE manner of presentation of Birkhot ha-Shaḥar is Zemirot (literally, "songs"; in this context it refers to songs of praise). The twenty-eight texts of Zemirot mostly consist of chapters from Psalms, combined with other biblical passages.[4] Like the previous liturgical section, Zemirot is recited during the week. However, unlike Birkhot ha-Shaḥar, Zemirot contains additional psalmodic texts for the Sabbath and omits certain texts (Psalms 67 and 100) that appear on the weekdays (Elbogen 1913 [1993], 95). The additional psalms for the Sabbath appear in the middle of the Zemirot section. A detailed comparison of the weekday and Sabbath renderings of the Zemirot section highlights important melodic and textual distinctions between the two. The weekday rendering is more informal, quicker, and less ornate with fewer participants (see table 7).

Table 7. *Zemirot liturgical section on Shabbat*

Liturgical section	Source of text	Weekday liturgy	*Maqām*
1. Hodu la-Shem Kir'u bi-Shemo	I Chronicles 16: 8–15	yes	*seyga*
Va-Ya'amideha le-Ya'akov le-Ḥok	I Chron. 16: 16–36 and various psalms	yes	
2. Kel Nekamot Ha-Shem	various psalms	yes	*seyga*
3. Aromimkha Ha-Shem	Psalm 30	yes	*seyga*
4. Ha-Shem Melekh*	various biblical passages	yes	*maqām* of day
5. Lamnazze'aḥ Mizmor le-David	Psalm 19	no	*seyga*
6. Rannenu Tsaddikim	Psalm 33	no	*seyga*
7. Le-David, be-Shannoto et Tamo	Psalm 34	no	*seyga*
8. Tefillah le-Moshe	Psalm 90	no	*seyga*
9. Yoshev be-Seter Elyon	Psalm 91	no	*seyga*
10. Mizmor, Shiru la-Shem	Psalm 98	no	*seyga*
11. Shir la-Ma'alot, Essa Einai	Psalm 121	no	*seyga*
12. Shir ha-Ma'alot le-David, Samaḥti	Psalm 122	no	*seyga*
13. Shir ha-Ma'alot, Elekha	Psalm 123	no	*seyga*
14. Shir ha-Ma'alot le-David, Lulei	Psalm 124	no	*seyga*
15. Halleluyah, Hallelu et Shem	Psalm 135	no	*seyga*
16. Hodu la-Shem Ki Tov	Psalm 136	no	*seyga*
17. Barukh she-Amar*	verses of praise	yes	fixed tune
18. Mizmor Shir le-Yom ha-Shabbat	Psalm 92	no	varies
19. Ha-Shem Malakh Ge'ut Lavesh	Psalm 93	no	varies
20. Yehi Khevod	various biblical passages	yes	*seyga*
21. Ashrei Yoshvei	Psalm 145	yes	*seyga*
22. Halleluyah, Halleli Nafshi	Psalm 146	yes	*seyga*

23. Halleluyah, Ki Tov Zamrah	Psalm 147	yes	*seyga*
24. Halleluyah, hallelu et Ha-Shem	Psalm 148	yes	*seyga*
25. Halleluyah, Shiru la-Shem	Psalm 149	yes	*seyga*
26. Halleluyah, Hallelu Kel be-Kadsho*	Psalm 150	yes	varies
27. Barukh Ha-Shem le-Olam	four psalm phrases; I Chronicles 29:10–13; Nehemiah 9:5–11	yes	*seyga*
28. Az Yashir Moshe (Shirt ha-Yam)	Exodus 14:30–15:19	yes	*seyga*

Note: An asterisk (*) indicates liturgical sections discussed in this chapter.

Zemirot begins at the conclusion of the recitation of the Kaddish with the congregation singing a fixed melody to Hodu la-Shem Kir'u bi-Shemo (Praise the Lord, Call on His Name; liturgical section [LS] 2.1; see table 6). Every week they use the same melody; no single individual initiates the singing. Next follows a recitation of the remaining portion of text by a seated congregant to the same *seyga* pattern used in Birkhot ha-Shaḥar. The next two texts are recited similarly.

The *ḥazzan* leads Ha-Shem Melekh (The Lord Is King; LS 2.4). The text reads, "Ha-Shem melekh, ha-Shem malakh, ha-Shem yimlokh le-olam va-ed" ("The Lord reigns, the Lord has reigned, the Lord will reign for ever and ever").[5] The *ḥazzan,* from his seat on the *bimah,* sings this single line of text, which is repeated by the congregation; the *ḥazzan* repeats the melody with the same text a second time, and the congregation again repeats. The melody is in the *maqām* of the day to be used during Shaḥarit (the next liturgical section). This melody is flexible since it will change, like the *maqām,* from week to week. As Moses Tawil explains:

> Ha-Shem Melekh always has a melody to it on Shabbatot [Sabbaths], Yamim Nora'im [High Holidays], and Yom Tovim [Holidays]. . . . The *ḥazzan* says it again, and they [the congregation] respond. And at times he will say a different melody for each time he says "Ha-Shem Melekh," depending on the *ḥazzan*'s mood and sophistication. . . . The proficient *ḥazzanim,* usually the *ḥazzan kavu'a* [6] [main *ḥazzan*], is the one that says "Ha-Shem Melekh." He usually uses the *maqām* that he is going to say the Nishmat [Kol Ḥai] [the first text of Shaḥarit (LS 3.1)], and that introduces to the knowledgeable ones that that's going to be the *maqām* for the day in the principal part of the *tefilah* [Shaḥarit]. (interview, October 6, 1991)

For Tawil the goal is to use the *maqām* of the day to foreshadow what will be heard later in Shaḥarit (see musical example 2). The congregation repeats the first verse the *ḥazzan* sings. The second verse differs; the *ḥazzan* sings a different melody, but the congregation sings the melody of the first verse. The melody Ha-Shem Melekh noticeably differs from the *seyga* recitation, a congregational melody with a defined rhythm.

After Ha-Shem Melekh, two congregants walk to the *teivah* and alternate reciting most of the remaining Zemirot. One of these two men is the leader; he performs this function from week to week. The second congregant, an assistant leader, rotates among a handful of congregants. The twelve psalms between Ha-Shem Melekh and Barukh she-Amar (LS 2.17) are recited in the *maqām seyga* formula. This formula can be characterized as an even recitation, giving equal prominence to each word with clear enunciation. The melodic components of the Zemirot formula emphasize the first and third notes of *maqām*

Example 2. *Ha-Shem Melekh. Sung in* maqām *bayat by David Shiro, October 6, 1999.*

seyga (E quarter flat and G, respectively) for each verse of the psalm text (see musical example 3). Occasionally, one verse may emphasize the first note of the *maqām,* and the next verse emphasizes the third. The formula is adapted to fit the text. It differs from the *maqām seyga* recitation used for Birkhot ha-Shaḥar (musical example 1) in that there is a greater emphasis in melodic shape. Ends of psalm texts are slightly melodically embellished. Occasionally, the leader gestures for someone else to continue, calling upon a member of the congregation to recite a psalm from his seat.

Example 3. *Zemirot* seyga *formula applied to Lamnataeʾah Mizmor le-David. Sung by David Tawil, July 28, 1995.*

The design of Zemirot, thus far, consists of three texts that precede Ha-Shem Melekh and twelve that follow. On the Sabbath, the three that precede are led from within the congregation and are rendered in the same manner as on weekdays. Ha-Shem Melekh serves as an introduction to the following twelve texts, which are specific to the Sabbath (see table 7). These twelve are rendered more formally by two leaders standing at the *teivah* rather than from within the congregation. While recited on weekdays, Ha-Shem Melekh receives emphasis on the Sabbath, most likely for its present, past, and future tense references to the reigning of the Lord. Highlighting this significant text, the *ḥazzan,* the important musical reciter, signals a change in the manner of recitation to follow and announces the *maqām* to be used later.

Similarly, Barukh she-Amar (LS 2.17) acts as a transition. It is sung by the entire congregation to a fixed melody in *nahawand* (see musical example 4). The Barukh she-Amar melody is widely known and not initiated by a leader. It is taken from Israel's national anthem, Hatikvah, showing the influence of Israel in the modern period. The first part of this text, sung by the congregation, differs from the second part, which is led by the *ḥazzan* or another knowledgeable member of the congregation and recited in a contrasting *maqām.* At Beth Torah the *ḥazzan* who does not lead Shaḥarit takes over at this point and recites the next two psalms (LSS 2.18 and 2.19). At other congregations, the second half of Barukh she-Amar may be recited by the *ḥazzan* of the day.

When Ḥazzan Moses Tawil attends Congregation Shaarei Zion as a congregant, he will begin with the second part of Barukh she-Amar after the congregational singing. The new *maqām* that he establishes will be used thereafter, up to and including Halleluyah, Hallelu Kel be-Kadsho (Hallelujah, Praise God in His Sanctuary, LS 2.26). Tawil elaborates on the prescribed change of *maqām* and the participation of others who recite from this point on during Zemirot:

Example 4. *Barukh she-Amar. Sung by Moses Tawil, October 6, 1991.*

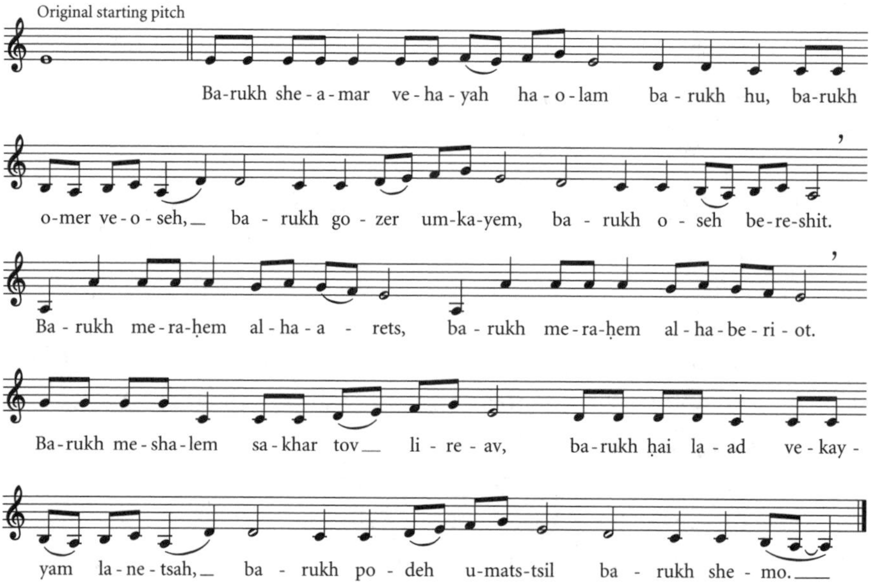

Moses Tawil: If I am present, I will take over from after the whole *kahal* [congregation] says "Barukh she-Amar" together until the *berakha* [blessing]. So at about the middle of the Barukh she-Amar, in this portion . . . we establish the *maqām* that we are going to say the Zemirot. . . . It is not the same *maqām* that we are going to pray from Nishmat and onwards, in order not to overdo the *maqām* and, on the other hand, give a chance to the *ḥazzan* that is going to start Nishmat to elaborate himself on that particular *maqām*. . . . Very often when it comes to Mizmor Shir le-Yom ha-Shabbat [LS 2.18], if there is someone who is proficient he is invited to say it out loud—to sing it. There it depends on the proficiency of the *ḥazzan*, how much he can elaborate on it.

Mark Kligman: What *maqām* would that be in?

MT: The *maqām* that they establish for the rest of the Zemirot. For example, this past Shabbat they sang it in *nahawand*. The *tefilah* [the prayers from Shaḥarit], the body of it, was in *rast*. The Zemirot before [Barukh she-Amar] were said in *seyga*, and soon as we got to Barukh she-Amar, I started and I switched to *nahawand*, and I made Mizmor Shir le-Yom ha-Shabbat in *nahawand*, and we finished the rest of these ([LSS 2.20–2.26] in *nahawand* until we get to this [Halleluyah, Hallelu Kel be-Kadsho (LS 2.26)], which is sung by the general public. Also in *nahawand*.

MK: Now this [Halleluyah, Hallelu Kel be-Kadsho (LS 2.26)] uses the same melody [from week to week] too?

MT: No, it varies. There are many tunes one can use in *nahawand*. For this Shabbat I used [he sings]; this is sung by the general public, and you set the pattern and you set the pace for it. (interview, October 6, 1991)

When the *ḥazzan* takes over from the blessing in Barukh she-Amar, the rendering is distinct from the even-paced formulaic style already heard during the Zemirot. The *ḥazzan* has a strong voice, and the improvisational style contrasts with the preceding application of the *seyga* formula: the cantor emphasizes certain words over others, elaborates some words melodically, and recites others very quickly. One of the other significant differences in the *ḥazzan*'s performance is the manner in which he cadences at the end of texts. In the cadence, the *ḥazzan* pauses before the last two or three words, which are recited by the congregation. The *ḥazzan* then elaborately repeats these words, producing a distinctive melodic cadence. This, like Ha-Shem Melekh, foreshadows what is to come during the *ḥazzan*'s rendering of Shaḥarit; the congregation hears the style of the forthcoming prayer style of the *ḥazzan*.

The rendering of the remaining Zemirot texts (LSS 2.20–2.28) is not unique to the Sabbath. The weekday recitation style may be used. Only a proficient reciter would employ a contrasting *maqām*, though the manner of recitation most often changes even if the reciters return to the *seyga* formula. The reciters at the *teivah* try to emulate the *ḥazzan*, usually by adding some slight cadential elaborations—although none as elaborate as those of the cantor. This is typically applied to the psalms that both begin and end with the word *halleluyah* ("praise the Lord") (Psalms 146–49, LSS 2.22–2.25). A slight melisma may emphasize the word *halleluyah*—often repeated or stated at the same time by the congregation.

It is during these sections of the service that members of the congregation proficient at reciting psalms are designated by the leader, signaled nonverbally with a hand gesture or a nod. Sometimes the leader may gesture to one of the two cantors to render a psalm. On the rare occasion when a guest cantor was present, he was designated to lead the text Yehi Khavod (May the Glory, LS 2.20), which is comprised of sentences or phrases from various psalms. The textual incipit reads, "May the glory of the Lord endure forever." The word *khavod*, translated here as "glory," could also be understood as "honor." Perhaps the honor of giving the guest *ḥazzan* this passage to read reflects in the word *khavod* at the beginning of the text. Another reason the Yehi Khavod text may be chosen for the guest cantor is that this is the first text that continues in the contrasting *maqām*. This assumes that the guest cantor is capable of continuing in the new *maqām* established earlier by one of the two regular *ḥazzanim*.

The next liturgical text emphasized is the final hallelujah psalm (Psalm 150), Halleluyah, Hallelu Kel be-Kadsho (LS 2.26). This last psalm in the book of Psalms praises God by listing various musical instruments and, appropriately, is sung by the congregation (see musical example 5 for an illustration of this liturgical section sung in *maqām nahawand)*. The text reads:

> *Praise God.*
> *Praise the Almighty in His sanctuary—*
> *praise Him in the firmament of His might.*
> *Praise Him for His mighty deeds—*
> *praise Him according to the abundance of His greatness.*
> *Praise Him with the blowing of the shofar—*

praise Him with lyre and harp.
Praise Him with drum and dance—
praise Him with stringed instruments and flute.
Praise Him with resounding cymbals—
praise Him with clanging cymbals.
Let every soul praise God—praise God.
Let every soul praise God—praise God.[7]

The musical rendering demonstrates a repetitive melody with a regular rhythm.

The two concluding texts of Zemirot (LSS 2.27 and 2.28), taken from biblical passages, are typically recited in *maqām seyga*. The reciter can vary the *maqām* in the first of these two passages. When Ḥazzan Moses Tawil leads this passage, he starts in *seyga* then goes to another *maqām* and returns to *seyga* (interview, October 6, 1991). The last section of Zemirot is recited in *maqām seyga* because it is a passage from the Torah, and like cantillation one recites

Example 5. *Halleluyah, Hallelu Kel be-Kadsho. Sung in* maqām nahawand *by Moses Tawil, October 6, 1991.*

Torah passages in the liturgy in this *maqām*.[8] Taken from Exodus 14:30–15:19, this final text is known as Shirat ha-Yam (Song of the Sea); it is said to have been sung by the Israelites after crossing the Red Sea following the Exodus from Egypt. The leader may embellish the song by decorating certain passages melodically. When this section from Exodus occurs in the weekly Torah reading, the entire congregation participates.[9] On the Sabbath known as Shabbat Shirah (the Sabbath of Song), the congregation at Beth joins the main leader during the recitation of Shirat ha-Yam. The congregational reading of Shirat ha-Yam on this particular Sabbath is a special Syrian practice (Dobrinsky 1986, 376).

In general, the Zemirot section of the service contains an increased level of musical activity or texture, a contrast to the prior declamatory style of Birkhot ha-Shaḥar. Zemirot employs a full range of recitation and vocal styles throughout. It is noteworthy that the manner of delivery articulates specific textual additions. Changes in recitation style, placement of the leader, and melodic choices all serve to accommodate psalms added to the liturgy for the Sabbath and make this organization of Zemirot unique for the day. The Zemirot section thus provides contrast. At certain times it allows for variety and personal expression with both fixed and flexible components.

The *ḥazzan* has a limited but important role in Zemirot. He recites the important textual portions, thereby signaling a change in the nature of the liturgical text and manner of recitation to follow. Three portions of the *ḥazzan*'s Zemirot activity express different musical elements: the responsorial singing of Ha-Shem Melekh (LS 2.4) introduces the *maqām* of the day; the second half of Barukh she-Amar (LS 2.17) and the two following psalms (LSS 2.17–2.19) introduce a contrasting *maqām* and an improvisatorial style; and Halleluyah, Hallelu Kel be-Kadsho (LS 2.26) introduces a song that is sung by the entire congregation with a different melody each week. All three of these elements, integrated strategically within Zemirot, offer to the congregation a taste of what is to come in the Shaḥarit section.[10] Variety of textual type does not determine the type of melodic style; function of the text is the determinant. Psalms added for the Sabbath receive more musical prominence. The dynamic relationship between music and text continues to another degree in Shaḥarit.

7

Shaḥarit

TOWARD THE CONCLUSION of Shirat ha-Yam, the final text of Zemirot, the *ḥazzan* of the day walks to the *teivah* in a white robe that distinguishes him from the previous prayer leaders.[1] Moses Tawil, who uses the term *ḥazzan* in a general sense to refer to any prayer leader, makes the following distinction: "As a rule, we have a *ḥazzan* who starts the *brakhot* [blessings] at the beginning of Birkhot ha-Shaḥar [LS 1], and usually another *ḥazzan* takes over when we reach 'Ha-Shem Melekh' [LS 2.4]—this *ḥazzan* is a little more sophisticated than the first one. And then the formal *ḥazzan* of the day starts from the *yotzer* [a liturgical section within Shaḥarit] of 'Nishmat Kol-Ḥai' [LS 3.1]" (interview, October 6, 1991) (see table 6).

Shaḥarit is the main part of the morning service because it contains the two mandatory liturgical components, the Shema and the Amidah, with a variety of prose styles.[2] Based on Moses Tawil's description of Shaḥarit, the discussion that follows begins with an explanation of the text. Comments on Arab musical components follow with an illustration of specific musical examples of Syrian liturgy. Since Shaḥarit contains the most varied and extensive musical treatment more background on Arab music provides further contextualization on the origins of melodies and the adaptation process. Specific musical examples demonstrate in detail the skill of the *ḥazzan* and the deep interconnection of Arab music and Syrian liturgy.

Figure 4. *Format of Shema in Syrian prayer book*

שחרית של שבת

שְׁמַע יִשְׂרָאֵל יְהוָה אֱלֹהֵינוּ יְהוָה ׀ אֶחָד:

בלחש:

בָּרוּךְ שֵׁם כְּבוֹד מַלְכוּתוֹ לְעוֹלָם וָעֶד:

וְאָהַבְתָּ אֵת יְהוָה אֱלֹהֶיךָ בְּכָל־לְבָבְךָ וּבְכָל־נַפְשְׁךָ
וּבְכָל־מְאֹדֶךָ: וְהָיוּ הַדְּבָרִים הָאֵלֶּה אֲשֶׁר אָנֹכִי
מְצַוְּךָ הַיּוֹם עַל־לְבָבֶךָ: וְשִׁנַּנְתָּם לְבָנֶיךָ וְדִבַּרְתָּ בָּם
בְּשִׁבְתְּךָ בְּבֵיתֶךָ וּבְלֶכְתְּךָ בַדֶּרֶךְ וּבְשָׁכְבְּךָ וּבְקוּמֶךָ:
וּקְשַׁרְתָּם לְאוֹת עַל־יָדֶךָ וְהָיוּ לְטֹטָפֹת בֵּין עֵינֶיךָ:
וּכְתַבְתָּם עַל־מְזֻזוֹת בֵּיתֶךָ וּבִשְׁעָרֶיךָ:

וְהָיָה אִם־שָׁמֹעַ תִּשְׁמְעוּ אֶל־מִצְוֹתַי אֲשֶׁר אָנֹכִי
מְצַוֶּה אֶתְכֶם הַיּוֹם לְאַהֲבָה אֶת־יְהוָה אֱלֹהֵיכֶם
וּלְעָבְדוֹ בְּכָל־לְבַבְכֶם וּבְכָל־נַפְשְׁכֶם: וְנָתַתִּי מְטַר־
אַרְצְכֶם בְּעִתּוֹ יוֹרֶה וּמַלְקוֹשׁ וְאָסַפְתָּ דְגָנֶךָ וְתִירֹשְׁךָ
וְיִצְהָרֶךָ: וְנָתַתִּי עֵשֶׂב בְּשָׂדְךָ לִבְהֶמְתֶּךָ וְאָכַלְתָּ
וְשָׂבָעְתָּ: הִשָּׁמְרוּ לָכֶם פֶּן־יִפְתֶּה לְבַבְכֶם וְסַרְתֶּם
וַעֲבַדְתֶּם אֱלֹהִים אֲחֵרִים וְהִשְׁתַּחֲוִיתֶם לָהֶם: וְחָרָה
להפסיק מעט ולומר בלחש אַף־יְהוָה בָּכֶם וְעָצַר אֶת־
הַשָּׁמַיִם וְלֹא־יִהְיֶה מָטָר וְהָאֲדָמָה לֹא תִתֵּן אֶת־

Description of Shaḥarit

THE SHAḤARIT TEXT is distinct from the rabbinic texts of Birkhot ha-Shaḥar and the psalms and biblical passages of Zemirot. Like Zemirot, the Shaḥarit text is also said on the weekdays. Unique textual insertions are added on the Sabbath. Other additions to Shaḥarit further underscore its importance as the core of the Sabbath morning service. The first addition is Nishmat Kol Ḥai (LS 3.1).[3] This text, an introduction to the Shema and Amidah to follow, emphasizes the physical, spiritual, and historical dependency upon God. An elaborate expression of praise and gratitude, the Kaddish (LS 3.2) follows in a short form.[4] The Bar'khu, the call to prayer, and the pre-Shema blessings (LS 3.3), contain additional passages for the Sabbath (LSS 3.3.2–3.3.5).[5] The first blessing, La-Kel Barukh (LS 3.3.7), focuses on the luminaries, and the second, Ahavat Olam (LS 3.3.8), on love of God. The Shema text (LS 3.4) follows, appearing in a format visually distinct from the other textual portions of Shaḥarit in the Syrian Prayer Book, with the *ta'amim* (Masoretic accents) of the Torah placed above or below each word (see figure 4). The post-Shema blessing (LS 3.5), which appears in the same form in the weekday liturgy, consists of several texts and concludes with a blessing for God as Redeemer of the people Israel. The Amidah (LS 3.6) follows. Only one of its six subsections is added for the Sabbath, Yismaḥ Moshe (LS 3.6.3).[6] This is followed by a complete, or full, Kaddish (LS 3.7) to mark the end of Shaḥarit.

The *ḥazzan*'s performance highlights seven sections of Shaḥarit (see table 8).[7] Interestingly, these seven musically emphasized portions are not the additional texts for the Sabbath, as with Zemirot. Furthermore, the two main liturgical portions are not accentuated with music. The recitation of the Shema is in *maqām seyga*, an interesting counterpart to the *maqām* of the day, and only one brief portion of the Amidah is sung. Musical emphasis is given primarily to portions that precede the Shema and to one portion that prefaces the Amidah.

Table 8. *Liturgical singing stations of the Syrian Sabbath morning service*

Liturgical portion	Liturgical section number (listed in table 6)	Liturgical section within Shahārit	Pillar	Music Sytle
Nishmat Kol Ḥai	3.1.1	Nishmat Kol Ḥai LS 3.1	Pillar #1	heavy
Shav'at Aniyyim	3.1.4	"		light
Kel ha-Hodaot	3.1.7	"		light
Kaddish	3.2	Kaddish LS 3.2	Pillar #2	heavy

Semeḥim be-Tseitam	3.3.4	pre-Shema blessings LS 3.3		light
Mi-mits'rayim Gealtanu	3.5.3	post-Shema blessing LS 3.5		light
Nak'dishakh	3.6.2	Amidah LS 3.6	Pillar #3	heavy

Ḥazzan Moses Tawil says, "there are seven parts of the *tefilah* [prayer] on Shabbat which are not improvised; they are set to a pattern" (interview, November 14, 1991). Tawil delineates the pattern, or the rules that a cantor follows: The *ḥazzan* begins by improvising a brief passage, Ki la-Shem ha-Melukhah; this gives him the opportunity to warm up his voice and "get a feel" for the *maqām* of the day (ibid.).[8] The *ḥazzan* continues with the text Nishmat Kol-Ḥai (LS 3.1.1). The first three lines of text are sung in the *maqām* to the melody of a *pizmon* or *bakkasha* as the first liturgical singing station; after singing the three lines, the *ḥazzan* continues by improvising a melody for the text. He stops at several points and cadences in the same manner discussed earlier as in the rendering of the second part of Barukh she-Amar (LS 2.17), creating interaction between the *ḥazzan* and the congregation. As Tawil explains, "They [the congregation] respond to these last two words, and I deliver it to them, and it's a closing response and they take part. I repeat [these words] and continue" (M. Tawil, interview, October 6, 1991).

Shaḥarit lasts forty to forty-five minutes. The improvisation between singing stations is at a deliberately slow pace to allow for clear enunciation. Certain words receive melodic embellishment and other portions quick recitation. The placement of the first three singing stations appear at the beginning, middle, and end of the Nishmat Kol-Ḥai liturgical text, creating a balanced form.

Ḥazzan Tawil explains the remaining portions of Shaḥarit:

> Moses Tawil: Then the *ḥazzan* says the Kaddish [LS 3.3, singing station 4], solo, of course, in his melody—whatever he picks. It has to be in the same *maqām*. There are a number of variations, and so on. [He sings three lines of the Kaddish.] The rest is adlibbed, whatever I feel like, I sing.[9] [He continues singing through Bar'khu.] Then the Kaddish is finished and you go into the *yotzer*, and there are two other portions that the *kahal* [congregation] sings. And that's Kel Adon [LS 3.3.3], [at] the end of Kel Adon [which is] Semeḥim be-Tseitam [LS 3.3.4, singing station 5].
>
> Mark Kligman: Now why do you start there? Is there any reason why?

MT: No, just tradition. It starts with Ki Tov [Because good], Semeḥim [They are happy].[10] But there is no reason for it. It is just closing the portion. It makes it interesting for the *kahal* to partake in the services. And they enjoy it. We try to instruct our *ḥazzanim* to select portions [melodies] that the *kahal* is familiar with so they could all sing together. This Semeḥim they sing. And [the] last one is Mi-mits'rayim [LS 3.5.3, singing station 6], in the last portion before the Amidah, before the Shemoneh-Esreh. . . . Then he continues with the prayers.

MK: And again this is all *bayat*? [In this interview all the melodies he sang were in *maqām bayat.*]

MT: Yes. Usually, I recommend from this portion on, if you want to give a variation of *maqāmāt,* you should do it over here.[11] Because they are through with the portions that they are going to give over to the *kahal* to sing in the same *maqām.* Generally, the proficient *ḥazzan* will now go over to a different *maqām* according to his mood and what he likes, providing that, in most cases, maybe by the end of one or two of these portions, he comes back to the same *maqām.* And then in Ahavat Olam Ahavtanu (LS 3.3.8), the last portion before the Kriyat Shema [reading of the Shema], they manage to touch a little on *seyga* because now they are going to Kriyat Shema, a part of the Torah, which is always sung in *seyga*—it has the regular *ta'amim* of the Torah. So here they can vary and go to different *maqāmāt* so as long as they come back to the same *bayat,* and even if they vary—here they touch on *seyga*—they close the portion in *bayat.* The same *maqām* that we have been praying before. And the Kriyat Shema, some *ḥazzanim* do it themselves while at the *teivah* and others may let somebody else do it, and then it is up to the *ḥazzan.* . . .

And then they say the Kriyat Shema in *seyga* up until "AdoShem Elokeikhem" [the last two words of the Shema], and as soon as they are going to start Ve-Yatsiv ve-Nakhon [LS 3.5.1] he goes back to the same *maqām* that he was before, in the [previous] part of the prayers. At Mi-mits'rayim (LS 3.5.3) they say a melody; this is the whole *kahal.*

And then [the] last melody I say is the Kedushah, which the *ḥazzan* starts it and the whole *kahal* joins in it.[12] And that is the last portion that is sung for the rest of Shaḥarit.

This melody [he sings "Kadosh, Kadosh, Kadosh," the thrice

holy congregational response] goes as they wish. And they [the cantors] finish the rest of the Kedushah also spontaneous, the way he feels like. This is the composed portion, and the whole *kahal* sings together. And that's it.

We make what you call *Dukhan Kohanim,* we make Birkat Kohanim [LS 3.6.5] every prayer, every Shaḥarit.[13] Then . . . the *ḥazzan* says the word and the *kohanim* repeat it—and here, also, they are usually in the same *maqām* as they are praying *tefilah,* or he could make many variations there because each word is stretched out quite a bit, I mean, they make a real song out of it. He could go to any variation that he wants—he can go to two, three *maqāmāt*—but he has to come back to the same *maqām* that he starts. He starts with the same *maqām* of the prayers, and then he varies according to his technique and to how nice he could make it and elaborate improvising. And when he prays the last word when he goes to say "Shalom" [the last word of Birkat Kohanim] it's got to close in the same *maqām bayat* as he has the prayers, and he finishes the Shemoneh-Esreh in that same *maqām.* And the last Kaddish . . . the Kaddish Titkabal [the complete Kaddish that follows the Shemoneh-Esreh, LS 3.7] is said plain.

MK: That's in the *maqām*?

MT: They have to close in the *maqām;* it is not a different *maqām,* no. But, I mean, it is said without a melody, they don't make a song out of it. Just like [the] other Kaddish.[14] (interview, October 6, 1991)

Organization of Shaḥarit

THE PATTERN ESTABLISHED with Nishmat Kol Ḥai continues throughout Shaḥarit. The *maqām* of the day is prominent. Each of the seven liturgical singing stations must use melodies taken from the same *maqām.* The placement of the last three singing stations, 5–7, appear midway through the third, fifth, and sixth sections of Shaḥarit (see table 8). The last Kaddish, said quickly by the *ḥazzan,* is not a singing station. As described by Moses Tawil, it is "said plain." With Shaḥarit taking forty to forty-five minutes to deliver, and with relatively few sung portions during this period of time (each of the singing stations consists of three to five lines of text), the majority of the *ḥazzan*'s melodic activity has the goal of initiating each of the singing stations and subsequent improvisation.

The Shema, which is the centerpiece of Shaḥarit, is not given musical prominence. Rather, it is read in *seyga* in the same way that the reader renders the Torah. In order for each congregant to fulfill his obligation to recite the Shema, one recites the text along with the *ḥazzan* at their own pace. The *ḥazzan*, however, may elaborate his recitation of the Shema in order to make it more interesting and enjoyable (M. Tawil, interview, October 22, 1991). Although the Shema itself is not given melodic emphasis, singing stations 5 and 6 frame it.

The melodic elaboration of Birkat Kohanim [the priestly blessing] (LS 3.6.5) within the Amidah is not considered a singing station. The *kohanim*, who number about fifty at Beth Torah, leave their seats and stand between the *bimah* and the *teivah*. They place their prayer shawls over their heads and face the *ḥazzan* standing at the *teivah*. The other congregants stand in front of the *kohanim* and face them. Shortly before this portion begins everyone shifts positions within the synagogue. The *ḥazzan* then recites each word of the three-fold blessing, drawn from Numbers 6:24–26; the *kohanim* repeat it.[15] The cantor can elaborate melodically on the blessing; at the end of each blessing the congregation responds with "Amen."

Three of the liturgical singing stations receive greater prominence. Tawil calls these the three crowns, or pillars: "There are three *keters*, there are three crowns, to the prayers, as far as the quality of the type of music. They are known as the Nishmat, the introduction of the *ḥazzan*. . . . The other one is the Kaddish of the *yotzer*, and the third one is the Kedushah. These are supposed to be classic pieces" (interview, November 14, 1991).[16] The pillars take prominence as the first, fourth, and seventh singing stations—the beginning, middle, and end (see table 8). Tawil characterizes the other sections as containing a "lighter type" of music. The "heavy," or classic, pieces typically use unmeasured melodies that are highly melismatic. The lighter pieces have a regular rhythm (these musical components are discussed later in this chapter). The imagery of pillars can be seen as the musical foundation that holds up, or organizes, Shaḥarit.

Use of the *Maqām* of the Day

THE MELODIC BASIS for all of Shaḥarit is the *maqām* of the day. This *maqām*, introduced earlier in the service during Zemirot, is the one with which the *ḥazzan* must begin and end. Cadences at the conclusion of prescribed portions must be in this *maqām*. While the *ḥazzan* can vary the *maqām* at certain places, this should not be overdone. As described earlier by Tawil, the liturgical singing stations must all make use of the *maqām* of the day. This point was underscored by other cantors as well.

When discussing the use of the *maqām* of the day in his *pizmonim* class, Cantor Isaac Cabasso stated that one must remain in that *maqām* and establish it for at least ten minutes before moving to another *maqām* (February 24, 1992). Arab singers like Umm Kulthūm and Muḥammad ʿAbd al-Wahhāb provide a model for this type of singing. Cabasso notes that the Israeli-trained Sephardic cantors adhere to the Yerushalmi Sephardi (Jerusalem Sephardic) style, not the Brooklyn Syrian style. These cantors, he says, "make use of up to five or six *maqāmāt* within the first page of text during Nishmat Kol Ḥai."[17] They are able to return to the *maqām* of the day but do not give it prominence. A young man in the *pizmonim* class who had studied in Israel said he was told to change *maqāmāt* frequently because it is too boring to have the majority of the prayers in the same *maqām*. The Aleppo-style cantors in Brooklyn, however, feel that frequent changes are distracting; instead, their goal is to render one *maqām* both prominent and interesting.

Musical Adaptation: Settings of the Liturgical Singing Stations

MUSICAL SETTINGS OF the liturgical singing stations more closely illustrate the adaptation of Arab music in Syrian Sabbath liturgy. In this musical process of adaptation, several changes and accommodations of the melody are made to suit the liturgical context. A background on components of Arab music provides a framework for viewing music in Syrian liturgy. Specific musical examples follow focusing on how a *ḥazzan* melodically realizes a *maqām* as a guiding principle for rendering of the liturgical singing stations.

Components of Arab Music

Song Genres of Adapted Melodies

Arab songs adapted for Syrian Jewish liturgical melodies derive from both vocal and instrumental repertories. Vocal genres represented include *muwashshaḥ, mawwāl, qaṣīdah, dawr, ṭaqṭūqah,* and possibly *layālī.* Instrumental genres are primarily from *bashārīf* or *samāī,* which is a specific form of a *bashārīf* (al-Faruqi 1981, 292).[18] The adaptation of secular vocal genres is more common in the liturgy than instrumental genres. Arab religious vocal genres, such as *adhān* or *dhikr,* are not adapted in Syrian liturgy. In general, Syrian liturgy makes use of Arab song forms (such as *muwashshaḥ, qaṣīdah, dawr,* and *ṭaqṭūqah*) rather than improvisational forms. The "heavy" and "light" liturgical singing stations differ in musical goal and the use of *maqām*. These differences center on the prominence of the song genre's rhythmic regularity and the presence of improvisation guided by the *maqām*.

Maqām and Its Role in Adapted Genres

THE MANNER IN which a *maqām* unfolds in a composition provides the structure for Arab music. Particularly in improvisation, the *maqām* determines a musical form's shape and design. Habib Hassan Touma provides a useful framework for viewing the realization of a *maqām* in Middle Eastern music, focusing on the relationship between tonal and rhythmic elements:

> The development of a *maqam* is always determined by two primary factors: space (tonal) and time (temporal). The structure of a *maqam* depends upon the extent to which these two factors exhibit a fixed or free organization. The tonal-spatial component is organized, molded, and emphasized to such a degree that it represents the essential and decisive factor in the *maqam;* whereas the temporal aspect in this music is not subject to any definite form of organization. In this unique circumstance lies the most essential feature of the *maqam* phenomenon, i.e., a free organization of the rhythmic-temporal and an obligatory and fixed organization of the tonal-spatial factor. (1971, 38)

Touma provides an analogy in Western musical terms. The waltz is an example of a composition type with a fixed rhythmic-temporal and an unspecified tonal-spatial structure (ibid.). While tonal and rhythmic features make up the characteristic musical elements in Arab music, the relationship of the two—or predominance of one over the other—also describes the view of musical genres by Middle Eastern musicians. Touma explains:

> The native musicians . . . quite consciously distinguish two melodic categories, which at the same time represent two different musical genres. In European terminology we might call one category the "melody," which has a fixed rhythmic-temporal and a free tonal-spatial organization (known in the Orient as *beste, bashraf, samai, tasnif, muwashshah,* etc.), and the other one the "melodic line," i.e., a free rhythmic-temporal but fixed tonal-spatial organization (which the Oriental musician calls *taqsim, gusheh, mugam,*

> *layali,* or *maqam*).[19] The Near Eastern musician is certainly not acquainted with such terms as "melody" and "melodic line," yet he is thoroughly aware of the difference between the two categories and assigns each of them an individual name. (ibid., 39)

Arab terms for melody are *beste, bistah,* or *bastah.* The improvisation of a melodic line is known as *taqsim.* Touma notes that while a melody, "with its organized rhythmic-temporal divisions provides the basis of the form, . . . only a modicum of musicianship" is required, a melodic line "shapes the respective form, [and] demands a high degree of inventiveness and a masterly technique" (ibid., 40). Therefore, it is logical to conclude that compositions of the melodic line genre have a higher degree of variability when comparing two or more performers' renditions. Hence, the performer becomes an integral component to the compositional process.

The progressive tonal levels of a composition guided by a *maqām* characterize the design of Arab improvisation. Touma expands on the concept of the tonal-spatial organization of a *maqām:* "The *maqam* phenomenon is a form which is represented by a fixed tonal-spatial organization peculiar to the respective mode. The singular feature of this form is that which is not built upon motifs, their elaboration, variation and development, but through a number of melodic passages of different lengths which realize one or more tone-levels in space and thus establish the various phases in the development of a *maqam*" (ibid., 41).[20] Viewing a *maqām* as the sequence of tone-levels rather than as a motif serves as a more dynamic characterization of a *maqām* usage. In fact, Touma rejects Western concepts like "motivic groups," "melody-model" or "melody-pattern" to depict *maqāmāt* previously subscribed to by Abraham Zvi Idelsohn (1913a, 1913b) and Edith Gerson-Kiwi (1967). Likewise, Scott Marcus and Lois Ibsen al-Faruqi conclude that melodic motives are not unique to specific *maqāmāt* since phrases that occur in one *maqām* are not exclusive to that *maqām* (al-Faruqi 1974, 101–2; Marcus 1989, 713–20).[21] Touma goes on to explain that the tone-levels typically progress upward from low to high and then return to the low tone-level (1971, 41), thus forming an arch where the climax is reached at the height of the melodic line (1976, 35).

Melodic Characteristics

Touma's approach—centered on the design of a composition determined by tone-levels—does aid in viewing musical adaptation in Syrian liturgy, particularly because Arab musicians see a melody as constantly changing. Before applying Touma's dichotomous model to Syrian liturgy, additional clarification in determining the specific surface features helps in characterizing Arab music and the changing nature of melodies.

In al-Faruqi's comparison of the interrelationship of ornamentation in Arab music and visual arts (1978), she employs several useful terms for the analysis of Middle Eastern music. Notably, she provides Western terms to convey indigenous Arab musical concepts. She uses the term "motif" to refer to the smallest unit of "raw material," and a "module" consists of "motif conglomerates" (1978, 19).[22] She then applies the term "design" or "pattern" to explain the tonal organization of the "structure itself and [the] plan which created it." A motif can vary in length from two notes to a phrase but is not the most important element. Al-Faruqi explains, "Arab genius is revealed primarily through the manipulation, the structuring of these motifs, through their combination with like and new elements to produce the visual or aural arabesque" (ibid., 20). Melodic material of a motif, and its subsequent module, consists of an undulating line of stepwise progressions interspersed with occasional leaps of a third or, less often, a fourth. The goal is not one of motivic development but motivic repetition and variation "by the infusion of ever-changing decorative devices" (ibid., 22). A *maqām* guides the specific motifs and modules unique to a composition.

Improvisation occurs on different levels in Arab music. Some genres are defined completely as improvisatory forms, such as the vocal *layālī* and the instrumental *taqāsīm*. However, other genres, like a *dawr,* contain improvisatory sections and a contrasting section with fixed melodies. Touma comments on melodic techniques in improvisation. He suggests that sudden changes arouse enthusiasm in Arab audiences. Sudden changes such as the dying away of a melodic sequence, changing tonal register, and modulating help to create tension in music that is later resolved (Touma 1976, 35). Ornamentation consists of varying tonal elements (sequences, octave change, tetrachord variation) and rhythmic elements (accent shift, rhythmic diminution) (al-Faruqi 1978, 22–23). Tonal additions are possible with grace notes, slides, mordents, trills, vibrato or tremolo, and terminal trail off or "an indefiniteness of pitch" (ibid., 23). Like Touma, al-Faruqi comments on the importance of melodic change as a musical element that adds interest: "The ornamentation or the restatement and variation of motifs in Arabian improvisatory music is therefore of utmost significance for understanding and appreciating this music" (ibid., 27).

The Changing Nature of Melodies

In Arab music the performer is given the freedom to play with a known melody through embellishments and other stylistic features. This creates a diffuse sense of the melody, since various renderings of the same melody by the same or different performers will yield slightly different results (Touma 1971, 47). As Salwa El-Shawan notes, "although a performer can add ornaments (*zakhārif*) to the core melody (*laḥn*) of a pre-composed structure and weave around it entirely new improvised sections (*ḥarakāt*), its main contours remain fixed and identifiable. Furthermore, the order of its segments is not altered" (1980, 32).[23] An existing song is identified by its "core melody" and its structure. Each performance recreates the melody anew, which gives the performer an important responsibility, equal to the role of the composer (Danielson 1991, 359). As a result, a particular feature of Arab music is the emphasis placed on performances by specific individuals rather than on the "specific melody." One finds:

> Autonomy given to the Arab musician in the realm of musical expression is ever present. Some musicians develop a particular phrase at length, others do so quite briefly; some extend the range of the tone-level to distances quite far from the central tone, other restrict themselves to a narrow *ambitus* around the central tone. But in all cases the central tone of a tone-level is of the utmost importance for the musician, because it is the nucleus of the entire phase. (Touma 1971, 41)

In particular, improvisation is the measure of individuality. By their very nature, the unspecified temporal-rhythmic features of improvisation produce variation. However, the mere fact that musicians try to vary musical phrases and never play the same thing twice indicates that individuality is part of all Arab music and not only a part of improvisation. Although the possibilities of elaboration can be far reaching, a core melody—an identifiable portion of a melody, usually found at the beginning of a piece of music, which remains relatively fixed in both tonal and rhythmic details—is indeed identifiable. Were that not the case, a song or melody could not have a unique identity.

Musical Examples

I draw upon the aforementioned musical characteristics of Arab music to show the process of adaptation in Syrian liturgy. Recordings from my fieldwork and other recordings available in the community are the sources. The examples that follow include the originating source, from Arab music or other genres of music, that were previously adapted in *pizmonim*. These *pizmonim* draw from the genres of *ṭaqṭūqah* and *dawr*. They explore melodies categorized in *maqām rast*, as well as in present-day usage in Brooklyn and represent the range and type of melodies found throughout the Syrian liturgy.

Within the Syrian community, charts circulate indicating which melody to sing for a particular liturgical singing station.[24] Table 9 indicates the melody of the *pizmon* or *bakkasha* that a *ḥazzan* can use during his rendering of Shaḥarit. Two examples are given in table 9, one for *maqām rast* and the other for *bayat.* In the case of Nishmat Kol Ḥai on a Sabbath when the *maqām* of the day is *rast,* a *ḥazzan* can use the melody of Mahalalakh. More specifically, when the *ḥazzan* sings the liturgical text Nishmat Kol Ḥai the melody is from Mahalalakh. In general, most melodies in the liturgy adapt *pizmonim; bakkashot* adaptations are rare. If a *bakkasha* melody is used it is set to one of the three pillars as a "heavy" melody. This attests to the serious nature of the *bakkashot.* They connote age and reverence. In terms of their musical characteristics, *bakkashot* are slower in tempo and melodically elaborate. It is more fitting for these melodies to be used as a "heavy" than a "light" singing station.

Table 9. *Melodies used for liturgical singing stations*

Liturgical Portion	*Maqām rast* *bakkasha* or *pizmon*	*Maqām bayat* *bakkasha* or *pizmon*
Nishmat Kol Ḥai	Mahalalakh	Kah Eli Maher
Shav'at Aniyyim	Magen Yish'i	Malki Yots'ri Kah
Kel ha-Hodaot	Navah Yafah Tsviyyah	Magen Baadi Meed'yo
Kaddish	Deleini Miyad ha-Zzari	Kel Naalah Refah
Semeḥim be-Tseitam	Ani Asaper	Middvash ve-Nofet Tsof
Mi-mits'rayim Gealtanu	Taan le-Shoni	Mam'lekhut ha-Arets
Nak'dishakh	Refah Tsiri	Kel Meod Naalah

The melodies designated in the charts of *SUHV* tend to be from older songs, composed before 1940. The *ḥazzan* is free to choose his own melodies; he does not need to adhere to any designation in a chart. In fact, some cantors have developed their own personal charts. However, the *bakkashot* and *pizmonim* designated for liturgical use in *SUHV* are the most commonly heard melodies in the Syrian community. Cantors are free to innovate their choice of melodies but must do so with caution. Their guiding principle is that the three pillars must use a "heavy" melody while the other portions must be set to "light" melodies.

Mahalalakh—Nishmat Kol Ḥai

Example 6 illustrates the use of the *bakkasha* Mahalalakh (*SUHV* #51) to Nishmat Kol Ḥai, the first liturgical singing station and the first pillar. Three renderings are given for both Mahalalakh and Nishmat Kol Ḥai. The comparative transcription illustrates the connection between the various renderings of this melody. Limitations of transcription make it difficult to convey individual pronunciation, enunciation, intonation, and vocal quality.[25]

Example 6. *Mahalalakh—Nishmat Kol Ḥai.*

Example 6. *Mahalalakh—Nishmat Kol Ḥai* (continued).

Example 6. *Mahalalakh—Nishmat Kol Ḥai* (continued).

Example 6. *Mahalalakh—Nishmat Kol Ḥai* (continued).

Example 6. *Mahalalakh—Nishmat Kol Ḥai* (continued).

a) Idelsohn—Mahalalakh. Transcription by A. Z. Idelsohn (1929a: 265, #447). Idelsohn's transcription includes a 4/4 time signature and barlines that are omitted in this comparative transcription.
b) Cabasso, Kaire, and Kairey—Mahalalakh. Transcription of "Bakashot [*sic*] and Saturday Night Songs," sung by Isaac Cabbasso [*sic*], Hyman Kaire, Meyer Kairey (Brooklyn: Sephardic Archives of the Sephardic Community Center, 1987), set of four cassette tapes. Vocal recordings with no accompaniment (tape #2, side B #42).
c and d) Shrem—Mahalalakh and Nishmat Kol Ḥai. Transcription of recording made for the Cantorial Institute of Yeshiva University and Yeshiva University High School by Cantor Gabriel Shrem (ca. 1975). This recording by Shrem is part of a set consisting of *bakkashot* and *pizmonim* with their use in the liturgy in various *maqāmāt:* twelve recordings total in various *maqāmāt* with no instrumental accompaniment *(maqām rast,* side A).
e) Cabasso—Nishmat Kol Ḥai. Transcription of recording by Cantor Isaac Cabasso from the Sephardic Archives of the Sephardic Community Center (recording no. 82, *maqām rast*, 1986), with instrumental accompaniment for *maqām rast.*
f) Avidani—Nishmat Kol Ḥai. "Nishmat Kol Hay [sic]: Saturday's Sephardic Prayers," sung by Yehezkel Zion and Ephraim Avidani (Jersusalem: Yehsivat Avidani, ca. 1985), set of eight cassettes with instrumental accompaniment. Example taken from tape 1, "Maqām Rāst," side A, sung by Ephraim Avidani.

Textual translations for Mahalalakh—Nishmat Kol Ḥai

Mahalalakh

A module: Your praise and abundance is Your greatness. He has no end.

A' module: There is also no one who will prepare for You. Total praise forever.

B module: And who is the man whose heart goes. To mention the praises of God.

Nishmat Kol Ḥai (translation taken from *Siddur kol ya'akov* 1995: 488)

A Module: The soul of every living being shall bless Your Name

A' module: God, our God, spirit of all flesh,

B module: shall glorify and exalt Your mention, our King continually.

B' module: From [this] world to [the] world [to Come], You are Almighty.

A comparison of the six renditions of this melody reveals considerable consistency among the three versions of Mahalalakh and the three versions of Nishmat Kol Ḥai. However, in order to have the words of Nishmat Kol Ḥai fit the melody, some accommodations are made. The differences among the versions concern the rhythm of certain phrases, the specific interval of an ascent within a melodic phrase, and the degree of embellishment. These variations reflect interpretation of what each singer perceives to be the melody as well as his personal style—each represents a version of the core melody.

The melody of Mahalalakh and the Nishmat Kol Ḥai adaptation is conjunct, consisting of mostly scalar passages with very few leaps, consistent with al-Faruqi's description of stepwise movement with occasional leaps (1978, 20). There is a moderate underlying rhythmic pulse, with pauses between modules. The ambitus of the melody is an octave, and the tessitura of the melodic line is between G and C. This emphasizes the lower tetrachord of *maqām rast.* Since Mahalalakh does not derive from an Arab song, there is no derivative genre that it follows.[26] This *bakkasha* is similar to the *qaṣīdah,* a vocal form set to poetry with the same meter throughout the text with several melodies, usually four, strung together. The text of Mahalalakh, written by Mordecai Abbadi, has six stanzas.[27] The melody consists of motifs that create modules. As shown in chart 1, module A consists of four motifs (a, b, c, and d) covering the first two stanzas of text—motifs a and b are set to the first stanza; motifs c and d are set to the second stanza. This pattern continues in module A and module B, and these modules form an organized and balanced structure. The Nishmat Kol Ḥai text consists of almost the same number of syllables and words as Mahalalakh but manages to include an added module. Thus, the *bakkasha* comprises three modules (A, A', and B), and the liturgical singing station is made up of four modules (A, A', B, and B'). Module B' in Nishmat Kol Ḥai is an additional melodic expansion that does not appear in the originating *bakkasha* melody.

Mahalalakh and Nishmat Kol Ḥai have traits of both fixed and free elements. Portions of the melody have a fixed temporal-rhythmic component, while other portions are not fixed. Likewise, the tonal-spatial plan has a fixed portion and a portion that is not fixed. Yet, the construction of the melody does closely follow a plan of specified central tones. Although not fully improvisatory, Mahalalakh contains fixed and free elements in both the tonal and temporal domains.

There are eight short motifs, designated by lower case letters. Each motif has a unique set of central tones. Motif a consists of a descent from the note G down to the tonic, C, followed by a fall to G below the C in some renderings and a rise up to F or E quarter flat. Motif b consists of a rise from D to F, with

Chart 1. *Text and melodic modules used in Mahalalakh and Nishmat Kol Ḥai*

Overall melodic design	A module	A' module	B module	B' module
Mahalalakh motif:	a b c d	a b c' e	f g h d	
Stanza:	1 2	3 4	5 6	
rhyme scheme	a b	a b	a C	
Nishmat Kol Ḥai motif:	a b c d	a b c' e	f g h e	f' g' h' d

Text and phrase structure

A module	a	b	c	d	syllables	words
Mahalalakh:	Ma-ha-la-lakh ve-rov	god-lakh.	Ein lo takh-lit ke-	zeh va-sof	16	8
Nishmat Kol Ḥai :	Nish- - - - - -mat	kol ḥai,	te - - va-rekh et	shim - kha	10	6

A' module	a	b	c'	e		
Mahalalakh:	Ein gam e-ḥad ya-a-	rokh lakh.	Hal-lel ga-mur	ad le - ein sof,	16	10
Nishmat Kol Ḥai :	A - - -do - shem e-lo-	kei - nu,	ve - - - ru - - - aḥ	kol ba-sar,	13	6

B module	f	g	h	e		
Mahalalakh :	U - - mi ha - ish	li-bo ha-lokh.	Yaz-kir te - hi - lot		16[a]	7
Nishmat Kol Ḥai :	te - - - - pa - er	ut - ro - -mem	zikh-re-kha mal-kei	nu ta - mid.	14	5

B' module	f'	g'	h'	d		
Mahalalakh:				A-do-Shem.		
Nishmat Kol Ḥai :	Min - - - - - - - -	ha - o - - lam	ve - ad ha - o -lam	a-tah Kel.	12	6

Totals	Mahalalakh	48	25
	Nishmat Kol Ḥai	49	22

Notes

a. The syllable and word counts for the last phrase of Mahalalakh, including the "d" melodic unit, are included in this line.

a specific eighth-eighth-quarter rhythmic pattern that is repeated two times. Motif c is similar to motif a, with a descent to C and an ascent to E quarter flat. Motif c differs slightly by starting on an A, but the descent is not direct. Motif d emphasizes the lower tetrachord of the *maqām* with a quick descent to C, followed by an ascent up to F or G, then a descent back to the tonic. Thus the melody is in *maqām rast.* The rhythm of motif d is not unified among the six renderings. The motifs a, b, c, and d form the first module (A).

The second module is a repeat of module A, with some changes to form module A'. Motifs a and b are essentially identical to the previous module A but are set to a different text. Changes are made to motif c, particularly in the rhythm. The six notes that end this motif, labeled as "x" in example 6, are the same in content, but they differ in rhythmic value. This is particularly noticeable in Gabriel Shrem's renderings of motif c (the two middle staves of the example). Motif e is an upward gesture toward G, A, or C. The goal of the ascent is the highest note in Mahalalakh and Nishmat Kol Ḥai; this represents the climax of the entire melody. As Touma explains, the climax occurs when the vocal line reaches the highest tone level (1976, 35). Module B expands the central tones and the melodic activity to emphasize the upper tetrachord of the *maqām.* Motifs f, g, and h are a series of downward gestures. Motifs f and g are the least consistent among the versions. The overall descent to a C in motifs f, g, and h, with an ascent to an E quarter flat, is similar to the design of motif c; this part of module B is as a development of motif c. Module B ends with motif d in Mahalalakh, which concludes the stanza, and motif e in Nishmat Kol Ḥai.[28] The latter continues with an altered melodic repetition of motifs f, g, and h, followed by cadence d. The use of motif d to close both songs creates a sense of balance; this parallels the cadence in module A.

The extension of the melodic line, module B', in Nishmat Kol Ḥai does not contain new melodic material. It is merely a reiteration and expansion of previous motifs. Most significant in module B' is the change in the upper tetrachord of the *maqām.* Both Shrem and Cabasso include an A flat at the end of motif f and at the beginning of motif g'. Slight tonal variation as well as more embellishments through rhythmic changes illustrate the nuances found in Arab improvisation, as described by al-Faruqi (1978, 20–22).

Although the three renditions of Mahalalakh and Nishmat Kol Ḥai are similar, each one is unique. Motif b is almost identical in all cantorial versions, but motif f varies, both tonally and temporally. This is especially notable in the melismatic embellishments in module B' of Nishmat Kol Ḥai. Other motifs, such as motif c, follow a melodic outline that gives emphasis to the same notes but differs in rhythmic details, an example of a cantor's individual expression.

Idelsohn's transcription of the melody is a basic presentation of Mahalalakh with no extended embellishments. The Cabasso, Kaire, and Kairey rendition of the *bakkasha* does not contain many embellishments. Additionally, the repetition of motifs a, b, and c in module A' is virtually exact, perhaps because of the unity needed for the group of three men to sing together.

Shrem's singing displays unique individual expression. For example, his reiteration of motif a in both Mahalalakh and Nishmat Kol Ḥai shows varied repetition. This illustrates the tendency in Arab music not to sing the same melodic module twice. As a result, the melody is re-created each time. Examples of his unique expression include filling in the third in motif b (the E quarter flat between the F and D) and adding a trill in the last few notes of the descent to the tonic in motifs c and d. Shrem's f' melodic line in module B' is the most melismatic of all the versions.

The individual styles of Mahalalakh and Nishmat Kol Ḥai confirm that there is a consistent core to the melody but also freedom of expression. Some rhythmic and tonal elements remain consistent, particularly in module A, and others are more varied.[29]

David Tawil describes the "heavy pieces" used in the three pillars as possessing more elaborate melodies that explore the full range of the *maqām* (interview, July 29, 1992). The heavy melodies of the three pillars are melismatic and rhythmically slower than the light melodies. In Nishmat Kol Ḥai, for example, the melody is elongated to fit the needs of the liturgical singing station through specific musical emphasis that matches textual needs. It is no surprise that modules B and B' are more ornate. In general, the heavy liturgical singing stations are more ornate at the end of that station's text with an improvisatory approach.

Shav'at Aniyyim and Light Liturgical Singing Stations

Two melodic examples of Shav'at Aniyyim (LS 3.1.4, the second liturgical singing station) and other light liturgical singing stations demonstrate some similarities and differences to the musical adaptation process illustrated in the heavy piece set to Nishmat Kol Ḥai. Where Nishmat Kol Ḥai emphasizes central tones of the *maqām*, the examples of Shav'at Aniyyim that follow show the adaptation of rhythmic elements from the originating song.

Ḥawwid Min Hina is an Arab song recorded, and most likely composed, by Zakī Murād (1880–1940) between 1915 and 1920.[30] The genre of this composition is known as a *ṭaqṭūqah*, which typically consists of several verses and a short refrain (Danielson 1991, 355). The text of a *ṭaqṭūqah*, like the music, is simple and straightforward, in colloquial Arab, on a light-hearted topic (ibid., 355–56), and uses a simple rhythmic mode (*wazn*) (al-Faruqi 1981, 349). The first verse of Ḥawwid Min Hina is in *maqām māhūr, rast faṣīlah* (see table 5), and the second verse is in *saba* (on A). The melody of the first verse only is set as a *pizmon* and liturgical station; the second verse melody is not used. Characteristic of *maqām māhūr,* this melody starts on the upper C of the *maqām* and progresses to the lower C. The rhythmic mode is a regular four-beat pattern; the name for the rhythmic mode is *waḥah.* The eighth-note motion of the melody emphasizes the third beat; there is slight variation to accommodate the text. The consistent rhythm provides regularity for this melody. Thus, according to Touma's dichotomy, Ḥawwid Min Hina is a *ṭaqṭūqah* with a fixed temporal-rhythmic pattern and a flexible tonal-spatial component. Anne Katharine Rasmussen discusses the endurance of the *ṭaqṭūqah* genre among Arab Americans because of its simplicity; she contrasts the "easy to sing" nature of this light genre with the so-called heavy stuff of other genres (1991, 95). Therefore, a *ṭaqṭūqah* provides a likely source for a light liturgical singing station.

A transcription of the melodies of the originating Arab song and the *pizmon* Bo'i be-Rinah (*SUHV* #156), the latter as sung by Isaac Cabasso, reveals a stable transmission in adaptation. The application of this melody to the Shav'at Aniyyim liturgical text, also sung by Cabasso, appears in musical example 7.[31] This melody, Bo'i be-Rinah, is also set to another liturgical station, Semeḥim be-Tseitam (LS 3.3.4, the fifth liturgical singing station), sung by Yeḥezkiel Zion and Ephraim Avidani; see track 14 on the CD. Semeḥim be-Tseitam also uses light pieces. While this example shows melody use for more than one liturgical singing station, the same melody would not be used for both liturgical singing stations on the same Sabbath.

There is a strong textual similarity between Bo'i be-Rinah and its originating Arab song text, Ḥawwid Min Hina. Both texts share the same rhyme scheme (aaba ccca); the text of the Hebrew closely follows the Arabic text as a model. The text of Ḥawwid Min Hina begins with the unrequited love of a woman to a man who ultimately calls on God to unite them. Bo'i be-Rinah starts with the expression of love to a woman that allegorically represents the love of humans for God.[32] The melody of Ḥawwid Min Hina, serves as the basis for the *pizmon* Bo'i be-Rinah and two possible liturgical singing stations, because each liturgical text comprises three, four, or five unrhymed syllable segments, each comprising two words, that fit the five or six notes of a motif (see motifs a1 and a2 in the first system of musical example 7). In essence, the Arab melody is easily adapted to these Hebrew texts since the liturgical texts contain short textual units. The texts for the liturgy convey rhetorical sense in this adaptation of the melodic motifs.

Example 7. *Ḥawwid Min Hina—Bo'i be-Rinah—Shav'at Aniyyim—Semeḥim be-Tseitam.*

Example 7. *Ḥawwid Min Hina—Bo'i be-Rinah—Shav'at Aniyyim—Semeḥim be-Tseitam* (continued).

a) Murrad—Ḥawwid Min Hina. Transcription of 78 LP recording by Zaki Murrad (ca. 1915–20).

b and c) Cabasso—Bo'i be-Rinah and Shav'at Aniyyim. Transcription of recording by Cantor Isaac Cabasso from the Sephardic Archives of the Sephardic Community Center (recording no. 82, *maqām rast*, 1986), with the instrumental accompaniment for *maqām rast*.

d) Zion and Avidani—Semeḥim be-Tseitam. "Nishmat Kol Hay [sic]: Saturday's Sephardic Prayers," sung by Yehezkel Zion and Ephraim Avidani (Jerusalem: Yeshivat Avidani, ca. 1985), set of eight cassettes with instrumental accompaniment. Example taken from tape 1, "Maqām Rāst," side B.

Translation of Texts

(each translated line corresponds to the line of each system in the transcription)

a) Ḥawwid Min Hina

Stop over, come to us.
Come on, let us love one another.
Joy is here, sorrow disappears.
My heart is enchanted. When shall we meet?

b) Bo'i be-Rinah

Come in Song, gentle graceful woman.
To my house now and with you I will dwell.
Your enemy fled your salvation blossomed.
Your light shined, time to be bestowed to her.

Example 7. *Ḥawwid Min Hina—Bo'i be-Rinah—Shav'at Aniyyim—Semeḥim be-Tseitam* (continued)

c) Shav'at Aniyyim (translation taken from *Siddur kol ya'akov* 1995:492)

You hear the cry of the impoverished;
You are attentive to the scream of weak and You give salvation.
And it is written: "Joyfully exult in God, [you] righteous ones,
for the upright, praise is fitting."
(This passage is taken from Psalms 33:1.)

Through the mouth of the upright, You are exalted;
and with the lips of the righteous You are blessed;
and by the tongue of the pious, You are sanctified,
and in the core of the holy, You are extolled.
(This second portion of the Shav'at Aniyyim liturgical text, a melodic repetition of the first portion, can be found on the fourth line of each system in the transcription.)

d) Semeḥim be-Tseitam (translation taken from Siddur kol ya'akov 1995:500)

Joyous in their rising and happy in their setting,
they perform with reverence the will of the Possessor.
Glory and honor, they give to His Name.
Jubilation and joyous song at the mention of His kingship.

He called to the sun and it shone with light.
He saw and fashioned the form of the moon.
All hosts on high give Him praise.
Glory and greatness.
(This second portion of the Semeḥim be-Tseitam liturgical text, a melodic repetition of the first portion, can be found on the sixth line of each system in the transcription.)

The liturgical setting of Shav'at Aniyyim and Semeḥim be-Tseitam consists of four modules. Each module contains two motifs. The second motif of each module is a slight variation of the first. The motifs are labeled as "a1," "a2" and "b1," "b2" accordingly. The first three modules emphasize the upper tetrachord of the *maqām*, and the last module emphasizes the lower tetrachord. One of the striking changes in the liturgical settings is the seaming of the motifs within a module, an element absent in the Arab song and the *pizmon*. For example, where Ḥawwid Min Hina pauses at the end of motif a1 with the words meaning "stop over" and likewise Bo'i be-Rinah pauses at the analogous point with the words meaning "come in song," the liturgical stations' renditions do not pause, producing a complete unit in one breath. This transformation is attributable to the need to provide consistency and regularity for congregational singing. While it is appropriate to pause as an expressive device to convey the Arab song and *pizmon* text, to do so in the liturgy is disruptive. Similar pauses appear in the third and fourth modules. The second module does not contain a pause due to the lengthy text.

The complex of melodic interpretations in example 7, like Mahalalakh and its setting to Nishmat Kol Ḥai, show slightly variant renderings. Textual reasons demand accommodations in rhythm and adjustment for individual style in adaptation. The few embellishments appear at the end of a module (see motifs a2, c2, and d2) through the use of passing tones and escape tones. These elaborations—individually applied—give the melody flavor (Cabasso, *pizmonim* class, December 2, 1991). A particular characteristic of this melody is the B flat at the beginning of motif c2. This is a striking gesture since it is not used earlier. The second module is repeated in Bo'i be-Rinah to the same text. This motif is not restated in the liturgical singing stations, because the liturgical text cannot be repeated (Cabasso, interview, May 29, 1992).[33]

The climax of this setting is in the third module. In the liturgical settings this occurs over the words meaning "And it is written: 'Joyfully exalt in God'" in Shav'at Aniyyim and "Glory and honor, they give to His Name" in Semeḥim be-Tseitam. These are both fitting textual lines for a musically expressive climax. The text of Ḥawwid Min Hina has a similar meaning of elation: "Joy is here, sorrow disappears." The liturgical singing stations thus take on the shape of the originating song.

Magen Yish'i—Shav'at Aniyyim

Pizmon Magen Yish'i (*SUHV* #127) is an example of the penetration of non-Arab melodies used in the liturgy.[34] The text of this *pizmon*, which first appeared in the 1928 edition of *Hallel v'zimrah* (Ashear 1928, 2), was written by Moses Ashear for the wedding of Ezra Obadiah Labaton.[35] The melodic source given in *SUHV* for this text is Margarita.[36] However, the first section of the melody of Magen Yish'i, corresponding to the first stanza of the *pizmon* (see the first four systems of musical example 8, sung by Cantor Moshe Dweck), is found in a Dutch folk song titled "Trip a Trop a Tronjes."[37] Frank Luther claims that this folk song is a lullaby sung by Dutch-Americans and is "generations old" (1942, 6). The Dutch origins of this melody may suggest an influence of Sephardic Jews of Dutch descent.[38]

This melody of Magen Yish'i is set to the Shav'at Aniyyim liturgical station. The syllabic setting of the text and fixed temporal-rhythmic design make this melody fitting for a light piece. *SUHV* lists Magen Yish'i in the *rast* section. Moshe Dweck's rendition of this melody for the *pizmon* and the liturgical station uses an E natural and not an E quarter flat, reflecting a change of the *maqām* to *ajam* (see table 5). David Tawil claims that some *pizmonim* are mislabeled in terms of their *maqām* because the people who compiled *SUHV* did not know how to read or write music (interview, July 29, 1992). Nevertheless, Magen Yish'i is categorized as a liturgical singing station in *rast;* although some cantors may sing this station in *rast,* Cantor Dweck does not.

In this second example of a Shav'at Aniyyim setting, the eight lines of the liturgical text use separate melodies. The last four lines of Shav'at Aniyyim in its adaptation of Bo'i be-Rinah repeated the first four lines. There is no clear climax in the Shav'at Aniyyim adaptation from Magen Yish'i. The height of the melody in the third line of Shav'at Aniyyim provides the climax. Again, the shape of the liturgical singing station follows the originating melody. Therefore, no textual point inherently needs emphasis. In adapting melodies, the sole criterion is for the tune to fit the text (D. Tawil, interview, July 29, 1992). The melody has to create rhetorical sense of the liturgical text.

The light liturgical singing stations generally adapt syllabic textual settings with short melodic motifs: five to eight notes. These source melodies comprise simple and regular rhythms, which are easy to sing because they are quicker in tempo than the heavy pieces. Light pieces fulfill an important function in Syrian liturgy: they facilitate congregational singing and contrast the melodically ornate heavy singing stations. The cantor does not usually sing a light liturgical station. He initiates a light melody, and then the congregation continues to sing without him, enabling the *ḥazzan* to rest his voice momentarily. Cantors do not describe the light pieces in detail. Typically their comments focus on the contrasting nature of light and heavy pieces.

Il-Ḥabib—Kel Ḥabib—Kaddish

The final musical example illustrates a unique heavy song used for Kaddish. The melody for *pizmon* Kel Ḥabib (Beloved God, *SUHV* #132a) is an adap-

Example 8. *Trip a Trop a Tronjes—Magen Yish'i—Shav'at Aniyyim*

Example 8. *Trip a Trop a Tronjes—Magen Yish'i—Shav'at Aniyyim*
(continued)

Example 8. *Trip a Trop a Tronjes—Magen Yish'i—Shav'at Aniyyim* (continued)

a) Luther—Trip a Trop a Tronjes. Taken from a song reproduced in Frank Luther, *Americans and Their Songs* (New York: Harper and Brothers, 1942), 6. This song includes a 2/4 time signature, barlines, and accompaniment.
b and c) Dweck—Magen Yish'i and Shav'at Aniyyim. Transcription of recording by Cantor Moshe Dweck from the Sephardic Archives of the Sephardic Community Center (recording number 54, *maqām rast*, no date given).

Translation of texts

(each translated line corresponds to the line of each system in the transcription)

a) Trip a Trop a Tronjes
Take a trip to Tronjes, up and down and over, the
pigs are in the bean patch, the cows are in the clover, the
ducks are in the water place, the calf is in the long grass
so big my baby is, Pope Jayvas.

b) Magen Yish'i (translated by author with assistance from Stanley Nash)
Shield of my salvation high and exalted God
I present my supplication to You in song and rejoicing
At the joyous occasion the groom and betrothed bride
They are the stock of Abraham the servant of God in their Joy.

My lips utter song and praise
And my tongue speaks your righteousness
Please make them [a thing of] glory and praise
And reestablish them as in days of old.

c) Shav'at Aniyyim (translation taken from *Siddur kol ya'akov* 1995:492)
You hear the cry of the impoverished;
You are attentive to the scream of weak and You give salvation.
And it is written: "Joyfully exult in God, [you] righteous ones,
for the upright, praise is fitting."
(This passage is taken from Psalms 33:1)

Through the mouth of the upright, You are exalted;
and with the lips of the righteous, You are blessed;
and by the tongue of the pious, You are sanctified,
and in the core of the holy, You are extolled

tation from a similarly titled Arab song, Il-Ḥabib (My Love).[39] Il-Ḥabib was composed and sung by Zakarīyā Aḥmad (1896–1961), best known in the Arab world for his compositions for Umm Kulthūm (Danielson 1991, 376). The Arab song, likely composed around 1925, is a *dawr*.[40] The period of *dawr* composition was from the mid–nineteenth century through the 1930s, this genre consists of a love poem in colloquial Arab cast in a poetic meter (Danielson 1991, 354–55; 1997, 70).[41] The *dawr* had two principal sections: a *madhab* and a *dawr*. The former is the opening section sung by the chorus; the latter is a longer solo section (al-Faruqi 1981, 58–59; Danielson 1991, 355). The *madhab* returns and is framed by different *dawr* sections, each of which may have instrumental interludes. Then the singer improvises on the syllable *ah* toward the end of the composition. Due to its complexity, the *dawr* is generally sung only by experienced or highly accomplished singers. It is appropriate for a composition of this complexity to be used for the Kaddish, the second pillar and second heavy piece in Shaḥarit.

The Kaddish adapts the *madhab* and first *dawr* (see musical example 9).[42] The melismatic *madhab,* in systems 1 to 5 continuing with an instrumental interlude through system 6, tonally begins on the upper C of *maqām rast* and proceeds to the lower C of the *maqām* at the end of the third system. Although starting on the upper C, Kel Ḥabib is not classified under the *mahur* section of *SUHV*. Rather, this *pizmon* appears in the *rast* section. The first two systems of the *madhab* emphasize the upper tetrachord of the *maqām,* but systems 3, 4, and the first half of system 5 emphasize the lower tetrachord. In system 5, both Il-Ḥabib and Kel Ḥabib end a line of text before the interlude. The Kaddish does not; instead, a portion of text for the Kaddish ends in the third system, and the congregation responds, "Amen." The liturgical portion does not complete the line of text in the fifth system. The textual line continues in the seventh system. Although slight variation of the *pizmon* and liturgical adaptations exist, the *madhab* is relatively stable rhythmically and tonally in all three renderings. A small amount of text is rendered in this *madhab;* the focus is on a descending and ascending scalar melodic line. Observe the use of notes that do not appear in the *maqām:* the D sharp in the first system, and the F sharp in the third system.

Due to the complexity of this *dawr,* the rendering of the *pizmon* and Kaddish liturgical station are unique interpretations, not exact adaptations. The *dawr* begins in the seventh system and continues through the twelfth. A brief instrumental interlude in system 9 precedes the climax in systems 10 and 11. Although the *dawr* section is traditionally improvised, Aḥmad's recorded performance provides a model for Moses Tawil's improvisation. The *dawr* begins on a B flat, a B quarter flat in Kel Ḥabib, in system 7 and modulates to a

Example 9. *Il-Ḥabib—Kel Ḥabib—Kaddish*

Example 9. *Il-Ḥabib—Kel Ḥabib—Kaddish* (continued)

Example 9. *Il-Ḥabib—Kel Ḥabib—Kaddish* (continued)

Example 9. *Il-Ḥabib—Kel Ḥabib—Kaddish* (continued)

a) Aḥmad—Il-Ḥabib. Transcription of 78 LP recording by Zakrīyā Aḥmad (ca. 1925).
b and c) Tawil—Kel Ḥabib and Kaddish. Transcription of field recording by Moses Tawil, Deal, New Jersey, November 14, 1991.

Translation of texts

(each translated line corresponds to the line of each system in the transcription; the number in parentheses before each line of text refers to the systems in the musical transcription)

a) Il-Ḥabib

1. My love
2. abandoned me.
3. for a long time.
4. My heart
5. yearns for her.
6. [instrumental interlude] (appears only in Il-Ḥabib)
7. O people,
8. I have shed enough tears over her Look at me, what can I
9. do. [instrumental interlude]
10. She left me for my foes, for my foes.
11. She left me for my foes. What
12. has become of this world. [instrumental interlude]

b) Kel Ḥabib

1. Beloved God,
2. forgive me God.
3. And Your name I will praise.
4. From Your goodness
5. bestow upon us.
7. God heal us.
8. To a poor nation who asks. God raise a flag to the poor nation. And Your Name
9. I will thank. [Tra-la-la . . .]
10. Oh! And redeem for me immediately all who are oppressed, all who are oppressed.
11. Oh! And redeem for me immediately. Because
12. in you I will trust, turn to me, God.

Example 9. *Il-Ḥabib—Kel Ḥabib—Kaddish* (continued)

c) Kaddish (Translation taken from *Siddur kol ya'akov* 1995:496)

1. Exalted
2. and sanctified
3. May His Great Name grow (Amen).
4. In the world
5. which He created according to His will [,]
7. and may He
8. Rule His kingdom [,] and may He bring forth His re-
9. demption and hasten the coming of His Messiah.
10. In your lifetimes and in your days,
11. and in the lifetime of the entire House of Israel,
12. speedily and in the near future—and say Amen.

---

different *maqām* and emphasizes G as a central tone. System 8 is a varied repetition with more text; the tension created through a modulation in *maqām* corresponds with a greater amount of text. Hence, system 8 is less melismatic. Musical and textual changes coincide. The specific *maqām* on G varies in the three renderings through the use of a B natural, B quarter flat, or B flat. These renderings correspond respectively to *ajam, rast,* or *nahawand* on G. Identifying the new *maqām* is not as significant as the tension created by the change of *maqām*. The instrumental interlude in the ninth system deflects the *maqām* back to *rast* on C; the E flat in the Kaddish rendering indicates the *maqām* as *nahawand* on C. Kel Ḥabib and the Kaddish adapt the instrumental interlude in the ninth system, whereas neither text did so in the previous interlude (systems 5 and 6). The tonal emphasis to C is essential in system 9, because it interrupts the tension created by the modulation to a tetrachord on G. The *pizmon* uses vocables (tra-la-la), and the Kaddish continues the text.

The improvisation continues in the tenth system with a sudden change that forms a climax. A sudden change of register is common in improvisation and vocal ornamentation (Touma 1976, 35; al-Faruqi 1978, 22). The tension of the passage in systems 7 and 8 continues in system 10 with a melodic ascent raising the tessitura. Consequently, the climax introduces a third tetrachord. Tonally the central tone begins on an F descending to a G and then ascending to a D natural in Il-Ḥabib or a D quarter flat in Kel Ḥabib and the Kaddish (last note of tenth system). Textually, the central tone emphasis on the second

D natural or D quarter flat at the end of the line repeats the last two words of the text in Il-Ḥabib and Kel Ḥabib—the words "ḥib-l `awaadhil" and "cal mis'tolel," respectively. The *ḥazzan* does not repeat words in the Kaddish, since he is admonished to do so in the liturgy. Each rendering explores a different series of intervening notes between the central tones in system 10. This creates different tetrachord possibilities. Moses Tawil's alternating use of a D sharp, D quarter flat, or D flat makes his renderings more elaborate than Aḥmad's. The Kaddish setting is less elaborate than the setting of the *pizmon*, which suggests that there are limits of ornamentation that are not to be employed in the liturgy. However distinct the three renderings, the central tones are similar and vary with a quarter-flat intervallic difference.

The increased tension produced in the climax resolves at the end of the improvisatory section in *rast* on C (middle of twelfth system). The eleventh system continues the emphasis on G in a less ornate fashion than does the embellished tenth system, a simplified repetition. This reduces the tension. Where Il-Ḥabib and Kel Ḥabib repeat the text of the tenth system, the Kaddish does not reiterate text. Instead, the liturgical text continues. The tension and its resolution of the climax of the three renderings illustrate the following characterization concerning improvisation in Arab music: "Each phrase is a new excursion into a tonal and durational unknown with its aesthetic tension, followed by an eventual relaxation as the performer returns to a point of music stability on tonic (*qarār*) or dominant (*ghammāz*) tone" (al-Faruqi 1978, 26). Unity in music is found in tonal and durational motivic material and tones of stability in the *maqām* rather than in structural unity that is commonly found in the developmental nature of Western music (ibid., 27).

The three renderings diverge at the end of system 12. Il-Ḥabib continues with an instrumental interlude and then repeats the *madhab*. In Moses Tawil's Kel Ḥabib rendering, an abbreviated interlude with vocables ends the section. The *madhab* is repeated in an abbreviated form with the second textual verse containing added improvisation including the "ah" section. The Kaddish no longer follows either the Arab song or the *pizmon;* the *ḥazzan*, in this case Moses Tawil, improvises the remaining section of the Kaddish text (not given in example 9). Note how he ends on a G; then he invites the congregation to respond with "Amen" on a G.

There are many accommodations made in the adaptation of this Arab melody for both the *pizmon* and the liturgy. The Arab song recording includes accompaniment with a choir and instruments. Tawil observes that he usually sings this *pizmon* without instrumental accompaniment and the other singers are not strong enough to sing the choral part (*madhab* section).[43] He recalls that it took him twenty minutes to sing Kel Ḥabib during a Sabbath afternoon gathering, including filling in the choral and instrumental parts vocally: "I was exhausted afterwards because it is a very demanding song. I did not get any relief. There was no choir or instruments" (interview, November 14, 1991). In group performance of the *pizmon* some of the instrumental interludes are omitted and one is sung to vocables (see systems 9 and 12 of the transcription).

The context of singing the Kaddish also creates unique conditions for the transformation of this *dawr* melody in the liturgy. The congregation is not allowed to sing along with the *ḥazzan* during Kaddish; they are required by Jewish law to listen and respond only with the word *amen* at the end of certain textual portions (D. Tawil, interview, June 9, 1994). Without choral response and instrumental accompaniment, the cantor sings the Kaddish alone. This gives a different character to the melody. Where the *madhab* section in Il-Ḥabib is cast in a regular rhythm, appropriate for choral singing, Ḥazzan Moses Tawil allows himself more freedom when singing solo, as in the Kaddish, by lengthening pauses between phrases and changing the tempo slightly. This is the reverse of the situation in Ḥawwid Min Hina as transformed in Shav'at Aniyyim. In its adaptation, the *ṭaqṭūqah* is regularized rhythmically; however in the case of the Kaddish, the melody is rendered more freely.

One specific melodic detail that Tawil brought to my attention was the initial descent to D sharp in Il-Ḥabib. The previous pitch is an E quarter flat creating a quarter-tone interval not part of *maqām rast* (see table 5). Tawil believes this results in a melody that has a unique flavor that many other cantors are not able to convey properly in performance. Demonstrating his own use of the melodic descent, including the interval from E quarter flat to D sharp, he contrasts the renditions by replicating cantors who omit this inflection (interview, November 14, 1991). The melodic move from E quarter flat to D sharp and other adjacent quarter-flat intervals is the source of Tawil's improvisation in the tenth system. Tawil's illustration conveys the subtle nuances that are the domain of the experienced *ḥazzan*.

All four musical examples (6-9) demonstrate that melodies are neither simply adapted from their non-Syrian models nor directly from the *pizmonim*. They are recast for the specific circumstances of the liturgy based upon the musical taste and ability of the *ḥazzan*. Whereas rhythmic regularity defines the light stations, tonal elaboration and improvisation characterize the heavy stations. The light stations are quicker in tempo, and the heavy stations are slower and more musically expressive—guided by the central tones of the *maqām*.

Musical Characteristics and Aesthetics of the Heavy Stations

THE THREE PILLARS use heavy pieces, unlike the other four liturgical singing stations. Additionally, the pillars have aesthetic distinction. Ḥakham David Tawil explains:

David Tawil: So also you find drama in expression . . . in the prayers; it depends on what you want to express, and that's the type of rhythm that you will apply to the music. . . . [E]ach area has a different format of expression—a different meaning, a different feeling, a different kind of praise. So you have Nishmat, and a Kaddish, and a Nak'dishakh. These are our three major parts in which we use very heavy music. What do I mean "heavy"? We use extensive melodies . . . you'll notice always it [has] a more extended kind of rhythm. It's not a chip-chop kind of deal. And in contrast you have Shav'at Aniyyim, which is a more small kind of "diddy" setup over there. But yet it could have a very appealing kind of melody, too. . . . In [Kel] ha-Hodaot [liturgical singing station 3] you'll always find this kind of rhythmy dance tune to it—a very fast kind of deal. Semeḥim be-Tseitam [liturgical singing station 5], you can express any *maqām* you want, but it could be a very flavorful kind of piece of music, happy, joyous, etc., etc. . . . And if you find a *ḥazzan* that, for instance, is not aware that rhythm has something to do with waking up the audience he's going to feel that his audience is going to fall asleep after a while. If every kind of piece he chooses is a dull, monotone kind of thing, they'll fall asleep on him. And his prayers will have very little expression in them. Because a guy . . . [might say], "When's he finishing? He's already been on there for fifteen minutes!" It takes forty minutes to finish Nishmat [of] Shaḥarit, but after ten, fifteen minutes, when it's dull, [there is a] problem.

Mark Kligman: You said Nishmat, Kaddish, and the Nak'dishakh each have separate meanings—how would you characterize that? What is different between Kaddish and Nishmat in terms of the character?

DT: Each one has a very central expressive tone of what . . . we try to worship God with. Nishmat Kol Ḥai is . . . self-advertising. We're speaking about all the souls of the world that at some time or other will turn on to God for their needs and for their blessings and for their worship. Yitgadal ve'yitkadash [the Kaddish], we've come to the point now while realization that God's grace is such and such, and now we bless Him with or praise Him with the most grandiose ways possible. So we use melodic systems that are long, and so on, very expressive, very differentiating, extensive in octave. . . . You'll find that we'll jump from one to two, and sometimes even to a third tetrachord to give the expression of the music, because of the grandiose of God's blessing at this point.

MK: And in Nishmat you wouldn't necessarily be as expansive in the scale?

DT: You will be expansive in a different manner. As a matter of fact, they're almost duplicating systems, the Nishmat, and the Kaddish, and the Kedushah [the Nak'dishakh]. . . . [Y]ou'll find very often that the same melodic pieces could be applied to either of the three systems—either of the three pieces. Yet other pieces of music, for instance Shav'at Aniyyim or Kel ha-Hoda'ot, and Semeḥim be-Tseitam, you can not even take those pieces of music and try to apply them to a Nishmat. It won't fit. It would sound like you're flat, or all of sudden you are repeating the phrase of music again and again, which creates monotony.[44] You can create monotony even in two phrases, in two lines you could create monotony. So we wouldn't even be using those pieces. Interestingly enough, the large pieces of music that we use for Nishmat [are] . . . more expressive, more variant. You want to use it in Nishmat, you want to use it in Kaddish, you want to use it in Kedusha—you can't squeeze it into Shav'at Aniyyim; you can't squeeze it into ha-Hoda'ot; you can't squeeze it into a Mi-mits'rayim [Ge'altanu, liturgical singing station 6] because . . . the feeling isn't the same, the meaning isn't the same. So why apply such a heavy piece of music to something like Shav'at Aniyyim or Mi-mits'rayim Ge'altanu, and so on? (interview, July 29, 1992)

Tawil's "thick description" highlights the complex musical and textual interconnection in Syrian liturgy. The two liturgical singing station types, heavy and light, describe both the music and the text. Musically, the heavy and light song stations are rhythmically and tonally distinct.[45] Textually, the heavy liturgical stations extol some aspect of God, while the light stations joyfully describe God. In Ḥakham Tawil's words, during Nishmat Kol Ḥai, "all the souls of the world . . . at some time or other will turn on to God for their needs and for their blessings" (example 6), and the text of the Kaddish blesses God "with the most grandiose ways possible" (example 9). The light texts are short, joyful statements describing God rather than elaborate and elongated praises (example 7). Note that musical realizations of the light and heavy texts are accomplished within the same *maqām* through differing rhythmic and tonal characteristics. Melodies in *maqām rast* in the aforementioned musical examples can therefore express both light and heavy texts.

The progression of musical and textual expression of the heavy pieces provides significant interest during Shaḥarit. Examples 6 and 9, respectively, illustrate the differences between Nishmat Kol Ḥai and the Kaddish described by Tawil. The former praises and extols God textually and musically, but the latter is more elaborate. The melismatic and ornate treatment of the Kaddish in example 9 demonstrates how the second pillar treats the text differently than the first pillar. The second pillar appears part way through the Shaḥarit section of the service at a point where extended embellishments expresses the text with different tetrachords of the *maqām*. The use of two or three tetrachords of a *maqām* is seen as the vehicle to musically express the meaning of the liturgy. Consistent with Arab music and Qur'anic recitation, word painting is not the musical goal of expressing the text (al-Faruqi 1987, 11); rather, conveying the *maqām* at appropriate points that coincide with the important text themes and statements is the ultimate purpose of Arab music and Syrian liturgy (see chapter 11 for a further discussion of this topic). Tonal and rhythmic elements are mutually employed to convey and express the meaning of prayers.

8

Torah Service and Musaf

WITH SHAḤARIT CONCLUDED, the remaining two sections, the Torah service and Musaf, continue and conclude the Sabbath morning service. The Torah service continues the formulaic and repetitive nature of Zemirot during the biblical reading; the quick-paced recitation of Birkhot ha-Shaḥar follows similarly in Musaf. Thus, these later two sections of the service present in a different manner musical styles heard earlier.

Torah Service

THE TORAH SERVICE, the fourth liturgical section of the Sabbath service, consists of the reading of the Torah and the Haftorah. The reading of biblical texts in a public setting is an ancient practice. Kabbalists consider the reading of Torah a dramatic reenactment of the revelation at Mount Sinai. Seeing the Torah, considered a holy object, provides the opportunity for various forms of expression to God. In some communities there are fervent emotional displays with repeated hand motions in parading the Torah around the synagogue; in other traditions, such as the Spanish and Portuguese, formality and dignity mark the ritual. Although there is no standard liturgy for the Torah service for all communities, its formulation developed over time. Ismar Elbogen comments that the liturgy before and after the Torah reading varies among communities:

> The most ancient sources do not know of any special prayers before, during, or after the reading of the Torah. The Torah was removed and replaced without any special ceremony, and the reading was not interrupted by prayers. This changed completely in the course of time. Removing the Torah and returning it to the Ark turned into solemn ceremonies with special prayers; the reading itself was accompanied by prayers, and, following the reading, several prayers were inserted before the Torah was returned to the ark. (1913 [1993], 158)

The liturgical texts recited and sung when removing and returning the Torah from and to the ark are biblical texts focused on hymns of praise and thanksgiving. Syrian liturgy follows the general Sephardic practice in the Torah service with some modifications.[1]

The Torah service comprises six subsections: taking out the Torah scrolls (LS 4.1), Torah reading (LS 4.2), prophetic reading (LS 4.3), prayers for government and blessing of new month (LS 4.4), Ashrei Yoshvei (LS 4.5), and returning the Torah to the ark (LS 4.6). The first and sixth subsections, taking the Torah from the ark and returning it, contain congregational singing.

Taking the Torah out of the *aron* (see figure 3), is dramatic. The Torah is written on parchment and rolled onto a scroll contained in a cylindrical case. The congregation has several Torah scrolls in the *aron.* An honored congregant takes the case out of the ark and carries it to the *teivah.*[2] The congregant walks with the Torah scrolls leading a procession from the *bimah* to the *teivah,* where the Torah is read. During the procession individuals point to the Torah scrolls acknowledging or affirming the presence of the Torah. The singing of fixed melodies creates a royal welcome during the parade from the *aron.* One of the melodies, Ashrei ha-Am (LS 4.1.3), is responsorial; the other, Romemu (LS 4.1.4), is sung by the *ḥazzan* and congregation together. The melodies sung for Ashrei ha-Am and Romemu today (see musical example 10) were introduced over twenty years ago by Raphael Elnadav, who was the cantor at Synagogue Shaarei Zion.

After Romemu the cantor may lead the singing of a *pizmon* (LS 4.1.4). The Torah is at the *teivah,* and congregants may have moved from their seats to stand for Birkat Kohanim or may have left their seat to stand near someone else. From the time of Birkat Kohanim until Romemu the congregation has been standing; after Romemu everyone returns to their seats. The singing of a *pizmon* at this point in the service is a brief break in the service. Approximately ten men gather around the *teivah* and join in the singing. The *pizmon* that is sung is not fixed and varies weekly. The *maqām* of the *pizmon* does not

Example 10. *Ashrei ha-Am and Romemu. Sung by Moses Tawil, October 6, 1991.*

need to be in the *maqām* of the day. The singing of a *pizmon* provides another opportunity for congregational participation.

On certain Sabbaths it is customary to sing specific *pizmonim*. This can either be done by using the melody of the *pizmon* during one of the liturgical singing stations—if the *pizmon* is in the *maqām* of the day—or by singing the *pizmon* itself at this point in the Torah service. For example, on the Sabbath when Bereshit (biblical reading [BR] 1.1; see table 10) is the biblical reading, two *pizmonim* are associated with this Sabbath: Ḥannun marom Melekh ozer (*SUHV* #109) and Kel ḥai ve-nora (*SUHV* #403).[3] The former is in *maqām rast*, and the latter is in *saba*. The first *pizmon* could be used as a melody for one of the singing stations—since *rast* is the *maqām* of the day for Bereshit—or it could be sung during the Torah service. The second *pizmon* could not be used for one of the singing stations, because it is not in *rast.* It would then be sung during the Torah service (M. Tawil, interview, November 14, 1991). On appropriate Sabbaths, choice of a *pizmon* can result from a reference to an approaching holiday or because the *ḥazzan* or congregation likes the *pizmon.*

The Torah is read in sections; each division provides an opportunity for the congregation to honor a different congregant who recites the blessings before and after the reading. *Pizmonim* can also be sung between sections of the biblical reading. They serve no liturgical function. The *pizmon* chosen for performance in between the reading of Torah sections may reflect the person who just received the honor of making the blessings. For example, individuals might be honored on the occasion of the birth of a son, a bar mitzvah, or a wedding.[4]

The Torah is read in a *seyga* formula that differs from the Zemirot formula.[5] A style of recitation with clear enunciation, as heard in Shirat ha-Yam (LS 2.28), is followed throughout the Torah reading. The *maqām* of the Torah reading is always the same each week, but the subject matter of the weekly biblical reading determines the *maqām* of the recitation of Shaḥarit. The proficient Torah reader will make tasteful embellishments (M. Tawil, interviews, October 6, 1991, October 22, 1991). It is not coincidental that the regular leader of Zemirot at Beth Torah is also the regular Torah reader. Ḥakham David Tawil and Ḥazzan Yeḥezkiel Zion perform this function when the regular Torah reader at Beth Torah is absent. Having a specialized person or prominent member of the congregation leading this section is common in most Syrian synagogues. Torah reading is an important skill for a *ḥazzan* to possess. Indeed, the ability to read the Torah is a basic skill that every young boy learns prior to his bar mitzvah (I. Cabasso, interview, May 29, 1992).

The Torah reading provides a different aesthetic to the morning service: its texture is new. Congregants listen to the Torah reading, and their response is passive; during the other portions of the service they participate, sometimes more actively than others. Others have commented on this dynamic: "There is an essential difference between the reading of the Torah and the other prayers. The latter are the call of Israel to its God—whereas the reading of the Torah represents the message of G-d [*sic*] to His people" (Munk 1961, 1:171).

After the reading of the Torah there are three other sections in this part of the service. The prophetic reading consists of the cantillation of a portion of the prophetic books. Blessings precede and follow the reading. After this, the rabbi reads the prayer for the government and for the new moon, if the holiday of Rosh Ḥodesh is upcoming in the week. The leader of the Musaf, the next section of the morning service, continues with Ashrei Yoshvei (LS 4.5) by stating the first few words of the prayer, and the congregation joins in. The returning of the Torah to the ark (LS 4.6) is the last section of Torah service. The congregation sings the melody, Yimlokh Ha-Shem le-Olam (see musical example 11), as the Torah is taken from the *teivah* back to the ark. The melodies are syllabic and rhythmic, conducive for congregational singing.

After the Torah reading, congregants sit, and the president of the congregation delivers announcements prior to the rabbi's sermon. The president begins with wishes of congratulations to congregants and their families on recent births, circumcisions, bar and bat mitzvah celebrations, engagements, weddings, and anniversaries, as well as condolences to the families of the deceased. Announcements provide information for upcoming activities and times of other prayer service for the remainder of the Sabbath day. Occasionally the president may introduce a guest or a member of the congregation for a fund raising appeal. Most often he concludes by asking that attention should be given to the rabbi. Rabbi Lieberman, the senior rabbi of Beth Torah during the time of fieldwork in the early 1990s, delivers the sermon in English. He has served for over forty years and speaks from the *bimah,* not the *teivah,* where the *ḥazzan* leads the prayers and the Torah reader reads the Bible (see figure 3). Rabbi Lieberman, like rabbis of other Jewish denominations and cultural traditions, speaks about a present-day topic but draws sources from the weekly biblical reading. He begins by reading a biblical passage; he offers traditional insights from a variety of Ashkenazic and Sephardic rabbis. Many times he directs his message toward interpersonal relations, and it is not uncommon for the sermon to focus on Jewish or national sovereignty, particularly in regards to Israel.[6] Rabbi Lieberman begins by standing behind a lectern on the *bimah,* but partway through he walks along the front of the *bimah,* providing direct eye contact with congregants and often emphatic gestures with his arms. After the sermon concludes, Musaf begins.

Musaf

MUSAF CONSISTS OF an Amidah (LS 6.2), preceded and followed by Kaddish (LS 6.1 and 6.3), and other short liturgical passages (6.4–6.7).[7] Another *ḥazzan* or a knowledgeable congregant, different from Shaḥarit, leads Musaf. Moses Tawil explains:

> Musaf, it's just simple. There is no melody, except the Keter [LS 6.2.2]; they make some sort of melody or whatever. And they don't say the Musaf in the same *maqām* that they said the Shaḥarit. . . . Very often they say it in *nahawand* or sometimes *ajam,* or some-

Example 11. *Yimlokh Ha-Shem le-Olam, Mizmor le-David.*
Sung by David Shiro, October 6, 1991.

> times in *seyga,* but it depends, whatever the *ḥazzan* feels like. In the Keter they very often use Western melodies, Israeli melodies; they use quite a variety of melodies for them. (interview, October 6, 1991)

Musaf is a brief liturgical section, and its musical treatment is rather informal in comparison to Zemirot and Shaḥarit. It contains only one text that receives melodic emphasis. The Keter of Musaf is liturgically and musically similar to and reminiscent of the Nak'dishakh of Shaḥarit (LS 3.6.2).[8] The choice of *maqām* for the Amidah is variable, and the only restriction is that it should be distinct from the *maqām* of the day. Macy Nulman writes, "Although any *maqām* is appropriate for this service the reader will sometimes introduce the *maqām* assigned to the [up]coming Sabbath" (Nulman 1977–78, 49).

Keter and Mysticism

LITURGICAL DEVELOPMENTS OVER the centuries both absorb and reflect a variety of influences. The text and musical expression of Keter was influenced by mysticism. During the early part of the second millennium, mystical and esoteric influences conveyed deeper religious meaning. In Judaism the quintessential text of the Zohar of the late thirteenth century established a new realm of understanding. The liturgy established prior to this period changed with new approaches and practices. As a liturgical moment reenacting union to the divine, Keter receives elaborate musical attention.

The main text distilling kabbalistic and mystical insights is *Sefer ha-Zohar* (late thirteenth century). The Zohar's theosophic approach enumerates prophetic revelation; the two primary prophetic visions are Ezekiel, chapter 1, and Isaiah, chapter 6. The esoteric imagery provides fertile ground for elaborate interpretations. In his seminal edition of the Zohar, Isaiah Tishby comments on prayer prior to the Zohar as consisting of two approaches: the external ritualistic and the internal spiritualistic. The ritualistic approach emphasizes the correct fulfillment of the practical commandments, whereas the internal spiritualistic approach places the highest value on the intellectual and spiritual striving to achieve emotional or rational contact with supernatural elements (1989, 941). The early mystics kept to the liturgical text but focused on *kavvanah* (concentration) prior to prayer. Their innovation is in the approach and engagement with prayer, not the creation of new texts for the liturgy. An essential goal of piety, as expressed in the Zohar, is careful adherence to biblical commandments to reflect in the lower earthly world the holiness of the upper heavenly world. The designation of the ten *sefirot* (attributes or divine realms) forms an important part of kabbalistic thought. Explaining the function of the *sefirot* Lawrence Fine states that "the ten *Sefirot,* or radiances of God, are *emanations* that flow out of the hidden wellsprings of *Ein-Sof* [infinite]. It is as if the concealed dimension of God gives birth to other, more manifest parts of Itself. . . . [E]ach of these *Sefirot* are known by different names and have highly distinctive characteristics" (Fine 1984, 318). The *sefirot* are not merely external traits but symbols of the essence of God (ibid., 319). The goal of Jewish practice is to unite the upper heavenly world and the lower earthly world through the *sefirot.* For medieval mystics, the practice of spiritual concentration and of directing the heart and mind was the *sefirot;* concentration of the *sefirot* was connected to the act of prayer (Tishby 1989, 947). In the words of the Zohar:

> The reward for prayer that is engaged in this kind of restoration occurs when the soul leaves the body to go to the future world. Just as [the worshiper] has honored the Shekhinah [lit., divine presence and name of one of the *sefirot*], and clothed her with beautiful clouds, called "clouds of glory," and raised her by his prayer to the Holy One, blessed be He, with songs and hymns, glorification, and praises in his prayer, so to the Holy One, blessed be He, will raise his soul to the world to come in a garment of clouds of glory, with many songs, glorification, and praises.[9] In the same way Israel came out of Egypt with clouds of glory and with music. This is the meaning of "Then sang Moses, and the children of Israel." (Exodus 15:1).[10]

Prayer as a means of connecting the lower and upper world is a concept articulated in a contemporary Syrian prayer book quoting the Zohar from *Parashat Terumah:*

> When Israel begins to bless (i.e., recite Barechu at the onset of Shabbat), a voice goes forth in all the heavens, which are sanctified with the sanctity of the onset of Shabbat: Fortunate are you, a holy people, that you bless and sanctify below so that many camps of lofty, holy ones may be blessed and sanctified above. Fortunate are they (Israel) in This World and fortunate are they in the World to Come. (*Siddur kol sassoon* 1995, xxi)

The mystical motivation in worship is kept alive in Syrian prayer.

Music plays a significant role in mysticism. Amnon Shiloah's survey of music in mysticism (1992, 131–56) shows a deep interconnection:

> Concepts relating to the importance and virtues of music that developed in the mystical doctrine and contributed to the enrichment of the musical repertoire are so interwoven with the symbols and concepts comprising the world of the kabbalah that it is often difficult to treat them separately. Hence in the writings of the kabbalists not only is there no systematic discussion of music or expression of opinions about it, but even in the few cases where these matters are explicitly raised, the focus is not on music in and of itself. . . . [T]he mystics maintained that music has its source in the divine; in their view, God created it on the third day, making angels out of his own breath to sing his glory, day, and night.(132)

Shiloah views established liturgical practices such as Kabbalat Shabbat (the welcoming of the Sabbath on Friday evening) and less frequently practiced rituals such as *tikkun ḥatsot* and *bakkashot* as having origins in mysticism. He divides the role of music in mystical world into two primary areas: music and meditation and music and prophecy (ibid., 135–37). Music and meditation describes the individual act of divine worship; in many instances speech becomes associated with musical sounds. Music and prophecy is an area that receives a good deal of discussion. The thirteenth-century mystic Abraham Abulafia used music to achieve a higher state of consciousness and saw the process of the body's response to music to be the same as speech (ibid., 136). Moshe Idel views prophecy and music as an analogy for the technique giving rise to prophecy and the prophetic experience (1982). Thus, music and mysticism weds both theory and practice, music and mysticism are wedded and since the medieval era music is an expression of the mystical text Keter.

The Kedushah for Musaf begins with the word *keter,* which means "crown." Keter is a liturgical moment to act out the reunification with the divine:

> In the mystics' zeal to disseminate their ideas, it is not surprising that they had great influence on the liturgy. . . . This is clearest in the Kedushah, the favorite prayer of the members of these circles, who saw themselves as divinely charged to cultivate and disseminate it, and who expected God's grateful recognition in return. . . . Above all the idea of the "crown" [*keter*] placed on the head of God simultaneously by the heavenly hosts and by Israel is authentically mystical. (Elbogen 1913 [1993], 287–88)

The Zohar conveys the importance of the thrice holy statement of the Kedushah:

> [Members of] Israel sanctify below in the same way as the celestial angels sanctify above, for it is written of them "And one called to the other and said: *Kadosh, [kadosh, kadosh]*" (Isaiah 6:3). When this Israel sanctify, they raise the celestial glory upward . . . the mystery of the supernal heavens, is raised upward. When the heavens are raised upward, *kodesh* shines in them and then it is called "*kadosh*" above. . . . The whole purpose is to bring some part of the sanctity of the upper world to the lower world, so that each individual may be hallowed by this sanctity, and receive it in order to clothe himself with a covering of sanctity. This is the mystical meaning of "I will be hallowed among the children of Israel." This is the first stage; subsequently, "I am the Lord who hallow you." (Leviticus 22:32)[11]

The format of Keter, like the Nak'dishakh (LS 3.6.2), begins with opening sentences chanted by the *ḥazzan* followed by one-sentence responses by the congregation. The first portion of the text is:

> *Ḥazzan:* Keter yitenue lekha, Adoshem Elokeinu, malakhim hamonei malah, im amekh yisrael kevutzei matah. Yaḥad kulam kedusah lekha yeshaleshu, kadavar haamur al yad neviakh, vekara zeh el-zeh veamar:
>
> Congregation: Kadosh, Kadosh, Kadosh Adoshem tzevaot, melocla-haaretz kevodo. (Isaiah 6:3)
>
> *Ḥazzan:* Kevodo melei olam umshartav shoalim ayei meko kevodo le-haaritzo.Leumatam meshabḥim veomrim:
>
> Congregation: Barukh kevod Adoshem Mimkomo (Ezekiel 3:12).

> *Ḥazzan:* They shall give a crown to you, Adoshem, our God the myriad of angels above together with your people Israel, who gather below. Together they shall all declare holiness thrice before You, as that which was said through Your prophet, each calls to the other and says:
>
> Congregation: Holy, Holy, Holy is Adoshem of Hosts, the entire world is filled with His glory (Isaiah 6:3).
>
> *Ḥazzan:* His glory fills the world and His ministering angels ask, Where is His place of glory to revere Him? Opposite themselves they praise and say:
>
> Congregation: Blessed is the glory of Adoshem from His place. (Ezekiel 3:12)[12]

For the mystic chanting the liturgy is reenacting the divine unification. Musical elaboration then serves to aid the process. Amnon Shiloah provides the connection between the historic practice and present prayer activity stating, "According to mystical theories, the *Qedushah* as sung concurrently in the synagogue and in the heavens is a supreme moment for both the angels and the people of Israel" (Shiloah 1992, 138). Shiloah further describes the musical significance of the cantor's chanting of Keter: "In many Sephardic communities, particularly in the Balkans and eastern regions of the Mediterranean, the *Qedushah* has become almost a bravura passage in which the cantors exhibit their full talent for improvisation and melismatic embellishment" (1992, 139).

Musical example 12 portrays the ornate cantorial approach to Keter. Like the singing of the heavy liturgical singing stations or pillars (see musical examples 6 and 9), musical elaboration extends this prayer by the solo singing of the *ḥazzan*. Melismatic vocal lines and changes of register are the primary musical devices to broaden chanting. In example 12 the range of the melodic line is nearly two octaves, certainly the realm of the experienced singer. Ḥazzan Ephraim Avidani begins starting on the upper D; the *maqām* is *nahawand*. His opening gesture is a scalar descent to the lower D; each note of the decent has a preceding changing note figure. The descent from the upper D to the lower D is a grand beginning to the opening of Keter: "Keter yitenue lekha" ("They shall give a crown to you"). The next few words ("yitenulekha Adoshem Elokeinnu malakhim hamonei malah"*)* remain within this octave. From there the tessitura rises (in the phrase beginning with the words "im a mekh") emphasizing the text "im amekh yisrael kevutsei matah" ("together with your people Israel, who gather below"). This phrase ends with a descent to the dominant A. From here the melodic line rises slightly above the dominant and returns to an A, which is then followed by a descent to the modal center (the gesture ends with the word *yeshaleshu*). This same melodic gesture repeats (beginning with the word *kadavar* and ending with *veamar*). At this point the congregation recites the thrice holy statement "Kadosh, Kadosh, Kadosh" from Isaiah 6:3. There is no specific melody sung by the congregation; each congregant recites this line. The cantor pauses and continues reciting this line after the congregation finishes. Beginning on the upper note D, the same note as the opening for the word "Keter," each of the three musical phrases for the word "Kadosh" is different. The first phrase leaps to a high A; the next two phrases include unique embellishments. The remainder of the text of this line descends to the lower D of *maqām nahwand*. The next phrase (beginning with the words "Kevodo malei olam") continues with a similar melodic gesture, beginning on the upper D and descending to the lower D.

Despite the designation by Moses Tawil, and other *ḥazzanim*, that there is no expressed overarching structure to the Keter prayer, there are indeed organizing features. Keter is not described as a liturgical section requiring either a heavy or light melody. Tawil's description that "they make some sort of melody or whatever" articulates the desire for freedom with no adaptation of a previously known melody. The cantor's portions are improvisatory, setting up the congregation to respond. Although the illustration of Keter in example 12 is improvisatory and free, it does follow a structure.[13] The cantorial line descends from the upper D to the lower D. Intervening passages emphasize the dominant A. The general nature of the melodic line follows the stylization in Arab music of scalar adjacent notes; there a few leaps. Keter follows the temporal freedom that Habib Hassan Touma describes.

A common congregational melody for a portion of Keter adapts a well-known Israeli folk song for the text Hu Elokeinu (toward the end of the Keter prayer). At Beth Torah, Yerushalayim Shel Zahav (*SUHV* #208a), a popular song by songwriter Naomi Shemer, is the melody used for Hu Elokeinu; the *maqām* is *nahawand*.[14] Although Moses Tawil discusses many other possible melodies for Keter, Yerushalayim Shel Zahav is the most common choice. When the *ḥazzan* initiates this melody, the congregation sings along, making this a highlighted moment.

Many Syrians would not describe the singing of Keter as a mystical experience, but the background of the text and its usage bears this history. The acknowledgement of the divine through cantorial elaboration makes this part of the liturgy stand out as unique; it is an interactive moment of the service with the verbal responses. Listening to the *ḥazzan* render these passages with melodic embellishments provides a contemplative experience.

The Continuation of Musaf

AFTER KETER, THE recitation pattern is rapid, since people are anxious for services to come to an end. The second portion of Musaf, from the second Kaddish until the end (LS 6.2–6.7), is similar to Birkhot ha-Shaḥar (LS 1). Like Birkhot ha-Shaḥar, the text comes from rabbinic literature and is recited with a *seyga* formula.

In many ways the Sabbath morning service ends anticlimactically. Given the formality of Shaḥarit with the seven liturgical singing stations, Musaf is considerably less formal. At the conclusion of Aleinu (LS 6.7) the service is complete. Aleinu, led by the *ḥazzan* or congregant, is recited by each individual in an undertone. In effect there is no formal conclusion to the service.

Example 12. *Keter (from Musaf). Sung by Yehezkel Zion and Ephraim Avidani.*

Example 12. *Keter (from Musaf). Sung by Yehezkel Zion and Ephraim Avidani* (continued).

Example 12. *Keter (from Musaf). Sung by Yehezkel Zion and Ephraim Avidani* (continued).

Transcription of Keter from "Nishmat Kol Hay [sic]: Saturday's Sephardic Prayers." Sung by Yehezkel Zion and Ephraim Avidani (Jerusalem: Yeshivat Avidani, ca. 1985), set of eight cassettes with instrumental accompaniment. Example taken from tape 2, "Maqām Nahawand," side B. The recording includes instrumental accompaniment (kanun and violin); this is included for the recording but would not have been used in a synagogue Sabbath service. "Interlude" indicates an instrumental interlude between verses. An asterisk indicates where the congregation would respond.

Edwin Seroussi comments that in many Middle Eastern Sephardic traditions the shape of the entire morning service can be represented by a bell-curve. At the beginning of the service the ritual activity is not intense, simply the recitation of biblical and rabbinic texts. During Zemirot, Shaḥarit, and the Torah reading the ritual and musical activity increases. At the end of the service, with the rabbinic texts at the end of Musaf the ritual activity is lessened. Some congregants walk out before the service is completed. Where in other traditions the service concludes with the hymn Adon Olam, the Syrian Sabbath morning service does not.

9

Overall Design of the Syrian Sabbath Morning Service

THE DESIGN OF the Sabbath morning service, like the music itself, reflects a Judeo-Arab synthesis. On both large and small scales, this Jewish service adapts Arab musical styles, genres, and predilections. The structure and design of the Sabbath morning service reveals the distinctive components that make this ritual event Syrian.

The musical rendering of the service is highly symmetrical.[1] Figure 5 illustrates the overall structure (Bateson 1974; Tambiah 1979). Each section possesses characteristics and organizing features of its own that closely follow the style and liturgical function of the text. The unique characteristics of these liturgical sections of the Sabbath morning service rest chiefly on the choice of *maqām* and the type of musical activity. Shaḥarit stands out as the main part of the service with regard to *maqām* and musical activity. The *ḥazzan,* the most experienced ritual specialist, delivers this portion of the service in the *maqām* of the day with precomposed melodies and improvisation. Zemirot foreshadows some of these elements, and Musaf, with the exception of Keter, balances the symmetry with a recitation formula like the opening liturgical section, Birkhot ha-Shaḥar. The formulaic singing in *maqām seyga* for Zemirot and the reading of the Torah, although their *seyga* formulas are different, provide an inner symmetry that frames Shaḥarit.

Maqām seyga serves as a unifying element for the symmetry of the overall design. Moses Tawil explains that *maqām seyga* is the basis for recitation because *seyga* is known by everyone, since all are trained to read the Torah. It is possible that *seyga* was chosen because of the importance of the Torah and

Figure 5. *Overall design of the Syrian Sabbath morning service*

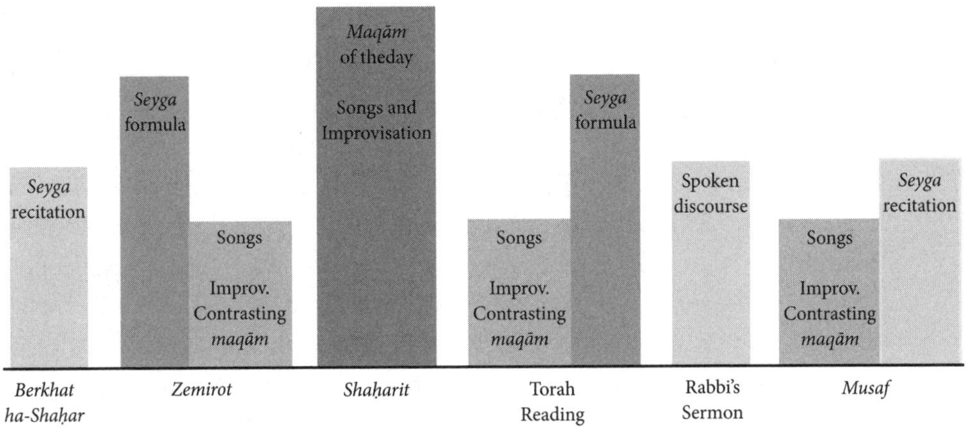

not only because of its familiarity. Thus, the *maqām* for reading the Torah unifies the overall organization of the service. Furthermore, the centerpiece of the Sabbath morning service, and Shaḥarit itself, is the reading of the Shema—also rendered in *maqām seyga.* The prominence of *seyga* cannot be overstated.

One finds contrasting *maqāmāt* and melodic styles within the design of the service. Shaḥarit is not rendered entirely within the *maqām* of the day; it features one *maqām* in the melodies of the seven liturgical singing stations. The *ḥazzan* has the choice to make use of other *maqāmāt,* but he must return to the *maqām* of the day at the end of the liturgical portions. Since changing *maqāmāt* creates interest for the knowledgeable congregants and displays the skill of the *ḥazzan,* it is recommended that a cantor not overemphasize the main *maqām.* But changing too often is also discouraged. Thus, the cantor must be suitably experienced not to cross the fine line between overemphasizing the main *maqām* and providing variety.

Sections other than Shaḥarit also make use of contrasting *maqāmāt* but each in a different manner. The latter portion within Zemirot introduces a *maqām* that is different from the *maqām* of the day (LSS 2.18–2.26). The fixed melodies sung at the beginning and end of the Torah reading are in various *maqāmāt* (LSS 4.1 and 4.6). And the *pizmonim* sung intermittently are not bound to any *maqām.* The first portion of Musaf makes use of a *maqām,* chosen from a limited number of possibilities, that contrasts with Shaḥarit.

Fixity and flexibility characterize the relationship between the liturgical structure and musical texture of Syrian liturgy. Approaches to the study of ritual have not always recognized flexibility as a part of the design. The invariant nature of ritual is a primary aspect of ritual structure repeatedly discussed by anthropologists. In his informative study “The Obvious Aspects of Ritual” (1979), Roy Rappaport states: “Invariance . . . is characteristic of all rituals, both human and nonhuman, and it may be that both the sacred and the supernatural arose out of union of words with the invariance of the speechless rituals of the beasts from whom we are descended. Be this as it may, both the sacred and the supernatural are, I believe, implied by liturgy’s invariance” (208). Casting his statement in general terms, Rappaport starts with the assumption that the necessity of formal structures makes ritual invariant. In fact, throughout his study he repeatedly emphasizes ritual invariance. Furthermore, Rapapport claims, “invariance leads to certainty which leads to sacred” (209). Formality and repetition foster a sense of austerity in ritual. Innovation in stylization of liturgy, he states, only occurs in more liberal rites. Others also hold ritual as sacred and “imagined in stasis” (see Kelly and Kaplan 1990, 120, 125).

Nevertheless, invariance is not what it may seem. No ritual will appear exactly the same way twice (Tambiah 1979, 115). Participants and officiants adapt new meaning to a ritual after participating or performing it repeatedly. Sections, as Rappaport claims, may be invariant generally, but variation becomes part of the system.

Stanley J. Tambiah applies performative approaches of ritual studies to the question of finding the viable components within a ritual. He comments on the dual aspects of ritual where the repeated enactments contain invariable sequences, chanted formulas, rules, and etiquette, which he contrasts with the anthropological reality that there is no single performance to a rite. Many aspects affect ritual: mode of recitation, social characteristics, and ability; all have a direct effect on attendance, audience interest, and the general tone of the ritual event (Tambiah 1979, 115).[2] Looking into ritual variability helps to determine the limits of the overall ritual and various sections allowing for the determination of the fusion of form and content (ibid., 139).

According to Tambiah, all rituals are flexible or variant to some degree. However, he approaches flexibility in terms of performance, not in terms of the rules for liturgical performance or ritual design. Syrian liturgy, like many other rituals of different faiths and cultures, builds flexibility into the fabric of its design. The texts of the prayers and certain musical elements are fixed. At the same time, the main parts of the prayers are flexible in terms of the use of melodies and melodic style. The Sabbath morning service of Syrian Jews is not unique in its use of flexibility. The application or set of rules that allows for *maqām* and melodic choice, however, is distinctive.

Charles Lafayette Boilés offers the following for considering music in ritual and the range of fixity and flexibility allowed:

> Some of the rituals are inflexibly rigid in their format whereas others are almost unstructured. Some occasions require an exact ceremonial, a rigidly followed protocol, although the music itself may vary considerably. Other occasions are characterized by permissible variables in event or participants. From all this, we may gather that humans have some sort of continuum regarding the relative amount of variation permitted in a musical occasion. . . .
>
> [I]t is possible to postulate something concerning the nature of this continuum related to musical events. Its priorities are defined according to the formal aspects of each musical occasion: who, what, when, where, and how. At one end, there is almost no ceremonial structure, and such musical events are relatively free in form. At the opposite extreme of the continuum, the format and musical artifact are rather rigid. Arbitrarily, I have selected two other points within the continuum and differentiate them with regard to the fixedness of their ceremonial format; these are *variable,* a category of occasions consisting of rites in alternative combinations, and *matrix,* in which category the ritual is fixed but rites may be added or taken from existing structure. (1978, 191)

Boilés's focus, however, is musical occasion. He is not concerned with the use of music in the ritual event. It is clear that the Sabbath morning service would not fit at either end of Boilés's continuum. However, Boilés's end point "variable" with "alternative combinations" is a useful designation. More of the Syrian liturgy is fixed than flexible because of the historically codified text. Overall, music provides the freedom to express the fixed text.

Since the text is a major determinant for musical activity within a liturgical context, viewing the interaction of music and text is necessary when studying liturgical music. Syrian liturgy employs three relationships of music and text: structure, context, and function. The structure of the text, the most general designation, describes origins of various textual types (biblical, rabbinic, poetic). The unique combination of textual types in each of the liturgical sections determines the type of musical rendering. The context of the text refers to textual usage in relation to other liturgical sections. Zemirot and the Torah reading primarily contain biblical texts. Hence *seyga* recitation formula comprise the musical approach. Shaḥarit and Birkhot ha-Shaḥar are maximally different in terms of text and music relationships. The function of Shaḥarit separates it from other liturgical sections and hence from the musical elaboration. The textual types—biblical, rabbinic, poetic—have different means of musical expression. Shaḥarit contains a different textual structure, and its context requires two mandated portions of prayer, the Shema and the Amidah. The most complex liturgical structure requires the most demanding music. Thus, Shaḥarit's texture is varied and dense.

Shaḥarit has a unique design worthy of further discussion. Its musical organization displays significant cultural traits by integrating Arab musical characteristics. The imagery of the seven liturgical singing stations as pillars suggests that these are foundations that hold up, or organize, Shaḥarit. Though they occur at the beginning, middle, and end, the musical emphasis does not coincide with the overall liturgical importance of the texts. The Shema, located between the fifth and sixth stations, is the textual centerpiece of the liturgy, one of the required components of the liturgy, and not highlighted musically.[3] Rather, the Shema is cantillated in *maqām seyga.* This important passage is given emphasis through means other than musical elaboration, simply rendering style change. For the Shema the cantor changes from singing and improvising in the *maqām* of the day to the Torah cantillation in *maqām seyga.* It may well be that the strategic placement of the singing stations came about to provide interest for the lengthy Shaḥarit service and to frame the Shema. The liturgical singing stations are moments of praise. At times, like Zemirot, they musically emphasize texts added for the Sabbath (liturgical singing stations 1, 2, 3, and 5 are added for the Sabbath). Textual type is not the only determinant of melodic style, liturgical function also influences the melodic rendering style. Thus, the musical design follows the function and structure of the service, but liturgically important items have various means of expressivity.

The melodic organization of Shaḥarit is similar to the Arab suite, or *waṣlah.* The characteristics of a *waṣlah* include the use of several melodies that are unified by the same *maqām;* the melodies may be drawn from a variety of genres and may differ in rhythmic content (al-Faruqi 1981, 388; Racy 1983). Typically, there is a rhythmic progression from slow melodies at the beginning to fast melodies later in the suite. Modulations to other *maqāmāt* are allowed in the *waṣlah,* but one must return to the principle *maqām* at the end of major sections. Shaḥarit has a parallel construction. Like the *waṣlah,* the use and centrality of one *maqām* unify it, and variety occurs through the choice of melodies in contrasting rhythms. However, a progression from slower to more lively rhythms is not found in Shaḥarit.[4] The *waṣlah* design, which Ali Jihad Racy sees as more of a process than a musical formal design (1983, 396), is adapted and a rhythmic progression is absent because of liturgical necessity. The last liturgical singing station, Nak'dishakh, is the highlight of the Amidah. It is the third pillar, and a slow or heavy melody expresses the words of the liturgy. In the *waṣlah* design, the last selection would be the quickest. During Shaḥarit each of the liturgical singing stations have their own function. This adaptability of the *waṣlah* design illustrates the point that Jewish liturgical demands override purely Arab musical concerns.

Kumiko Yayama's study of *bakkashot* singing among Syrian Jews from Aleppo in Jerusalem (2003) reveals similar design characteristics. The four-hour singing of *bakkashot* from three o'clock to seven o'clock Saturday morning, prior to the Sabbath morning service, consists of more than sixty texts. These texts divide into ten sections. Yayama delineates the opening of each section, the *petiḥa*, as having unique features: improvisatory singing with frequent changes of *maqām* (271–316, xviii–xix). After the opening of each section several *bakkashot* are sung; they differ musically from the *petiḥa* with measured melodies, some adapted (like the *pizmonim*) from known predominantly Arab melodies (191–271, xv–xvii). Yayama describes sections 1 through 5 as melodies and improvisation in predominantly *maqām bayat* and sections 6 through 9 as predominantly in *maqām rast* or *huzam*. Section 10, the final grouping of texts before the start of the morning service, are sung in the *maqām* of the day.[5] So the design of *bakkashot* performance contains measured and unmeasured melodies, a directed progression, and organization guided by *maqām*. Moving from *maqām bayat* to *rast* and *huzam*, the singing ends in the *maqām* of the day for Sabbath morning service; no one *maqām* becomes predominant overall. Thus, the prelude *bakkashot* performance sets the stage for the Sabbath morning service.

The design of Syrian liturgy is not necessarily unique in its use of various melodic styles. The eastern European system also uses various prayer modes to shape the rendering of the liturgy with Magen Avot as a didactic mode and specific affectual attributes to the HaShem Malaḥ and Ahavah Rabbah prayer modes. However, the eastern European system remains constant from week to week in regards to the use of a mode. The fact that the mode changes every week in the Syrian tradition for the Shaḥarit section enhances a unique mode of expression.

The overarching design of the Sabbath morning service rests on an aesthetic approach to music and text in a ritual setting. The more complex the variety of texts, context, and function, the more varied the musical elaboration. Two contrasting uses of music describe the music and text interaction, music that propels and music that highlights the text. Music propels recitation of the text when the musical texture consists of melodic formula (evident in Zemirot and the Torah reading). However, the liturgically important text of Shaḥarit uses elaborate rendering styles, thus highlighting specific texts to enhance expression and meaning. There are significant ritual moments of contrast in the morning service, points where music and text maximally propel and highlight the text. For example, when one views the Shema within the liturgical design, its musical approach to propel the text is striking in comparison to the liturgical singing stations. Each liturgical section in the Syrian Sabbath morning service—Birkhot ha-Shaḥar, Zemirot, Shaḥarit, the Torah reading, and Musaf—has its unique mix of musical styles. The degree or significant amount of highlighted moments within Shaḥarit grants further evidence for its prominence. Shaḥarit is a highly fused ritual structure; its varied texture is distinct in this regard. Balance forms the entire morning service; each section is a part of the overall design.

Adapting Arab music on a variety of direct musical levels certainly displays the intricate and complex Judeo-Arab synthesis found in the liturgy. Other forms and aspects of this Judeo-Arab synthesis are the subject of part 3.

Part Three

A Judeo-Arab Synthesis

10

The *Maqāmāt* and the Weekly Biblical Reading

Syrian Jews in Brooklyn carefully maintain a practice of associating a *maqām* with the weekly biblical reading; the associated *maqām* then serves as the *maqām* of the day for use in the main part of Sabbath morning prayers. The orderly use of Arab melodies in the same *maqām* comprises the main musical process of the Shaḥarit portion of the Sabbath morning liturgy.

Table 10. Maqām *and biblical reading associations*

Biblical reading	Brooklyn system[1]	Israel associations[2]	Early-twentieth-century compilation by Idelsohn[3]
Genesis			
1.1. Bereshit	*rast*	*rast*	*rast*
1.2. No'aḥ	*seyga*	*bayat*	*iraq*
1.3. Lekh Lekha	*saba*	*saba*	*saba*
1.4. Va-Yera	*rahaw (nawa)*	*nawa*	*nawa*
1.5. Ḥayyei Sarah	*hijaz*	*hijaz*	*hijaz*
1.6. Toledot	*mahur*	*mahur*	*mahur*
1.7. Va-Yetse	*ajam*	*ajam*	*jaharkah*[4]
1.8. Va-Yishlaḥ	*saba or seyga*	*bayat*	*iraq*
1.9. Va-Yeshev	*rahaw or nahawand*	*rahaw*	*rahaw*
1.10. Mi-Kets	*seyga*	*seyga*	*seyga*
1.11. Va-Yiggash	*bayat*	*bayat or saba*	*bayat*
1.12. Va-Yeḥi	*hijaz*	*hijaz*	*hijaz*

Exodus			
2.1. Shemot	*rast or bayat*	*bayat*	*rast*
2.2. Va-Era	*ḥuseini or rast*	*nahawand*	*ḥuseini or nawa*
2.3. Bo	*seyga*	*seyga*	*iraq*
2.4. Be-Shallaḥ	*ajam*	*ajam*	*ajam*
2.5. Yitro	*ḥuseini*	*ḥuseini*	*seyga*[5]
2.6. Mishpatim	*saba*	*saba*	*saba*
2.7. Terumah	*ḥuseini*	*bayat*	*seyga*
2.8. Tetsavveh	*seyga*	*seyga*	*seyga*
2.9. Ki Tissa	*hijaz*	*hijaz*	*hijaz*
2.10. Va-Yakhel	*ḥuseini*	*ḥuseini*	*ḥuseini*
2.11. Pekudei	*rahaw (nawa)*	*nawa*	*nawa*
2.12. Va-Yakhel-Pekudei	*bayat*		
Leviticus			
3.1. Va-Yikra	*rast*	*rast*	*rast*
3.2. Tsav	*rahaw (nawa)*	*nawa*	*iraq*
3.3. Shemini	*ḥuseini*	*ḥuseini*	*ḥuseini*
3.4. Tazri'a	*saba or bayat*	*saba*	*bayat*
3.5. Taḥor	*nahawand or seyga*	*saba or seyga*	*iraq*
3.6. Tazri'a-Taḥor	*saba*		
3.7. Aḥarei Mot	*hijaz*	*hijaz*	*hijaz*
3.8. Kedoshim	*saba*	*saba*	*saba*
3.9. Aḥarei Mot-Kedoshim	*bayat-hijaz*		
3.10. Emor	*seyga ḥuseini*	*seyga*	*ushayran*[6]
3.11. Be-Har	*saba or nahawand*	*nawa*	*nawa*
3.12. Be-Ḥukkotai	*nahawand*	*bayat*	*bayat or nawa*
3.13. Be-Har-Be-Ḥukkotai	*saba*		
Numbers			
4.1. Be-Midbar	*ḥuseini or rast*	*bayat*	*muḥayyar*
4.2. Naso	*rast-saba*	*ḥuseini or saba*	*saba*
4.3. Be-Ha'alotkha	*seyga*	*seyga*	*seyga*
4.4. Shelaḥ Lekha	*hijaz*	*nahawand*	*iraq*
4.5. Koraḥ	*nahawand*	*ḥuseini*	*ḥuseini*
4.6. Ḥukkat	*ḥuseini*	*rast*	*rast*
4.7. Balak	*mahur*	*bayat*	*bayat*
4.8. Ḥukkat-Balak	*ḥuseini*		
4.9. Pinḥas	*saba*	*saba*	*saba*
4.10. Mattot	*nahawand or rahaw*	*nawa*	*nawa*
4.11. Masei	*saba*	*saba*	*saba?*
4.12. Mattot-Masei	*nahawand*		
Dueteronomy			
5.1. Devarim	*hijaz*	*hijaz*	*hijaz*
5.2. Va-Etḥannan	*ḥuseini*	*ḥuseini*	*ḥuseini*

5.3. Ekev	*seyga*	*seyga*	*seyga*
5.4. Re'eh	*rast*	*rast*	*iraq*
5.5. Shofetim	*ajam*	*ajam*	*seyga*
5.6. Ki Tetse	*saba*	*saba*	*saba*
5.7. Ki Tavo	*seyga*	*seyga*	*iraq*
5.8. Nitsavim	*nahawand*	*nawa*	*nawa*
5.9. Va-Yelekh	*hijaz*	*rast*	
5.10. Nitsavim-Va-Yelekh	*nahawand*		
5.11. Ha'azinu	*muḥayyar*	*ḥuseini*	*ḥuseini*
5.12. Ve-zot Ha-Brakhah	*ajam*	*ajam*	*ajam*

1. This column is taken from the chart in *SUHV* (565–66). The chart is a reprint of one taken from *Hallel v'zimrah* (1928), an earlier publication used by Syrian Jews in Brooklyn.
2. This column is taken from *Shirei zimrah ha-shaleim* (1988), a collection of *bakkashot* and *pizmonim*, analogous to *SUHV*, used by Sephardic Jews in Israel.
3. This column is taken from the scholarly work of Abraham Zvi Idelsohn from the first quarter of the twentieth century; it is a composite based upon three studies, two of which are found in the fourth volume of his *Hebräish-orientalisher Melodienschatz*, in German (1923a) and Hebrew (1923b) versions. The third study is an article on the *maqāmāt* and poetry, "Die Makamen in der hebräischen Poesie der orientalischen Juden," published in 1913.
4. Idelsohn states that this *maqām* is similar to *sasgar* (1923a:104), a transposition of *ajam* (89), starting on the note F (the Arabic name of this note is *jahārkāh*), with a change in the upper tetrachords. This is also found in S. Marcus 1989 (844).
5. Idelsohn 1923a and 1923b list "*seyga*," and Idelsohn 1913 lists "*seyga* or *ḥuseini*." This is the only difference among Idelsohn's three charts.
6. *Ushayrān* is defined by Idelsohn as a transposed *ḥuseini*. He also states that *ushayrān* is little known in Syria (1923a, 97; 1923b, 80). S. Marcus lists *ushayrān* under the *bayat faṣīlah* as *ḥuseini ushayrān—ḥuseini* starting on the note *ushayrān* (the Arabic name for the note A) (1989, 529).

Extramusical associations of modes and other musical elements are a part of the early history of Western music—as seen in Greek writings and the early music of the church—and in non-Western cultures. This cross-cultural phenomenon has been discussed by Bruno Nettl as one aspect of the particular power of music "to symbolize in distilled and abstract form the character and values of a culture" (1983, 182; see also Powers 1981, 525, Sharma 1981, 525–30, and Becker 1981, 530–36). Inherent in these extramusical associations are, according to Powers, three interrelated domains: "the universal macrocosm of times, seasons, and the heavens; the human microcosm of humors, passions, and psychological character; and the domain of symbolic actions accompanied by music, that is, of liturgy and drama" (1981, 525). Extramusical associations illustrate important features such as music's meaning in a culture, a way to imbue music with significance.

Extramusical associations refers to connecting meaning to music or a musical practice. Emotion, literary features, holidays, and events are associated to music in various cultures through modes. In many cases the close connection between musical activity, theory, or the music itself with a non-musical element enables a deeper purpose for the use of music in many religious contexts.

The organization of extramusical associations is interconnected with the systematic use of modes. The structuring of liturgy with a modal framework is common to rituals of many cultures. For example, modes are used to organize Christian chant by season since specific modes are used for particular periods of the ecclesiastical year (Apel 1958; Powers 1980, 382–83) or specific chant type (Treitler 1975; Crocker 1986; Robertson 1988); *nusaḥ*, the system of Jewish prayer modes in the Ashkenazic tradition, signifies a time of the week, year, or a holiday through known melodic phrases in specific modes set to particular prayers (Cohon 1950; Avenary 1971; Levine 1980–81); *raga* demarcates the daily prayer cycle in addition to its evocable sentiments, a range of moods of feeling are associated with an hour of the day (Sharma 1981, 525); *pathet* organizes a performance of *wayang kulit* in Southeast Asia, different modes are connected with particular activities (Becker 1980; Wong and Lysloff 1991); and *maqām* guides the recitation of the Qur'an, beginning in *maqām bayyātī* the reader then moves to other *maqāmāt* but must return to *bayyātī* (Nelson 1982, 1985). The use of modes in religious traditions provides symbolic meaning that carries powerful associations that are often enduring. An investigation of the modal practices within a tradition depends on the various contexts of that tradition to uncover historical meaning and characteristics of present usage. Local practices may play a prominent role in creating unique associations not found in a wider cultural context.

Syrian Jews carefully maintain an effective combination of extramusical associations of a modal tradition that also serves to organize and shape their liturgy. This practice does touch upon associations of the first and second domains identified by Powers, but it is in the last domain that their associations should be positioned since the system that governs them organizes their liturgical music. Syrian extramusical associations contain a rich dimension of the interconnection between textual and musical meaning. Perpetuating the *maqām* extramusical associations is a fundamental aspect to the liturgical tradition. Meaning ascribed to music associated with the biblical text plays a significant role in shaping the music, the Sabbath morning liturgy in particular.

My focus here is on the associations of the *maqāmāt* with the weekly biblical reading. In order to accomplish this task, I look at how these associations are used and understood by the Syrian community in Brooklyn. I compare the Brooklyn practice with that of others, including scholarly investigations on this topic (Shiloah 1979 and 1981; S. Marcus 1989). The extramusical associations found in theoretical writings on Arab music and among practicing Arab musicians today serve to contextualize the Syrian extramusical associations. Consideration of the affect of the *maqāmāt* in Arab musical practices at large places the associations of the Brooklyn community in a wider perspective. I show how Syrian Jews use this system, as well as what it represents in order to uncover a key component anchoring the Syrian community and its liturgical practices in an Arab aesthetic yet shaped by their own experience.

Extramusical Associations

AMNON SHILOAH'S STUDY of over twelve hundred Arabic sources on music from the tenth to the nineteenth century, summarized in "The Arabic Concept of Mode," shows multiple associations of individual modes to ethical and cosmological values (1981, 38).[1] Detailed lists of correspondences include planets, signs of the zodiac, seasons, day and night, hours, elements, humors, temperaments, virtues, colors, and odors. These extramusical associations are significant, since "these multiple correspondences were considered important to the musician, who was expected to select the appropriate mode for each circumstance. They were also useful to the physician, enabling him to administer the suitable treatment for each disease" (ibid.). Extramusical associations are commonly found in treatises during the tenth to the nineteenth centuries.[2] Although these associations were not standardized and varied to a considerable extent, their regular appearance illustrates the desire to order music with the world (e.g., *maqām rāst* was understood to correspond to either Aries or Cancer; see items 219 and 235 in Shiloah 1979).

Scott Marcus characterizes extramusical associations as an important part of the Arab past: "By the beginning of the modern period . . . a large portion of the associations were either forgotten or consciously rejected. Most modern writers omit any mention of extra-musical associations. Nevertheless, a few statements do continue to appear in the modern literature. . . . [E]xtra-musical associations have continued to exist throughout the modern period" (1989, 747). He particularly notes that these associations are not consistent in modern sources (748). Marcus distinguishes between two layers of statements about extramusical associations, those that claim that a *maqām* may convey a specific mood to the listener and those that indicate that a type of song is commonly associated with a specific *maqām* (749). Marcus quotes a theorist in the modern period who states that any emotion evoked from a *maqām* derives from habit; it is not based upon an intrinsic quality of the *maqām* (748).

The doubt about a *maqām* explicitly conveying emotions is most likely responsible for the decline of extramusical associations in modern Arabic musical practice. Marcus offers several common song-type associations that include associating "religious" music, or music in a sacred context, with *rāst*, *ḥijāz* and *bayyātī,* but are not exclusive to them. The chanting of the Qur'an begins in *maqām bayyātī.* He states that some writers and musicians have associated wedding songs with *bayyātī,* love songs with *nahāwand* and *kurdy,* and nationalistic songs with *ajam* (ibid., 750).

The extramusical connections of a *maqām* to emotions are rarely and inconsistently presented in modern sources, but when they do occur, they appear to follow some general patterns. While not every *maqām* has an emotion associated with it, a handful are discussed in this fashion. Marcus gathers together characterizations recorded by a few Arab writers who associate *rāst,* and occasionally *ajam,* with conveying glory, dignity, joy, and liveliness; *ḥijāz* is thought of as "simple" and "pretty," used for pastoral melodies; and *ṣabā* is "delicate" and "tender" and used for sad songs, as is *nahāwand,* which is said also to have a "sweet character" (ibid., 749–52). Marcus elaborates on the characterization of *ṣabā:* "The association of *ṣabā* with feelings of sadness (*ḥuzn*) is the most commonly acknowledged mood/emotional association in the present day, both in the recent literature and among my Cairo and United States informants" (ibid., 749–50). He concludes that associations are left to the realm of the individual musician, since "those so inclined are free to subscribe to such associations on whatever level or to whatever extent he or she chooses. Most seem to limit such associations to a few general thoughts involving a number of adjectives, a few song types, and a few of the most common modes" (ibid., 752).

Both emotional and song-type associations are found among Brooklyn Syrians. However, Syrian Jews associate different emotions and song-types with *maqāmāt* than do a few Arab sources. While extramusical associations are a part of the past for Arab musicians, for Syrian Jews a fundamental component of the liturgy is the *maqām* associations.

Associating the *Maqāmāt* with Prayers

THE SYRIANS' UNDERSTANDING and application of the *maqām* associations reveal how they understand and make use of the *maqāmāt,* how they synthesize their Arab aesthetic with Jewish life, and how they realize their musical sensibilities in actual practice. The Syrian Jewish community's associations as practiced and maintained in their liturgical tradition provide a way of understanding their view of themselves and their culture.

The specific textual thematic association of a *maqām* with the weekly biblical reading and the resulting application of a *maqām* to the prayers of the Sabbath morning service is not unique to Syrian Jews. Other Jewish communities from Arab lands share this practice: Turkish, Egyptian, Lebanese, Iraqi,

Bukharian, and Sephardic Jews in Jerusalem. The most detailed practice today is the Syrian system.[3] No studies have yet compared the various communities' usage of this type of system.

While the *maqām* used for the Torah reading itself—*maqām seyga*—does not vary from week to week, the *maqām* employed during the *ḥazzan*'s rendering of Shaḥarit is chosen for its connection to the theme of the Torah reading for that day.[4] Therefore, the weekly Torah is always read in the same *maqām*—a *seyga* formula is used to recite the text—but the weekly Torah portions determines the *maqām* to be used for the Shaḥarit section of the morning liturgy.

The Brooklyn System

MOSES TAWIL COMMENTS that the adherence to the proper *maqām* for a Sabbath is a unique feature of the Syrian community, saying, "Our system is quite strict" (interview, June 6, 1993). I apply his term "system" to refer to the associations of the *maqāmāt*. Prominent members of the Syrian community believe that these associations are over one hundred years old and were first arranged by Rabbi Raphael Antebi "Taboush." Rabbi Moses Ashear documented the Aleppo practice from his teacher, Taboush, and codified the Brooklyn system (see figure 6) (Lieberman, interview, June 26, 1992; D. Tawil, interview, June 1, 1993).[5]

Four principles characterize the use of the *maqāmāt* in the Brooklyn system: affect, theory, melody, and variety. Each principle is unique and explains a different type of association. The principle of affect relates to three *maqāmāt* in particular: *saba, hijaz,* and *ajam.* Each one of these *maqāmāt* is said to convey a unique emotion that is then related to the thematic content of the biblical reading. The second association principle, theory, explains the use of *maqām rast* in the opening reading of each of the five books of the Bible. Since *maqām rast* is seen as the first *maqām* in Arab music theory, it is therefore applied to the first reading of each of the five books of the Bible. There are exceptions to this rule, which will be discussed later in the chapter. The principle of melody describes the following phenomenon: the content of a *pizmon* mentions a biblical event and, if it is a prominent *pizmon,* the *maqām* of that *pizmon* is then associated with the corresponding Sabbath. The melody association can also refer to an upcoming holiday with which a *pizmon* is associated, and, likewise, this is the *maqām* used the Sabbath preceding the week of the holiday. This is an example of the song-type association described by Marcus. The principle of variety explains the use of *bayat, ḥuseini, nahawand, rahaw nawa, seyga,* and *mahur,* in particular, creating diversity so that a *ḥazzan* does not employ the same *maqām* in two adjacent weeks.

Figure 6. Shir ush'vaḥa, hallel v'zimrah maqām *association chart*

פרשה	מקאם
בראשית	ראשט
נח	שיגא
לך לך	צבא
וירא	רהאוו (נאווה)
חיי שרה	חג׳אז
תולדות	מאהור
ויצא	עג׳ם
וישלח	צבא או שיגא
וישב	רהאוו או נהוונד
מקץ	שיגא
ויגש	ביאת
ויחי	חג׳אז
שמות	ראשט או ביאת
וארא	חוסיני או ראשט
בא	שיגא
בשלח	עג׳ם
יתרו	חוסיני
משפטים	צבא
תרומה	חוסיני
תצוה	שיגא
כי תשא	חג׳אז
ויקהל	חוסיני
פקודי	רהאוו (נאווה)
ויקהל-פקו׳	מחוברות ביאת
ויקרא	ראשט
צו	רהאוו (נאווה)

פרשה	מקאם
שמיני	חוסיני
תזריע	צבא או ביאת
טהור	נהוונד או שיגא
תזריע טהור	מחוברות צבא
אחרי	חג׳אז
קדושים	צבא
אחרי קדו׳	מחוברות ביאת־וחג׳ז
אמור	שיגא חוסיני
בהר סיני	צבא או נאווה
בחוקותי	נהוונד
בהר בחוקו׳	מחוברות צבא
במדבר	חוסיני או ראשט
נשא	ראשט-צבא
בהעלותך	שיגא
שלח לך	חג׳אז
קרח	נהוונד
חֻקת	חוסיני
בלק	מאהור
חקת בלק	מחוברות חוסיני
פינחס	צבא
מטות	נהוונד או רהאוו
מסעי	צבא
מטות ומסעי	מחוברות נהוונד
דברים	חג׳אז
ואתחנן	חוסיני
עקב	שיגא

פרשה	מקאם
ראה	ראשט
שופטים	עג׳ם
תצא	צבא
תבא	שיגא
נצבים	נהוונד
וילך	חוסיני
נצבים־וילך	מחוברות נהוונד
האזינו	מחייאר (שבת שובה)
וזאת הברכה	עג׳ם (יום שמחת תורה)

זמן	מקאם
סוכות	
יום א׳	שיגא
יום ב׳	עג׳ם
שבת חול המועד	ביאת
יום א׳ ״	איראק
יום ב׳ ״	ראשט
יום ג׳ ״	נהוונד
יום ד׳ ״	חוסיני
הושענא רבא	ענין כִּפּור
שמיני עצרת	צבא או סיגא
יום שמחת תורה	עג׳ם
חנוכה	
יום א׳	רהאוו
יום ב׳	איראק

זמן	מקאם
חנוכה	
יום ג׳	שיגא
יום ד׳	צבא
יום ה׳	ראשט
יום ו׳	נהוונד
יום ז׳	שיגא
יום ח׳	ביאת
פורים	
יום א׳	אוג׳
יום ב׳	שיגא
שבת קודם פורים	שיגא
פסח	
שבת קודם חג פסח	רהאוו
יום א׳	שיגא
יום ב׳	עג׳ם
שבת חול המועד	ביאת
יום א׳ ״	איראק
יום ב׳ ״	רהאוו
יום ג׳ ״	ראשט
יום ד׳ ״	ביאת
יום שביעי של פסח	עג׳ם
יום אחרון של פסח	צבא
שבועות	
שבת קודם חג שבועות	חוסיני
יום א׳	שיגא
יום ב׳	עג׳ם

A *maqām* is not exclusive to one association principle. Although affective associations are exclusive to three *maqāmāt* (*saba, hijaz,* and *ajam*) and the theoretical association is exclusive to one *maqām* (*rast*), the melody and variety principles can make use of almost all eleven *maqāmāt. Maqāmāt* of the affect and theory principles are also found in the melody and variety principles. For example, *hijaz* chiefly appears as an affective association, but it can also be employed as a melody association. While *rast* is the only *maqām* of the theory principle, *rast* is also used for variety. Therefore, a *maqām* is not associated exclusively with one principle. Occasionally an association of one principle may override the designated *maqām* by another principle. This study will refer to situations of interrelated principles since such instances are instructive in defining extramusical associations of the *maqāmāt.*

Affective Associations

The three *maqāmāt* that are grouped here—*saba, hijaz,* and *ajam*—separate into two categories. The first (*saba*) refers to an important event that ushers in a serious but unarticulated emotion. The second (*hijaz* and *ajam*) is a direct emotional connotation. *Maqām saba* is associated in the Bible with the event of circumcision, seen as important and serious. Although there is no reference to a particular emotion in this reading, the act of circumcision marks both an important biblical event and turning point in every Jewish boy's life. There is a direct emotional connotation for each of the other two *maqāmāt—hijaz* is associated with sadness and *ajam* with happiness. In general, more is said by Syrian *ḥazzanim* and laymen alike about these three *maqāmāt* than any other, which separates this principle of affective associations as significant and different from the three other principles.

Maqām Saba—*Circumcision Association*

The event of Abraham's circumcision (Heb., *brit milah*)(Genesis 17:1–17:27), recalled in Lekh-Lekha (Genesis 12:1–17:27; biblical reading [BR] 1.3), is the first occurrence of circumcision in the Bible.[6] For the week of the reading of this Torah portion, the *ḥazzan* uses *maqām saba* during the Shaḥarit portion of the prayers: Lekh-Lekha is associated with *saba*. Other biblical readings associated with this *maqām* are Pinḥas (BR 4.9) and Ki Tetse (BR 5.6) (D. Tawil, interview, June 6, 1993).[7] Other occurrences of *saba* also exist (see BRS 2.6, 3.4, 3.8, 4.2, and 4.11).

Ḥakham David Tawil comments on the connection of *maqām saba* and circumcision:

> That we don't know. This is not *halakhah le-Moshe mi-sinai* [a law according to Moses from Mount Sinai, meaning a divine law]—we don't know. It just happens that tradition adapted that format of a melody to identify basic laws [such as circumcision] from the Torah, which in itself is very interesting. The same way that you might tell me why would you use a minor scale against a major scale? Why? . . . The drama in back of it may be more expressive. There is drama in back of this music—there is no doubt about it. . . . Interestingly enough you'll notice, if you come and pray on the High Holidays, we use *saba* in very intimate expressions of worship on the High Holidays.[8] You'll notice that everything is in *saba*—our prayer is saturated with *saba* on the High Holidays. . . . From *saba* are ramifications of many other *maqāms*, but that doesn't matter.[9] The point is what is it expressing, and we find [in] it that kind of feeling. The same feeling that you get when you go from a major scale to a minor scale. You say, "A minor scale! Oh!" You know, it's

> like your mind wanders because, shall we say, [there] is a sense of delicacy to it—very fine threads of music in it. The same stuff that happens with *saba.* (interview, July 29, 1992)

A reason for the association of *saba* with circumcision is not given by Tawil; nor is an explanation deemed necessary for continuing the practice.[10] Tawil tells us the reason for the use of *saba*, or any *maqām*, is not a law decreed "to Moses from Mount Sinai." This is a most interesting point because it is a phrase from rabbinic literature associated with laws whose reasons are not known. His statement that this is their tradition and that it became the format was the general explanation for not only *saba* but the other *maqāmāt* with associations as well, a point reiterated several times by other cantors. The sense of delicacy or means of conveying intimate expressions is the affect associated with *saba.*

Maqām Hijaz—*Death and Sadness*

Hijaz is connected with sections of the Bible where a death or tragic event is recalled, such as the following:

Ḥayyei Sarah (BR 1.5)	death of matriarch Sarah
Va-Yeḥi (BR 1.12)	death of patriarch Jacob
Ki Tissa (BR 2.9)	sin of the golden calf
Aḥarei Mot (BR 3.7)	death of Aaron's sons
Devarim (BR 5.1)	precedes Tisha b'Av holiday

In these five examples, three tell of deaths of biblical figures and two mark pivotal events in Jewish history—one mentioned in the Bible (the sin of the golden calf), and the other connected to a holiday commemorating the destruction of the Temple (Tisha b'Av). The use of *hijaz* for Devarim (BR 5.1) and Tisha b'Av goes beyond the biblical narrative and is an example of an association based on melody creating an intersection with the third association principle, an example of relationship between principles.

Like *maqām saba,* the feeling associated with *maqām hijaz* arises through customary usage. Ḥazzan Moses Tawil says he does not feel that *hijaz* is particularly sad but that it can have that effect (interview, June 6, 1993). In other words, this *maqām* may not be inherently sad but could be rendered in a way that conveys sadness.

The perception is that *hijaz* has a unique character associated with sad events. Thus, it can only be used, like *saba,* at appropriate times. As explained by Moses Tawil in his comments on the performance of *havdalah* (a short liturgical section recited to mark the end of the Sabbath and the beginning of the week), *hijaz* is

> defined for sad occasions—although I love the *maqām hijaz.* I think it is a beautiful *maqām,* and you Ashkenazim, they use it all the time.[11] I love it, but we associate it already with something sad. . . . Nahari [a student of Moses Tawil] touched on *hijaz* twice during *havdalah.* I was saying to him, "Don't stick to it. You know I love it, but don't stick to it." Because the fifteen or twenty that could understand *hijaz* would say, "on Saturday night he is making *hijaz* for us?" You are supposed to laugh; it is suppose to be happy. . . . You are already coming out from the Shabbat.
>
> So, in other words, what I am saying is, there are certain *maqāmāt* which if you do say them at the wrong time you will get criticized; the others, it is not so critical—except this is the tradition, this is what we follow. So they open this book [referring to the *maqām* and biblical reading chart in *Shir ush'vaḥa hallel v'zimrah,* represented in figure 6]. (interview, June 6, 1993)

Maqām Ajam—*Happiness*

For each of the previous associations there is one example that serves as a paradigm. For *saba,* it is Abraham's circumcision in Lekh-Lekha (BR 1.3); for *hijaz,* it is Sarah's death in Ḥayyei Sarah (BR 1.5). The main example of the association of happiness with *ajam* is the portion Be-Shallaḥ (BR 2.4), the section in the biblical narrative where the Jewish people are freed from slavery and leave Egypt (Exodus 13:17–17:15). Three other biblical readings are associated with *ajam:* Va-Yetsi (BR 1.7), Shofetim (BR 5.5), and Ve-zot Ha-Brakhah (5.12).

Several members of the community have their own personal associations with *ajam.* Ḥazzan Isaac Cabasso says that *ajam* is connected with the Exodus from Egypt, the subject of Be-Shallaḥ (BR 2.4) (*pizmon* class, November 18, 1991; interview, May 29, 1992). For Cabasso, happiness is a factor in the association, but the Exodus from Egypt is a trigger that causes the association with *maqām ajam.* Moses Tawil's explanation for the association of Va-Yetse (BR 1.7) with *ajam* is the happy result of Jacob's departure to go out and search for a wife (interview, June 6, 1993). He also characterizes *maqām nahawand* as "happy."

Theoretical Association

The second principle is the theoretical association, that is, the use of *maqām rast* for the opening of each of the five books of the Bible. All the Syrian cantors consulted stated that *rast* is the fundamental *maqām* from which all other *maqāmāt* can be derived. Indeed, this concept is also found in Arabic theoretical writings since the thirteenth century (Shiloah 1981, 35). *Pizmonim* set in *rast* are listed first in *Shir ush'vaḥa hallel v'zimrah*. It is appropriate, therefore, that this *maqām* is associated with the beginning of each book of the Bible.

While the association of theory exists, there are exceptions: *rast* is employed in Bereshit (Genesis; BR 1.1), Shemot (Exodus; BR 2.1), and Va-Yikra (Leviticus; 3.1). Although *bayat* is indicated as an alternate *maqām* for Shemot, *rast* is more commonly used. The reason *bayat* may be employed here, and also why the opening portions of the last two books of the Torah—Be-Midbar (BR 4.1) and Devarim (BR 5.1)—are, in fact, not in *rast,* intersects with the third principle, melodic associations. As mentioned, *rast* is the *maqām* most commonly associated with Shemot (BR 2.1). The other choice is *bayat* (explained in the next section). If *bayat* is used, *rast* will be employed the following week for Va-Era (BR 2.2). Ḥakham Tawil explains that "you still need a *rast* that you missed in order to complete the cycle" (D. Tawil, interview, June 1, 1993). In other words, if one of the five books does not start with *rast,* then *rast* will be employed the following week, or shortly thereafter. Be-Midbar (BR 4.1) and Devarim (BR 5.1) operate in a similar manner due to melodies of *pizmonim* associated with holidays following these biblical readings.

Maqām rast is only listed when it is associated with the beginning of each of the five books of the Bible. Exceptions for this rule are discussed later in this chapter. There are no other associations for *rast* in the *maqām* and biblical reading chart. It is significant that while *maqām rast* does not appear as a *maqām,* it does as a *faṣīlah. Maqām mahur,* a *maqām* belonging to the *rast faṣīlah* (see table 5), is used for Toledot (BR 1.6), Balak (4.7), and Ha'azinu (BR 5.11) so that there should be a variety of *maqāmāt* employed throughout the system (M. Tawil, interview, June 6, 1993). The use of *rast* only for the first biblical reading, in practice or in concept, reinforces its unique principle: Arabic theory privileging *rāst* as a starting point to understand *maqām* theory is equated with the opening of a book of the Bible. Thus, the theoretical association demonstrates an external musical reason as an association principle that contrasts with the affect principle equating an emotion to an event in the biblical reading.

Melodic Association

A *pizmon* is often associated with particular biblical readings or a holiday. For a holiday association, the melody of the *pizmon* provides the basis for the *maqām* of the day. *Pizmon* El Me'od Na'alah (*SUHV* #266) is in *maqām bayat;* based on its textual content, this *pizmon* is connected with the biblical reading of Shemot (BR 2.1).[12] Since *bayat* is the *maqām* of this *pizmon,* it may be used for that Sabbath. The use of *saba* to announce a circumcision, discussed earlier, and the use of *bayat* for Shemot are two examples of a melody of a *pizmon* determining the *maqām* for the prayers. The former announces an event in the Bible or a ceremonial occasion such as a circumcision (as described by Moses Tawil). The latter is simply a *pizmon* whose content mentions aspects of the associated biblical reading.

The cases of Be-Midbar (BR 4.1) and Devarim (BR 5.1) serve as examples of association by melody for reasons based on a holiday association—a different type of association for this third principle. There are several *pizmonim* associated with the holiday of Shavuot (a two-day holiday, as celebrated outside of Israel) in *bayat, ḥuseini,* and *ajam.*[13] *Pizmon* Da'at u-mizmah (*Shir ush'vaḥa hallel v'zimrah,* #334), is in *ḥuseini;* the originating melody is Tsari ba'al agfun and most commonly employed to represent this holiday. The melody of this *pizmon* is used on the Sabbath before the holiday (Cabasso, interview, May 29, 1992). Therefore, just as *saba* announces a circumcision, *ḥuseini* announces the impending holiday of Shavuot. The biblical reading of Be-Midbar, the first reading for the book of Numbers, usually precedes the Shavuot holiday. The *maqām* for this Sabbath is *ḥuseini,* not *rast* because of the association by melody. If *rast* is not used for Be-Midbar, it will be used for the following Sabbath to maintain the theoretical association of beginning each book of the Pentateuch in *rast.*

Similarly, since Devarim precedes the Tisha b'Av holiday, *maqām hijaz* is used in order to reflect the sadness of this holiday. The "missed" *rast* appears three weeks later with Re'eh (BR 5.4) because Va-Etḥannan (BR 5.2) and Ekev (BR 5.3) each have their own *maqām* associations that preclude the use of *rast* (D. Tawil, interview, June 1, 1993). Both of these examples also illustrate the interrelationship between the first three principles, that affective and melodic associations can override the theoretical association. The theoretical association will appear in future weeks, when no affective or melodic associations conflict.

The association by melody identified with a holiday differs from the melody association determined by a *pizmon* in that the former signals to the congregation that something is about to take place during the upcoming week. This is similar to the Ashkenazic liturgical practice of announcing the new month on the Sabbath preceding the week in which the new month begins. Both Sephardic and Ashkenazic liturgy bless the new Hebrew month on the preceding Sabbath. It is common in Ashkenazic musical liturgical practice to employ a melody associated with a holiday appearing in the upcoming month for the text of the blessing for the new month. This musical custom is followed in concept by the Syrians but to a different extent. Whereas Ashkenazic Jews make use of a melody to sing the blessing for the new month, the Syrians use both the associated melody and the appropriate *maqām* throughout the cantor's recitation of the service.

Variety

Some biblical readings have a clear *maqām* designation, as seen in the three previous principles. In other cases there are no associations to be found within the biblical reading or holiday. The principle of variety specifies a *maqām,* somewhat loosely defined when it happens. In order to provide an assortment of *maqāmāt* from week to week, the Brooklyn system indicates the use of *seyga, nahawand, rahaw nawa, bayat, ḥuseini,* and *mahur.* These six are the main *maqāmāt* employed for variety. In some instances *rast* and *saba* can be used for variety; when that is the case, the reason for their use in the Brooklyn system is not based on only one principle. All of the cantors assert that the same *maqām* will not be used in two successive weeks; indeed, no *maqām* repeats in contiguous weeks (see table 10). It is even uncommon to have a *maqām* repeated two weeks after its use. One exception is the use of *ḥuseini* for Yitro (BR 2.5) and again two weeks later for Terumah (BR 2.7).

Seyga is unique because it is the *maqām* for the biblical reading. Since its use is so common within the service, four of the five sections of the Sabbath morning service are based on this *maqām.* The appearance of *seyga* in the *maqām* and biblical reading association system is not unexpected. Many *pizmonim* for the holiday of Purim are in *seyga;* Tetsavveh (BR 2.8) precedes this holiday, so *seyga* is used on that Sabbath (Cabasso, *pizmonim* class, March 9, 1992). Moses Tawil reasons that *seyga* or *saba* could be used for Va-Yishlaḥ (BR 1.8) only for variety. The need for variety also describes the use of *saba* not only for circumcision (M. Tawil, interview, June 6, 1993). David Tawil explains the possibility of substitution of either *maqām* in Va-Yishlaḥ by the fact that they both mention commandments (interview, July 29, 1992). He says, "They switch off for variety [especially] if they are in close proximity" (interview, June 1, 1993). This adds another dimension to *saba.* It can have two associations: affect and variety. Thus, the desire for variety can add to the possible uses of a *maqām*.

Double Parashah

Certain circumstances create the need for two biblical readings on a Sabbath; this is known as a double parashah (Heb., portion). The first occurrence of a double parashah is Va-Yakhel-Pekudei (BR 2.12).[14] According to Jewish law, the prophetic reading associated with the Sabbath reflects the second biblical portion.[15] In the case of Va-Yakhel-Pekudei, the prophetic reading is the reading associated with Pekudei. The Syrian practice is to take the *maqām* of the first biblical portion but read the second prophetic reading as prescribed. In the case of the double parashah under discussion, *ḥuseini* is associated with Va-Yakhel (BR 2.10) and *rahaw nawa* with Pekudei (BR 2.11). When these portions are brought together (doubled), *maqām bayat*, the principal mode of the *faṣīlah* to which *ḥuseini* belongs, is used. One suggestion for reconciling the difference between the practice of the prophetic reading and *maqām* association during a double parashah is that they can be seen to balance each other. The prophetic reading continues the theme of the last biblical reading, while the *maqām* maintains the continuity with the first biblical reading.

One exception to this rule is the double biblical reading Aḥarei Mot-Kedoshim (BR 3.9). Aḥarei Mot (BR 3.7) is associated with *hijaz,* as discussed earlier, and Kedoshim is associated with *saba.* This double parashah should be *hijaz,* but it is not. Instead, both *bayat* and *hijaz* are used. This is unusual for several reasons. *Hijaz* is not used by itself. Two *maqāmāt* are used instead of one. If two are to be used, one would expect *hijaz* and *saba,* not *hijaz* and *bayat.* David Tawil explains that Aḥarei Mot (BR 3.7) has a strong association with *hijaz* because of the death of Aaron's sons. The second reading, Kedoshim (BR 3.8), relates to *saba* because circumcision is mentioned. Therefore, the *ḥazzan* needs to incorporate both musical aesthetics. This, according to Tawil, could not be done through *hijaz* and *saba; hijaz* and *saba* would not have enough contrast.[16] He claims that while one could go to *saba* from *hijaz,* this is not done. Instead, the melancholy feeling of *hijaz* contrasts with what he described in this instance as the "energetic and pleasing quality of *bayat.*" The modulation takes place halfway through the cantor's recitation of Shaḥarit. Tawil explains, "The important thing is did he [a cantor] mention *ḥijaz* and *bayat* in his prayers. . . . [Instead of one] main *maqām* there are two. How this is done depends on how clever you are" (interview, June 1, 1993). Tawil's discussion shows how a dual or competing association is accommodated musically. It once again underscores the perceived unique characteristics of specific *maqāmāt.*

Personal Choice

There is some freedom for *ḥazzanim* to make choices in the use of *maqāmāt*, but only during specific weeks. On some days a *ḥazzan* who does not make use of the correct *maqām* will appear as if he does not know what he is doing (D. Tawil, interviews, July 29, 1993, June 1, 1993; M. Tawil, interview, June 6, 1993). The choice of which *maqām* to use at certain times gives the *ḥazzan* the opportunity to express his individual associations.

Isaac Cabasso feels there is a problem with Va-Yishlaḥ (BR 1.8), because, according to the Brooklyn system, the *maqām* would be either *saba* or *seyga*. He feels *seyga* should not be used, because it will be used for Mi-Kets (1.10) two weeks later. Using it for Va-Yishlaḥ will not provide enough variety. Ḥazzan Cabasso, expressing an interpretation not followed by Moses Tawil, also says there is a problem with using *saba*, since this *maqām* is usually associated with circumcision. Cabasso feels that the specific circumcision discussed in this biblical reading does not lend itself to *maqām saba*. The circumcision described in Va-Yishlaḥ occurs when the men of the city of Shekhem decide to convert after Shekhem, the son of Ḥamor, rapes Jacob's daughter Dina. After the community's circumcisions, Shimon and Levi kill all the men of Shekhem (Genesis 34:1–34:31). Therefore, Cabasso chooses to use *rast*—his favorite *maqām*—instead of *saba* to express the biblical reading (*pizmonim* class, November 18, 1991). He does not feel that the circumcision described in Va-Yishlaḥ merits placement at the same level as other circumcisions discussed in the Bible. This shows how personal association and interpretation can effect the choice of *maqām* and thereby reshape its meaning.

In summary, the Brooklyn system of associations between *maqām* and biblical reading can be organized according to four principles: affect, theory, melody, and variety. There are certain strong associations that must be followed; the affective associations must be followed by Syrian cantors in Brooklyn, as not to do so would be considered wrong. There is room for personal interpretations as well, particularly when a *maqām* is used for variety. The principal of variety is an important component that dictates rules such as not repeating a *maqām* from one week to the next. Ḥakham David Tawil puts this into perspective: "Looking for a reason for each parashah [biblical reading] is incorrect. One can only think in generalities. This is not *halakhah le-Moshe mi-Sinai*. Be careful not to make ironclad theories. . . . There may have been a *maqām* associated with a *pizmon* [and, consequently, with a biblical reading]. At this stage of the game we lost track. . . . The goal is to provide pleasant programming, and this has become standardized through usage" (interview, June 1, 1993). Associations of the *maqāmāt* are a contemporary part of organizing the liturgy of the Syrians in Brooklyn. The overall system has fixed requirements with the overall goal of achieving variety.

Israel Associations and Other Scholarly Studies

THE FOLLOWING COMMENTS on the Israel associations are based on a chart in *Shirei zimrah ha-shaleim* (1988) and an interview with a Syrian cantor in Israel—Ḥazzan Yaakov Bozo.[17]

Cantor Bozo's explanations for maqām associations are similar to those I discovered in Brooklyn with some slight differences. The theoretical and melodic associations are common. The melodic association principle, not the principle of affect, in Cantor Bozo's opinion explains the use of *saba, hijaz,* and *ajam.* Since there are *pizmonim* whose texts mention circumcision, *saba* is then necessary when it appears in the biblical reading for the Sabbath. Likewise, happy events are described in *ajam pizmonim,* hence the use of *ajam* for happy events mentioned in a biblical reading. For Cantor Bozo both are associations of melody rather then affect. He also uses the association of melody to explain *ḥuseini.* Since many *pizmonim* in *ḥuseini* mention the receiving of the Torah, biblical readings that refer to the receiving of the Law use this *maqām,* as in Yitro (BR 2.5) and Va-Etḥannan (BR 5.2). In effect, the affective princi-

Table 11. Maqām *and biblical reading associations with Cantor Bozo and Idelsohn Explanations*

Biblical reading	Israel associations		Early-twentieth-century compilation	
	maqām	Cantor Bozo's reason	*maqām*	Idelsohn's reason
Genesis				
1.1. Bereshit	*rast*	start of book	*rast*	
1.2. No'aḥ	*bayat*		*iraq*	
1.3. Lekh Lekha	*saba*	Abraham and Isaac's circumcisions	*saba*	circumcision
1.4. Va-Yera	*nawa*		*nawa*	
1.5. Ḥayyei Sarah	*hijaz*	Sarah's death	*hijaz*	death
1.6. Toledot	*mahur*		*mahur*	
1.7. Va-Yetse	*ajam*	Jacob's wedding	*jaharkah*	
1.8. Va-Yishlaḥ	*bayat*		*iraq*	
1.9. Va-Yeshev	*rahaw*	Joseph in jail	*rahaw*	selling of Joseph
1.10. Mi-Kets	*seyga*		*seyga*	Hanukkah; Inauguration of altar
1.11. Va-Yiggash	*bayat or saba*		*bayat*	
1.12. Va-Yeḥi	*hijaz*	Jacob's death	*hijaz*	Jacob's death

Exodus				
2.1. Shemot	*bayat*		*rast*	
2.2. Va-Era	*nahawand*		*ḥuseini* or *nawa*	
2.3. Bo	*seyga*		*iraq*	
2.4. Be-Shallaḥ	*ajam*	leaving Egypt, happy	*ajam*	Song of the Sea
2.5. Yitro	*ḥuseini*	giving of the Torah	*seyga* (or *ḥuseini*)	giving of the Torah
2.6. Mishpatim	*saba*	circumcision	*saba*	remembering covenant
2.7. Terumah	*bayat*		*seyga*	Torah, and checking of Temple
2.8. Tetsavveh	*seyga*		*seyga*	Tabernacle
2.9. Ki Tissa	*hijaz*	building of the golden calf	*hijaz*	death
2.10. Va-Yakhel	*ḥuseini*		*ḥuseini*	
2.11. Pekudei	*nawa*		*nawa*	
Leviticus				
3.1. Va-Yikra	*rast*	start of book	*rast*	
3.2. Tsav	*nawa*		*iraq*	
3.3. Shemini	*ḥuseini*		*ḥuseini*	
3.4. Tazri'a	*saba*	circumcision after childbirth	*bayat*	
3.5. Taḥor	*saba or seyga*		*iraq*	
3.7. Aḥarei Mot	*hijaz*	death of Aaron's sons	*hijaz*	death
3.8. Kedoshim	*saba*		*saba*	circumcision
3.10. Emor	*seyga*		*ushayran*	
3.11. Be-Har	*nawa*		*nawa*	
3.12. Be-Ḥukkotai	*bayat*		*nawa* or *bayat*	
Numbers				
4.1. Be-Midbar	*bayat*		*muḥayyar*	
4.2. Naso	*ḥuseini* or *saba*		*saba*	circumcision
4.3. Be-Ha'alotkha	*seyga*		*seyga*	Tabernacle
4.4. Shelaḥ Lekha	*nahawand*		*iraq*	
4.5. Koraḥ	*ḥuseini*		*ḥuseini*	
4.6. Ḥukkat	*rast*		*rast*	
4.7. Balak	*bayat*		*bayat*	
4.9. Pinḥas	*saba*	circumcision	*saba*	circumcision
4.10. Mattot	*nawa*		*nawa*	
4.11. Masei	*saba*		*saba?*	
Deuteronomy				
5.1. Devarim	*hijaz*	before holiday of Tisha B'Av	*hijaz*	death

5.2. Va-Etḥannan	*ḥuseini*	Ten Commandments	*ḥuseini*	
5.3. Ekev	*seyga*		*seyga*	Torah making tablets
5.4. Re'eh	*rast*		*iraq*	
5.5. Shofetim	*ajam*		*seyga*	Torah
5.6. Ki Tetse	*saba*		*saba*	circumcision
5.7. Ki Tavo	*seyga*		*iraq*	
5.8. Nitsavim	*nawa*		*nawa*	
5.9. Va-Yelekh	*rast*			
5.11. Ha'azinu	*ḥuseini*		*ḥuseini*	
5.12. Ve-zot Ha-Brakhah	*ajam*		*ajam*	blessing and joy

ple can be deduced, but it is not emphasized. Instead, melodic associations, because of related *pizmonim,* are the main determinant for Ḥazzan Bozo.

Kumiko Yayama, in her work on *bakkashot* in Israel, confirms the happy association with *rast* and *ajam.* She documents that *maqām bayat* is "thought to represent the typical and unique feelings of the Middle Eastern people" (2003, 189). Indeed *hijaz* is seen as conveying sadness, and for some this is also true of *saba.* She also states that some *maqāmāt* are associated with groups of people: *saba* with Iraqi Jews and *huseini* with Kurdish Jews (ibid., xv and 189).

Personal choice is clearly articulated by Cantor Bozo, but variety is not; perhaps personal choice incorporates variety. For example, in Va-Yeshev (BR 1.9) the selling of Joseph and his subsequent imprisonment necessitates the use of *maqām rahaw* because there are *pizmonim* in this *maqām* that mention a jail.[18] Bozo explains that *rahaw* is used in some instances, although not exclusively, where a jail is mentioned in the biblical text. However, he says *ḥazzanim* are free to "make what they want if they are not happy with this." There are certain instances, such as the strong affective associations, where the specified *maqām* must be used; in other instances it is not imperative to follow the chart exactly.

The publication of *Shirei Zimrah* reflects the practice of Syrian Jews in Israel, mainly in Jerusalem.[19] To date there have been four publications of *Shirei Zimrah,* the full text of the publication is *Sefer Shirei Zimrah haShalem.* The book contains a collection of *piyyutim* and also lists particular *piyyut* texts to be sung for various celebrations and liturgical singing stations, and it includes a *maqām* and biblical reading chart. The first publication was by Hayyim Shaul Abbud, in 1936, who also published a revised edition in 1953. Abbud died in 1977, and his son Shlomo published one edition in 1988 and the fourth edition in 1995.[20]

A comparison of the *maqām* and biblical reading charts of these editions reveals interesting issues regarding this practice. The tables in the 1936 and 1953 editions of *Shirei Zimrah* are identical. When comparing the 1936/1953 and 1988 versions, forty-two of the fifty-seven associations of the biblical reading are the same (table 12 lists the discrepancies). The significant difference in the two editions is that the 1936/1953 table lists choices between two *maqāmāt*, where the 1988 edition only includes a single *maqām*. Many of the differences deal with *maqām bayat*. The 1936/1953 table offers more choices on certain occasions where bayat is one of the choices; in these instances the 1988 edition only has one *maqām* that is listed. For example, for No'aḥ (BR 1.2) the 1936/1953 edition lists *iraq* or *bayat*, where the 1988 edition indicates only *bayat*. In other instances two different *maqāmāt* are listed in the 1936/1953 edition and *bayat* is indicated in the 1988 editions (see BRS 1.8 and 4.1). The 1936/1953 table reflects an older practice in Israel. Where the 1936/1953 edition of *Shirei Zimrah* lists *maqām iraq*, the same practice appears in Abraham Zvi Idelsohn's compilations (BRS 1.2, 3.2, 4.4). Other instances indicate similar practices between the 1936/1953 table and the Brooklyn practice (BRS 1.8, 2.1, 3.10). While the 1936/1953 table is closely related to the 1988 edition, it is clear that there has been some changes with the weekly associations. Viewing the 1936/1953 table as a benchmark in this practice over time, the 1988 edition has become more like the Brooklyn tradition, showing the maintenance of this practice in Israel and Brooklyn with similar changes.[21] Thus, many elements of the Brooklyn system find their parallel here. In addition, there are some unique characteristics that are either found in the Israel system or are personal preferences of Cantor Bozo. Clearly, the Brooklyn and the Israel associations emanate from a similar tradition.

Table 12. *Discrepancies in Shirei Zimrah 1936/1953 and 1988 charts*

Biblical reading	Shirei Zimrah 1936 and 1953	Shirei Zimrah 1988
Genesis		
1.1. Bereshit	*rast* or *bayat*	*rast*
1.2. No'aḥ	*iraq* or *bayat*	*bayat*
1.8. Va-Yishlaḥ	*saba* or *seyga*	*bayat*
Exodus		
2.1. Shemot	*bayat* or *rast*	*bayat*
2.2. Va-Era	*ḥuseini* or *seyga*	*nahawand*
2.3. Bo	*seyga* or *rast*	*seyga*
2.7. Terumah	*bayat* or *saba*	*bayat*
Leviticus		
3.2. Tsav	*iraq*	*nawa*
3.4. Tazri'a	*bayat* or *rast*	*saba*
3.10. Emor	*ḥuseini* or *seyga*	*seyga*

Numbers		
4.1. Be-Midbar	*saba* or *rast*	*bayat*
4.4. Shelaḥ Lekha	*iraq* or *nawa*	*nahawand*
Dueteronomy		
5.4. Re'eh	*seyga* or *rast*	*rast*
5.5. Shofetim	*saba*	*ajam*
5.6. Ki Tetse	*rast*	*saba*

Idelsohn provides more information to understand this Syrian Jewish practice.[22] His presentation of the *maqām* and biblical reading associations, published in three sources in the early twentieth century, highlight the main points found in the Brooklyn system and include additional associations as well as reasons for the associations.[23] The information provided by Idelsohn is based upon his work with Syrian Jews in Israel in the early twentieth century. The value of his study lies in his comparative knowledge of the musical practices of other Jewish communities and his broad knowledge of Arab *maqām* usage (1916, 1923a, 1923b).

Table 11 lists Idelsohn's reasons for specific associations, particularly the three *maqāmāt* with affective associations. Additionally, Idelsohn offers affective descriptions of *maqāmāt* and the general principles for applying the associations. Idelsohn explains, "[One] establishes respectively to the contents of the weekly order [biblical reading] an existing character of an analogous *maqām*" (1923a, 37); this is similarly explicated in the Hebrew (Idelsohn 1923b, 107). A summary of Idelsohn's maqām associations is as follows:

maqām	affect	association
saba	purity or innocence	circumcision
hijaz	sorrow	death
ajam	liveliness	departure from Egypt
simḥat	Torah	bridegroom called to Torah

The reasons for the associations parallel the affective association found in the Brooklyn system and go a step further by attaching affect to *maqām saba*. Idelsohn also asserts that *seyga* is used for the Torah reading and is associated with biblical portions concerning the Tabernacle and Jewish law (1923a, 39; 1923b, 107). Each occurrence of *seyga* has an explanation of either "Tabernacle" or "Torah"; the latter refers to laws that are mentioned in the reading. *Maqām ḥuseini* is described as being associated with readings of rebukes, intercessions, and warning cries (see Idelsohn 1923a, 39).[24] No explanation for this is given in any of the charts; nor is this association found in the Brooklyn system.

Idelsohn points out that associations are not always followed exactly but asserts that generally the connections are observed with the Exodus from Egypt (*ajam*), Torah and Tabernacle (*seyga*), circumcision (*saba*), and death (*hijaz*) (1923b, 108). At the beginning of the twentieth century affective associations were fixed and variety was intrinsic to the application of other *maqāmāt*. Both features still practiced among Brooklyn Syrians.

Idelsohn makes no mention of the theoretical and melodic principles. He does, however, offer an explanation for why *hijaz* is associated with death and sorrow: "For the Sabbath in which its biblical reading discusses death they established *maqām hijaz,* which is sad and is the melody of sorrow. The Arabs sing in this *maqām* songs of sorrow and of accompanying the dead (and this goes for the Eastern Christians)." (1923b, 107). According to Idelsohn, the melodies used in Arabic music that reflect sorrow and death are in *hijaz,* clearly generating or reinforcing association with sorrow and death in Syrian liturgy. However, this contradicts widely held eastern Arab musical notion of the use of *saba* for sadness. In his reference to the use of *ḥuseini* for rebukes, intercessions, and warning cries, Idelsohn says that *ḥuseini* "is also used by the Shiites for these purposes" (1923a, 39). His claim suggests a further connection with some particular Arab religious musical practices. Unfortunately, he does not elaborate further.

Comparison of the Brooklyn System, Israel Associations, and Other Scholarly Studies

A COMPARISON OF the Brooklyn system, Israel associations, and Idelsohn's compilation is useful for analytical purposes and provides another level of understanding of Syrian extramusical associations.[25] All three Syrian examples of associations have a large amount of agreement in their usage of a specific *maqām* for the same biblical reading, as seen in the three *maqām* columns of table 10. In other instances, two are in agreement and the third indicates a different *maqām*. The Israel associations and Idelsohn's compilation use *nawa* instead of *rahaw nawa*. In most cases, practices charted by Idelsohn in the early twentieth century have been maintained in Jerusalem and Brooklyn, demonstrating historical depth to present usage. The three examples of Syrian *maqām* associations disagree completely only during a few weeks of the year; for instance, Va-Yishlaḥ (BR 1.8) and Shelaḥ Lekha (BR 4.4) call for three fundamentally different *maqāmāt*.

If the *maqām* of a given week is considered by *faṣīlah*, regrouping each *maqām* by its family type, the agreement of all three systems of association is more pronounced (see table 13). In general, Idelsohn is more precise in regard to the specific *maqām* variant that should be used for a given week. He indicates the use of *iraq, jaharkah,* and *ushayran,* none of which are found in the Brooklyn system or Israel associations (see table 10). The readings in the first, second, and fifth books have a higher degree of agreement in Syrian *maqām* associations, with more variability in the third and fourth books. This is most likely a result of the lack of specific subjects in Leviticus and Numbers that carry strong associations, such as those of circumcision, death, joy, or holidays that have an association by melody.

Table 13. Maqām *and biblical reading associations (by* faṣīlah*)*

Biblical Reading	Brooklyn system	Israel associations	Early-twentieth-century compilation by Idelsohn
Genesis			
1.1. Bereshit	*rast*	*rast*	*rast*
1.2. No'aḥ	*seyga*	*bayat*	*seyga*
1.3. Lekh Lekha	*saba*	*saba*	*saba*
1.4 Va-Yera	*rahaw* (*nawa*)	*nawa*	*nawa*
1.5. Ḥayyei Sarah	*hijaz*	*hijaz*	*hijaz*
1.6. Toledot	*rast*	*rast*	*rast*
1.7. Va-Yetse	*ajam*	*ajam*	*ajam*
1.8. Va-Yishlaḥ	*saba* or *seyga*	*bayat*	*seyga*
1.9. Va-Yeshev	*rahaw* or *nahawand*	*rahaw*	*rahaw*
1.10. Mi-Kets	*seyga*	*seyga*	*seyga*
1.11. Va-Yiggash	*bayat*	*bayat or saba*	*bayat*
1.12. Va-Yeḥi	*hijaz*	*hijaz*	*hijaz*
Exodus			
2.1. Shemot	*rast* or *bayat*	*bayat*	*rast*
2.2. Va-Era	*bayat* or *rast*	*nahawand*	*bayat* or *nawa*
2.3. Bo	*seyga*	*seyga*	*seyga*
2.4. Be-Shallaḥ	*ajam*	*ajam*	*ajam*
2.5. Yitro	*bayat*	*bayat*	*seyga* [or *bayat*]
2.6. Mishpatim	*saba*	*saba*	*saba*
2.7. Terumah	*bayat*	*bayat*	*seyga*
2.8. Tetsavveh	*seyga*	*seyga*	*seyga*
2.9. Ki Tissa	*hijaz*	*hijaz*	*hijaz*
2.10. Va-Yakhel	*bayat*	*bayat*	*bayat*
2.11. Pekudei	*rahaw* (*nawa*)	*nawa*	*nawa*
2.12. Va-Yakhel-Pekudei	*bayat*		

Leviticus			
3.1. Va-Yikra	*rast*	*rast*	*rast*
3.2. Tsav	*rahaw* (*nawa*)	*nawa*	*seyga*
3.3. Shemini	*bayat*	*bayat*	*bayat*
3.4. Tazri'a	*saba* or *bayat*	*saba*	*bayat*
3.5. Taḥor	*nahawand* or *seyga*	*saba* or *seyga*	*seyga*
3.6. Tazri'a-Taḥor	*saba*		
3.7. Aḥarei Mot	*hijaz*	*hijaz*	*hijaz*
3.8. Kedoshim	*saba*	*saba*	*saba*
3.9. Aḥarei Mot-Kedoshim	*bayat-hijaz*		
3.10. Emor	*seyga bayat*	*seyga*	*bayat*
3.11. Be-Har	*saba* or *nahawand*	*nawa*	*nawa*
3.12. Be-Ḥukkotai	*nahawand*	*bayat*	*nawa* or *bayat*
3.13. Be-Har-Be-Ḥukkotai	*saba*		
Numbers			
4.1. Be-Midbar	*bayat* or *rast*	*bayat*	*bayat*
4.2. Naso	*rast-saba*	*bayat* or *saba*	*saba*
4.3. Be-Ha'alotkha	*seyga*	*seyga*	*seyga*
4.4. Shelaḥ Lekha	*hijaz*	*nahawand*	*seyga*
4.5. Koraḥ	*nahawand*	*bayat*	*bayat*
4.6. Ḥukkat	*bayat*	*rast*	*rast*
4.7. Balak	*rast*	*bayat*	*bayat*
4.8. Ḥukkat-Balak	*bayat*		
4.9. Pinḥas	*saba*	*saba*	*saba*
4.10. Mattot	*nahawand* or *rahaw*	*nawa*	*nawa*
4.11. Masei	*saba*	*saba*	*saba?*
4.12. Mattot-Masei	*nahawand*		
Deuteronomy			
5.1. Devarim	*hijaz*	*hijaz*	*hijaz*
5.2. Va-Etḥannan	*bayat*	*bayat*	*bayat*
5.3. Ekev	*seyga*	*seyga*	*seyga*
5.4. Re'eh	*rast*	*rast*	*seyga*
5.5. Shofetim	*ajam*	*ajam*	*seyga*
5.6. Ki Tetse	*saba*	*saba*	*saba*
5.7. Ki Tavo	*seyga*	*seyga*	*seyga*
5.8. Nitsavim	*nahawand*	*nawa*	*nawa*
5.9. Va-Yelekh	*hijaz*	*rast*	
5.10. Nitsavim-Va-Yelekh	*nahawand*		
5.11. Ha'azinu	*bayat*	*bayat*	*bayat*
5.12. Ve-zot Ha-Brakhah	*ajam*	*ajam*	*ajam*

The association based on the affective principle provides the most agreement in Syrian *maqām* associations. The theoretical principle is also employed in Syrian *maqām* associations even though it is not an articulated feature within Idelsohn's explanation. Thus, the four *maqāmāt* connected with affective and theoretical associations (*saba, hijaz, ajam,* and *rast*) are employed for specific purposes and are used similarly. Table 14 lists the number and percentage of use of the *maqāmāt* in Syrian *maqām* associations; the first half of table 14 refers to the associations found in table 10, and the second half refers to the regrouped *maqām* associations by *fașīlah* in table 13.[26] The usage of *saba* is the most flexible of the four *maqāmāt.* This is because of its use beyond the association to circumcision, which is not clearly articulated in any of three practices of Syrian *maqām* associations. The consistency of occurrences based on affect and function, the affective and theoretical principles, respectively, are more consistent in Syrian *maqām* associations than the principles of melody and variety.

Table 14. Maqāmāt *used in* maqām *and biblical reading associations*

	All *maqāmāt* used in table 10					
	Brooklyn system		Israel associations		Idelsohn compilation	
	Number	Percentage	Number	Percentage	Number	Percentage
ajam	4	5	4	7	2	4
jaharkah	0	0	0	0	1	2
rast	7	10	5	9	4	7
mahur	2	3	1	2	1	2
nahawand	9	12	2	4	0	0
bayat	5	7	8	14	4	7
ḥuseini	10	14	7	12	7	13
ushayran	0	0	0	0	1	2
muḥayyar	1	1	0	0	1	2
saba	12	16	10	18	7	13
hijaz	8	11	5	9	5	9
seyga	10	14	8	14	7	13
iraq	0	0	0	0	8	14
rahaw nawa	5	7	7	12	8	14
Total	73		57		56	

Grouped by *faṣīlah*						
ajam	4	5	4	7	3	5
rast	9	12	6	11	5	9
nahawand	9	12	2	4	0	0
bayat	16	22	15	26	13	23
saba	12	16	10	18	7	13
hijaz	8	11	5	9	5	9
seyga	10	14	8	14	15	27
rahaw nawa	5	7	7	12	8	14
Total	73		57		56	

The *bayat faṣīlah* comprises nearly one-quarter of the occurrences in Syrian *maqām* associations, making *bayat* the most frequently used *maqām* in the Brooklyn system and Israel associations. *Seyga* is most commonly used according to Idelsohn. This recurrent use of *bayat* in Brooklyn is not surprising, for it is the *maqām* with the largest number of *pizmonim* and *bakkashot* in *Shir ush'vaḥa hallel v'zimrah* (see table 4). *Maqām ḥuseini* is used quite consistently in Syrian *maqām* associations. This is surprising because there is no reason articulated for the associations of *bayat* or *ḥuseini,* that is, no affect is attributed to either *maqām.* Occasional statements were made in Brooklyn regarding an association of melody for *ḥuseini* on specific holidays such as Shavuot—used for Be-Midbar (BR 4.1). Bozo claims *ḥuseini* was associated with the giving of the Torah, whereas Idelsohn holds that it was used for rebukes, intercessions, and warning cries. When comparing the usage of *bayat* and *ḥuseini* in the charts of *Shirei Zimrah,* there is also some inconsistency (see table 12). The 1936/1953 table of *Shirei Zimrah* makes use of *ḥuseini,* while the 1988 version does not. Despite this lack of agreement in the explanation of *bayat* and *ḥuseini,* these two *maqāmāt* are consistently associated with the same biblical readings. This suggests that although no explanation for their use is articulated in Brooklyn, a reason once existed that is now forgotten.

Greater variability in usage is found with *seyga, nahawand,* and *rahaw nawa.* According to Idelsohn, *seyga* is used for 27 percent of the readings (see table 14), almost twice the total found in the other two. He lists seven instances of *seyga* usage and eight for *iraq.* While he always gives a reason when *seyga* is used, he provides only one for *iraq. Nahawand* is the most variable in its degree of occurrence throughout Syrian *maqām* associations. In the Brooklyn system, *nahawand* is commonly used. It is not commonly used in Israel and not at all according to Idelsohn. Perhaps the frequent use in Brooklyn reflects Western influence, since *nahawand* is theoretically near equivalent to a minor scale; this may indicate the inclusion of more European melodies during the twentieth century.

Some *maqāmāt* are highly variable in both their usage and explanations of their use. Variety is the principle for such circumstances in Brooklyn. Some biblical readings may have been determined by a *maqām* that is no longer known through an associated *pizmon*. It is even logical to assume that the affective association may have been a melodic association at an earlier date. Since Cantor Bozo stated each of the affective associations were based on *pizmonim* melodies, these *pizmonim* may not be practiced in Brooklyn. Indeed Ḥakham David Tawil says, as quoted earlier, "There may have been a *maqām* associated with a *pizmon*. At this stage of the game we lost track." (D. Tawil, interview, June 1, 1993). The comparison of the Brooklyn system to contemporary practice in Israel and historical practices, documented by Idelsohn, suggests that the affective associations were a particular type of melody associations, but the melodies are no longer practiced. Further research of other Syrian cantors in Israel and in other locations is needed to confirm or develop these insights.

Analysis on a Wider Level

CONSIDERATION OF THE Brooklyn system within a broader framework through its relation to Arab practices demonstrates the Judeo-Arabic synthesis. The Brooklyn association of *ajam* with joy is consistent with the occasional comment suggesting similar modern Arab associations. *Hijaz* and *saba*, on the other hand, are associated in an opposite way among Syrian Jews in comparison to Arab extramusical associations. Sadness is associated with *hijaz* for the Syrian Jews, while *saba* commonly carries this signification for Arabic musicians. This is significant particularly since sadness associated with *ṣabā*, the most common association found in modern Arab musical sources, among Arab musicians is routine, and the sadness affect is not found among Syrian Jews in Brooklyn, Israel, or in accordance with Idelsohn. The Syrian Jewish affective associations reflect their own practice, diverging from common practices found among Arab musicians.

Unique to Syrian Jews is the adherence to their system of associations. The affective associations for *saba* and *hijaz* and the melodic associations reflect Syrian Jewish local style, which is independent of Arab musical practices, emphasizing that the systematic organization of the *maqāmāt* can reflect local styles (Shiloah 1981, 39). Melodic associations, a derivative of song-type associations found on occasion in Arab practice, is a significant feature to Syrian Jewish *maqām* associations. A similar principle found between Arab Islamic practice and Syrian Jews is the recitation of scripture. The recitation of the

Qur'an most commonly begins in *maqām bayyātī*; the reader can modulate to other *maqāmāt*, but he returns to *bayyātī*. Similarly Syrian Jews, as well as other Jews from the Levant, recite the Torah in *maqām seyga.*[27] Likewise they modulate to emphasize a word or passage but return to *seyga*. In the Syrian Jewish tradition, modulating to other *maqāmāt* during the Torah reading is less frequent than is modulation in the recitation of the Qur'an.

Usage of the *maqām* of the day within the morning service aids in assessing the application of the *maqām* in Syrian liturgy. During the cantor's recitation of Shaḥarit, seven liturgical sections are sung to *pizmonim* or *bakkashot* melodies in the *maqām* of the day (see chapter 7). Certain sections are considered more important and call for a more elaborate form of musical expression. The other sections make use of lighter pieces in a quicker tempo. The variety of moods is deemed necessary in order to hold the congregation's interest and to involve them during the forty-five minutes of Shaḥarit. With this entire portion of the service sung in the same *maqām*, the *maqām* of the day needs to express both the drama and expressive character of the heavy liturgical sections and the contrasting character of the light liturgical singing stations. Therefore, one might ask, if *maqām hijaz* is used, is there *dramatic* sadness and *lighter* sadness expressed in the prayers? When *ajam* is used, is there, likewise, dramatic joy and lighter joy? To ask the question in a different way, how are the extramusical association of the *maqām*, determined by the biblical reading, reconciled with the need for a variety of moods within Shaḥarit?

The answer lies in the fact that ultimately the associations of the *maqāmāt* with the prayers provide a system of variety that achieves what David Tawil describes as "pleasant programming." The chosen *maqām* is a meaningful representation of the biblical reading, but the reason for this association is not expressed musically throughout Shaḥarit. Shaḥarit has its own moods to be conveyed. The sadness associated with *maqām hijaz* is an association made through tradition, but the overall character of *hijaz*—or any other *maqām*, for that matter—will change when expressing the liturgical needs of Shaḥarit.

This explanation of the Syrian use of *maqām* within their liturgy is consistent with a similar practice in Qur'anic recitation. Kristina Nelson claims the meaning of the text in the Qur'an may dictate the choice of *maqām* (Nelson 1985, 125–26). However, Nelson does not demonstrate her point with musical examples; only statements from her informants are offered. The *maqām* associations of Nelson's informants parallel those set forth by Scott L. Marcus. In contrast, Lois Ibsen al-Faruqi rejects the notion that the text of the Qur'an may dictate the *maqām* used for its rendering; she states that the reader can have two or more associations with the same *maqām:*

> One salient feature of Quranic recitation is its avoidance of programmatic effects. . . . Changes in pitch, duration or volume do not correspond to or musically 'portray' literary meanings. Textual repetitions are not coupled with repetitions of melodic phrases. Changes of mode or register and musical leitmotifs cannot be related to persons, objects or events mentioned in the text. Narrative or programmatic elements are singularly absent. Moods and emotions implied in the text are not represented by corresponding musical materials. There is no tone painting. Register, ambitus, *maqām, jins* [tetrachord of a *maqām*], melodic or rhythmic motif—all of these may change during the course of a recitation, at a point of literary continuity or at one of literary disjunction. They seem to have no correspondence to poetic discursive content. (al-Faruqi 1987, 11)

Both Nelson and al-Faruqi agree that the important function of music in Qur'anic recitation is to convey the text, which is done through clear and comprehensive delivery and through the use of musical devices, such as melodic embellishments and cadences that correspond to the ending rhymes of the text (Nelson 1985, 127–28; al-Faruqi 1987, 13). The *maqām* functions as a reference point; returning to the original *maqām* at the end of a section of text in the Qur'an organizes the reading by a coincidence of musical and literary elements. For Syrian Jews the role of *maqām* in the liturgy operates in the same fashion. Qur'an recitation serves as model for understanding the delivery of Shaḥarit by a *ḥazzan.* The associations govern the choice and use of a *maqām* for a particular week but do not guide all facets of the rendering of a *maqām* during the Sabbath service. Syrian cantors do modulate to other *maqāmāt,* but at specific points in Shaḥarit a *ḥazzan* returns to the *maqām* of the day. Likewise, programmatic elements of the text do not determine the choice of the *maqām.* A *maqām* is linked to the Bible and then used in the liturgy. The liturgical usage allows for hearing a variety of melodies from week to week.

For Syrian Jews in Brooklyn, the process of acquiring Arab music also extends to a complex network of extramusical associations. Syrian Jews perpetuate a practice found among Arab musicians in the premodern period, although details differ. Indeed Syrians in Brooklyn have developed their own unique usage of extramusical associations. When the Brooklyn system is compared to one currently practiced in Israel, as well as a historic compilation provided by Idelsohn, they have a great deal in common. But the understanding of certain particulars is different between Syrians in Brooklyn and Israel.

The music and the associations that come with the music utilized by the Syrians, consciously and unconsciously, are an adaptation of Arab models and precedents. Arab models of association are infused into the Jewish tradition. Perpetuating this practice of extramusical associations is vital to the ritual of prayer; it is intrinsic to the process. Extramusical associations provide a mechanism for meaning, variety, and personalization. Syrian Jews are steeped in the Jewish tradition religiously and express their liturgy in an Arab fashion culturally.

The interrelated domains of extramusical associations of time, affect, and symbolic action reflect the purpose of this practice. However, associations go beyond shaping the liturgical year; they reflect the essence of a people and the allied tradition. Perpetuating the biblical associations of the *maqām* for Syrian Jews displays usage of a local tradition shaped by strong ties to the past; biblical events and images of antiquity become relevant for the present day. Thus extramusical associations are intertwined with religious knowledge, aesthetic tastes, and desires. The Torah, the central text of Jewish life, informs the *maqām*, in turn shaping the liturgy. Modern Arab melodies are then incorporated into the liturgy through a religiously driven and culturally shaped system. Past and present are intrinsically wedded.

11

Aesthetics, Performance Practice, and Maintenance of Syrian Liturgy

THE DYNAMIC NATURE of the melodic rendering of Syrian liturgy is a process, understanding of which can be gained from viewing employment of Arab performance practices. While a description of liturgical melodies through melodic transcriptions is useful for demonstrating the concrete adaptation of Arab music, it does not convey the essence of the musical endeavor (Seeger 1988, xiv–xv), specifically, in this case, the liturgy. While the adaptation of sung melodies to the liturgy plainly draws upon Arab musical elements, the incorporation of Arab performance practices is more indirect. Adapting known melodies relies more on the practices of paraphrasing and borrowing, whereas performance customs more fittingly demonstrate simulating and modeling (see Meyer 1967 [1994], 195–208).[1] The needs of Syrian liturgy dictate specific requirements that adapt Arab performance models in a new context.

Through the course of my fieldwork during the early 1990s, it became evident that the Aleppo tradition in Brooklyn was in a state of transition. Noted cantors such as Moses Tawil, David Tawil, and Isaac Cabasso, who at the time of research were in their seventies or eighties, were each involved at some level in educating the next generation of Aleppo cantors in Brooklyn. Members of the Brooklyn community participate in a range of cantorial activities, based on experience and expertise. Some members of the community are interested in learning the melodies of the *pizmonim* and their application to prayers in order to participate more fully as congregants. Others desire to lead portions of the service; many people in this group lead the Zemirot and Musaf sections of the prayers. It is the expert *ḥazzan* that leads Shaḥarit. Since the 1980s few cantors in the Syrian community are Brooklyn natives, cantors from Israel, part of the Mizraḥi (Arab eastern), and Yerushalmi-Sephardi communities are retrained by the three experienced men in Brooklyn to conform to the desired customs of Brooklyn Aleppo Jews. It is believed that the musical and ritual experience of these Israeli cantors, as well as their exposure to Arab music in the Middle East, can be adapted to fit the preferred Brooklyn style. The aim of this chapter is to convey the perceptions of Syrian cantors concerning the desired aesthetic of the Brooklyn Aleppo-style *ḥazzan.*

The *Ḥazzan* as Worship Facilitator

MOSES TAWIL DESCRIBES the musical role of the *ḥazzan* as dynamic; his goal is to make the music and prayers feel spontaneous (interview, November 14, 1991). In describing the use of a particular *maqām* for a Sabbath in the liturgy, Ḥazzan Tawil typically says, "we make *ajam,*" or "we make *seyga*" (ibid.).[2] Both Moses Tawil and David Tawil have remarked that "we say" a *maqām* when referring to applying a *maqām* to a particular point in the liturgy (M. Tawil, interviews, October 6, 1991, June 1, 1993; D. Tawil, interview, July 29, 1992).[3] The use of the word "make" or "say" connotes an active stance that underscores the dynamic and flexible nature of the melodic rendering of the liturgy. The phrase "we say," in particular, underscores the musical connection to the text; a text is "made" or "said" through a *maqām.*

The *ḥazzan*'s improvisatory sections of Shaḥarit are guided by musical rules and liturgical requirements. The musical rules focus on the *maqām.* One *maqām* is made prominent during Shaḥarit. Although the cantor is free to modulate to other *maqāmāt,* he must always return to the *maqām* of the day. The significant liturgical requirements are as follows: the cantor (1) must clearly deliver the text, (2) cannot repeat words, and (3) cannot use melodies or be melodically elaborate so that the music detracts from the text.[4] The melody always needs to fit the text (M. Tawil, interviews, November 11, 1991, and June 6, 1993; D. Tawil, interview, July 29, 1992). The improvised sections usually consist of a declamatory recitation of the liturgical text where certain portions are emphasized through melodic elaboration. Emphasis is achieved through sudden shifts to a higher tessitura, movement to other tetrachords, or modulation to a different *maqām.*[5]

Moses Tawil stresses that the *ḥazzan* should first "get into the *maqām* of the day," develop the music, and then change to other *maqāmāt* (interview, November 14, 1991). Cantors have various strategies to "get into the *maqām.*" Some may have favorite melodic phrases in a *maqām* that they use throughout their improvisation. For example, Cantor Yeḥezkiel Zion often recites the improvisatory section of the Kaddish with a melodic phrase in *maqām saba*, regardless of the *maqām* of the day.[6] His recurrent use of the melodic phrase suggests that portions of the improvisatory sections are, in effect, precomposed and not derived spontaneously. Pacing, that is, knowing when to speed up and when to slow down, is important (M. Tawil, interview, October 22, 1991); rhythmic differentiation is crucial to be an effective *ḥazzan* (D. Tawil, interview, July 29, 1992). The cantor's freedom in the improvisatory process, controlled by fixed portions at singing stations, gives rise to the active, creative nature of the service.

The description of a good *ḥazzan* varies. Many of the same characteristics are valued but emphasized to different degrees. The primary qualification is that the *ḥazzan* should have a sweet and pleasant, not necessarily strong, voice that people like (Shrem, interview, January 9, 1986). The main function of the *ḥazzan* is to pray and to encourage everyone else to do so. Cabasso also suggests that a *ḥazzan* should look around and see that people are praying with him (*pizmon* class, February 24, 1992). The cantor should also be knowledgeable of the melodic settings for the liturgy and choose melodies that people know (M. Tawil, interview, November 14, 1991). As the late Cantor Gabriel Shrem explained:

> I'll tell you. My secret is this: they like me, let's say, [a] little bit more than the average *ḥazzan*. I try to give them something old, old *pizmonim*, and medium—which is not so old—and something new. I try to give them all in one session. This way you please the young [and] the old like that. And any given time you come to any of our congregations you will find a six year old, twenty year old, forty year old, sixty year old, and hundred year old—if there is a hundred year old. They all enjoy it . . . you feel it. (interview, January 9, 1986)

The cantor needs to be careful not to cross the fine line of "becoming a singer"—or, as Cabasso remonstrates, the *ḥazzan* is not and should not be a "Caruso," referring to the famous Italian opera singer Enrico Caruso (1873–1921) (interview, May 29, 1992). The *ḥazzan* is praying to God, not performing a concert. Moses Tawil cautions that the *ḥazzan* should not hold a note so long that the congregation focuses on his singing (interview, October 6, 1991). He also recognizes that the *ḥazzan* has more limitations than an Arab singer because of the stylistic requirements of the liturgical singing stations and the need to express the meaning of the prayers:

> The singer['s goal is] just to sing, you know not *tefliah* [pray]; he [the singer] has other freedoms that he could use in developing

> his music in his taste and his feel. In the *tefilot* [prayers] he [the *ḥazzan*] is a little limited and cannot be as free. Of course he has to develop music and elaborate on it, but it is a little more restricted. To me the proficient *ḥazzan,* the melody that he is using has to fit, more or less, the words that he is saying in the *tefliah.* If it's praises it has to sound like praises, if it's prayers and beseeching it has to sound like beseeching, and so on. This is the artistry of the main body [the improvisatory sections]; I'm not talking about the fixed melodies, the little melodies that everybody sings together [liturgical singing stations]. . . . [I]f there is giving thanks it needs to be in a thankful way to express that musically and melodiously. This is the artistry of the *ḥazzanut.* (interview, October 6, 1991)

Nahari, a student of Moses Tawil, states that it is not enough to solely take an Arab song of a famous singer: "I'd take a song of Umm Kulthūm, I'd take a song of many, many singers, and I'd copy from them. . . . But when it comes to be a cantor, not only did you have to listen to the original song, you have to be the one to create a music" (Shelemay 1998, 125).

The Syrian cantor, like his Sephardic and Ashkenazic counterparts, is a melodic arbiter (Shiloah 1992, 67). The cantor's role is dynamic. He not only must know the main melodies used in the liturgy but also, on occasion, he must introduce new melodies. The cantors in the community are variously active in the singing of *pizmonim* and *bakkashot* and the reading of the Torah. Primarily functioning as a prayer leader, the *ḥazzan* is the melodic facilitator for the liturgy. In a sense, he is the bridge between the secular and the sacred.[7] Secular music can be appropriated for liturgical use because it is newly recreated by the *ḥazzan* with authoritative "religious" approval given. Melodies added to the liturgy in the past two decades do not include the intervening *pizmonim* process; instead, melodies are adapted to the liturgy directly from Arab music (M. Tawil, interview, October 22, 1991).[8] This use of existing melodies reflects the fluidity of Syrian musical repertoire and the dynamic nature of music as a performance-oriented medium for cantors. In Syrian liturgy, creating a melody anew is connected with creating prayers.

Interaction of Cantor and Congregation

THE *ḤAZZAN* ENGAGES the congregants and facilitates their response by choosing known melodies for the singing stations and setting up a cadential response at other textual points during Shaḥarit. This process is similar to the audience response during Qur'anic recitation. The reader of the Qur'an may pause in his delivery, with members of the audience saying, "Alah," or other words of praise, during these pauses (Nelson 1982, 43). Likewise, the audience will release their tension during short pauses "by uttering words of praise or loud shouts" in a concert of Arab secular music (Touma 1976, 35). During his rendering of Shaḥarit, the *ḥazzan* pauses after completing the cadence or at other moments of repose. This gap is commonly filled by some members of the congregation anticipating the next word of the liturgical text. Some cantors facilitate this interaction by lengthening their pauses.[9] Sudden changes in register, *maqām,* tetrachord, or central tone produce tension. The climatic moment of the Kaddish liturgical singing station is filled with tension in Moses Tawil's rendering (see systems 10 and 11 of example 10); the only release of the tension, and appropriate response in the liturgy, is the congregational response of "Amen."

The ecstatic experience in Arab music, known as *ṭarab,* provides an interesting parallel to Syrian liturgy. However, such parallels do have their limitations. Ali Jihad Racy describes *ṭarab* as a style emphasizing live musical performances that "gives prominence to instantaneous modal creations and treats music as an ecstatic experience" (1991a, 9). Momentum, emotional efficacy, and aesthetic consistency in *ṭarab* are derived through a "feedback process involving active and direct communication between the artist and the initiated listener" (ibid., 11). The act of listening, *samā,* has been historically linked to both profound mystical transcendence and excessive mundane indulgence. As *ṭarab* artists say, "al-fann Iḥsās" ("art is feeling" or "music is to be felt").[10] Hence, the ecstatic experience can be viewed as a musical and emotional process. Racy explains:

> Musically, *Iḥsās* [feeling] implies correct intonation, rhythmic accuracy, and good judgment regarding modal progressions and tonal emphasis. "Feeling" also refers to an intuitive ability to affect, for example, finding the desirable delicate musical balance between renditions that are too static and too repetitive to be emotionally engaging, and those that are too excessive and digressive to generate and maintain a true sense of musical ecstasy. A talented *muṭrib,* or *ṭarab* singer, is someone who knows how to manipulate the music in order to engage the initiated listeners, a skill that requires that the performer be able to "feel" the music himself as well. (ibid., 12)

For Arab performers, *salṭana* refers to "modal ecstasy" experienced prior to the generation of *ṭarab* proper as well as during it (ibid., 13).[11]

Syrian cantors use many of the same explanations when referring to Syrian liturgy. The dynamic role of the cantor, particularly as described by Moses Tawil, focuses on the spontaneity of musical improvisation and the need to provide a balance in terms of rhythmic pace and melodic choice. Congregants, like Arab audience members, respond appropriately during their service. However, affective comments concerning the Syrian liturgy differ from those in the Arab tradition in an important detail. While the goal of Arab improvisation is to involve the audience for all to experience ecstasy, encouraging others to pray is the ultimate goal of the Syrian *ḥazzan*. That intent is highlighted in the introduction to *SUHV:*

> In recent generations, this [the creation of *pizmonim*] holy tradition was perpetuated by Aleppo's two outstanding poets, Raphael Taboush and Moses Ashear HaCohen. They developed the usage of tunes and melodies of the Middle East in our Sabbath and Holiday prayers. Thus, led by the gifted *ḥazzan,* the congregants participated in the services and reached new heights in the worship of the Almighty.
>
> The tradition of singing and chanting the Bakashot took place between midnight and dawn each Sabbath morning. This ancient custom continues till this very day in Syrian Synagogues the world over. The participants reach a sublime feeling of fervor and ecstasy. (3)

The worship is enhanced by the use of Arab melodies; ecstasy is not the desired end. The goal of singing *bakkashot* within their own context, however, is to achieve an ecstatic experience. Therefore, Arab performance practices are paralleled in Syrian liturgy with certain limitations. Like the unique extra-musical associations of the *maqāmāt* to the biblical readings, Syrian liturgical performance practices simulate and model Middle Eastern processes. At the same time, improvisation for Syrian cantors and the appropriate congregational response and participation achieves its own end: to facilitate prayer. A congregant "should be able to sense the meaning of the words and feel it" (D. Tawil, interview, July 28, 1995). Arab performance practices are accommodated to a new context in Jewish worship.

In Syrian liturgy, the congregation has certain expectations of the cantor. In turn, the cantor has expectations of the congregation. In order for a service to be completed in the proper manner, both parties must interact in an agreeable fashion. It is the cantor's responsibility to connect the various parts of Shaḥarit together with nuance and expression. The cantor's proficiency will determine how effectively this can be accomplished. For example, a young cantor from Israel at a Syrian synagogue tried to incorporate new Arab melodies into the service. There was resistance by some members of the congregation because they were not familiar with these melodies. As a result, most people were frustrated when this young cantor led the prayers; they could not interact with him musically. Although he has a beautiful voice and people enjoyed his skill as a singer, it was evident that they felt he needed to continue to develop as a cantor. This young cantor has learned melodies known by the congregation, but he hopes that the congregation will allow him to innovate over time.

The service is also affected by the presence of certain guests. On one occasion, Ḥazzan Moses Tawil came for Sabbath services to Beth Torah. His student, a new Israeli cantor, led Shaḥarit. Many congregants reported the exceptional clarity by this Israeli cantor. They further observed that he was more careful than usual in the recitation of the prayers. On another occasion, a close friend of this Israeli cantor, who is himself a noted cantor, was present. The visiting cantor was asked to lead various psalms during the Zemirot section. His experienced voice encouraged others to recite with more excitement. Afterward, the Israeli cantor led Shaḥarit, with more ornate embellishments. Some commented that perhaps he was trying to impress his friend or was inspired by him.

The congregation and cantor interact in a relational manner such that unique personalities emerge. Specific congregations are know for their desire to sing certain melodies over others. Likewise, cantors become known for the choice of melodies and specific nuances of vocal delivery. Additionally, participants interact in a manner that can significantly effect the musical rendering of the liturgy.

Individual Traits of Cantors

THE COMMUNITY PROVIDES a range of melodic choices, but these choices are interpreted and practiced individually. Ḥazzan Moses Tawil has a preference, particularly in the heavy pieces, for complex, artful songs. Cantor Cabasso, on the other hand, typically likes to use melodies of *bakkashot* and *pizmonim* written by Moses Ashear—primarily because of his personal bond to this important cantor in the community (*pizmon* class, March 23, 1992). The late Cantor Shrem, like others, chose to use both new and old melodies in order to provide variety and to hold the interest of young and old. Individuality is expressed both by the melodies chosen and by the style in which a melody is rendered.

Another factor is personal choice of a melody for the liturgy. At a *pizmon* class on December 9, 1991, Cantor Cabasso reviewed the strategy of his rendering on the previous Sabbath. In response to a question from a student concerning his performance of Musaf on the prior Saturday, Cabasso discussed his use of the melody "My Country 'Tis of Thee," for Keter (LS 6.2.2). Cabasso indicated that he used this melody because of the anniversary of Pearl Harbor Day.[12] Just as the *maqām* is associated with a biblical reading, a non-"Jewish" event—in this case an American war commemoration—similarly influences the choice of melody to be used for the prayers.

After the conclusion of one Sabbath service in the spring of 1992, a group from the *pizmon* class gathered to ask Cantor Cabasso questions. When asked if one of the melodies he used for Nishmat Kol Ḥai was from a *pizmon* he taught us that particular week, Cantor Cabasso was pleased that the students were paying such close attention to the liturgy. His strategies included the involvement of specific members of the congregation. For him the process was not complete until he knew that people were aware of which melodies were used in the prayers and why they were chosen.

Another illustration of the power of individual expression is the manner in which the cantorial tradition is discussed, whether conveyed in formal and informal musical terms. Cantor Cabasso emphasizes practical concerns, explaining the use of charts that indicate the *bakkasha* or *pizmon* melody according to *maqām* in *SUHV* (table 10) as a useful way for the *ḥazzan* to "get into" a *maqām* (*pizmon* class, November 18, 1991). For Cabasso, the *bakkasha* or *pizmon* source serves to remind the *ḥazzan* of a *maqām* through a specific melody. This guides him by making sure the chosen melodies are in the *maqām* of the day. His focus is on practical pedagogical purposes where *maqāmāt* are learned through a song; through singing the song melody in the liturgy, the cantor knows the *maqām* to continue in his prayers. Ḥazzan Moses Tawil, on the other hand, always stresses the fine, subtle qualities of Aleppo *ḥazzanut*, as in the particular melodic stylization of his rendition of the Kaddish in example 10. The goal of the *ḥazzan*, according to Tawil, is to render the prayers in an artful and meaningful way—not simply to go from one prayer to another. For Tawil, the *bakkashot* and *pizmonim* melodies provide a source for elaboration when used for creating prayers.

Melodic Identity

MELODIES IN THE Syrian liturgy are known in various forms: as an original Arab or non-Arab song, as a *bakkasha* or *pizmon*, or as a liturgical melody.

In particular, many *pizmonim* melodies are well known in the community and are sung regularly at ritual circumcisions, domestic gatherings, or in the synagogue.[13] While all *bakkashot* and *pizmonim* melodies are not used in the liturgy, some are heard more often in Syrian life in the application to the liturgical text than as a *bakkasha* or *pizmon.*[14] The main association an individual has for a specific melody depends on that individual's knowledge of music and the use of the melody within the community. In general, while most members of the community listen to Arab music sung in Arabic, the melodies from Arab songs are discussed using the *pizmon* title rather than the title of the originating song or the name of a liturgical singing station. *Pizmonim* and some *bakkashot* are recoded and resignified in a liturgical context like popular music in other cultures (Manuel 1992/1993, 96). Syrian liturgy is learned and experienced through live performance, not recordings. Although there are recordings of *pizmonim, bakkashot,* and liturgical singing stations, they are not widely used in the community. Syrian liturgy in particular is experienced as a regular part of religious life. Community members do not listen to recorded Syrian liturgy as they would recorded Arab music.

Clearly there is a preference for Arab music as the main source of liturgical melodies. Non-Arab melodies are used, but as Cantor Cabasso states, "One should not use melodies like 'Oh Christmas Tree,' 'Santa Lucia,' or 'Fiddler on the Roof,' not because it is sinful, but because it generates talking. People will say, 'Look what he is using, is this all that he knows?' There are so many melodies to use, and there is no reason to use the melodies that will provoke talking" (*pizmon* class, November 18, 1991). His reasoning is that borrowing of well known non-Arab tunes can create talking in the synagogue; he is less concerned that these melodies may be inappropriate. Perhaps this is because the source melodies are so well known that they would be immediately associated with other contexts. This is not true for most of the Arab melodies, although many are equally secular and widely popular. There is a proclivity for Arab melodies over non-Arab due to familiarity and aesthetic preference.

The musical repertoire of the Syrian liturgy, like Arab music in general, absorbs new influences. The origin of the melody is not as important as the manner in which it is rendered. New influences motivate not only the choice of new melodies but also the stylization of existing melodies; a cantor may render a melody differently by adding new, or employing alternative, embellishments after hearing someone else sing—either live or recorded. The dynamic nature of a melody adds to the variable nature of the service. No two services are ever the same; the variables of *maqāmāt* and potential melodies on a given Sabbath allow for endless possibilities.

Nonmusical Factors that Affect Performance

ONE ASPECT OF describing a ritual is determining what factors have an effect upon it. This includes musical influences as well as nonmusical influences. At Beth Torah the attendance was often a key determinant of the tone and nature of a service. For example, three to four hundred people, mostly men, regularly attend services at Beth Torah during the fall, winter, and spring. During the summer, however, most members of the Brooklyn Syrian community reside in Deal, New Jersey. Services are held at Beth Torah during the summer, but only approximately fifty people attend. As a result, the worship service is moved from the large sanctuary to a smaller social hall. The synagogue personnel also change; Beth Torah's cantors and other participants also reside in Deal for the summer. Ḥakham David Tawil is the *ḥazzan* for Shaḥarit and the Torah reader for the main services in the summer at Beth Torah.[15] The organization of the service is the same, but he and other leaders do not elaborate as extensively during melodic renderings. The rabbi also is not present during the summer, and there is no sermon. As a result, the services are shorter, more informal, and the general atmosphere is more relaxed.

Like other influences in the service, the physical space of the prayer setting affects performance. In the large Brooklyn Syrian synagogues that accommodate hundreds of people, the placement of the cantor at the *teivah* is crucial to establish a more intimate relationship with the large congregation. Ali Jihad Racy comments that Arab singers are sensitive to their mood and surroundings in order to be effective in performance (1991a, 12, 17). Likewise, Syrian cantors vary their approach to the factors that affect the setting of the service.

In order to explain further how personnel can affect musical performance, it is first necessary to comment on the difference between the rabbi and the cantor in the Syrian community. Rabbis are respected figures; in the words of one Syrian congregant, "we never contradict a rabbi." The rabbis of a congregation, as well as rabbinical instructors in Syrian religious schools, wear hats (Zenner and Kligman 2000, 167–72). Many consider this custom to be an Ashkenazic influence since Sephardic rabbis have not been known to dress in this manner in the past. Congregants show their respect to a rabbi by standing when he walks by them. Additionally, the rabbi sits on the *bimah* (see figure 3) for the entire service. Guest rabbis also sit on the *bimah* and are sometimes invited to address the congregation before the resident rabbi's sermon. Synagogue rabbis are paid professionals who may also serve as a teacher at one of several religious schools in the community.

The cantor's role in the community and in the service is distinct from the rabbi. Generally, cantors do not wear hats. Cantors have not been financially remunerated for their participation in the service until recently. They too are respected by the community, but respect is demonstrated in a different way. Congregants do not stand up when cantors walk by, yet congregants appreciate and admire their participation in the service. Guest cantors may be asked to participate during Zemirot, but they do not sit on the *bimah* and are not usually invited to lead Shaḥarit. Both cantors at Beth Torah sit on the *bimah* during Birkhot ha-Shaḥar and Zemirot. The *ḥazzan* of the day renders Shaḥarit from the *teivah* (see figure 3) wearing a white robe. When the Torah scrolls are taken out of the *aron* and placed on the *teivah* during the opening part of the Torah service after Shaḥarit, the *ḥazzan* of the day returns to his seat on the *bimah* after derobing. At Beth Torah it was very common for both cantors to leave their seats on the *bimah* to sit in the congregation toward the end of the Torah service. They remain seated in the congregation until the conclusion of Musaf. Both their location in the synagogue during liturgical performance and their dress signify the cantor's role as *shaliaḥ tsibbur* (messenger of the congregation). When his task as prayer leader has been completed the cantor returns to his position among the congregants—having removed his robe as a visually distinct marker. The cantor's liturgical role is as one of the congregants, appointed as their messenger to pray on their behalf and, consequently, to encourage them to pray. His placement at the *teivah* puts him in the midst of the congregation to be the messenger.

It is significant that the rabbi delivers his sermon from the lectern on the *bimah*. The distinction in ritual roles of the cantor and rabbi are reflected in the service; the congregation interacts with and is physically close to the cantor but does not interact with nor is physically close to the rabbi. When the rabbi of Beth Torah is absent during the nonsummer months, the tone of the service is more informal and resembles summer services. The rabbi's presence is always notable, despite the lack of interaction between him and the congregation. Ezra Barnea says the rabbi can not be compared to the *ḥazzan*. The rabbi, he says, historically was the leader of a city or neighborhood. If a *ḥazzan*'s reputation precedes him, though, people will sing his melodies (1996–97, 19).

The content of the rabbi's sermon injects a nonmusical element that may affect the musical performance. Although congregants may not always agree with the rabbi's opinions, nevertheless, his intellect and his person are highly respected. One Sabbath morning in the fall of 1992, an article appeared in the Saturday morning *New York Times* quoting Rav Ovadia Yosef, the past chief Sephardic rabbi in Israel—perhaps the most revered rabbi among the Syrians in Brooklyn. Rabbi Ovadia suggested that it is permissible according to Jewish law for Israel to give up portions of the West Bank in the interest of peace. The rabbi of the Brooklyn synagogue, while claiming complete respect for the past chief Sephardic rabbi of Israel, disagreed with this conclusion. He went on to say in no uncertain terms that all of the land in the West Bank belonged to Israel and quoted several biblical passages in support his position.

There was a great deal of murmuring by the congregants during this sermon. A man sitting next to me leaned over and said, "I don't believe what we are seeing. This is history. How could anybody disagree with Rav Ovadia Yosef?" This feeling was shared by others.

Immediately following the sermon, the cantor led the Musaf liturgical section. On the Saturday of this sermon, the cantor—one of Rabbi Ovadia Yosef's rabbinical students—was devastated by what the rabbi of the synagogue had said; he had vehemently contradicted the cantor's mentor. While his usual recitation of Musaf was ornate, the cantor recited the Musaf text in a cursory fashion with no melodic singing or embellishments. It was apparent that the cantor was gravely affected by the rabbi's sermon. Many congregants commented on what had transpired; whether congregants agreed or disagreed with the rabbi, the cantor's perfunctory recitation of Musaf was unsettling for all.

This event demonstrates how the interaction between all the officiants is vitally important to the musical performance. It also serves as an example of musical performance as commentary to the events within a ritual.

Maintenance of Brooklyn System

THE MUSICAL REQUIREMENTS for Brooklyn Syrian cantors are adhering to the *maqām* of the day and, preferably, using known melodies. It is also preferable to stay in the *maqām* of the day, deviating only momentarily once the *maqām* of the day has been established. The extramusical association of the *maqām* and biblical reading chart (represented in table 10) and the suggestions of melodies for the liturgical singing stations (represented in table 9) equip the new cantors with a system to follow, thus enabling them to perpetuate the Brooklyn system. The cantor is given occasional liberty, which perhaps accounts for the variability found within this system. In fact, variability is a part of any ritual system (Turner 1967, 33, 46; Geertz 1973, 17–18; Daniel 1984, 24, 35–39).

Adherence to the Brooklyn system is seen as conforming to the Aleppo cantorial style, which is important for the longevity of Syrian Jewish liturgical practices. The approach distinguishes that practice from Ashkenazic and other Sephardic Jews. After giving a lecture at the Coalition for the Advancement of Jewish Education (CAJE), Moses Tawil stated the following:

> And this [the Brooklyn system] is very unique and it is very broad. I mean if you talk to Ashkenazim [they will say] "What are they talking about? [Why do you have] all this variation in the prayers?" It's mind-boggling. When I gave the lecture at CAJE, . . . they were all pretty sophisticated—the ones that attended the lecture I gave. They said, "Aren't you afraid you will lose some of your beautiful minhagim? This, your beautiful tradition that you have?" And I told them, "No, we're not, because so long as we are adhering to the *maqām* we only gain and we don't lose." In other words, we are not giving up anything. . . .
>
> Other Sephardim . . . [are] not as organized in their *tefilah* as we are—we are very strict. Our system is quite strict. For example, if they are praying *saba,* and if they don't end and use it as a base for their whole *tefilah* it is okay. Where with us . . . eventually you have to finish, you have to wind up [praying] everything in that *maqām.* (interview, June 6, 1993)

Adherence to this system of extramusical associations is an important part of Syrian Sabbath liturgical practice and something in which they take great pride. Keeping to the *maqāmāt* as the central component of their prayers is crucial for the community's survival.

Congregants that attend services vary in their knowledge of the system of associations. The majority have a vague familiarity. In large measure this is based on an individual's knowledge of Arab music and the liturgy; a congregant's awareness of *maqāmāt,* Arab music, and how the liturgy is organized is directly related to their knowledge of the extramusical associations of the *maqāmāt* with the prayers (see also Shelemay 1998, 36). Congregation Beth Torah publishes a yearly calendar that is distributed to its members. The calendar lists the Jewish holidays and the appropriate times of the lighting of candles for Sabbaths and holidays. In the calendar the names of the biblical and prophetic readings for each Sabbath are given, as commonly found in other Jewish calendars. At Beth Torah the *maqām* that will be used in the prayers is also given. This certainly indicates that the *maqām* of the Sabbath may not be unknown to the congregants.[16]

At Beth Torah, the members of the *pizmonim* class were generally in their twenties, thirties, and forties. Many are experienced with leading the prayers for Zemirot and Musaf. These members of the class are also the main singers in the congregation during the Torah service when *pizmonim* are sung. Thus, a small group, about twenty, are actively involved in participating in Syrian liturgical and paraliturgical songs. During the experienced cantor's rendering of Shaḥarit, about half the congregation respond with the appropriate responses. Clearly, not all the congregants know how to respond aloud during the prayers; others may not wish to respond aloud.

The expertise and awareness of the Syrian liturgical tradition can be viewed within several concentric circles. The expert *ḥazzan* is situated in the center. Those that lead Zemirot or Musaf are in the next circle. And those that respond during prayers are in the next. Experienced listeners either learn from habit or classes.[17]

Cantor Cabasso was particularly reflective about the present state of transition in the education of new cantors, declaring that it is hard to teach the *maqāmāt* to the present generation Brooklyn-born Syrians.[18] While some are avid listeners of Arab music, there are not many opportunities to learn Arab music in Brooklyn. Efforts are being made to teach Syrian children *pizmonim* with the addition of active singing of the twenty-five or so popular *pizmonim* in the Syrian day schools, a practice that began in the early 1980s. Cantor Cabasso was particularly surprised when he heard his granddaughter sing a *pizmon* that she learned from school. However, these efforts have not produced expert cantors for the community. Currently most Syrian synagogues employ a *ḥazzan* who is financially compensated, a practice that was unheard of many decades ago (see also Shelemay 1998, 50). Cabasso agrees with this practice because it is necessary to perpetuate the tradition. However, the Israeli-born and retrained cantors are changing the tradition. Cabasso and others point toward the more frequent change of *maqām* in Shaḥarit during Israeli cantors' improvisatory sections. In addition, these new cantors bring fresh melodies with them that they have slowly introduced to the community. These new melodies supplant other already known melodies in the community. Cabasso is concerned about these differences and sees the changes as the "wave of the future." He prefers to stay in one *maqām* and to develop the *maqām* after five to ten minutes before modulating. Cabasso's models for remaining in the *maqām* of the day for an extended period of time are taken from recordings of famous Arab singers Muḥammad 'Abd al-Wahhāb and Umm Kulthūm. Ezra Barnea provides a comment by Rabbi Yaakov Levi (1890–1983) that focuses on the change in cantorial practice:

> The Sephardic *hazzanut* is the most original and pure in the world, especially in Jerusalem. For about sixty years the immigrants from Eastern countries who speak Arabic increased in number and brought with them new melodies adulterated with Arab *lahanim* [melodies].
>
> The melody of the *Bakkashot,* of those who came from Aleppo,

had a serious influence on the *hazzanut* heard today in the Sephardic synagogues. Would that this was the melody of the *Bakkashot* heard with music accompanying the prayers and Kaddishim; but we have perverted the synagogues into a center of cheap Arabic music with melismatic imitations. The young *hazzanim* were not privileged to hear the original from older and veteran *hazzanim* who were knowledgeable in tradition. Rather they gathered here and there from the lips of favorite singers, and built themselves a *hazzanut* which is completely torn and patched without any system, without a program, and far from the esteemed and longed-for tradition. (1996–97, 25)

Future research will be needed to chart the developments to see how present practices may change the stylization of the liturgy. Recent trends suggests that while the melodies for the liturgy change slowly, the style of delivery by the *ḥazzan* is changing more rapidly. Younger cantors prefer to change *maqāmāt* more frequently during the improvisatory passages during Shaḥarit.

Creating Prayers

THE EFFICACY OF Syrian liturgy is vested in individual and communal prayer. The cantor uses various choices available to him, much like the reciter of the Qur'an (Nelson 1982, 1985; al-Faruqi 1987), to create his prayers. This practice encourages others to pray. Cantors in Brooklyn make their prayers meaningful through individual strategies in the choice of *maqām,* repertoire, and specific songs for particular occasions. Arab aesthetics and performance practices are likewise accommodated but with limitations. While ecstasy is the goal for Arab musicians, Syrian cantors seek to achieve prayer in Sabbath worship through involvement. Similar tools are used in both contexts but modified in the latter. Adaptation is, therefore, more than merely the use of melodies recast into a new context.

For Moses Tawil, the closeness of the community has been crucial for the survival of the Aleppo liturgy tradition he enjoys and endeavors to perpetuate:

> It is a beautiful way of delivering the *tefilah.* It is very moving and, you know, like everything else we take it for granted. With us we just do it; we take it for granted. It is very unique. There are many other Sephardi types of prayers, but none of them are like ours, the Ḥalabi. Of course I'm partial and from my aesthetic point-of-

view, from a musical point of view Ḥalabi, I think, is really the most beautiful prayers in the Sephardic world. Because also many of the other Sephardim are also intermixed with whatever other culture surrounded it. For example, if they were in Yemen they had much of that culture that they picked up; if they were in Greece, there are other areas where the Sephardim come from so they picked up some of that. The Ḥalabi, naturally, is restricted to the Ḥalabi culture. . . .

We are very much together, the Ḥalabi people. The people from Egypt most of them came from Ḥalab. People that come from Beirut, it's close enough to Ḥalab or from Damascus which is close enough to Ḥalab. So all of these groups had the same background and the same culture and we are very, very clannish. We are very closely knit. So we are able to perpetuate it because of our closeness. (interview, October 6, 1991)

For Syrian Jews, prayer reinforces their history and heritage and builds comradery.

Conclusion

Judeo-Arab Synthesis in the Syrian Sabbath Liturgy

Syrian liturgy presents an opportunity to view the contact between Jewish and Arab culture. One can only explain the dynamic processes of Syrian liturgy through identifying its constituent Arab and Jewish elements and their combination into a Judeo-Arab synthesis. This synthesis operates on many levels in Syrian liturgy. From the overall design of the Sabbath service (chapter 9) to performance practices (chapter 11) and the use of specific melodies (chapters 6–8), Syrian liturgy adapts and innovates Arab music in order to accommodate Jewish liturgical requirements. Specifically, the *maqāmāt* play a crucial role in the adaptation process as they organize and structure Syrian liturgy and provide the means to reassociate and use Arab melodies (chapter 10). Despite the correspondences between pan-Arab and Syrian Jewish use of the same musical system, differences do exist. Examining these differences is instructive toward understanding Syrian Sabbath prayers and identity, as well as defining them. Ultimately the process of synthesis in the liturgy affords a provocative example of culture contact: the adaptation of Arab musical aesthetic desires within a Jewish religious context.

The Distinctive Components of Syrian Liturgy

In order to show the contact of Jewish and Arab culture in Syrian liturgy, I have focused on the relationship of music and text. Both employ a process of adaptation. The textual process describes the formation of paraliturgical textual construction: the culling of texts from the Jewish tradition.[1] In regard to *pizmonim* texts specifically, an Arab song text serves as a model for the newly composed Hebrew text. This new Hebrew text employs rhyme patterns, textual assonance, and subject matter from the originating Arab text. However, as discussed in chapter 4, *pizmonim* texts are not merely adaptations of Arab song texts; the newly composed Hebrew texts follow a tradition first established in medieval Spain, where Hebrew poetry, *piyyutim,* flourished. These *piyyutim* adapt texts from biblical, rabbinic, and mystical Jewish texts. Likewise, Syrian *pizmonim* follow not only aspects of Arab poetry but *piyyutim* as well. The result is a unique creation of Jewish and Arab influences reflecting Syrian Jewish history. Jews living in Aleppo coexisted with their Arab neighbors and interacted with and were inspired by a variety of influences. Today in Brooklyn they retain the practice of singing these poetic texts in their religious practices. Their close family ties and an insular social milieu not only characterize Aleppo Jewish society in Syria during the eighteenth and nineteenth centuries but likewise describe Syrian Jewish life in Brooklyn today (see chapter 2). Singing *pizmonim* retains a link to Jewish life in Aleppo (see also Shelemay 1998, 25, 171).

The musical expression of the liturgy consists of Arab melodies, extramusical associations, and performance practices that are incorporated through adaptation and development, similar to the textual process of *pizmonim* creation, to form the Syrian Sabbath morning service. Melodies of Arab origin, first adapted into the community through the paraliturgical practice of the *pizmonim,* are incorporated into the liturgy. Depending upon its function, the liturgy adapts appropriate melodies to seven liturgical singing stations of the Shaḥarit portion of the Sabbath morning service; apropos tempo, adaptability to the liturgical text, and suitability for congregational singing govern melody choice (chapter 7). The use of *maqāmāt* gives rise to extramusical associations taken from Arab musical practices adapted into a Jewish context. The unique network of Syrian *maqām* associations is the result of both culture contact and developments internal to Jewish life alone—Syrian extramusical associations build upon and move beyond Arab practice (chapter 10). Syrian liturgical performance practices, which are similar to Arab musical practices, provide the basis for the *ḥazzan* to facilitate participation of the congregation (chapter 11). The transformation of Arab elements in Jewish religious life perpetuated in liturgy also exists in other facets of Syrian musical life, particularly in their understanding of the pan-Arab *maqām* system (see chapter 4).

The primary distinction between Arab music and Jewish liturgy relates to context and goal. In the performance of Arab music, ecstasy is the goal, whereas the goal of Jewish liturgy is worship (described in the previous chapter). Additionally, although Qur'anic recitation and Jewish liturgy share musical similarities, the role of music in Islam and Judaism differs greatly. In Islam, music is forbidden for religious use, while it is allowed in Judaism. The reader of the Qur'an must not act like nor imitate a singer (Nelson 1982, 46). Indeed, there are sharp religious and social distinctions between readers and singers (Nelson 1982; al-Faruqi 1987). The Syrian Jewish cantor's rendering is an amalgamation of recitation techniques and singing. Like the Qur'an reader, the *ḥazzan* must deliver the text clearly and not act like a singer; the musical improvisation must serve the text. However, the *ḥazzan* is given the freedom to use known melodies from Arab songs, a practice forbidden for Qur'an readers (Nelson 1982, 41; al-Faruqi 1987, 7). Therefore, the freedom given to the Syrian *ḥazzan* differs from the one given to the Qur'an reader. The spontaneous nature of the cantor's improvisation must fit the text to facilitate the meaningful creation of prayers.

The fixed Jewish liturgical texts place demands on emphasis and extension through the flexible nature of the music. The *ḥazzan* renders Shaḥarit through singing, reciting, and improvising, all of which serve to highlight this section of the service. Within Shaḥarit, various musical means highlight liturgical passages (the seven liturgical singing stations). The flexible application of music during Shaḥarit demonstrates this liturgical section's uniqueness and the dynamic musical role of the *ḥazzan*. The appropriate technique heightens textual declamation in key moments, and through this the cantor seeks to engage the congregation in worship. The improvisatory nature of the *ḥazzan*'s rendering of Shaḥarit must also accommodate the contrasting musical characteristics of the singing stations while simultaneously adhering to the *maqām* of the day. This organization of Shaḥarit parallels the overall design of the Arab suite (*waṣlah*); however, the seven liturgical singing stations of Shaḥarit provide a musical design that uniquely transforms the Arab suite model. Syrian Jewish liturgy requires three of the seven stations, appearing at the beginning, middle, and end of Shaḥarit, to be emphasized, which express the important textual themes of the liturgy. Fittingly, the musical approach to emphasize these three texts consists of elaboration of melodies in a slow tempo. Alternation follows liturgical requirements. The musical organization of the Sabbath morning service as a whole, and Shaḥarit in particular, gives rise to the unique design of Syrian liturgy.

Synthesis in the Syrian Sabbath Liturgy

FIGURE 7 ILLUSTRATES the interrelationships of Jewish and Arab elements in the Syrian Sabbath liturgy. This depiction is on a horizontal continuum, with

the Arab-derived elements in relative proximity to that realm. The same holds true for the Jewish-derived elements. The Arab realm consists of musical elements, the Jewish realm of textual elements. The two simultaneously interact to form Syrian liturgy.

Figure 7. *Judeo-Arab synthesis in the Syrian Sabbath liturgy*

Arab musical elements	Jewish textual elements
Arab poetry and music	Biblical texts
Arab songs	Rabbinic texts
LITURGY	
Arab musical style	Piyyitim (paraliturgical texts pizmonim and *bakkashot*)
Extramusical associations of *maqām*	Reading of the Torah

The Arab realm incorporates the constituent elements of Arab music, including Arab poetry, songs, and performance practices that encompass the interaction between singer and listener. It offers a direct influence on Jewish liturgy with the use of melodies from Arab songs. Additional Arab aesthetics influence the liturgy through extramusical associations of the *maqāmāt.* A more indirect influence in the dynamic nature of musical performance and the reading of the Qur'an. Jewish worship alters Arab performance practice techniques.

Textually based, the Jewish realm comprises biblical, rabbinic, and paraliturgical texts. All three textual types are in the liturgy. The *pizmonim* and *bakkashot*—prominent collections of paraliturgical texts used in a variety of ritual contexts but not included in the liturgy—are directly influenced by the *piyyutim.* Biblical and rabbinic texts indirectly influence these *pizmonim* and *bakkashot* on the level of subject matter. The *pizmonim* also make mention of Jewish ritual life while having an effect upon it at the same time.[2] The melodies of *pizmonim and bakkashot* serve as the stock set of melodies for Shaḥarit.

The textual process found in paraliturgical practices serves as a model for the Sabbath liturgy: Jewish elements influence the texts of the *pizmonim* and *bakkashot;* the music comes from the Arab realm.[3] Likewise, the liturgy adapts various Jewish texts and Arab music. Non-Arab melodies have an indirect influence on the liturgy, since some *pizmonim* and melodies in the liturgy derive from non-Arab sources. However, the *pizmonim* serve as an intermediary melodic stage in a three-part process of melodic adaptation in the liturgy.

First, melodies brought into Syrian religious life within the context of *pizmonim* originate from Arab songs, previously adapted melodies. Second, a *pizmon*'s *maqām* classification and musical quality ("heavy" or "light") determines its specific use during Shaḥarit. Third, biblical reading associations determines the *maqām* of the day; this narrows the melodic choices. Within this three-part process of melodic adaptation, the *pizmonim* and the *maqām* and biblical reading associations are intermediary stages in the overall liturgical synthesis. Arab and Jewish elements directly influence both the *pizmonim* and the extra-musical associations (see figure 7). Therefore, the adaptation of Arab music through the *pizmonim* and the extramusical associations of the *maqāmāt* with the biblical readings provide an organizing structure that transforms melodies absorbed into the service. The *pizmonim* and extramusical associations infuse the liturgy with meaning; both influence the melody a cantor employs in his rendering of the service. Consequently, Syrian liturgy is not at the midpoint between Arab and Jewish elements since it is already mediated by other factors. Syrian liturgy itself, the result of the process, is a synthesis of Arab elements mediated, in some form, by components that have already been made "Jewish."

The deep and complex interaction of music and text in Syrian liturgy can be seen as forming its own ritual language (Feld and Fox 1994). Within the overall design of the Sabbath morning service, structural components of the texts determine melodic style. As a result, various musical and textual relationships emerge. The aesthetic qualities of a *maqām,* determined by its various associations to the biblical reading, add an additional influence to the liturgy. Musical and textual influences, interacting with one another, simultaneously create and recreate the liturgy. Ḥakham Ovadia Yosef's rabbinic permission to use Arab melodies underscores the re-creative act of music, because melodies are intangible and created anew each time they are sung (see chapter 4). Thus, the *ḥazzan* and congregation create Syrian liturgy each Sabbath. The *ḥazzan* provides the appropriate rendering style or melody to express the text at a given moment within the liturgy to create and re-create worship by selecting the melody from a variety of possibilities.

The resulting similarity between the Sabbath service and these elements of Arab music is an outgrowth of a shared musical and cultural experience. The use of popular or secular music for the sacred context of the Sabbath service is not met with objections. Likewise, Syrian Jews do not make the sacred and secular distinction in paraliturgical music (Shelemay 1994, 32). Music of the Arab world provides a fertile source for blurring this ostensible divide, since the same musical repertory permeates various forms and genres in Syrian liturgy.

While it is beneficial to view Syrian liturgy as a synthesis, such an approach is also limiting. As discussed in chapter 9, the *waṣlah* provides a means of organizing various song genres within the same *maqām* during an Arab musical performance. Although Shaḥarit makes use of various song genres for its seven liturgical singing stations, viewing Shaḥarit only in terms of its relationships to a *waṣlah* does not leave room to see the unique organization of the "heavy" and "light" song types governed by liturgical necessity. Similarly, the customary nature of Arab song performance and the interaction of the audience does not fully provide the means to view the interaction of the *ḥazzan* and the congregation. The organization of the liturgical singing stations and performance practice of Shaḥarit serve to produce worship.

Although focusing primarily on the organization and effective rendering of Shaḥarit, it is worthwhile to consider the overall structure of Syrian liturgy itself, namely, the relationship of Syrian worship to Qur'anic recitation. The recitation of the Qur'an in Islam is in one of two styles: *murattal,* a type of recitation that is close to normal speech, and *mujawwad,* which uses musical elaboration (Nelson 1985, xxiii–xxiv, 105–11; al-Faruqi 1987, 8–9). Birkhot ha-Shaḥar, Zemirot, the Torah reading, and Musaf follow the *murattal* style—each makes use of formulas with emphasis on textual word accents. Shaḥarit, on the other hand, makes use of the more musically elaborate *mujawwad* manner; musical and textual issues share an equal role in guiding the recitation of the liturgy.[4] While use of the *murattal* style is for private devotions and the *ṣalāt* (five daily ritual prayers), the *mujawwad* style is used for public occasions of recitation (Nelson 1985, xiii). This latter, more ornate, style is generally heard on recordings and broadcasts in the Arab world; it is more characteristic of the artistry of Qur'anic recitation. Given the ban on music in Islam, the *mujawwad* style is not considered to be music by Islamic adherents. Specific rules govern Qur'anic recitation (Nelson 1982, 41, 1985, xv), including the lack of melodic fixity (Nelson 1985, 110) in order to prevent approaching music: "The ideal in the *mujawwad* style is that a spontaneously crafted melody be executed on the fixed text. . . . This issue of fixity versus freedom is basic to the *mujawwad* style and directly affects several aspects of its performance" (ibid., 110–11). Muslim worship does not use this ornate style of recitation.[5] The parallels of the *mujawwad* style and the *ḥazzan*'s rendering of Shaḥarit are obvious; both focus on textual clarity and spontaneity but serve different purposes.

Recitation of the Qur'an is a basis for Syrian liturgy, but there remain important distinctions. Although Syrian liturgy and Qur'an recitation both use music, rabbis sanction the use of music, while Islamic adherents do not. As a result, in Islam adherents clearly distinguish Qur'anic recitation from music (ibid., 189).[6] In Judaism there is no such ban on music; the use of known songs is permitted and encouraged by rabbinic authorities. Syrian regard the process of adaptation as an avenue toward enhancing the service in order to enhance the prayer experience. Like Syrian liturgy, Qur'anic reading uses music to "engage the emotions and heighten the listener's involvement in recitation" (ibid., 188). However, the Qur'an recitation achieves an ecstatic rather than a prayerful end. Kristina Nelson notes that the "sincere participant in recitation [of the Qur'an] is, and indeed should be, moved to tears by the wonder and beauty of the event, by the awe of God, and by humility in the face of His omnipotence" (ibid.). The respective Jewish and Islamic contexts achieve different ends. Regarding Syrian liturgy, in the words of Margaret J. Kartomi, "the 'hybrid' has become a new species" (1981, 233). Viewed on its own terms, Syrian liturgy, while based on Arab practices, transforms these familiar devices into a new form.

Re-creating the liturgy is also a part of re-creating a sense of self influenced by the past that forms the present. Kay Kaufman Shelemay views the *pizmonim* as maintaining a connection to a "delocalized and, perhaps idealized 'Oriental' past" (1998, 230). In the same way, the liturgy blurs their view of the past since it contains biblical, rabbinic, and postrabbinic texts representing Jewish history from ancient Jewish times through the medieval period. Taking into account the *pizmonim* and *bakkashot*, Syrian-composed Hebrew poetry as a part of the liturgical process, these more recent texts fill the gap historically between the postrabbinic texts of the medieval period to the twenty-first century. Thus, Syrian liturgy surveys Jewish history from biblical times to the present. At the same time, the variety of musical styles in the service expresses the liturgical text and reflects the community members' identity as Jews from an Arab land. The liturgy pulls various pasts together for Syrian Jews in order to connect them to their Jewish heritage and Arab sensibilities.

Mark Slobin, in his study of the American Ashkenazic cantorate, comments on the parallel task of the *ḥazzan* and the Talmudic scholar. Just as the latter incorporates the past to inform ongoing learning in the present, the *ḥazzan* "based on the past, moves ever forward into a musical present as part of an unfinished commentary on the sacred texts" (1989, 10). Returning to the land of Israel and rebuilding the Temple remain central textual themes in Jewish liturgy. So too Syrian cantors provide commentary "on the sacred texts." Their rendering of the Sabbath service synthesizes time and place, thereby shaping the present. As Barbara Kirshenblatt-Gimblett suggests, "folklore is made[,] not found" (1995, 369). Each Sabbath, Syrian Jewish identity is made and remade. Drawing from various pasts and places, Syrian liturgy forms and reinforces a Judeo-Arab synthesis.

Adaptive Process: Reassociating Meaning through *Maqāmāt*

THE *MAQĀM* PROVIDES the thread of continuity in the process of music and meaning reformulation. The choice of fitting a melody to a "heavy" or "light" liturgical singing station is not determined by the meaning of the text of the Arab song or of the *pizmon* (chapter 7). A melody's *maqām* and rhythm are the criteria for use of the particular melody in the liturgy. The goal for Syrian cantors is adherence to the *maqām* of the day; if the proper *maqām* is not employed, a cantor is seen as one who does not follow the Syrian liturgical system. In his discussion of the double biblical reading mentioned in chapter 10, Cantor David Tawil remarked that two *maqāmāt* need to be used in certain instances. He claims that it is important for the cantor to "mention" two specific *maqāmāt* in his prayers.[7] Note that the emphasis is on mentioning a *maqām* and not on a melody. The prayers are somehow incomplete unless the cantor uses a specific *maqām*—or in unique instances two *maqāmāt*—during Shaḥarit.

The *maqām* carries extramusical associations in its liturgical usage. Although no objective criteria verifies the mood or affect of the association, Syrian cantors do discuss extramusical meaning attached to the *maqām*. What then is the relationship of the *maqām* to the liturgy? What meaning is derived from a *maqām*'s usage in the Syrian liturgical system? Ali Jihad Racy comments on *maqām* associations and the notion of *salṭana* ("modal ecstasy" in Arab musical performance):

> Today musicians attribute *salṭana* to a number of factors. Some established musicians from Cairo, Damascus, and Aleppo, including Sabāḥ Fakhrī, are aware of medieval Arab treatises on musical cosmology and the general implication of celestial modal influence upon humans on certain days or at specific times of the day. . . . [T]he notion implies direct causalities between the momentary appeal of specific modes and the momentary configurations of heavenly entities. . . . The cosmological explanation as to why at certain times we feel inclined to perform in specific *maqāmāt* is not explicitly subscribed to by practicing musicians in general. However, such musicians still allude to a possible external source for *salṭana,* primarily because at times modes "impose" themselves in ways that appear too mystifying and compelling. (1991a, 13)

Perhaps it is the "mystifying and compelling" or appealing aspects of historical associations and usage of a *maqām* that Syrian cantors desire to perpetuate in Syrian liturgy. The extramusical associations also offer the means to disassociate a melody with its Arab source and allow the creation of new meaning for the melody. Consequently, the extramusical association of a *maqām* transforms a melody into the liturgy.

In order to offer interpretive insights into the meaning of *maqāmāt* in Syrian liturgy, it is important to view the Sabbath morning service within the context of the entire Sabbath day. In this manner, using the *maqām* of the day becomes intrinsically linked to the Sabbath. In contrast to the weekday service, the Sabbath liturgy centers on appropriate textual themes from the Bible and elsewhere that present God as the creator of the world. Since God rested, humans are instructed to rest. The added prayers for the Sabbath focus on affirming God as creator, God's closeness to the Jewish people, and the promise of *olam haba* (the world to come). Abraham Joshua Heschel focuses on the Sabbath's temporal aspects stating that "the meaning of the Sabbath is to celebrate time rather than space. Six days a week we live under the tyranny of things of space; on the Sabbath we try to become attuned to *holiness in time*" (Heschel 1951 [1986], 10). In the introduction to a Syrian prayer book the editor discusses the special nature of Shabbat:

> Shabbat is more than just rest in the physical sense, whereby one takes a respite and relaxes from his strenuous weekday affairs. Rather, after a week of being immersed in mundane, material and worldly matters, on the Shabbat, a Jew mentally, emotionally and spiritually discards his weekday existence and enters a state of tranquility and holiness, utilizing the Shabbat to rejuvenate his soul and elevate his spirit.
>
> Thus, every aspect of a Jew's existence is different on Shabbat: his demeanor is different; his talk is different; his walk is different; his dress is different; his meals are different;
>
> . . . and his prayers are different. . . . (*Siddur kol sassoon* 1995, xx)

Reciting Syrian liturgy in the *maqām* of the day parallels the Sabbath's liminal time. Cantor Moses Tawil commented that he vividly remembers his older brother Naphtali's rendering of the liturgy. He admired Naphtali's ability to clearly focus the *maqām* of the day in all the singing stations and his subsequent improvisations. Tawil remarked, "after my brother [Naphtali] prayed Shaḥarit I heard the *maqām* in my head all day" (M. Tawil, interview, June 6,

1993). For Tawil, there is an inherent association between the Sabbath and the *maqām* for the entire day and not just for the Sabbath morning service. Just as the entire Sabbath is liminal in contradistinction to the remaining days of the week and thereby creates a different status of time, the *maqām* of the day becomes a sonic element that differentiates a distinctive state of musical sound. The three heavy liturgical singing stations of Shaḥarit particularly suspend time; their slow tempo melodies extend the prayers for meaningful expression. The *ḥazzan's* freedom to improvise includes melodic ornamentation, elongation of phrases and the opportunity for exploration of two or more tetrachords of the *maqām*. Hence, sound that becomes sacred, the *maqām* of the day, is a part of time that becomes sacred, the Sabbath. A *maqām,* then, does not only resignify an Arab song, it resignifies the realm of sound during holy time. Thus, holiness of sound coincides with "holiness in time."

Music and Culture Contact

MUSICAL, AESTHETIC, AND cultural tastes are highly fluid among Syrian Jews in Brooklyn. Arab music and culture are valued but not in every facet of Syrian Jewish life. The liturgy holds a special place that retains a synthesis formed in, and representing, the past. Kay Kaufman Shelemay states: "If the conceptual and affective doubleness of the Syrian pizmon is at once an expression of a dual Jewish and Arab identity, it may also serve to conceal that symbiosis" (Shelemay 1998, 226). No doubt this doubleness is even more complex in the liturgy. Sabbath liturgy forms a Judeo-Arab identity regularly experienced in Syrian Jewish life.

Syrian liturgy illustrates the adaptive capacity of a Jewish musical tradition, namely, the acceptance in Jewish ritual practices of Arab music.[8] For many Syrian Jews, singing the melodies, as a cantor or congregant, allows the individual to maintain his identity by being Jewish and Arab in his own way. Since they are great devotees of Arab culture, it is not unexpected to find the Jewish ritual practices of Syrian Jews laced with Arab music. It is not just a simple borrowing. The complex network, as represented in figure 7, shows how Syrian Jews play with and adapt elements of Arab culture for Jewish purposes. Melodies in liturgy are changing slowly with the emergence of a new generation of Israeli-born cantors. Despite this change in melodies, style of performance and reliance on *maqām,* both Arab components, remain the mainstay of the liturgical design. This suggests that performance practice may be more significant than the melodies themselves. The goal for an Aleppo-style *ḥazzan* is to deliver prayers through reciting in a refined and spontaneous manner that evokes the meaning of the text and to elicit the participation of the congregation through a variety of melodies. The essence of Syrian liturgy consists of the dynamic interaction between the *ḥazzan* and the congregation such that members of the synagogue participate and thus worship.

The music-culture contact categories of Bruno Nettl (1978, 1985) and Margaret J. Kartomi (1981) provide the foundation to view music of culture contact where two musical systems are synthesized. However, Syrian liturgy is a unique form of culture contact since Syrian prayer synthesizes an Arab musical system and a Jewish religious tradition within a ritual context. Like the *pizmonim* process of adapting paraliturgical texts, deeply embedded Arab components are found in the liturgy. In the Sabbath morning prayer, the organized use of the *maqāmāt* and the design of the service provide a clear case of nontangible musical components that have penetrated cultural boundaries. Thus, these components of Syrian liturgy contrast Kartomi's observation of usually surface features only found in music culture contact: "But it is likely that in this [*kroncong*-Portuguese-Malay folk songs in Tugu] and other cases of contact, aesthetic tastes and standards, together with many of the extramusical meanings attached to music, have tended to cross cultural boundaries with far greater difficulty than have tangible objects such as musical instruments" (1981, 244). Judeo-Arab synthesis of Syrian liturgy offers an example of musical features that go beyond the difficulty of "tangible objects." The persistence of the extramusical associations of the *maqāmāt* allows the liturgy to absorb and innovate music of other cultures.

The penetration of nontangible musical components is less difficult in the context of Syrian liturgy when considering that Syrian Jews are not entirely culturally distinct from Arabs. Cultural interaction was a part of Jewish life in Aleppo. Two complementary cultures have interacted historically, and the process of this synthesis continues in Brooklyn. Syrian liturgy is a unique case of culture contact where two musical cultures are not combined. Two entities, Arab music and Jewish liturgical texts, synthesize through adaptable artistic forms in Arab music and the allowance of such modes of expression in Judaism. Music in Syrian liturgy is music that is the result of cultures in contact, not the result of musical culture contact. Music, religion, and culture intersect in a complementary manner.

Concluding Thoughts

THE SYRIAN LITURGICAL tradition in Brooklyn faces a significant test in the future. The current generation is presently training Israeli-born cantors in the

Aleppo style. These younger cantors bring with them a new repertoire of melodies and a different style of rendering *maqāmāt.*[9] While the pre-1950s *pizmonim* are the core of liturgical melodies, there is some ambivalence toward straying too far from these foundations of the liturgy. As these new cantors adapt to the community they will undoubtedly have an influence on the repertoire and the nature of the service. The process of creating prayers offered by the Syrians promises a dynamic and resilient liturgical practice.

Walter Paul Zenner's comment that "the most Arab of cultural forms for Syrian Jews in Brooklyn is paradoxically one of the most Jewish" (2002, 166) refers to the Arab nature of their Jewish prayer. Thus, Syrians perform Jewish ritual with Arab melodies and aesthetics effectively blurring boundaries of "Jewish" and "Arab." Despite Middle Eastern political tensions between Jews and Arabs, Syrians re-create or enact their identity as Jews. In other domains of Syrian life, such as food and literature, they also display a Judeo-Arab synthesis; ritual shows the most intensely rooted cultural aesthetics. Religious expression, therefore, is at times porous, absorbing many influences. Syrian Jewish religious expression fuses identity, ethnicity, and heritage.

The structure and design of Syrian Sabbath liturgy allows for the continued expression of deeply embedded Arab elements within the Syrian Jew's religious life. If the goal of a ritual is to organize and make sense of the world (Geertz 1973, 89; Ortner 1978, 5), the Syrian Jewish Sabbath liturgy provides a salient example. This musical liturgical organization rests on a synthesis of Jewish religious meaning with related Arab extramusical associations. Sherry B. Ortner states: "The ritual process, then is a matter of shaping actors in such a way that they wind up appropriating cultural meaning as personally held orientations" (Ortner 1978, 5). Giving new meaning to Arab music and aesthetics provides a new context, making Syrian rituals personally significant for cantors and members of the community. Music as an activity within ritual including melodies, aesthetics, extramusical associations, and performance are part of the cultural process that transcend time and place. Syrian Sabbath liturgy in Brooklyn expresses and affirms a particular Judeo-Arab heritage.

Notes

Introduction

1. Yitgadal v'Yitkadash is an important liturgical passage sung by the *ḥazzan* during the Sabbath morning service.
2. He is referring to the segmentation of a *maqām* that guides the melodic rendering of the service.
3. Population estimates vary between twenty-four and thirty-five thousand: Daniel J. Elazar estimates the size of the Brooklyn community to be twenty-four thousand (1989, 171); Jonathan Schachter, thirty thousand (1991, 9); and Rabbi Zevulun Lieberman, thirty-five thousand (1991). Robert Chira states there are forty thousand Aleppo immigrants and their descendants in the United States and Canada (1994, 1, 21).
4. "Ashkenazic" and "Sephardic" refer to two groups of different geographical origins in Judaism, each with distinct liturgical rites and customs. Further divisions are made within each group; see Zimmels 1958. The Syrian Jews are a particular group of Sephardic Jews. Further distinctions of Sephardic Jewry and its relation to Syrian Jews are discussed in chapter 2.
5. Obadia, a Jew who was born in Iraq, emigrated to America in 1952 and currently lives on Long Island. He is a renowned violinist and *ūd* player and has made close to one hundred recordings of Arab music. He is also trained in Western music with an undergraduate degree in music from the University of California at Berkeley. Obadia is now retired after twenty-five years of teaching music in the public school system in Long Island, New York. Although not of Syrian origin, he is actively involved as a performer for the Brooklyn Syrian Jewish and Arab communities of New York City and the vicinity.
6. The recordings in the Sephardic Archives contain interviews with members of the community and melodic examples of *bakkashot, pizmonim,* and portions of the liturgy. Some recordings were deposited by the New York University Urban Ethnomusicology seminar, and others were completed by members of the community interested in documenting their tradition.
7. Tawil is not an ordained rabbi but is often given the traditional title *ḥakham* because of his learned devotion to religious texts.

8. Jeffrey A. Summit describes similar experiences (2000, 8).
9. Summit notes similar experiences in what he describes as "recording unrecordable music" (2000, 9–11).

Chapter 1

1. Abraham Zvi Idelsohn's study compares Syrian liturgical practices to other Sephardic traditions. Macy Nulman focuses solely on the liturgy of the Syrian Jews for the Sabbath and other occasions, but the article-length study is too brief to explore the subject fully.
2. Walter Paul Zenner has focused primarily on Syrian Jews in Israel (1965, 1968, 1980, 1982a, 1982b, 2000) and, to a limited extent, other locales, including Manchester, England (1990, 2000), and Buenos Aires (2000).
3. See Joan Vincent's review article "System and Process, 1974–1985" (1986) for an investigation of anthropological studies of ecological and judicial processes in addition to ritual.
4. Non-Arab melodies of Western origin are used, but their appearance is not nearly as common.
5. The extramusical associations of a mode—such as ethos and mood—are found in other cultures throughout music history (Powers 1981, 525) and a feature common to modes in many cultures (Hood 1971, 324).
6. In later centuries the use of known melodies markedly declined: "Contrafacta virtually disappeared in nineteenth- and twentieth-century art music. This can be attributed to the premium placed on originality and the belief in the uniqueness of the individual work of art that has prevailed since the 19th century" (Picker 1980, 701).
7. For a useful summary of studies focusing on Judeo-Arab syntheses, see Wasserstrom 1990, 43–47, and 1995, 3–12. Historians S. D. Goitein (1955) and Bernard Lewis (1984), e.g., explore the historical and cultural dimensions of a Judeo-Arab synthesis, focusing on the religious organization of Judaism and Islam and its cultural dimensions (see particularly Goitein 1955, 59–60; Lewis 1984, 73). Goitein states that Jews did not create a Jewish culture in Arab lands but rather a "Judaeo-Arab symbiosis" (10). Lewis uses the term "Judaeo-Islamic symbiosis" to denote the religious influences of Arab culture on Judaism (77). I have chosen to use the term "Judeo-Arab synthesis" to show the composite tradition between cultures that includes both secular and religious elements.
8. The breadth and depth of Arab inquiries into science and the humanities encouraged and profoundly influenced Jewish cultural and religious life in Muslim Spain. Jews had the opportunity to adhere freely to their religious practices, and prominent Jews encouraged creativity alongside the developments of Arab culture in Spain; the Jews sought to fuse the two cultures.
9. Goitein, Lewis, and others (Rosen 1972; Goldberg 1978; Stillman 1979, 1991; Deshen and Zenner 1982; Zenner 1980; Wasserstrom 1995) focus on cultural syntheses of the past.
10. Harvey E. Goldberg (1990) looks at Jewish life in Muslim Libya, examining the customs that unite and divide Jews and their Muslim neighbors.
11. Much of Shamosh's literature deals with being an Aleppo-Syrian Jew in Israel, in America, and in other locations; for an overview of his works, see Zenner 1988.
12. Kartomi clarifies her terminology: ethnomusicologists, she claims, took from various disciplines in the sciences and used words such as *hybrid, crossfertilized, pastiche, transplanted, exotic, fused, blended,* and *integrated* (1981, 228). Kartomi criticizes such terms since they favor a "pure" tradition often approached with negative attitudes. The term *hybrid* for example, draws "attention to the music's parentage or ancestors . . . rather than to the musical offspring, which is the primary object of interest and value to the people identifying with it.

The union of the parent musics is a necessary but not sufficient condition for musical synthesis and transformation to take place" (ibid.). Kartomi prefers to use the "proper names" of synthesized music rather than "undifferentiated terms like 'hybrid'" (229).

13. Nettl also offers various categories of responses, but his focus is the Western influence on non-Western cultures; see particularly 1978, 130–34.
14. The syncretism of musical traditions is discussed in the studies of many cultures throughout the world (Merriam 1964, 313–15; Manuel 1988, 91).
15. Religious life in the Syrian community since the 1950s has been influenced significantly by Orthodox Ashkenazic Jews. See Zenner and Kligman 2000, 168–71.
16. Zenner's work on Syrian identity in Israel views Syrian identity vis-à-vis Ashkenazic and Sephardic Jews (1965) and Syrian communities globally (2000).

Chapter 2

1. Although the focus of this study is on the Jews from Aleppo, I will refer to the history of Jews from both Aleppo and Damascus, since their pasts are interrelated. For a discussion of the difference between Aleppo and Damascus Jewry, see Zenner 1965, 58, 65, 96, and Cohen 1973, 99, 137–39, 176.
2. Aram-Tsoba is mentioned in II Samuel 10:6, 8 and Psalms 60:2; the location Tzoba is mentioned in II Samuel 8:3. Aram-Damasek is mentioned in Chronicles 18:5, 6, and Damasek is mentioned in II Samuel 8:5–6 and II Kings 5:12.
3. This legend was first recorded by a twelfth-century traveler, Pethahiah of Regensburg (Cohen 1972, 562). Syrian Jews believe that King David's general Joab Ben Seruyah conquered Aram-Tsoba; some Aleppo Jews claim that the general established a synagogue and Jews lived in Aleppo uninterrupted since that time (Sutton 1979, 155).
4. A scarcity of sources presents difficulties for further explication for early Jewish history in Aleppo.
5. Sephardic Jews are those whose descent is from the "Mediterranean and western Asia, including their eastern and western diasporas" (Elazar 1989, 14). The definition of Sephardic Jewry is a debated subject. At issue is the application of the label "Sephardic" for Jews who are not from Spain or descendants of Jews from Spain; a concise discussion of the use of the term appears in Elazar 1989 (14–17). In this study I will use the term "Sephardic" to refer to the larger body of non-Ashkenazic Jewry. Since the Syrian Jews in Brooklyn identify themselves as Sephardim, most likely they claim a legacy to Spanish Jewry. See also Shelemay 1998 (72–73) for further consideration of Syrians as Sephardim.
6. For an extended treatment of this subject, see Lutzky 1940.
7. This was not true, however, of Damascus (Cohen 1973, 137). The effects of the Frankish Jews upon the religious tradition are discussed by scholars but not in detail (see Lutzky 1940; Stillman 1979, 318). There were apparently conflicts between the Frankish and indigenous Jews in Aleppo. However, by the twentieth century the distinctions between these subgroups had faded and they had merged into one community (Zenner 1965, 34–35; 1982a, 157–59).
8. In fact, Shabbatai Tzvi (1625–76), a self-proclaimed messiah, sought popular support in the Ottoman Empire during an economically depressed period (Shaw 1991, 131). Due to economic limitations and social opportunities, mysticism offered an alternative to present realities. Shabbatai Tzvi represented a messianic option. He gained support for his cause in Aleppo in 1665 (135).
9. The current estimates of Sephardic Jews in the United States, 150,000 to 200,000 (Papo 1992, 303), suggest that they make up approximately 2.8 percent of the general Jewish population

in the country (Elazar 1989, 166). The Sephardic population is dwarfed in comparison to the Ashkenazic mainstream.

10. Rabbi Kassin was born in Palestine and was ordained at a seminary in Jerusalem. He was brought to New York by the community to serve in this capacity (Kassin 1980, 6–7; Sutton 1988, 80). He was a revered leader, and his death in December 1994 was covered in New York Jewish newspapers (Yellin 1995) and the *New York Times* (Herszenhorn 1994).
11. His Hebrew name was Moshe Ashkar. See Shelemay 1998 (33) for a further description. The Arabic pronunciation of this name would be "Ash'ar".
12. These traits, particularly pertaining to the cantors, are discussed in chapter 11.
13. In Israel, Ashkenazic and Syrian Jews are more involved with one another and share many of the same institutions (Zenner 1965, 359; 2000, 97).
14. Syrians are pleased with their low intermarriage rate, since this is a major issue for American Jewry. The then chief rabbi of the Syrian community, Rabbi Kassin, issued a decree against interreligious marriage in 1935. This decree stipulated that any Syrian Jew who married a non-Jew, even one who converted to Judaism, would not be given honors in the synagogue or buried in a Jewish cemetery. This decree has been renewed in subsequent years, most recently in 1984 (see Sutton 1988, 84a–d), and a laminated copy of the decree, signed by representatives from thirty-five synagogues and organizations, is prominently displayed in every Syrian synagogue. Although converts are permitted historically in Judaism according to Jewish law, Syrian rabbis strictly forbid this practice out of a concern to preserve the integrity of their Jewish commitment (Chira 1994, 65n5).
15. Although the coffeehouses are no longer in existence, they were important centers for culture contact in the first half of the century in Manhattan's Lower East Side. Zenner claims coffeehouses were more readily found in Brooklyn than in Israel (1983, 183).

Chapter 3

1. Since the focus of this study is the Sabbath morning service, my comments on the liturgical text are likewise taken from this liturgy. Few piyyutim are incorporated into the Sabbath liturgy, but the liturgy of the Three Festivals and High Holidays make prominent use of piyyutim.
2. The Shema is discussed extensively in the Talmud (Babylonian Talmud, Tractate Berakhot, chapters 1–3) and rabbinic literature (*Shulḥan Arukh: Oraḥ Ḥayyim* §58–88). The Shema is recited twice a day, with the second recitation during the evening prayers. The Amidah, also discussed extensively in the Talmud (Babylonian Talmud, Tractate Berakhot, chapters 3–6) and rabbinic literature (*Shulḥan Arukh: Oraḥ Ḥayyim* §59–127), is said three times a day during the week and four times daily on the Sabbath and festivals.
3. See Lawrence Hoffman's discussion of rites and reevaluation of earlier scholarship, "Rites: A Case of Social Space" (1987, 46–59).
4. For a listing of specific practices by Syrians in Brooklyn see Dobrinsky 1986 (171–74). For a discussion of Syrian and Spanish and Portuguese ritual practices in Manchester, England, see Zenner 2000 (67).
5. Since the publication of *Maḥzor aram-tzoba*, no specific prayer book for the Syrian Jews has been published. The Hebrew printing house in Livorno, Italy, supplied prayer books, and books of *pizmonim*, for the North African and Levantine communities in pre- and early-modern times; see Attilio Milano and Cecil Roth, "Leghorn," *Encyclopaedia Judaica* 1972, 1572–73. My thanks to Isaac Ades, who showed me several prayer books that were printed in Livorno and used by his family in Aleppo; Mr. Ades is a great-nephew of Raphael Antebi Taboush.

6. The English version of the siddur is *Siddur Kol Yaakob Hashalem: Daily Prayer Book According to the Minhag of Aleppo (Aram Soba)* (New York: Sephardic Heritage Foundation, 1990, 1995). An earlier version, printed in 1985, was edited and arranged by Rabbi David Bitton. Several holiday prayer books have been printed under the name *Maḥzor shelom yerushalayim*. The full title of the first volume is *Maḥzor shelom yerushalayim (ha-shalem), ḥeilek rishon: seder tefilot le-rosh ha-shannah ke-minhag b'nei aram tzoba be-khol artzot megurehem ha-shem aleihem yiḥyu* (Maḥzor Shelom Yerushalayim [complete], volume 1, the order of the prayers for Rosh ha-Shannah according to the customs of the people of Aleppo in all lands, may God dwell with them). The English version is *Mahazor Shelom Yerushalayim Volume One: Prayers for the Rosh Hashanah*, edited and arranged by Ezekiel H. Albeg (New York: Sephardic Heritage Foundation, 1990). The English title page gives the date of 1970 and indicates this is the seventh printing, but the Hebrew page gives the Hebrew date of 5749, which corresponds to 1989–90. The publication dates of the other volumes are as follows: volume 2 for Yom Kippur, 1989; volume 3 for Sukkot, 1990; volume 4 for Pesaḥ, 1991; volume 5 for Shavuot, 1994.
7. Here Catton refers to *Siddur tefilat yeshurun: ke-minhag kehilot ha-kodesh shel ha-yehudim ha-sephardim be-artzot ha-mizraḥ me-kodemet moshvoteihem* (New York: Hebrew Publishing Company, [1935]). Other prayer books used in the Brooklyn Syrian community include *Seder ha-tefilot: ke-fi minhag ha-sephardim be-amerika im targum angli* [*Book of Prayer: According to the Customs of the Spanish and Portuguese Jews*], 2nd ed., ed. and trans., David De Sola Pool (New York: Union of Sephardic Congregations, 1947) [in Hebrew and English]; and *Siddur sukkat david yerushalayim: le-sephardim u-b'nei edot ha-mizraḥ* (New York: American Friends of Sucath David, 1985–86).

   One example of a Syrian liturgical practice that is reflected in the prayer books is Kabbalat Shabbat, the portion of the liturgy that immediately precedes the Sabbath evening prayers. General Sephardic practice is to recite seven psalms, followed by a piyyut called Lekha dodi, followed by Psalms 92 and 93, then concluding with a section from rabbinic literature (see *Siddur tefilat yeshurun*, 133–40, and *Siddur sukkat david*, 177–86—both reflect general Sephardic practice). The Syrian practice is to recite one of the seven psalms, followed by an abbreviated form of Lekha dodi, Psalms 92 and 93, then recite the same passage from rabbinic literature and follow that with a repetition of Psalms 92 and 93 (see *Siddur kol ya'akov* [1990], 189–96, and *Siddur beit yosef* [1979–80], 197–203). This is an Aleppo custom not practiced by Damascus Jews (Cabasso, interview, May 29, 1992); the prayer book that reflects the Damascus practice follows the general Sephardic convention (see *Siddur eit ratzon: kulal ha-tefilot le-khol ha-shannah le-ḥol le-shabbatot le-roshei ḥadashim u-le-mo'adim*, 4th ed. [Brooklyn: Ahiezer (*sic*) Congregation, 1987], 157–63).
8. The first Aleppo prayer book published in the Brooklyn community was compiled by Gabriel Shrem, who died in 1986. The prayer book is *Siddur beit yosef ve-ohel avraham: ke-minhag aram tzoba le-eidot ha-sephardim be-khol mekomoteihem* (Jerusalem: Aleppian Publication Society, 5740 [1979–80]). *Siddur beit ratzon*, a prayer book prepared for the Aḥi Ezer Congregation of Brooklyn, follows the Damascus Syrian tradition.
9. The title page of *Siddur kol sassoon* includes the following information: "A new linear, Sephardic Siddur with English translation and an anthologized commentary including the laws and customs of Sephardic communities in all parts of the world."
10. This practice is common among other Sephardic Jews. See Dobrinsky 1986 (233–34), which discusses the highlighted textual portions according to Moroccan Jewish practice. See chapter 7 for a discussion on the use of Nishmat Kol Ḥai in Syrian liturgy.
11. All four of these prayer books have been or are currently being used in the Syrian community.

12. Other sung portions of the service are presented in the same manner in the recent publications.
13. From personal experience in learning Syrian liturgy, the visual cues created by the layout of the last figure made following the service significantly easier.
14. Ezra Albeg, the editor of *Maḥzor shelom yerushalayim,* states in his introduction to the first two volumes that they are compiled in the tradition of *Seder Rav Amram* and the later prayer books through *Maḥzor aram tsoba* (1:[4]; 2:[4]). Additionally, the title page of *Maḥzor aram tsoba* is reproduced in the respective High Holiday prayer books (1:[8]; 2:[8]), another instance of paying homage to and representing the past with the new printing.
15. Perez Smolenskin (1842–85) asserts that the term *ḥazzan* is derived from the Hebrew word *ḥarzan,* meaning versifier or rhymester, whose function was to supplant the prayers with his own poems and hymns (Nulman 1975, 102).
16. For more on this subject, see Shiloah 1992, (111–29).
17. *Bakkashot* literally means "requests," and the poetry typically contains petitions to God. *Pizmonim* are synonymous with piyyutim, since they do not always occur in a particular poetic form. A later designation of the term refers to a rhymed poem or hymn arranged in strophic form with a refrain for congregational response (Nulman 1975, 196). This is a good characterization for most Syrian *pizmonim.* Other communities are also active in the composing of piyyutim, most notably in Israel; see Seroussi 1993a.
18. *Bakkashot* are more actively performed in the liturgy in Jerusalem. My thanks to Geoffrey Goldberg for allowing me to consult his study of Syrian *bakkashot:* "Syrian-Jewish Religious and Social Song: A Literary and Ethnomusicological Enquiry, with Particular Reference to *Bakkashot,*" master's thesis, New York University, 1988. Zenner refers to the *bakkashot* practice in Israel (1965, 195–96, 219–20; 2000, 99; see also Yayama 2003). For the treatment of this subject in another community, see Seroussi 1985. On the publication of *bakkashot* books in the nineteenth century, see Seroussi 1993a. Shelemay discusses the contextual usage of *bakkashot* and *pizmonim* as well as the *petichot,* introductory texts sung before a piyyut (1998, 150–55); she also compares the practice of these genres in Brooklyn, Israel, and Mexico (1998, 87–88).
19 An earlier *pizmonim* collection by Moshe Ashear, *Hallel ve-zimrah* (Jerusalem, 1928), is in the possession of only a few members of the community in Brooklyn. *SUHV* combines the contents and the titles of the two earlier works and is a reprinting of this 1928 publication with additions from another collection of *pizmonim* by Raphael Hayyim, *Shir u-shevaḥah* (Jerusalem, 1905 and 1921). For a discussion of the publication of books by Aleppo poets in the late nineteenth century and early twentieth century, see Seroussi 1993a.
20. For a reproduction of this title page, see Shelemay 1998 (39).
21. For a further description of the close association of the Arabic song texts as models for the *pizmonim,* see Kligman 1997 (146) and Shelemay 1998 (95). For further investigation of the *pizmonim* texts, see Kligman 1997 (132–55, 166–80) and the prelude to each chapter in Shelemay 1998.
22. This is the subject of investigation in Shelemay and Weiss 1985 and Shelemay 1988, 1994, and 1998.
23. There are several *pizmonim* by Taboush with the melodic indication of *muzikah* in the *nahawand* section of *pizmonim* in *SUHV* (#210–13). One *pizmon* in *maqām ajam,* Sharim roznim (*SUHV* #205), has the melodic designation "Turkey." For a further discussion of non-Arab melodies, see Shelemay 1998 (205).
24. The *nahawand pizmonim* correspond to the Western minor scale, and *ajam* to a major scale. Hence, European melodies are used as source material for the composition of *pizmonim.* Ḥazzan Isaac Cabasso said that Asher was a great admirer of opera (*Pizmonim* Class, Novermber 11, 1991). See chapter 4 for a further discussion of *maqām.*

Chapter 4

1. A *qaṣā'id*'s textual source can derive from classical or folk poetry (al-Faruqi 1981, 260–61).
2. Taken from an interview with Morris Antebi, who was born in Aleppo and immigrated to the United States in 1980.
3. After the opening of the Suez Canal in 1869, European dignitaries came to Cairo to hear Verdi's *Rigoletto* at the opera house in Cairo (Hournai 1991, 283).
4. Shelemay discusses the topic of the Judeo-Arab musical practices of Syrian Jews in Brooklyn in detail in chapter 3, "The Judeo-Arab Musical Tradition," 104–34. On the transmission of Arab music through recordings, see 33, 43, 106, 108, 113.
5. Morris Antebi takes great pride in stating that Muḥammad ʿAbd al-Wahhāb got his start as a musician in Aleppo (see Sutton 1988, 228).
6. Shelemay notes that weddings contain a mix of Arab music and popular American music (1998, 139). Zenner notes a similar experience at a wedding he observed in 1963; he comments on both Arab and American music and food (1983, 182; see also Zenner and Kligman 2000, 170–71).
7. *Ḥaflāt* are formal private music parties. *Mahrajānāt* are three-day outdoor events with hundreds or thousands of participants involving community interaction, storytelling, networking and matchmaking, eating, and dancing. These were fundraisers for churches and Syrian/Lebanese organizations (Rasmussen 1991, 78).
8. Eddie "the Sheik" Kochak and Hakki Obadia are credited with creating "Amerabic," a synthesis of American and Arab music. Through innovation and assimilation, bands used Western electronic instruments. The quarter tones used in the *maqāmāt* started disappearing, and many instrumental and vocal genres were forgotten (Rasmussen 1989, 94, 1997).
9. For further detail on the practice and usage of *maqāmāt* among Brooklyn Syrian Jews see Kligman 1997 (88–111) and Shelemay 1998 (118–27).
10. The spellings of the *maqāmāt* that will be used in the following discussion, and throughout this study, follow the spellings and pronunciation as practiced among Syrian Jews in Brooklyn. Ḥakham Tawil teaches *maqām* to members of the community, he created several handouts detailing the names and characteristics of the *maqāmāt*. He is inconsistent with the spellings of three *maqāmāt: nahawand* appears as "nahwand," (in its Hebrew spelling of the consonants, the second *a* vowel is missing; thus the pronunciation may vary); *seyga* may also appear as "seygah" or "sigah"; and *saba* also appears as "sabah." These differences are due to variances in transliteration. The main reference book for the use of *maqāmāt* in the liturgy is *SUHV*; the *maqāmāt* are listed with Hebrew letters.

    When referring to the practice of Arab musicians the names of the *maqāmāt* will follow the standard Arabic transliterations taken from Lois Ibsen al-Faruqi's *An Annotated Glossary of Arabic Musical Terms* (1981).
11. The order of Ḥakham Tawil's chart is slightly different than what is presented in this example. His order is as follows: *ajam, nahawand, rast, bayat, kurdy, hijaz, saba, seyga.* Additionally, Ḥakham Tawil's chart includes a section titled "Names of Notes in Arabic Music (Commonly Used)" for two octaves—from G two ledger lines below the treble clef staff to G above the staff.
12. More accurately this should be called a trichord rather than a tetrachord.
13. See Marcus's appendix 7 (833–36) for a listing of *maqāmāt* in published sources and chapter 8, "How Many *Maqāmāt* Are There?" (330–67).
14. "Nine or eleven" is not an approximation. The difference is due to the specificity of the *sīkāh faṣīlah;* some theorists include *huzām* and *'irāq* as separate *faṣā'il,* while others include these two as variants within the *sīkāh faṣīlah* (S. Marcus 1989, 381). Marcus's appendix 9, "Modal

Scales According to Present-Day Theory," lists nine standard *faṣā'il* and their related variants, including *huzām* and *'irāq* in the *sīkāh faṣīlah* (844).

15. The *bayat* tetrachord that Tawil refers to appears in the middle of *maqām 'irāq* rather than at the end as described with *maqāmāt rast* and *māhūr* (diagram from S. Marcus 1989, 523, 534):

maqām sīkāh:	E𝄳 F G A B𝄳 C D E𝄳
	¾ 1 1 ¾ ¾ 1 ¾
	sīkāh rast
maqām 'irāq:	B𝄳 C D E𝄳 F G A B𝄳
	¾ 1 ¾ ¾ 1 1 ¾
	sīkāh bayātī

The term *jins,* Arabic for the defining trichord or tetrachord of a *faṣīlah,* is more useful. The *sīkāh faṣīlah* typically begins on the note E quarter flat and is commonly transposed to B quarter flat. Marcus shows that the B quarter flat and E quarter flat *maqāmāt* make use of three *ajnās*: the first *jins* is *sīkāh,* with the variation in the second and third *ajnās.* The second *jins* in *maqām sīkāh* is *rast,* whereas the second *jins* in *'irāq* is *bayātī.* The third *jins* is not represented in the diagram.

16. Throughout the quotation of transcripts presented, the pronunciation of the *maqām,* if it is not one of the eight basic *maqāmāt,* is in the manner that it was stated in the interview with the standard Arab transliteration, for means of identification, in square brackets. If there is no difference between the two, the standard Arab transliteration will stand.

17.

Maqām nahawand:	C D E♭ F G A♭ B♭ C
maqām nawa anthar:	C D E♭ F♯ G A♭ B C
maqām ḥijāz:	D E♭ F♯ G A B♭ C D

(S. Marcus 1989, 842, 843)

The essential difference between *nahawand* and *nawa anthar* is the fourth note of each *maqām*—F in the former and F sharp in the latter. The resulting augmented second interval in *nawa anthar* creates a similarity with *maqām ḥijāz.*

18. In addition to the piyyutim, *SUHV* contains prayers that are associated with household rituals, like blessings for foods. It also includes two indices of the book's texts: one is alphabetic and the other is by *maqām.*
19. The *bakkashot* in *SUHV* are in order of textual usage, that is, they are sung in the order that they appear.
20. There are four *bakkashot* with alternate melodic renderings in two different *maqāmāt.* Therefore, the number of actual *bakkashot* texts is sixty-four, not sixty-eight. In table 4 both *maqāmāt* are indicated for each of these four texts (see *SUHV,* 45, 48, 61, 69). Two *bakkashot* marked as *seyga* include instructions above the text to sing the *bakkasha* in the *maqām* of the given Sabbath (see 69 and 70—these two appear at the end of the *bakkashot* section).
21. Isaac Cabasso claims to know half of the *pizmonim* in *SUHV;* see Sutton 1988 (484). Shelemay states that less than two hundred are in active transmission (see 1998, 199–204, particularly 202). Some say that a few pizmonim are misclassified by *maqām.*
22. This includes both *nahawand and rahaw nawa.* The typical designation of *rahaw,* a *maqām* only rarely used in general Arab music, is a *rast maqām* with "high focus," that is, melodic emphasis on the upper tetrachord of the *maqām* (Marcus 1989, 842, where it is spelled "rahāwī"). According to Ḥakham Tawil, "the *rahaw* that we adopted and emasculated and transformed really is *nahawand.* . . . This word *rahaw* should never be in existence because nobody knows what it really means" (interview, July 29, 1993). *Rahaw nawa* is included

under the *nahawand faṣīlah* in table 5 (see also Kligman 1997, 101–7, particularly note 29).

23. One chart (pp. 567–68) appeared in the first edition of *SUHV,* and the second and third charts (pp. 568a–568b and 568c–568d, located after p. 569) were printed in later editions. This is discussed in more detail in chapter 7; see table 9. The first two charts list ten *maqāmāt,* and the third lists eight. The ten *maqāmāt* of the first two charts make use of ten of the eleven given in table 5, excluding *muḥayyar;* its absence is not surprising, since its pitch content is identical to *bayat,* with melodic emphasis on the upper part of the *maqām.* Marcus lists *muḥayyar* as "*bayāt* with high focus" (1989, 843).
24. Since *maqām rast* is typically defined as starting on the note C, the characteristic third note of this tetrachord, or *faṣīlah,* is E quarter flat, creating a three-quarter interval between the second and third notes. In fact, *rast* and *seyga* consist of the same set of pitches, though they begin on different notes (see table 5).
25. Maimonides, a major twelfth-century rabbinic figure, responded to a letter from the Jews in Aleppo asking if it was permissible to listen to Arab songs. He responded that it was not permitted because it might lead Jewish people away from being a "holy nation" (letter reproduced in Adler 1975, 240–42; discussed in Shiloah 1992, 85). This opinion was not followed by all in later generations.
26. For a more extended discussion on this topic, see Shiloah 1992, chapter 3, "Music and Religion" (65–86).
27. *Responsa* literature is known in Hebrew as *she'eilot u-teshuvot* (questions and answers), where questions are asked of a major rabbinic figure and answered in a written response. A *responsa* is a specific ruling by an authority of Jewish law on difficult and practical matters.
28. A. Antebi, *Ḥokhmah uMusar* (Jerusalem 1960–61 [Jewish Year 5721]), 10; translation found in Zenner 1982b (200). The 1960 date of Antebi's work is a modern rendition of his nineteenth-century rabbinic text that was printed in Israel.
29. These ideas are also expressed at length by Rabbi Ya'akov Kassin (Jacob Kassin), the chief rabbi of the Syrian community in Brooklyn since 1935; see *SUHV* (28–33).
30. Ashear's introduction is reproduced in the recent edition of *SUHV* (9–10).
31. Ḥakham Yosef mentions several opinions of major medieval rabbis that prohibit the use of a building for Jewish purposes if it was originally used for what is deemed idol worship. He does mention one opinion that does permit the use of such a building, with some restrictions, but cautions that this is a minority view—in the rabbinic reasoning process it is preferable to side with the majority. He reasons that since a physical object is possibly permitted for Jewish use, then surely a melody—a nonphysical object—can be used even if it came from idolatrous origins. My thanks to Rabbi David Levine who helped me understand this text.
32. This response is taken from Ḥakham Yosef's weekly radio addresses in Israel, which are not as technical as the aforementioned written *responsa.*
33. The phrase "chooses songs of praise" is taken from the liturgy from the last sentence of *U-ve-khen yishtabaḥ,* found in *Siddur kol ya'akov* (1990, 50, 260). This portion appears both in the weekday and the Sabbath liturgy. The liturgical passage taken from the *Kedushah; Siddur kol ya'akov* (1990, 61, 273).
34. Yosef states that this principle of reasoning appears in the Jerusalem Talmud, Tractate *Ma'aser sheini,* chapter 5, section 2.
35. In *Siddur kol sassoon* sources quoted regularly draw upon kabbalistic insights, including the Zohar, a classic thirteenth-century text of mysticism; the writings of Rabbi Ḥayyim Vital (1543–1620), who was born in Safed and died in Damascus; and *Ben Ish Ḥai,* by Rabbi Yosef Ḥayyim (1834–1909) of Baghdad.
36. My thanks to Rabbi David Barnett, who shared with me his insights on this text.

Chapter 5

1. The liturgy for the Sabbath is similar to the liturgy for the three pilgrimage festivals with specific extensions reflecting the tone of the festival being observed.
2. Other Sephardic Jews share this feature. Ashkenazic Jews, on the other hand, recite the majority of texts individually. The Ashkenazic *ḥazzan* initiates the liturgical text—this is done by reciting the opening and closing lines of a liturgical text—and leads the singing of important liturgical portions. This is a very different practice than the rendering of the entire service aloud as done by Sephardic Jews.
3. These synagogues include Shaarei Zion, Benai Yosef, and Kol Israel. I also attended one Sabbath service of the Syrian minyan at the Fifth Avenue Synagogue in Manhattan; this is an Ashkenazic synagogue that houses a small Syrian service of about thirty men in a small chapel.
4. My descriptive account focuses on the text and activities that influence the rendering of the music and is based on divisions of the service made by Syrian cantors as well as their explanations. This description is not a complete delineation of every activity in the service.
5. Ashkenazic Jews refer to Zemirot as Pesukei de-Zimrah (verses of song).
6. See Bell 1992 (88–89) for historical background on the use of the term *ritualization*. Bell defines it as "ritual as activity" (89).
7. On one occasion a guest rabbi from Damascus, Syria, spoke at Shaarei Zion in Arabic. The rabbi of the synagogue at the time of the research, Rabbi Abraham Hecht, regularly delivered his sermons in English. The former chief rabbi of the Syrian community in Brooklyn, Rabbi Ḥakham Jacob Saul Kassin, used to give sermons on the High Holy Days in Arabic with some interspersed English phrases (Sutton 1979, 84).
8. Table 6 provides a detailed summary of the Sabbath morning service. For a listing of distinct Syrian practices for Shaḥarit, see Dobrinsky 1986 (171–73). Dobrinsky lists specific wording variants and pronunciation patterns that are distinctive to the Syrian community. In general, his remarks focus on the practices of the Aleppo tradition; he occasionally refers to differences between the Aleppo and Damascus traditions. For an English translation of the Sabbath morning service, see *Siddur kol ya'akov* 1995 (61–70, 443–560).

Chapter 6

1. For a full treatment of the texts of Birkhot ha-Shaḥar, see Freehof 1950–51 (339–55); Hoffman 1979 (127–34); Elbogen 1913 [1993] (76–80). For a succinct discussion of this liturgical section see "Morning Benedictions," *Encyclopaedia Judaica.*
2. Bibliography on the Kaddish is vast. Some important sources are: Pool 1909; "Kaddish," in Elbogen 1913 [1993], 12a, 80–83; Hoffman 1979, 56–65; "Kaddish," *Encyclopaedia Judaica* 10:660–62. The Kaddish occurs at the end of sections of the service as a division marker, appearing in slightly different forms (Elbogen 1913 [1993], 82–83; Hoffman 1979, 191).
3. This form of the Kaddish is recited by the mourners after rendering a section of rabbinic text. According to Jewish Law, mourners recite the Kaddish for a deceased relative for eleven months following the death (*Shulḥan Arukh: Yoreh Deah* 376:4). Another Kaddish recited by the mourners at the end of the service is known as the mourners' Kaddish.
4. For a bibliography of this liturgical section see "The Morning Psalms," in Elbogen 1913 [1993], 11:72–76, 95; Hoffman 1979, 127–34; Herman Kieval, "Pesukei De-Zimra," *Encyclopaedia Judaica.* The Zemirot section of Sephardic liturgy is in a different order and includes more psalms than the corresponding Ashkenazic Pesukei de-Zimra.

5. This phrase is a combination of three separate biblical clauses from Psalms 10:16, Psalms 93:1 and Exodus 15:18.
6. Literally, the "permanent *ḥazzan.*" In this context he means the main *ḥazzan* who will start at Shaḥarit.
7. Translation taken from *Siddur kol ya'akov* 1995 (480).
8. See chapter 10 for a discussion of the association of *maqām seyga* with the Torah.
9. The name of the biblical reading for this Sabbath is Be-Shallaḥ (biblical reading [BR] 2.4, see table 10). The *maqām* for this Sabbath is *ajam* for the joy of leaving Egypt and the successful crossing of the sea.
10. This point can be developed further to include the recitation of Shirat ha-Yam (LS 2.28) in the manner in which the Torah is read. This can be seen to provide a preview of the Torah reading section (LS 4).

Chapter 7

1. The two cantors of Beth Torah alternate leading Shaḥarit. Ḥazzan Cabasso leads for three consecutive weeks, and Yeḥezkiel Zion leads the fourth week. Whoever does not lead Shaḥarit usually leads Musaf.
2. The additional Amidah for the Sabbath is contained within Musaf (see table 6, LS 6.2). The Amidah is also known as the Shemoneh-Esreh (literally, "eighteen"), referring to the eighteen blessings of the liturgical passage; in its present-day form it consists of nineteen blessings, yet it retains the title Shemoneh-Esreh. The Syrians, like other Sephardic Jews, refer to this as the Amidah, which is the term I will use throughout my discussion.
3. Additions for the Sabbath include LSS 3.1.1–3.1.5, while LSS 3.1.6 and 3.1.7 are also said during the week.
4. This form of the Kaddish is known as the Ḥatzi Kaddish ("half Kaddish") since it is not stated in its full form.
5. See Elbogen, "The *Shema* and Its Benedictions," in Elbogen 1913 [1993] (§7:16–24, 96–97). For a historical discussion, see Hoffman 1979 (24–49). This liturgical passage, also known as the *yotzer,* refers to the postbiblical poetry that precedes and follows the Shema. See Elbogen 1913 [1993] (168–70) and Ezra Fleischer, "*Yozerot,*" *Encyclopaedia Judaica.* Moses Tawil frequently uses the term *yotzer.*
6. The nineteen blessings of the Amidah of the weekday liturgy are reduced to seven for the Sabbath. The first and last three blessings (for a total of six) are the same in both the weekday and Sabbath liturgies. The middle thirteen blessings of the weekday are omitted and replaced with Yismaḥ Moshe for the Sabbath.
7. I will refer to these seven sections as "liturgical singing stations." This term is a translation of the Hebrew phrase *taḥanat liturgi* (liturgical stations), which was used to refer to the sung improvised portions of the *piyyutim* by cantors in the sixth to eighth centuries (Carmi 1981, 19). I have adapted the concept to fit the liturgical context for the sung liturgical portions. I thank Professor Edwin Seroussi for suggesting this term.
8. The vocal improvisation that begins Shaḥarit proper is found elsewhere in Syrian musical performance. Kay Kaufman Shelemay notes that the *layālī,* Arab introductory vocal solo improvisation, also opened performances of *pizmonim* at concerts (1998, 152–53, 193). The Hebrew word for opening, *petiḥa,* is the equivalent to the Arab *layālī*; see *SUHV*: 97–106 for examples. Kumiko Yayama also investigates the singing of *petiḥot* (see 2003, 271–316).
9. He means the improvisation of the latter part of the Kaddish.
10. The first line of Semeḥim be-Tseitam translates, "Splendor and glory they bestow upon His Name."

11. This portion extends from after Semeḥim be-Tseitam (La-Kel Asher Shavat, LS 3.3.5) until a few lines before the Shema (through most of Ahavat Olam, LS 3.3.8).
12. Kedusha refers to the section that begins with the word "nak'dishakh" (LS 3.6.2, singing station 7). The Amidah is first recited silently by everyone, and then it is repeated out loud by the *ḥazzan*. This is a portion within the Amidah that proclaims the holiness of God. Included is the thrice holy state of God taken from Isaiah 6:3, which appears as the Sanctus in Christian liturgies.
13. Here he is referring to the section within the Amidah where the members of the priestly class (*kohanim*) bless the congregation. The term *Dukhan Kohanim* is used by Ashkenazic Jews. This illustrates Ḥazzan Tawil's knowledge of Sephardic as well as Ashkenazic liturgical terminology. The Ashkenazic custom is for the *kohanim* to bless the congregation only on the High Holidays and the three pilgrimage festivals.
14. Tawil is referring to the Kaddish of Birkhot ha-Shaḥar (LS 2.17), which is declaimed in the *seyga* recitation pattern. He feels that this recitation is not a "melody" and, therefore, is "said plain."
15. The specific laws for reciting the priestly benediction in the Syrian community appear in a festival prayer book for the holiday of Sukkot; see *Maḥzor shelom yerushalayim: Ḥelek Shelishi, Seder Tefilot le-Khavod Ḥag ha-Sukkot* (1990, 191).
16. Ḥakham David Tawil uses the same terminology as well as "the three major parts of the prayers" (interview, July 29, 1992). The term *keter* (crown) is the first of the ten heavenly spheres, or emanations of God, in the Kabbalah, or Jewish Mysticism (Scholem 1972, 570–71). The Hebrew term *shlosha ketarim* [three crowns] is mentioned in *Pirke Avot* (*The Sayings of the Fathers*, 4:17). The three crowns mentioned are Torah, priesthood, and kingship.
17. Yayama discusses the frequent changes of *maqāmāt* in *bakkashot* performance (see 2003, 274–89, 556–67).
18 For examples of *pizmonim* adapted from instrumental genres, see Shelemay and Weiss 1985 and the compact disc to Shelemay 1998, which contains an example of a *bashārīf* and a *samāī*. Yaḥid Ram (#238, Shelemay and Weiss 1985, A1) is an example of a *bashārīf* (see Shelemay 1998, track 9; transcription pp. 164–66). Tzur Ya'el (#313, Shelemay and Weiss 1985, B1) is taken from `Abd al-Wahhāb's Bint al-balad (see Shelemay 1998, track 1; transcription and discussion pp. 15–24).
19. Here he uses the term *maqām* to refer to the technique of melodic improvisation; see al-Faruqi 1981 (170).
20. Touma defines a phase as "the characteristic central tone" (1971, 41; 1996, 40).
21. Marcus provides common phrases found in the *taqāsīm* but states that these are not unique to a specific *maqām* (1989, 718–20).
22. Specific Arab terminology are found in al-Faruqi's annotated glossary (1981). An Arab term for motif is *jam* (ibid., 118–21). The Arab term for musical phrase is *juz* (133).
23. El-Shawan's conclusion is based on her analysis of the rendering of the same song by various artists; see El-Shawan 1980 (222–61). Touma also discusses not altering segments (1971, 41).
24. Three charts appear in *SUHV*; see pp. 567–68, 568a–568b, 568c–568d.
25. The intonation of the E quarter flat, the third note of this *maqām*, is not always the same with each singer. Occasionally the E quarter flat is sung higher, approaching an E flat. There is also no consistency in the use of B flat and B quarter flat in this example. This illustrates the flexible nature of the upper tetrachord of the *maqām*. The quality of some of the recordings in the Sephardic archives does not provide the clarity needed to discern some of the ornamentation. In addition most of the cantors in the these recordings are in their mid-

seventies. Thus, declining vocal quality hinders the determination of certain notes—these notes appear in square brackets in the example.

26. Curiously, Touma states that the *qaṣīdah* was popular among "*ṣūfī* [*sic*] fraternities of Islamic mysticism throughout the Arabian world" (1996, 96). Since the purpose of *bakkashot* singing is for spiritual elevation prior to Sabbath prayers, it is logical to assume that the formal adaptation of the *qaṣīdah* follows a similar context in Arab musical practices.
27. For a further explanation on the text of Mahalalakh, see Kligman 1997 (132–38 and 167–70, and 318–34 for further details on the music). Yayama also analyzes and transcribes this *bakkasha* (2003, 484–89).
28. To illustrate the similar endings of Mahalalakh and Nishmat Kol Ḥai, the final motif d of Mahalalakh is placed with the corresponding ending module of Nishmat Kol Ḥai in example 6.
29. See Kligman 1997 (328–34) for further discussion of individual expression.
30. Zakī Murād is known by members of the Syrian community in Brooklyn—of particular interest are his Jewish origins (Shelemay 1998, 112; see also Rasmussen 1991, 216–17). Ḥawwid Min Hina is not a well-known Arab song, and information on the date of the recording and the song itself is difficult to obtain. The dating of this piece is based on the form of the composition, a *ṭaqṭūqah,* and the time period it was most likely written (Virginia Danielson and Hakki Obadia, oral communications).
31. In the setting of this melody to Shav'at Aniyyim, the melody is heard twice. The first time through, the melody is sung to the text beginning with the words "Shav'at aniyyim" (on the third staff of both systems of example 7). During the second singing, the melody is sung to the words "Be-Fi yesharim" (on the fourth staff). Occasionally, separate melodies may be used for the latter text.

    Cantor Cabasso's rendition of Bo'i be-Rinah includes the use of B natural throughout the first half of the melody. He uses a B quarter flat in most of the equivalent points in the melody in his singing of Shav'at Aniyyim. *Rast* can use either note for the seventh note of the *maqām,* since, as also seen in Mahalalakh, the upper tetrachord is not fixed.

    There are two instances where a syllable is missing from the text in Cantor Cabbaso's rendering of Shav'at Aniyyim. This is marked with an asterisk (*) in example 7.
32. For a further discussion, see Kligman 1997 (138–46, esp. examples 4.2c, p. 143; also 170–75). See also Shelemay 1998 (95) and Yayama 2003 (104–5, 366–91).
33. The repetition of words in the rendering of the liturgical text is forbidden by rabbinic authorities (Yosef 1976, 20–21).
34. Isaac Cain, a cantor in the Syrian community in Mexico, discusses his use of non-Arab music, which includes melodies from Beethoven, Mozart, and Tchaikovsky, as well as music from American films (Shelemay 1998, 194).
35. Rabbi Ezra Labaton in Deal, New Jersey, said that Magen Yish'i was written for his grandfather Ezra Obadiah Labaton, for whom he is named. Family names are incorporated into this text: Obadiah appears in the first verse of the text, Ezra in the third verse, and Mordekhai in the fourth verse (Mordekhai Labaton was a famous rabbi and poet who lived in Aleppo). Rabbi Ezra Labaton stated that when he is called to the Torah for a celebration, birth of a child, or other happy occasion, the congregation sings this *pizmon* after his aliyah to the Torah.
36. While David Tawil says that this melody is taken from a European song (interview, June 9, 1994), I am unable to find a concordance in European songbooks.
37. Special thanks to Jessica Kligman for remembering this melody from her youth, which aided in the exploration of the melody's origin. The second module of the Dutch folk song differs from Magen Yish'i. The latter repeats the second module with a different cadence and continues with a contrasting module.

38. The text of this folk song appears in Ferris 1890–91 (243); with a slight variation it also appears in Goodwin 1921 (110–11). The Dutch American sources that list this folk song date it to New York immigrants during colonial times (Luther 1942, 6; Goodwin 1890–91, 1921, 110). Sephardic Jews of Spanish and Dutch origin, some from Amsterdam, found refugee in the Dutch colony in the seventeenth century in New Amsterdam (Roth and Cohen 1972, 1173). Dutch Jews were very active in the religious and social life of New York City, particularly in the nineteenth century (Hershkowitz 1972, 1062, 1071). This raises speculation about the transmission of this song to Syrian immigrants from Dutch or other Sephardic immigrants living in New York. There is no documented use of the melody of Trip a Trop a Tronjes or Magen Yish'i by Sephardic Jews (confirmed by Israel J. Katz, personal communication, May 17, 1993).
39. For a further discussion, see Kligman 1997 (146–54, 175–79).
40. Aḥmad composed for Umm Kulthūm from 1931–47 and again in 1960 (Danielson 1991, 376). He composed religious as well as secular songs (ibid., 168). For a longer discussion, see Danielson 1991 (164–76), and Danielson 1997 (33–35, 102–8). Shelemay lists Aḥmad among other musicians discussed by Syrian Jewish men (1998, 109). Dating of this song is approximate and based on stylistic characteristics (Hakki Obadia, personal communication, October 10, 1993) and its place in Aḥmad's oeuvre (Virginia Danielson, personal communications, November 15, 1993).
41. Ali Jihad Racy states that the *dawr* was both the climatic point of the *waṣlah* (suite) and its longest segment. Certain singers are known as acclaimed *dawr* singers (1983, 398–99).
42. Il-Ḥabib has an instrumental introduction that is not included in example 9. The systems are numerically labeled for reference in the following discussion.
43. According to traditional Jewish law, since the Temple was destroyed, playing of instruments is forbidden both inside and outside the synagogue on the Sabbath (*Shulchan Aruch, Orach Chayyim* 338:1).
44. The reiteration of a musical phrase permissable in a light liturgical station, such as Shav'at Aniyyim in example 8, would be undesirable in heavy liturgical stations.
45. For Arab musicians *thaqīl* means "heavy" and refers to a melody "slow in tempo" (al-Faruqi 1981, 367) and *hafīf*, or *khafīf*, means "light" and refers to a melody "rapid in tempo" (ibid., 142). For Syrian cantors "heavy" and "light" are not only rhythmically differentiated but also tonally or a melody type.

Chapter 8

1. One example of the similarity and difference is in the taking out of the Torah (see table 6, LSS 4.1.1–4.1.4). In the Sephardic tradition, the first two texts are Atah Har'eita and Berikh Shmeh; Syrian liturgy follows this tradition. Berikh Shmeh traditions differ; some traditions, such as the Syrian tradition, have a blessings for the State of Israel or the government. Ashrei ha-Am is the next text in Syrian liturgy; in other Sephardic traditions, the text at this point may be Ki Mitziyon or Barukh ha-Makom.
2. On certain occasions during the liturgical year two Torah scrolls are taken out of the ark. In this instance two congregants are honored by carrying the Torah scrolls around the *teivah*. See Dobrinsky 1986 (164–69) for a discussion of Syrian customs related to honors given to congregants for the Torah.
3. Both of these *pizmonim* have an indication on their respective pages in *SUHV* that they should be sung on the Sabbath of Bereshit. A list of *pizmonim* for specific Sabbaths appears in *SUHV*, 572–73.
4. See Shelemay 1998 (161). For a listing of *pizmonim* for specific occasions, see *SUHV*, 570–72.

5. The melodic components of the Torah cantillation are documented elsewhere. For melodic formulas according to the Syrian tradition, see Idelsohn 1929 (44–46), which contains various melodies; see also Idelsohn 1923a and 1923b. Avishai Ya'ar's dissertation, "The Cantillation of the Bible—the Aleppo Tradition (Pentateuch)," focuses on the Torah reading of Syrian Jews.
6. See chapter 11 for a further discussion of the rabbi's sermons and their potential effect on the service. For a discussion of other Syrian sermons related to Israel, see Zenner and Kligman 2000 (165).
7. The Amidah of Shaḥarit replaces the daily Temple sacrifice. Musaf is said to be performed in place of the additional sacrifice on the Sabbath and holidays (Elbogen 1913 [1993], 98).
8. Another portion in Musaf that is similar to Shaḥarit is Birkat Kohanim (see LSS 6.2.5 and 3.6.5).
9. The phrase "cloud of glory" most likely refers to the image of the presence of God in the form of a cloud; see Exodus 16:10 and 19:16 and Ezekiel 1:4.
10. Taken from Zohar Ḥadash, Tikkunim (96a–97a), found in Tishby 1989 (1058).
11. Zohar III, 93a, Raya Mehemna; qtd. in Tishby 1989 (1031–32).
12. Translation is from *Siddur kol sassoon* (1995, 454–55).
13. The opening melody adapts the *pizmon* Rayoni Yaḥid (*SUHV* #215), composed by Rabbi Raphael Antebi Taboush. In *SUHV* there is no indication for an originating Arab melody.
14. Amnon Shiloah discusses the popularity of this melody and its use in the liturgy of various Jewish communities (1992, 65–66).

Chapter 9

1. The musical design of the service is symmetrical; the rabbi's spoken sermon interrupts the symmetry.
2. Furthermore, Tambiah discusses formality, conventionality, stereotypy, and rigidity as elements to examine in ritual performance (1979, 122–34).
3. The fifth liturgical singing station, Semeḥim be-Tseitam precedes the Shema, and the sixth, Mi-mits'rayim Gealtanu, follows it; see tables 8 and 9.
4. Kay Kaufman Shelemay notes that Syrian *pizmonim* concerts more closely follow the *waṣlah* design, since the selections at the end of performance are faster rhythmically (1998, 132–34).
5. See Yayama 2003, chapter 9, "The Overall Musical Structure of the Singing of *Baqqashot*" (317–30), particularly the table on pp. 322–24.

Chapter 10

1. These associations are also made to the *āwāzāt*—a secondary mode derived from a primary mode. For a more detailed study, see Shiloah 1979.
2. E.g., see item numbers 86, 107, 168, 219, 220, 275, 308, and 334 in Shiloah 1979.
3. For a brief discussion of the Turkish tradition, see Dorn 1991 (160–63). Ezra Barnea compiles a composite chart representing the practices of Syrians in Brooklyn, Yerushalmi-Sephardim, and Bukharians in Israel (1996–97, 26–27).
4. Precedents in the Jewish tradition at large associate liturgical or paraliturgical practices with the Torah reading. E.g., a portion of the books of the Prophets follows the Torah reading. The prophetic portion is connected to the Torah reading by a shared theme. Some prayer books further associate a Psalm chapter with a biblical reading. One such example can be found in Seligman Isaac Baer's prayer book, *Siddur Avodat Israel* (Germany: Roedelheim, 1868). This provides a "stringing together" of the Pentateuch, Prophets, and Psalms for any given Sabbath.

5. The title of the chart in *Shir ush'vaḥa hallel v'zimrah* reads as follows: "Seder niggun tefilot le-shabbatot ha-shanah u-le-mo'adim" ("Order of the prayer melodies for the Sabbaths of the year and for festivals" see figure 6). The Hebrew word *niggun* is translated as "melody" or "tune," indicating the functional use of this chart. Although the word *maqām* is not used in the title, and neither is there a Hebrew equivalent for the term, *niggun* is the closest Hebrew word for *maqām.* The purpose of the chart is to provide a source for melodies that are used during the course of the services. The *maqām* of the day, or, as the cantors refer to it, the *maqām* of the *tefilah* (prayer), establishes the foundation of the prayers on which the cantor bases his rendering of the Shaḥarit portion of the service.
6. The biblical readings are listed in table 10.
7. Ḥakham David Tawil did not give a reason for this last biblical reading's association with *saba,* which is particularly interesting because circumcision is not mentioned in it.
8. Macy Nulman discusses the use of *saba* on Rosh ha-Shanah (1977–78, 44–45).
9. He indicates that one can easily move to another *maqām* from *saba.*
10. A rationale for connecting *saba* with circumcision is offered by Morris Arking: *sabi* in Arabic means "baby boy" (cited in Shelemay 1998, 156).
11. He is referring to the use of the augmented second interval in the Ashkenazic prayer mode Ahavah Rabah, with a flat second and major third.
12. The originating melody of El Me'od Na'alah is a polka from Istanbul (*Shir ush'vaḥa hallel v'zimrah,* 26). See *Shir ush'vaḥa hallel v'zimrah,* 572–73, for a listing of *pizmonim* associated with particular biblical readings.
13. *Maqām ḥuseini* is found in the *bayat faṣīlah;* see table 5.
14. Other examples of a double parashah are BRS 3.6, 3.9, 3.13, 4.8, 4.12, 5.10, and 5.12. During a Jewish leap year an additional month is added to the calendar. During nonleap years there are more biblical readings than Sabbaths. Therefore, a double parashah is not uncommon.
15. *Shulḥan Arukh: Orakh Ḥayyim* 284:7; this Code of Jewish Law, first printed in 1565, was compiled by Rabbi Joseph Caro and is the main legal codification for both Ashkenazic and Sephardic Jews.
16. The distinction of a great contrast between *hijaz* and *bayat,* as opposed to *hijaz* and *saba,* is based primarily on Tawil's perception of the "character" or "quality" differences between *bayat* and *saba.* The intervallic content of *bayat* and *saba* has many shared elements; they are both *maqāmāt* based on the note D and differ in the fourth note of the lower tetrachord, a G for the former and G flat for the latter (see table 5).

bayat	D	E♭	F	G	A	B♭	C	D
saba	D	E♭	F	G♭	A	B♭	C	D
hijaz	D	E♭	F♯	G	A	B♭	C	D

Bayat is deemed by Tawil as more unique than *saba.* Note that *maqām saba* has a *hijaz* tertrachord on the note F (an augmented second interval between the G flat and A). Thus, *saba* and *hijaz* do not have enough contrast.

17. Cantor Bozo was born around 1910 and lived in Aleppo, Syria, until 1948, when he left for Israel. He is the oldest living Syrian-born cantor in Israel, where he has trained many cantors. Our discussion focused on associations between the *maqām* and biblical reading. The following comments on the Israel associations must be seen as tentative based solely on this one useful interview. Cantor Bozo's comments on the associations of the biblical reading are included in table 11 and are based upon the liturgical practices of Syrians in Israel, particularly those at the Ades Synagogue in the Maḥaneh Yehudah neighborhood in Jerusalem. He stated that he knows the reason for some of the *maqām* associations but not all.

18. Unfortunately, Cantor Bozo did not identify *pizmonim* where jail is mentioned in the text. He also suggests that "*rahaw* and *nawa* are really the same thing. . . . It [*rahaw*] is a difficult *maqām* and nobody knows it" (interview, June 29, 1993).
19. This publication also reflects the practice of Yerushalmi-Sephardim, Sephardic Jews from the Levant whose traditions have merged while in Israel. Their liturgical practices are very similar to Syrian Jews from Aleppo (see Barnea 1996–97).
20. For a further discussion, see Seroussi 1993a.
21. In the various recent editions of *SUHV,* compilers have included texts from *Shirei Zimrah* (see Sam Catton's comments found in Shelemay 1998, 237n31).
22. Macy Nulman's article on Syrian *maqām* associations offers some additional insights (1977–78). Nulman focuses on the reason for the associations of four *maqāmāt: saba, hijaz, ajam,* and *seyga.* He offers additional interpretations based upon textual exegesis. For further comments on Nulman, see Kligman 1997 (289–91). In Ezra Barnea's composite table of *maqām* and biblical readings, he includes a brief explanation of the reason for the associations, which are almost identical to the ideas discussed (1996–97, 28).
23. There are minor differences between Idelsohn's three charts. These are specified in the notes to table 10.
24. This point is mentioned in the German edition but not in the Hebrew. The essence of the *maqām* and biblical reading associations is explained in both Idelsohn editions, but they are expressed differently in the two languages. The German edition specifically lists the affect of each *maqām,* which is not included in the Hebrew edition. Likewise, the Hebrew edition gives specific explanations for why certain biblical readings are associated with given *maqāmāt;* this is not done the same way in the German. A possible explanation for the difference in presentation is that Idelsohn is reaching two separate audiences. The respective German and Hebrew volumes of the thesaurus (Idelsohn 1923a and Idelsohn 1923b) are not direct translations, since slightly different information is conveyed in each. For a description of the general differences in editions of Idelsohn's *Thesaurus of Hebrew Oriental Melodies,* see Schleifer 1986 (63–92) for a description of the thesaurus (esp. 75–77 for volume 4).
25. The following discussion of the Israel associations is based upon the 1988 edition of *Shire Zimrah,* since this is the systems of associations currently practiced.
26. The percentage column is more useful for comparative purposes because the number of *maqāmāt* listed for each of the three practices of Syrian *maqām* associations differs. The Brooklyn system contains more *maqāmāt* because it includes associations for a double parashah that do not appear in the Israel associations nor in Idelsohn's compilation. The assumption of these tallies and percentages is that where two *maqāmāt* are listed for a biblical reading, such as Va-Yishlaḥ (BR 1.8), which lists *saba* or *seyga,* both are counted. Since more choices are found in the Brooklyn system and it also lists the *maqām* of a double parashah where Idelsohn and the Israel associations do not, there is a higher number of *maqāmāt* used in the Brooklyn system. Idelsohn and the Israel associations only differ by one. *Rahaw nawa* is not regrouped to a *faṣīlah,* because its use is ambiguous.
27. Idelsohn refers to *maqām seyga* as mode II (1929, 25–26), stating that for the recitation of the Torah it is "common in all Oriental and Italian synagogues with the exception of the Yemenite and Spanish-Oriental" (43).

Chapter 11

1. The extramusical associations of a *maqām* to the biblical reading (see chapter 10) is one example of an indirect process of adaptation. The Brooklyn system of extramusical asso-

ciations simulates and models Arab practices; Syrian associations are unique adaptations based on an Arab model. In addition, the more ornate renderings of the liturgical singing stations, such as Moses Tawil's setting of the Kaddish (see example 10), simulate and model the originating Arab song and improvisation.

2. Ḥazzan Yaakov Bozo used the Hebrew phrase "Anaḥnu osim ajam," which, directly translated, means "we make *ajam*" (interview, June 29, 1993).
3. See extended interview transcripts provided in chapter 7 that mention the word "say" when referring to the application of a *maqām* in the liturgy. Kay Kaufman Shelemay also discusses the phrase "to say" a *maqām* encountered in her fieldwork; she comments that it is reflective of Islamic attitudes concerning the "exclusion of liturgical chant from the category of music" (1998, 119). I would add that "to say" underscores the importance of conveying the text with a *maqām* during liturgical performance: one says, not sings, the prayers.
4. The desired qualities of a good Qur'an reciter are similar. One is required (1) to use correct pronunciation, (2) to contain dignity by choosing an appropriate tune, (3) to have a beautiful voice with a richness in sound and clarity, (4) to be musical, and (5) to make proper use of breath control (al-Faruqi 1987, 18).
5. For an example of melodic elaboration see the melodic figurations described in examples 7 and 10.
6. A possible explanation for Zion's reliance on *maqām saba* for the Kaddish improvisation is the intervallic nuances afforded by the *maqām* (D-E♭̸-F-G♭, which produce the intervals ¾–¾–½; see tables 2 and 5). Ali Jihad Racy notes that "feeling the music" for performers includes playing or singing the microtonal intervals correctly in order to "feel" their musical effect (1991a, 11). Perhaps Zion feels he can best express the Kaddish with the subtle intervallic changes afforded through *saba.*
7. For a discussion of the uses of popular songs in the *pizmonim,* see Shelemay 1994 (26) and Shelemay 1998 (chapter 1).
8. Shelemay records a similar process among Syrians in Mexico (1998, 194).
9. This practice is akin to differing audience responses to various readers and reading styles as described by Kristina Nelson (1982, 46).
10. Both Ali Jihad Racy and Lois Ibsen al-Faruqi confirm that the modern notion of *samā* is related to the *sūfī* concept (Racy 1991a, 11; al-Faruqi 1981, 291–92). Al-Faruqi adds that *samā* refers to engaged listening through performance (ibid.).
11. Racy clarifies the distinction between *ṭarab* and *salṭana. Ṭarab* refers to both traditional secular music as a genre and to the overall ecstatic sensation connected with that music and the experience of various participants in the musical process. *Salṭana* refers to the ecstasy of the performer (1991a, 13).
12. This demonstrates the importance of memorializing the events of World War II in the community. See Marianne Sanua, "From the Pages of the *Victory Bulletin:* The Syrian Jews of Brooklyn During World War II," *YIVO Annual,* vol. 19 (1990):283–330.
13. Some of the well-known *pizmonim* are recorded on *Pizmon: Syrian-Jewish Religious and Social Song* (Shelemay and Weiss 1995; also on the accompanying CD for Shelemay 1998).
14. A few melodies used for the liturgical singing stations and other parts of the liturgy do not originate from a known Arab song, a non-Arab song, nor a *bakkasha;* these melodies are only used in the liturgy (D. Tawil, interview, June 9, 1994). Two possibilities can account for this: either the melody is from an unpopular or forgotten song or the melody was composed for use in the liturgy.
15. Tawil fulfills this same function at various times during the year for a separate service at Beth Torah that begins earlier on Sabbath morning.
16. Joseph A. D. Sutton states that Beth Torah is particularly known for its adherence to the *maqāmāt* in Syrian prayers for the Sabbath and holidays (1988, 95–96).

17. Racy states, "In the absence of good listeners, members of a performing ensemble usually play the double role of musicians and *sammī,* thus supporting and ecstatically reinforcing the performances of one another" (1991a, 25). Although the context is different in Syrian liturgy, similarly not all members of the congregations are actively involved in their participation through responses.
18. The following comments are taken from my interview with Cabasso on May 29, 1992, unless otherwise noted.

Conclusion

1. Similarly, rabbinic literature and discourse, such as the classical sermon, also cull from texts for new insights.
2. Kay Kaufman Shelemay discusses how key individuals have formed and perpetuated this tradition; see her discussion of *pizmon* Ramach everai (*SUHV* #204)(1994, 28–31; see also 1998, 135–47 and chapter 4).
3. The *pizmonim* directly adapt Arab melodies, whereas the *bakkashot* indirectly adapt from Arab music since new *bakkashot* melodies were composed in an Arab musical style.
4. Additional similarities between Qur'anic and Syrian liturgical recitation include the desire to avoid approaching the rendering as a singer (Nelson 1982, 46) and to refrain from the use of instruments (al-Faruqi 1987, 8).
5. It is difficult to draw parallels between Islamic and Jewish music during prayer, since prayers in Islam are spoken and not recited like Jewish prayer. Additionally, there are few musical studies of Islamic prayer rituals; see Denny 1985.
6. Kristina Nelson also states that viewing Qur'anic recitation as music would make the enterprise a human endeavor rather than a divine one (1985, 190).
7. See the discussion of the double parashah Aḥarei Mot and Kedoshim (BR 3.7 and BR. 3.8) in chapter 10. *Hijaz* and *bayat* are used in this instance (D. Tawil, interview, June 1, 1993).
8. Other products of music culture contact in Arab music include the influence of Western traits and others in pan-Arab popular recorded music (Danielson 1988, 142) and "Amerabic" in the United States in the 1960s and 1970s. "Amerabic" is defined as "music with a Middle Eastern flavor geared to the American ear" (Rasmussen 1991, 89); quarter tones were minimized and electronic instruments were included in nightclub ensembles.
9. Here I am specifically referring to the use of the *maqām* of the day within the service. The preferred Syrian practice is to establish the *maqām* of the day for about ten minutes before using other *maqāmāt;* when another *maqām* is used it should not detract from the prominence of the *maqām* of the day (chapter 11). The Israeli style may be characterized as starting in the *maqām* of the day and then frequently departing from this *maqām* to demonstrate one's skill in changing *maqāmāt.* For a discussion of the Sephardi-Yerushalmi cantorial style, see Yayama 2003 (83–85).

Bibliography

Abu-Lughod, Lila. 1991. "Writing against Culture." In *Recapturing Anthropology: Working in the Present,* ed. Richard G. Fox, 137–62. Santa Fe: School of American Research Press.

Adler, Israel. 1966. *La pratique musicale savante dans quelques communautés juives en Europe aux XVIIe–XVIIIe siècles.* 2 vols. Paris: Mouton.

———. 1975. *Hebrew Writings Concerning Music: In Manuscripts and Printed Books from Geonic Times up to 1800. Répertoire International des Sources Musicales* BIX². München: G. Henle Verlag.

Alcalay, Ammiel. 1993. *After Jews and Arabs: Remaking Levatine Culture.* Minneapolis: University of Minnesota Press.

Apel, Willi. 1958. *Gregorian Chant.* Bloomington: Indiana University Press.

Ashear, Amerik. 1985. "Moses Ashear." In *Shir ush'vaḥa, hallel v'zimrah,* 11–13. New York: Sephardic Heritage foundation.

Ashtor, Eliyahu. 1972. "Dhimma, Dhimmi." *Encyclopaedia Judaica* 5:1604–6.

———. 1973. *The Jews of Moslem Spain.* Trans. from Hebrew by Aaron Klein and Jenny Machlowitz Klein. 3 vols. Philadelphia: Jewish Publication Society of America.

Avenary, Hanoch. 1971. "The Concept of Mode in European Synagogue Chant." *Yuval: Studies of the Jewish Music Research Centre* 2:11–21.

Barnea, Ezra. 1996–97. "The Tradition of the Jerusalemite-Sephardic Hazzanut: A Clarification of Nusah Hatefillah as Dominant in Our Era." *Journal of Jewish Music and Liturgy* 19:19–30.

Baron, Salo. 1957. *A Social and Religious History of the Jews.* 3 vols. New York: Columbia University Press.

Barz, Gregory F., and Timothy J. Cooley, eds. 1997. *Shadows in the Field: New Perspectives for Fieldwork in Ethnomusicology.* New York: Oxford University Press.

Bateson, Mary Catherine. 1974. "Ritualization: A Study in Texture and Texture Change." In *Religious Movements in Contemporary America,* ed. Irving I. Zarestsky and Mark P. Leone, 150–65. Princeton: Princeton University Press.

Bauman, Richard. 1977. *Verbal Art as Performance.* Rowley: Newbury House.

Bauman, Richard, and Charles L. Briggs. 1990. "Poetics and Performance as Critical Perspectives on Language and Social Life." *Annual Review of Anthropology* 19:59–88.

Becker, Judith. 1981. "Some Thoughts about *Pathet.*" In *Report of the Twelfth Congress, Berkeley, 1977,* ed. Daniel Heartz and Bonnie Wade, 530–36. Basel: American Musicological Society.

Béhague, Gerard. 1984. *Performance Practice: Ethnomusicological Perspectives.* Westport: Greenwood Press.

Bell, Catherine M. 1992. *Ritual Theory, Ritual Practice.* New York: Oxford University Press.

Blacking, John. 1978. "Some Problems of Theory and Method in the Study of Musical Change." *Yearbook of the International Folk Music Council* 9:1–26.

———. 1981. "Summaries of the Papers Presented: The Ethnography of Musical Performances." In *Report of the Twelfth Congress, Berkeley, 1977,* ed. Daniel Heartz and Bonnie Wade. Basel: American Musicological Society.

———. 1986. "Identifying Processes of Musical Change." *The World of Music* 28:3–12.

Blum, Stephen. 1994. "Conclusion: Music in an Age of Cultural Confrontation." In *Music-Cultures in Contact: Convergences and Collisions,* ed. Margaret J. Kartomi and Stephen Blum, 250–77. Switzerland: Gordon and Breach.

Boilès, Charles Lafayette. 1978. *Man, Magic, and Musical Occasions.* Columbus: Collegiate.

Bokser, Baruch M. 1984. *The Origins of the Seder: The Passover Rite and Early Rabbinic Judaism.* Berkeley: University of California Press.

Boyarin, Jonathan. 1989. "Voices around the Text: The Ethnography of Reading at Mesivta Tifereth Jerusalem." *Cultural Anthropology* 4:399–421.

Briggs, Charles L. 1988. *Competence in Performance: The Creativity of Tradition in Mexicano Verbal Art.* Philadelphia: University of Pennsylvania Press.

Burkholder, J. Peter. 1995. *All Made of Tunes: Charles Ives and the Uses of Musical Borrowing.* New Haven: Yale University Press.

Carmi, T. 1981. "Introduction." In *The Penguin Book of Hebrew Verse,* ed. T. Carmi. England: Penguin.

Chira, Robert. 1994. *From Aleppo to America: The Story of Two Families.* New York: Rivercross.

Clifford, James. 1988. *The Predicament of Culture.* Cambridge: Harvard University Press.

———. 1994. "Diasporas." *Cultural Anthropology* 9:302–38.

Clifford, James, and George Marcus, eds. 1986. *Writing Culture.* Berkeley: University of California Press.

Cohen, Hayyim. 1972. "Aleppo." *Encyclopaedia Judaica* 2:562–65.

———. 1973. *The Jews of the Middle East, 1860–1972.* Jerusalem: Israel University Press.

Cohen, Erik, and Amnon Shiloah. 1985. "Major Trends of Change in Jewish Oriental Ethnic Music in Israel." *Popular Music* 5:199–224.

Cohon, Baruch J. 1950. "Structure of the Synagogue Prayer Chant." *Journal of the American Musicological Society* 3:17–32.

Crocker, Richard. 1986. "Martins Antiphons at St. Denis." *Journal of the American Musicological Society* 39:441–90.

Daniel, E. Valentine. 1984. *Fluid Signs: Being a Person the Tamil Way.* Berkeley: University of California Press.

Danielson, Virginia. 1988. "The Arab Middle East." In *Popular Musics of the Non-Western World,* ed. Peter Manuel, 141–60. New York: Oxford University Press.

———. 1991. *Shaping Tradition in Arabic Song: The Career and Repertory of Umm Kulthum.* PhD diss., University of Illinois.

———. 1997. *The Voice of Egypt: Umm Kulthum, Arabic Song, and Egyptian Society in the Twentieth Century.* Chicago: University of Chicago Press.

Denny, Frederick M. 1985. "Islamic Ritual: Perspectives and Theories." In *Approaches to Islam in Religious Studies,* ed. Richard C. Martin, 63–77. Tucson: University of Arizona Press.

Deshen, Shlomo. 1979. "The *Kol Nidre* Enigma: An Anthropological View of the Day of Atonement Liturgy." *Ethnology* 18:121–33.

Deshen, Shlomo, and Walter Zenner. 1982. *Jewish Societies in the Middle East: Culture, Community and Authority.* Lanham, MD: University Press of America.

Dobrinsky, Herbert. 1986. *Treasury of Sephardic Laws and Customs: The Ritual Practices of Syrian Moroccan, Judeo-Spanish and Spanish and Portuguese Jews of North America.* Hoboken: KTAV and New York: Yeshiva University Press.

Elazar, Daniel J. 1989. *The Other Jews: The Sephardim Today.* New York: Basic Books.

Elbogen, Ismar. 1913 [1993]. *Jewish Liturgy: A Comprehensive History.* Trans. Raymon P. Scheindlin. Philadelphia: Jewish Publication Society and New York and Jerusalem: Jewish Theological Seminary of America. Based on *Der jüdische Gottesdienst in seiner geschichtlichen Entwicklung* 1913; reprint, Hildesheim: Georg Olms, 1962. And *Hatefila beyisra'el behitpatḥutah Hahistorit.* Ed. Joseph Heinemann et al. Tel Aviv: Devir, 1972.

El-Shawan, Salwa A. 1980. *Al-Mūsīka al-'Arabiyyah: A Category of Urban Music in Cairo, Egypt, 1927–1977.* Ph.D. diss., Columbia University.

Falck, Robert. 1980. "Contrafactum, before 1450." *New Grove Dictionary* 4:700–701.

al-Faruqi, Lois Ibsen. 1974. *The Nature of the Musical Art of Islamic Culture: A Theoretical and Empirical Study of Arabian Music.* Ph.D. diss., Syracuse University, Syracuse, New York.

———. 1978. "Ornamentation in Arabian Improvisational Music: A Study on Interrelatedness in the Arts." *World of Music* 20:17–28.

———. 1981. *An Annotated Glossary of Arabic Musical Terms.* Westport, CT: Greenwood Press.

———. 1987. "The Cantillation of the Qur'an." *Asian Music* 19:2–25.

Feld, Steven. 1982 [1990]. *Sound and Sentiment: Birds, Weeping, Poetics, and Song in Kaluli Expression.* Philadelphia: University of Pennsylvania Press.

Feld, Steven, and Aaron A. Fox. 1994. "Music and Language." *Annual Review of Anthropology* 23:25–53.

Fenton, Paul. 1975. "Baqqašht d'Orient et d'Occident." *Revue des études juives* 134:101–21.

———. 1982. "A Jewish Sufi on the Influence of Music." *Yuval: Studies of the Jewish Music Research Centre* 4:124–30.

Ferris, M.P. 1890–91. "Dutch Nursery Rhymes of Colonial Times." *Holland Society of New York Yearbook.*

Fine, Lawrence. 1984. "Kabbalistic Texts." *Back to the Sources: Reading the Classic Jewish Texts,* 305–59. New York: Simon and Schuster.

Fleischer, Ezra. 1972a. "Piyyut." *Encyclopaedia Judaica* 13:573–602.

———. 1972b. "Yotzerot." *Encyclopaedia Judaica* 16:865–66.

Fredman, Ruth G. 1981. *The Passover Seder: Afikoman in Exile.* Philadelphia: University of Pennsylvania Press.

Freehof, Solomon. 1950–51. "The Structure of the Birchos HaShachar." *Hebrew Union College Annual,* pt. 2, 23: 339–55.

Geertz, Clifford. 1973. *The Interpretations of Culture.* New York: Basic Books.

Gerson-Kiwi, Edith. 1967. "Maqam." *Riemann Musik Lexikon.* Mainz: B. Schott's Sohne.

Goitein, S. D. 1955. *Jews and Arabs: Their Contacts through the Ages.* New York: Schocken.

Goldberg, Geoffrey. 1988. "Syrian-Jewish Religious and Social Song: A Literary and Ethnomusicological Enquiry, with Particular Reference to *Bakkashot.*" Master's thesis. New York University.

Goldberg, Harvey E. 1978. "The Mimuna and the Minority Status of Moroccan Jews." *Ethnology* 17:75–87.

———. 1987. "Introduction: Reflections on the Mutual Relevance of Anthropology and Judaic

Studies." In *Judaism Viewed from Within and from Without: Anthropological Studies*, ed. Harvey E. Goldberg. Albany: State University of New York Press.

———. 1990. *Jewish Life in Muslim Libya: Rivals and Relatives.* Chicago: University of Chicago Press.

Goldschmidt, Ernst Daniel. 1972. "Liturgy: Liturgical Rites." *Encyclopaedia Judaica* 11:397–402.

Goodwin, Maud Wilder. 1921. *Dutch and English on the Hudson: A Chronicle of Colonial New York.* In the Chronicles of America series, set 2, vol. 7, ed., Allen Johnson. New Haven: Yale University Press.

Heilman, Samuel C. 1976. *Synagogue Life: A Study in Symbolic Interaction.* Chicago: University of Chicago Press.

———. 1982. "Prayer in the Orthodox Synagogue: An Analysis of Ritual Display." *Contemporary Jewry* 6:2–17.

Heinemann, Joseph. 1972. "Amidah." *Encyclopaedia Judaica* 2:838–45.

Herndon, Marcia. 1987. "Toward Evaluating Musical Change through Musical Potential." *Ethnomusicology* 31:455–68.

Herndon, Marcia, and Norma McLeod. 1980. *Music as Culture.* Darby: Norwood.

Hershkowitz, Leo. 1972. "New York City." *Encyclopaedia Judaica* 12:1062–75.

Herszenhorn David M. 1994. "Sephardic Jews Shift Leadership, Father to Son." *New York Times* 25 December.

Heschel, Abraham Joshua. 1951 [1986]. *The Sabbath: Its Meaning for Modern Man.* New York: Farrar, Straus and Giroux.

Hrushovski, Benjamin. 1972. "Prosody, Hebrew." *Encyclopaedia Judaica* 13:1196–1240.

Hoffman, Lawrence A. 1979. *The Canonization of the Synagogue Service.* Notre Dame: University of Notre Dame Press.

———. 1987. *Beyond the Text: A Holistic Approach to Liturgy.* Bloomington: Indiana University Press.

Hood, Mantle. 1971. *The Ethnomusicologist.* New York: McGraw-Hill.

Hournai, Albert. 1991. *A History of the Arab Peoples.* Cambridge: Harvard University Press.

Idel, Moshe. 1982. "Music and Prophetic Kabbalah." *Yuval: Studies of the Jewish Music Research Centre* 4:150–69.

Idelsohn, Abraham Zvi. 1913a. "Die Makamen in der hebräischen Poesie der orientalischen Juden." *Monatsschrift für Geschichte und Wissenschaft des Judentums* 57:314–25.

———. [Idelsohn P]. 1913b. "Die Maqamen der arabischen Musik." *Sammelbände der Internationale Musikgesellschaft* 15. Jg., H.1:1–63.

———. 1916. "Der jüdische Volksgesang im Lichte der orientalischen Musik." *Ost und West* 16, H. 6/7:253–58; H. 8/9:331–44.

———. 1923a. *Gesänge der orientalischen Sefardim.* Vol. 4 of *Hebräish-orientalisher Melodienschatz.* Jerusalem: Benjamin Hartz Verlag.

———. 1923b. *Neginot sefaradei ha-mizraḥ.* Vol. 4 of *Otzer neginot yisrael.* Jerusalem: Benjamin Harz Verlag.

———. 1929. *Jewish Music in Its Historical Development.* New York: Tudor; Repr., New York: Schocken.

———. 1932. *Jewish Liturgy and Its Development.* New York: Sacred Music Press.

Kartomi, Margaret J. 1981. "The Processes and Results of Musical Culture Contact: A Discussion of Terminology and Concepts." *Ethnomusicology* 25:227–49.

———. 1991. Preface. In *Music-Cultures in Contact: Convergences and Collisions*, ed. Margaret J. Kartomi and Stephen Blum, ix–xiii. Switzerland: Gordon and Breach.

Kartomi, Margaret J., and Stephen Blum, eds. 1994. *Music-Cultures in Contact: Convergences and Collisions.* Switzerland: Gordon and Breach.

Kassin, Rabbi Jacob Saul. 1980. "Genealogy of the Kassin Family of Aleppo (Haleb), Syria." Translation of Hebrew found in Saul J. Kassin *The Light of the Law.* New York: Shengold. English translation in *Image* 6(1996):6–7.

Katz, Ruth. 1968. "The Singing of *Baqqashot* by Aleppo Jews: A Study in Musical Acculturation." *Acta Musicologica* 40:65–85.

Kelly, John D., and Martha Kaplan. 1990. "History, Structure, and Ritual." *Annual Review of Anthropology* 19:119–50.

Kirshenblatt-Gimblett, Barbara. 1995. "Theorizing Heritage." *Ethnomusicology* 39:367–80.

Kligman, Mark. 1997. *Modes of Prayer: Arabic Maqāmāt in the Sabbath Morning Liturgical Music of the Syrian Jews in Brooklyn.* PhD diss., New York University.

———. 2001. "The Bible, Prayer, and Maqām: Extra-Musical Associations of Syrian Jews," *Ethnomusicology: Journal for the Society of Ethnomusicology* 45/3:443–79.

———. 2003. "Chanting Psalms Today: The *Zemirot* in Syrian Sabbath Prayers." In *Psalms in Community: Jewish and Christian Textual, Liturgical and Artistic Traditions,* ed. Harold Attridge and Margot Fassler, 325–40. Atlanta: Society of Biblical Literature.

———. 2005. "Prayers in an Arabic Mode: Liturgical Performance of Syrian Jews in Brooklyn." In *Liturgy in the Life of the Synagogue: Studies in the History of Jewish Prayer,* ed. Ruth Langer and Steven Fine, 177–204. Winona Lake: Eisenbrauns.

———. 2005–2006. "Arab Music and Aesthetics as a Basis for Liturgical Structure in the Sabbath Morning Service of the Syrian Jews in Brooklyn, New York." *Musica Judaica* 18: 87–105.

Koskoff, Ellen. 1978. "Contemporary Nigun Composition in an American Hasidic Community." *Selected Reports in Ethnomusicology* 3:153–73.

———. 2001. *Music in Lubavitcher Life.* Urbana: University of Illinois Press.

Kugelmass, Jack, ed. 1988. *Between Two Worlds: Ethnographic Essays on American Jewry.* Ithaca: Cornell University Press.

Lachmann, Robert. 1940. *Ges¬nge der Juden auf der Insel Djerba.* Repr., Yuval Monograph Series VII. Jerusalem: Magnes Press/ Hebrew University, 1978.

Levine, Joseph. 1980–81. "Toward Defining the Jewish Prayer Modes with Particular Emphasis on the *Adonay Malakh* Mode." *Musica Judaica* 3:13–41.

Lewis, Bernard. 1984. *The Jews of Islam.* Princeton: Princeton University Press.

Lieberman, Rabbi Zevulun. 1991. "History and Development of Syrian Community in America." Lecture delivered at Sephardic House, New York, New York.

Lockwood, Lewis. 1966. "On 'Parody' as Term and Concept in 16th-Century Music." In *Aspects of Medieval and Renaissance Music: A Birthday Offering to Gustave Reese,* ed. Jan LaRue, 560–79. New York: Norton.

Luther, Frank. 1942. *Americans and Their Songs.* New York: Harper and Brothers.

Lutzky, A. Dothan. 1940. "The Francos and the Effects of the Capitulations on the Jews of Aleppo" [in Hebrew]. *Zion* 6:46–79.

Lomax, Alan. 1968. *Folk Song Style and Culture.* Washington: American Association for the Advancement of Science.

Manuel, Peter. 1988. *Popular Musics of the Non-Western World: An Introductory Survey.* New York: Oxford University Press.

Marcus, Abraham. 1989. *Middle East on the Eve of Modernity: Aleppo in the Eighteenth Century.* New York: Columbia University Press.

Marcus, Scott L. 1989. *Arab Music Theory in the Modern Period.* PhD diss., University of California, Los Angeles.

———. 1992. "Modulation in Arab Music: Documenting Oral Concepts, Performance Rules and Strategies." *Ethnomusicology* 36:171–96.

Merriam, Alan P. 1964. *The Anthropology of Music.* Evanston: Northwestern University Press.

Meyer, Leonard B. 1967 [1994]. *Music, the Arts, and Ideas: Patterns and Predictions in Twentieth-Century Culture.* Repr., with a new postlude. Chicago: University of Chicago Press.

McLeod, Norma, and Marcia Herndon. 1980. *The Ethnography of Musical Performance.* Norwood: Norwood Editions.

Milano, Attilio, and Cecil Roth. 1972. "Leghorn." *Encyclopaedia Judaica* 10:1570–73.

Munk, Elie. 1961. *The World of Prayer* [*Olam Ha-Tefilot*]. Trans. Henry Bieberfeld. 2 vols. New York: Philipp Fledheim.

Naff, Alixa. 1983. "Arabs in America: A Historical Overview." In *Arabs in the New World,* ed. Sameer Y. Abraham and Nabeel Abraham, 8–29. Detroit: Wayne State University Press.

———. 1994. "The Early Arab Immigrant Experience." In *The Development of Arab-American Identity,* ed. Ernest McCarus, 23–35. Ann Arbor: University of Michigan Press.

Nelson, Kristina. 1982. "Reciter and Listener: Some Factors Shaping the *Mujawwad* Style of Qur'anic Reciting." *Ethnomusicology* 26:41–47.

———. 1985. *The Art of Reciting the Qur'an.* Austin: University of Texas Press.

Nettl, Bruno. 1978. "Some Aspects of the History of World Music in the Twentieth Century: Questions, Problems, and Concepts." *Ethnomusicology* 22:123–36.

———. 1983. *The Study of Ethnomusicology: Twenty-nine Issue and Concepts.* Urbana: University of Illinois Press.

———. 1985. *The Western Impact on World Music: Change, Adaptation, and Survival.* New York: Schirmer Books.

———. 1992. "Recent Directions in Ethnomusicology." In *Ethnomusicology: An Introduction,* ed. Helen Myers, 375–399. New York: Norton.

Nulman, Macy. 1975. *Concise Encyclopedia of Jewish Music.* New York: McGraw-Hill.

———. 1977–78. "Musical Service of Syrian Synagogue: Its Structure and Design." *Journal of Jewish Music and Liturgy* 2:34–56.

Ortner, Sherry B. 1978. *Sherpas through Their Rituals.* Cambridge: Cambridge University Press.

Papo, Joseph M. 1992. "The Sephardim in North America in the Twentieth Century." In *Sephardim in the Americas,* special issue of *American Jewish Archives* XLIV, no. 1 (1992), guest editor Martin A. Cohen, 267–308.

Picker, Martin. 1980. "Contrafactum, after 1450." *New Grove Dictionary* 4:701.

Pool, David de Sola. 1909. *The Old Jewish Aramaic Prayer: The Kaddish.* Leipzig: Rudolf Haupt. Also appears as *The Kaddish.* 1964. 3rd printing. Jerusalem: Sivan Press.

Powers, Harold S. 1980. "Mode." *New Grove Dictionary* 12:376–450.

———. 1981. "Eastern and Western Concepts of Mode." In *Report of the Twelfth Congress, Berkeley, 1977,* ed. Daniel Heartz and Bonnie Wade, 501–49. Basel: American Musicological Society.

Prell, Riv-Ellen. 1988a. *Prayer and Community: The Havurah Movement and the Recreation of American Judaism.* Detroit: Wayne State University Press.

———. 1988b. "Laughter That Hurts: Ritual Humor and Ritual Change in an American Jewish Community." In *Between Two Worlds: Ethnographic Essays on American Jewry,* ed. Jack Kugelmass, 192–221. Ithaca: Cornell University Press.

Quataert, Donald. 2000. *The Ottoman Empire, 1700*–1922. Cambridge: Cambridge University Press.

Qureshi, Regula B. 1987. "Musical Sound and Contextual Input: A Performance Model for Musical Analysis." *Ethnomusicology* 31:56–86.

Racy, Ali Jihad. 1978. "Arabian Music and the Effects of Commercial Recording." *The World of Music* 20:47–58.

———. 1981. "Music in Contemporary Cairo." *Asian Music* 13:4–26.

———. 1983. "The Waslah: A Compound Form Principle in Egyptian Music." *Arab Studies Quarterly* 5:396–403.

———. 1991a. "Creativity and Ambience: An Ecstatic Feedback Model from Arab Music." *World of Music* 33:7–28.

———. 1991b. "Historical Worldviews of Early Ethnomusicologists: An East-West Encounter in Cairo, 1932." In *Ethnomusicology and Modern Music History,* ed. Stephen Blum, Philip V. Bohlman, and Daniel M. Neuman, 68–91. Urbana: University of Illinois Press.

Rappaport, Roy A. 1979. "The Obvious Aspects of Ritual." *Ecology, Meaning, and Religion,* 173–221. Richmond: North Atlantic Books.

Rashid, Stanley. 2002. "Cultural Traditions of Early Arab Immigrants to New York." In *A Community of Many Worlds: Arab Americans in New York City,* ed. Kathleen Benson and Philip M. Kayal, 74–82. New York: Museum of the City of New York and Syracuse University Press.

Rasmussen, Anne Katharine. 1989. "The Musical Life of Arab Americans: Performance Contexts and Musical Transformation." *Pacific Review of Ethnomusicology* 5:15–33.

———. 1991. *Individuality and Social Change in the Music of Arab-Americans.* Ph.D. dissertation, University of California, Los Angeles.

———. 1997. The Music of Arab Americans: A Retrospective Collection Rounder Records Corp., Rounder CD 1133. One compact disc with 24-page booklet including photos, songs texts with transliteration and translation. Translations by John Eisele and Ali Jihad Racy.

Reyes-Schramm, Adelaida. 1986. "Tradition in the Guise of Innovation: Music Among a Refugee Population." *Yearbook for Traditional Music* 18:91–101.

———. 1989. "Music and Tradition: From Native to Adopted Land through the Refugee Experience". *Yearbook for Traditional Music* 21:25–35.

Robertson, Anne Walters. 1988. "*Benedicamus Domino:* The Unwritten Tradition." *Journal of the American Musicological Society* 41:1–62.

Roseman, Marina. 1991. *Healing Sounds from the Malaysian Rainforest: Temiar Music and Medicine.* Berkeley: University of California Press.

Rosen, Lawrence. 1972. "Muslim-Jewish Relations in a Moroccan City." *International Journal of Middle Eastern Studies* 3:435–449.

Roth, Cecil, and Hayyim Cohen. 1972. "Sephardim." *Encyclopaedia Judaica* 14:1164–77.

Roth, Norman. 1983. "Jewish Reaction to the `*Arabiyya*' and the Renaissance of Hebrew in Spain." *Journal of Semitic Studies* 28:63–84.

Russell, Alexander. 1756. *The Natural History of Aleppo.* 2nd ed. London. 2 vols.

Sáenz-Badillos, Angel. 1993. *A History of the Hebrew Language.* Trans. John Elwolde. Cambridge: University of Cambridge Press.

Saliba, Najib E. 1983. "Emigration from Syria." In *Arabs in the New World,* ed. Sameer Y. Abraham and Nabeel Abraham, 30–43. Detroit: Wayne State University Press.

Sanua, Marianne. 1990. "From the Pages of the *Victory Bulletin:* The Syrian Jews of Brooklyn during World War II." *Yivo Annual* 19:283–330.

Sanua, Victor D. 1977. "Contemporary Studies of Sephardi Jews in the United States." In *A Coat of Many Colors: Jewish Subcommunities in the United States,* ed. Abraham D. Lavender, 281–88. Westport: Greenwood Press.

Schachter, Jonathan. 1991. "NY's Syrian Jews: An Insular Lot." *The Jerusalem Post International Edition.* 22 June, 9.

Scheindlin, Raymond. 1986. *Wine, Women, and Death: Medieval Hebrew Poems on the Good Life.* Philadelphia: Jewish Publication Society.

———. 1991. *The Gazelle: Medieval Hebrew Poems on God, Israel, and the Soul.* Philadelphia: Jewish Publication Society.

Schirmann, Jefim. 1953–54. "Hebrew Liturgical Poetry and Christian Hymnology." *Jewish Quarterly Review* 44:123–61.

———. 1954. "The Function of the Hebrew Poet in Medieval Spain." *Jewish Social Studies* 16:235–52.

Schleifer, Eliyahu. "Idelsohn's Scholarly and Literary Publications: An Annotated Bibliography." *Yuval: Studies of the Jewish Music Research Centre* 5 (1986): 53–180.

Scholem, Gershon. 1972. "Kabbalah." *Encyclopaedia Judaica* 10:489–653.

Schrade, Leo. 1955. "A Fourteenth-Century Parody Mass." *Acta Musicologica* 27:13–25.

Schwartzfuchs, Simon R. 1972. "Alliance Israélite Universelle." *Encyclopaedia Judaica* 2:648–54.

Seeger, Anthony. 1988. *Why Suya Sing: A Musical Anthropology of an Amazonian People.* Cambridge: Cambridge University Press.

Seroussi, Edwin. 1985. "Politics, Ethnic Identity and Music in Israel: The Case of the Moroccan *Bakkashot.*" *Asian Music* 17:32–45.

———. 1989. *Mizimrat Qedem: The Life and Music of R. Isaac Algazi from Turkey.* Jerusalem: Renanot Institute for Jewish Music.

———. 1990a. "Rabbi Israel Najara: Modeler of Hebrew Sacred Singing after the Expulsion from Spain" [In Hebrew]. *Assufot* 4:285–310.

———. 1990b. "Turkish *Maqām* in the Musical Culture of the Ottoman Jews: Sources and Examples." *Israel Studies in Musicology* 5:43–68.

———. 1993a. "The Beginnings of *Bakkashot* Poetry in Jerusalem in the Nineteenth Century" [In Hebrew]. *Pe'amim* 56:116–20.

———. 1993b. "New Directions in the Music of the Sephardic Jews." In *Modern Jews and Their Musical Agendas, Studies in Contemporary Jewry, an Annual,* ed. Ezra Mendelsohn, 9:61–77.

———. 1999. "The Liturgical Music of the Sephardi Jews: East and West." In *Judeo-Spanish Studies X: London 1997,* ed. A. Benaim. London, 289–98.

———. 2000. "Jewish Music III Liturgical and Paraliturgical: Sephardi." *The New Grove Dictionary of Music and Musicians,* ed. Stanley Sadie. New York: Gove's Dictionaries.

Seroussi, Edwin, and Susana Weich-Shahak. 1990–91. "Judeo-Spanish Contrafacts and Musical Adaptations: The Oral Tradition." *Orbis Musicae* 10:164–92.

Shamosh, Amnon. 1979. *My Sister the Bride.* Trans. Judy Levi. Israel: Massada, Peli Printing.

Sharma, Prem Lata. 1981. "*Raga* and *Rasa.*" In *Report of the Twelfth Congress, Berkeley, 1977,* ed. Daniel Heartz and Bonnie Wade, 525–30. Basel: American Musicological Society.

Shaw, Stanford J. 1991. *The Jews of the Ottoman Empire and the Turkish Republic.* New York: New York University Press.

Shelemay, Kay Kaufman. 1988. "Together in the Field: Team Research among Syrian Jews in Brooklyn, New York." *Ethnomusicology* 32:369–84.

———. 1994. "The Study of Sacred Music: A Perspective from Ethnomusicology." In *Reflections on the Sacred: The Musicological Perspective.* Yale Studies in Sacred Music Worship and the Arts, ed. Paul Brainard, 26–33. New Haven: Yale Institute of Sacred Music.

———. 1998. *Let Jasmine Rain Down: Song and Remembrance among Syrian Jews.* Chicago: University of Chicago Press.

Shelemay, Kay Kaufman, and Sarah Weiss. 1985. *Pizmon: Syrian-Jewish Religious and Social Song.* Hohokus, NJ: Meadowlark. ML 105.

Shiloah, Amnon. 1979. *The Theory of Music in Arabic Writings, (c. 900–1900). Répertoire International des Sources Musicales* B/X. München: G. Henle Verlag.

———. 1981. "The Arabic Concept of Mode." *Journal of the American Musicological Society* 34:19–42.

———. 1982. "The Medieval Arab World." In *Proceedings of the World Congress of Jewish Music,*

Jerusalem, 1978, ed. Judith Cohen, 35–36. Tel Aviv: Institute for the Translation of Hebrew Literature.

———. 1992. *Jewish Musical Traditions.* Detroit: Wayne State University Press.

———. 1993. *The Dimension of Music in Islamic and Jewish Culture.* Aldershot, Hampshire, UK.: Variorum.

Shiloah, Amnon, and Erik Cohen. 1983. "The Dynamics of Change in Jewish Oriental Ethnic Music in Israel." *Ethnomusicology* 27:227–52. Reprinted in *Studies in Israeli Ethnicity,* ed. Alexander Weingrod, 317–40. New York: Gordon and Breach.

Shir ush'vaḥa, hallel v'zimrah. 1964–95. New York: Sephardic Heritage Foundation. First edition 1964, second edition 1976, third edition [revised and expanded] 1983, fifth edition 1988, seventh edition 1995.

Siddur kol sassoon. 1995. *Siddur kol Sassoon: The Orot Sephardic Shabbat Siddur.* Ed. Rabbi Eliezer Toledano. Lakewood, NJ: Orot.

Siddur kol ya'akov. 1985. *Siddur kol ya'akov: ke-minhag aram tsoba* [English title page reads: *Siddur Kol Yaakob: Daily Prayer Book According to the Minhag of Aleppo (Aram Soba)*]. Ed. and arranged by Rabbi David Bitton.

———. 1990. *Siddur kol ya'akov: ke-minhag aram tsoba ha-shalem,* [English title page reads: *Siddur Kol Yaakob Hashalem: Daily Prayer Book According to the Minhag of Aleppo (Aram Soba)*]. Ed. Rabbi Shimon H. Alouf, Sam Catton, Dennis Dweck and David A. Tawil. New York: Sephardic Heritage Foundation.

———. 1995. *Siddur kol ya'akov: ke-minhag aram tsoba ha-shalem, Im Targum Anglei* [English title page reads: *Siddur Kol Yaakob Hashalem: Daily Prayer Book According to the Minhag of Aleppo with English Translation*]. Ed. Rabbi Shimon H. Alouf, Sam Catton, and David A. Tawil. New York: Sephardic Heritage Foundation.

Slobin, Mark. 1989. *Chosen Voices: The Story of the American Cantorate.* Urbana: University of Illinois Press.

———. 1992. "Micromusics of the West: A Comparative Approach." *Ethnomusicology* 36:1–87.

———. 1993. *Subcultural Sounds: Micromusics of the West.* Hanover, NH: University Press of New England.

Soloveitchik, Haym. 1994. "Rupture and Reconstruction: The Transformation of Contemporary Orthodoxy." *Tradition* 28:64–130.

Stillman, Norman. 1979. *The Jews of Arab Lands: A History and Source Book.* Philadelphia: Jewish Publication Society.

———. 1991. *The Jews of Arab Lands in Modern Times.* Philadelphia: Jewish Publication Society.

———. 1996. "Middle Eastern and North African Jewries confront Modernity: Orientation, Disorientation, Reorientation." In *Sephardi and Middle Eastern Jewries: History and Culture in the Modern Era,* ed. Harvey E. Goldberg, 59–72. Bloomington: Indiana University Press; New York: Jewish Theological Seminary of America.

Summit, Jeffrey A. 1993. "I'm a Yankee Doodle Dandy?": Identity and Melody at an American *Simḥat Torah* Celebration." *Ethnomusicology* 37:41–62.

———. 2000. *The Lord's Song in a Strange Land: Musica and Identity in Contemporary Jewish Worship.* New York: Oxford University Press.

Sutton, Joseph A. D. 1979. *Magic Carpet: Aleppo in Flatbush, The Story of a Unique Ethnic Jewish Community.* New York: Thayer-Jacoby.

———. 1988. *Aleppo Chronicles: The Story of the Unique Sephardeem of the Ancient Near-East in Their Own Words.* New York: Thayer-Jacoby.

Sweet, Jill Drayson. 1983. "Ritual and Theater in Tewa Ceremonial Performances." *Ethnomusicology* 27:253–69.

Tambiah, Stanley J. 1979. "A Performative Approach to Ritual." *Proceedings of the British Academy* 65:113–69.

Tilmouth, Michael. 1980. "Parody." *New Grove Dictionary* 14:238–39.

Tishby, Isaiah. 1989. *The Wisdom of the Zohar: An Anthology of Texts.* Trans. David Goldstein. 3 vols. New York: Oxford University Press.

Titon, Jeff Todd. 1988. *Powerhouse for God: Speech, Chant, and Song in an Appalachian Baptist Church.* Austin: University of Texas Press.

Touma, Habib Hassan. 1971. "The *Maqam* Phenomenon: An Improvisation Technique in the Music of the Middle East." *Ethnomusicology* 15:38–48.

———. 1976. "Relations between Aesthetics and Improvisation in Arab Music." *World of Music* 18:33–36.

———. 1996. *The Music of the Arabs.* Trans. Laurie Schwartz. Originally published as *Die Musik der Araber* 1989. Portland: Amadeus Press.

Treitler, Leo. 1975. "Centonate Chant: *Übles Flickwerk* or *E pluribus unus*?" *Journal of the American Musicological Society* 28:1–23.

Turino, Thomas. 1993. *Moving Away from Silence: Music of the Peruvian Altiplano and the Experience of Urban Migration.* Chicago: University of Chicago Press.

Turner, Victor W. 1967. *The Forest of Symbols: Aspects of Ndembu Ritual.* Ithaca: Cornell University Press.

———. 1969. *The Ritual Process: Structure and Anti-Structure.* Chicago: Aldine.

———. 1974. "Liminal to Liminoid, in Play, Flow, and Ritual: an Essay in Comparative Symbology." *Rice University Studies* 60:53–92.

van Gennep, Arnold. 1908 [1960]. *The Rites of Passage.* Chicago: University of Chicago Press. Translated from the French *Les rites de passage* 1908 by Monika B. Vizedom and Gabrielle L. Caffee.

Vincent, Joan. 1986. "System and Process, 1974–1985." *Annual Review of Anthropology* 15:99–119.

Wade, Bonnie C. 1976. "Fixity and Flexibility: From Musical Structure to Cultural Structure." *Anthropologica* 18:15–26.

Wagner, Roy. 1984. "Ritual as Communication: Order, Meaning, and Secrecy in Melanesian Initiation Rites." *Annual Review of Anthropology* 13:143–55.

Wasserstrom, Steven M. 1990. "Recent Works on the Creative Symbiosis' of Judaism and Islam." *Religious Studies Review* 16:43–47.

———. 1995. *Between Muslim and Jew: The Problem of Symbiosis Under Early Islam.* Princeton: Princeton University Press.

Werner, Eric. 1976. *A Voice Still Heard . . . The Sacred Songs of the Ashkenazic Jews.* University Park: Pennsylvania State University Press.

Wolf, Richard. 2001. "Emotional Dimensions of Ritual Music Among the Kotas, a South Indian Tribe." *Ethnomusicology* 45/3:379–422.

Wong, Deborah A. 1991. *The Empowered Teacher: Ritual, Performance, and Epistemology in Contemporary Bangkok.* PhD diss., University of Michigan.

Wong, Deborah A., and René T. A. Lysloff. 1991. "Threshold to the Sacred: The Overture in Thai and Javanese Ritual Performance." *Ethnomusicology* 35:315–48.

Ya'ar, Avishai. 1996. *The Cantillation of the Bible—the Aleppo Tradition (Pentateuch).* PhD diss., City University of New York.

Yayama, Kumiko. 2003. *The Singing of Baqqashot of the Aleppo Jewish Tradition in Jerusalem: The Modal System and the Vocal Style.* PhD diss., Hebrew University, Jerusalem.

Yellin, Deena. 1995. "A Legacy Continues." *The Jewish Week* 24 February 1995:16–17.

Yosef, Ovadiah. 1976. *Sefer she'eilot u-teshuvot yabi'a omer* 6:18–21.

———. 1978. *Sefer she'eilot u-teshuvot yehaveh da'at* 2, no. 5:24–28.

Zenner, Walter Paul. 1965. *Syrian Jewish Identification in Israel.* PhD diss., Columbia University.

———. 1968. "Syrian Jews in Three Social Settings." *Journal of Jewish Sociology.* 10:101–20.

———. 1980. "Censorship and Syncretism: Some Social Anthropological Approaches to the Study of Middle Eastern Jews." In *Studies in Jewish Folklore: Proceedings of a Regional Conference of the Association for Jewish Studies Held at the Spertus College of Judaica, Chicago May 1–3, 1977,* ed. Frank Talmage, 377–94. New York: Ktav for the Association for Jewish Studies.

———. 1982a. "Jews in Late Ottoman Syria: External Relations." In Deshen and Zenner, 155–86.

———. 1982b. "Jews in Late Ottoman Syria: Community, Family and Religion." In Deshen and Zenner, 187–209; also appears as "The Inner Life of the Jews in Late Ottoman Syria" [In Hebrew]. *Pe'amim* 3(1979):45–58.

———. 1983. "Syrian Jews in New York Twenty Years Ago." In *Fields of Offerings: Studies in Honor of Raphael Patai,* ed. Victor D. Sanua, 173–93. London: Associated University Presses.

———. 1988. "Aleppo and the Kibbutz in the Fiction of Amnon Shamosh." *Shofar* 6:25–35.

———. 1990. "Bourgeois Immigrants: Syrian Sephardim in Manchester." Paper presented at the Annual Meeting of the American Anthropological Association, 29 November.

———. 2000. *A Global Community: The Jews from Aleppo, Syria.* Detroit: Wayne State University Press.

———. 2002. "The Syrian Jews of Brooklyn." In *A Community of Many Worlds: Arab Americans in New York City,* ed. Kathleen Benson and Philip M. Kayal, 156–69. New York: Museum of the City of New York and Syracuse University Press.

Zenner, Walter P., and Mark Kligman. 2000. "Brooklyn's Syrian Sephardim in the 1990s: Diversification and Ethnic Persistence." In *A Global Community: The Jews from Aleppo, Syria,* 155–76. Detroit: Wayne State University Press.

Zimmels, H. J. 1958. *Ashkenazim and Sephardim: Their Relations, Differences, and Problems as Reflected in the Rabbinical Responsa.* Repr., London: Marla, 1976.

Interviews

Bozo, Yaakov. June 29, 1993. Jerusalem.

Cabasso, Isaac. May 29, 1992. Manhattan.

Catton, Sam. November 22, 1991. Brooklyn.

Lieberman, Rabbi Zevulun. June 26, 1992. Congregation Bet Torah, Brooklyn, New York.

Shrem, Gabriel. January 9, 1986. Interview by Kay Kaufman Shelemay.

Tawil, David. July 29, 1992. Congregation Bet Torah, Brooklyn, New York.

———. June 1, 1993. Congregation Bet Torah, Brooklyn, New York.

———. July 28, 1995. Brooklyn, New York.

———. 6 October 1999. At B'nai Yitachak Synagogue in Brooklyn.

Tawil, Moses. August 21, 1991. Deal, New Jersey.

———. October 6, 1991. Deal, New Jersey.

———. October 22, 1991. Brooklyn, New York.

———. November 14, 1991. Deal, New Jersey.

———. June 6, 1993. Brooklyn, New York.

———. October 6, 1999. B'nai Yitzchak Synagogue, Brooklyn, New York.

Zalta, Benjamin. March 16, 1990. Interview by Kay Kaufman Shelemay.

Index

bar mitzvahs, and performance of Arab music, 55
Barnea, Ezra, 12, 13, 201, 204, 235n22
Barukh she-Amar, 88, 90, 94, 98
bashārif, 53, 102
bashraf, 67, 103
bastah, 104
bastanikā faṣīlah, 62
Bateson, Mary, 75, 80
bayat faṣīlah, 61
bayātī, 67
Be-Fi Yesharim, 80
Beit Kenneset Ades, Jerusalem, 56
Be-Midbar, 172, 173
Bensonhurst, 57
Bereshit, 139
Berikh Shmeh, 232n1
Be-Shallaḥ, 171
beste, 104
biblical passages, 37
bimah, 81, 82, 87, 101, 138, 141, 200, 201
Birkat Kohanim, 100, 101, 138–39, 233n7
Birkhot ha-Shaḥar, 3, 74, 84–85, 155, 158, 201; blessings, scriptural readings, and rabbinic texts, 84; formulaic recitation in *maqām seyga,* 81, 84, 85, 94, 148, 152; Kaddish of, 85, 230n14; *murattal* style, 212
bistah, 104
Bitton, David, 223n6
Bo'i be-Rinah, 117, 118–19, 122
Boilès, Charles Lafayette, 14, 80, 154
borrowing, 17
Bozo, Yaakov, 177, 180, 186, 187, 234n17, 235n18, 236n2
Bradley Beach, 35
brakhot, 95
Brit Mihal, 46, 169. *See also* circumcision
Brooklyn Syrian rabbis and cantors, responses to use of non-Jewish melodies, 70
Brooklyn system of extramusical associations, 167–77; affective associations, 168–69, 176, 185; association of *ajam* with joy, 187; association of different emotions and song-types with *maqāmāt,* 166; association of *hijaz* with death and sadness, 169, 170–71, 179, 182, 187, 188; association of *ḥuseini* with rebukes, intercessions, and warning cries, 182; association of *rast* with happiness, 179; association of *saba* with circumcision, 169–70, 173; *bayat faṣīlah,* 61; comparison of with Israel associations and other studies, 182–87; maintenance of, 202–5; *nahawand,* 186; theoretical associations, 172, 176
Bukharian Jews, 34
Burkholder, J. Peter, 17

Cabasso, Isaac, 4, 5, 56, 68, 115, 229n1; on *ajam,* 171; discussion of *maqām* of the day, 102; on improvisatory sections, 204; involvement of specific members of congregation, 198; photograph of, 57; *pizmonim* knowledge, 226n21; preference for Arab music, 199; on present state of cantorial education, 191, 204; on role of *ḥazzan,* 193; singing of Bo'i be-Rinah, 117; song preferences, 197; strategy of rendering, 198; on Va-Yishlaḥ, 176
Cain, Isaac, 231n34
canonization period, 45
Catton, Sam, 39, 40, 45
Chevalier, Maurice, 19
Chira, Robert, 219n3
choreography, 39, 40
Christian Americans, antisemitic stereotypes of Jews, 36
Christian chant, 164
circumcision, 169–70, 173
Clifford, James, 19
Coalition for the Advancement of Jewish Education (CAJE), 202
coffeehouses, Arab and Turkish, 35, 54, 222n15
Cohen, Eric, 13
concentration, 144

setting of, 102–3; style requirements of, 193; three crowns or pillars, 101, 107, 116, 134–36, 156; use of melodies from same *maqām,* 100
love songs, with *nadawand* and *kurdy,* 166
Luther, Frank, 122

madhab, 126, 132
Magan Avot, 157
Magen David Congregation, 31, 57
Magen David Yeshiva, 57
Magen Yish'i, 121–22, 125, 231n35
Mahalalakh, 107–16
mahrajānāt, 55, 225n7
māhūr, 63, 66, 167, 174
maḥzor, 39
Maḥzor aram-tzoba, 38, 222n5
Maḥzor shelom yerushalayim, ḥlek shelishi, 44
Maimonides, Moses, 24, 227n25
Malakhei marom, 49
maqām ajam, 66, 68, 122, 131; association with happiness, 169, 171, 179; extramusical associations, 166, 167, 168–69, 173; intervallic values of, 60
maqām bayat, 62, 63, 66; and *bakkashot,* 157; and *biblical reading associations,* 177–80; and double parashah, 175; Ha-Shem Melekh, 88; intervallic values of, 60; *intervallic values of,* 60; Israel associations, 179; and principle of variety, 167, 174; and Shaḥarit, 99, 100, 107; and Shemot, 172, 173; in *Shirei Zimrah,* 186; starting pitch, 59; tetrachord, 226n15
maqām bayyātī, 164
maqām hijaz, 66, 175, 226n17; affective associations, 167, 168; association with death and sadness, 169, 170–71, 179, 182, 187, 188; starting pitch, 59; and Tisha b'Av, 173
maqām ḥuseini, 66, 234n13; announces holiday of Shavuot, 173; association with rebukes, intercessions, and warning cries, 181, 182; and biblical readings that refer to the receiving of the Law, 177; and principle of variety, 167; use of for Yitro and Terumah, 174; use of in *Shirei Zimrah,* 186
maqām huzam, 67, 157
maqām kurdy, 59, 62, 65–66, 67
maqām māhūr, 62, 63, 172
maqām māhūr, rast faṣīlah, 116–21
maqām/maqāmāt: aesthetic qualities of, 211; affective associations, 168–69, 185; allow cantor to express individual associations, 176; in Arab musical practices, 164; association with prayers, 166–67; characteristics of, 2; contemporary Arab usage of, 16; conveying of emotions, 165; as defined by modern Arab theorists, 61–64; eight basic, 59–60, 63–64; guide recitation of Qur'an, 164; improvisation of, 4; intervallic value of adjacent notes in eight basic, 60; and Israel biblical reading associations, 177–79; number of, 61, 66; as "open system," 61; practice of, 64–65; primary organizational tool of liturgy, 2, 3, 15; and principle of variety, 174–75; reassociation of meaning through, 213, 214–16; role in adaptation process, 103–33, 207, 214–16; segmentation of, 219n2; in Sephardic liturgical traditions, 12; system as defined and practiced in Brooklyn, 53–72; temporal aspect, 103; theoretical associations, 185; tonal-spatial component, 103, 104; for Torah reading, 153; transformation of melody into liturgy, 215; two tetrachords, 59, 60, 61, 62; used for variety, 176; used in *Shir ush'vaḥa, hallel v'zimrah,* 65; and weekly biblical reading, 161–90. *See also* Brooklyn system of extramusical associations

maqām nahawand, 63, 66, 68, 91, 131, 226n17, 226n22; Barukh she-Amar in, 90; biblical reading associations, 161; characterized by Moses Tawil, 171; Halleluyah, Hallelu Kel be-Kadsho in, 93; intervallic values of, 60; Keter in, 147, 148; lower tetrachord definition, 61; and principle of variety, 167, 174; starting pitch, 59; used by Syrian Jews in Brooklyn, 67; use for sad songs, 166
maqām nawa anthar, 226n17
maqām of the day, 98, 161; establishment before using other *maqāmāt,* 237n9; expresses both drama of heavy sections and contrasting character of light sections, 188; *ḥazzan* adherence to, 202, 209; melody of *pizmon* basis for on holiday, 173; in Shaḥarit, 100, 192; sonic element that differentiates a distinctive musical sound, 215–16; use of, 101–2
maqām rahaw, 179
maqām rahaw nawa, 66, 69, 167, 174, 182, 226n22
maqām rast, 66, 91, 106, 107, 115, 166, 227n24; association with happiness, 179; and *bakkashot,* 157; in Bereshit, 172; biblical reading associations, 161; first *maqām* in Arab music theory, 167; Ḥannun marom Melekh ozer, 139; intervallic values of, 60; and Kaddish, 126, 131–33; and light and heavy texts, 136; most commonly associated with Shemot, 172; opening of each of five books of the Bible, 167, 172; and *seyga,* 68; starting pitch, 59; tetrachords, 62, 113; theoretical association exclusive to, 168; used by Syrian Jews in Brooklyn, 67; in Va-Yikra, 172
maqām saba, 66, 117, 139, 181; association with circumcision, 169–70, 173; association with sadness, 179, 182, 187; intervallic value of, 60; and Kedoshim, 175; most flexible of four *maqāmāt* associated with affect and theory, 185; starting pitch, 59
maqām seyga, 66, 181, 227n24, 235n27; and *bastanik,* 64; Birkhot ha-Shaḥar in, 84; lower tetrachord definition, 61; *maqām* for biblical reading, 174; and principle of variety, 74; and *rast,* 68; Shema in, 75, 97, 99, 101, 153, 156; starting pitch, 59; Torah reading in, 140, 155, 157, 167, 181, 188; as unifying element of Sabbath service, 152–53; Zemirot in, 82, 87, 88–89, 89, 91, 92, 93, 137, 152, 155
Marcus, Abraham, 26, 27, 53
Marcus, Scott, 59, 62, 67, 104, 164, 165–66, 167 188, 225n13, 225n14, 226n15, 226n17, 226n22, 226n23, 230n21; "Arab Music Theory in the Modern Period," 61
Margarita, 122
mawwāl, 67, 102–3
medieval mystics, 144
melismatic embellishments, 92, 115, 116, 121, 126, 131, 140, 147, 151
melodic association, 173–74, 176
Menaged, Eliyahu, 56
Meyer, Leonard, 17
Middle Eastern Jews: musical practices, 12; view of by historians of past, 23
Middle Eastern music. *See* Arab music
Middle Eastern–style restaurants, New York, 35–36
"middle-of-the-road Orthodoxy," 32
Mif'alot elokim, 49
Mi-Kets, 176
Mi-mits'rayim, 99
mimuna, 18
minhag aram-tsoba, 38
minhagim, 21
Mishhah, 37
Mizmor le-David, sung by Moses Tawil, 142
Mizmor Shir le-Yom ha-Shabbat, 80, 91
Mizraḥim Jews (Musta'rab, Arabized), 24
"modal ecstasy," 195, 214
modeling, 17
"modes of action," 75

modules, 115, 121
mordents, 105
motifs, 113, 115–16, 121
Mount Sinai, 137
muḥayyar, 66
mujawwad, 212
Murād, Zakī, 116, 231n30
murattal, 212
Musaf, 3, 74, 137, 140, 141–43, 158, 233n7; alternation of singing and reciting of texts, 81; Amidah for, 80; Amidah preceded and followed by Kaddish, 141; continuation of after Keter, 148, 151; informality, 83; Kedushah for, 145; Keter of, 143; *maqām* that contrasts with Shaḥarit, 153; *murattal* style, 212; musical treatment, 143; recitation formula, 152
music: in Aleppo, 53–54; and culture contact, 216–18; forbidden for religious use in Islamic practice, 209, 212; and meditation, 145; and prayer, 11; and prophecy, 145; and ritual process, 13–15; role in mysticism, 144–45. *See also* Arab music; Syrian Sabbath morning service
musical performance: Arab practices, 15, 16, 189; effect of rabbi's sermon on, 201–2; ethnography of, 13–14
music and text, interaction of: in *pizmonim*, 48–49; in Sabbath morning service, 2, 15–18, 153, 154, 155, 157, 211; in Shaḥarit, 136, 209; in Shema, 158
music culture contact, 8, 21, 207, 208, 216–17; product of, 20
muwashashāḥ, 53, 67, 102–3
"muzikah," 48–49, 49
"My Country 'Tis of Thee," 198
mysticism: in Aleppo Jewish life, 27; feature of Syrian and Mizraḥi, 72; and Keter, 143–48; role of music in, 144–45

Naff, Alixa, 29, 31
Nahari, 194
nahawand faṣīlah, 62, 64
nahawand pizmonim, 224n24
Najara, Israel, 69–70
Nak'dishakh, 143, 146; "heavy" music, 134; highlight of the Amidah, 156
nakrīz faṣīlah, 62
nationalistic songs, with *ajam*, 166
nawa anthar faṣīlah, 62, 64
Nelson, Kristina, 188, 189, 213, 237n6
Nettl, Bruno, 14, 20, 163, 217
Nishmat Kol-Ḥai, 95, 101, 107–16, 134–35, 136, 198; addition to Shaḥarit on Sabbath, 97, 98; both fixed and free elements, 113; "heavy" music, 134; in Syrian prayer books, 40; text and melodic modules used in, 113, 114; textual translation for, 112
No'aḥ, 179
non-Jewish melodies: Hasidic response to, 69; used for liturgical and paraliturgical purposes, 69
Nulman, Macy, 143, 220n1, 224n17, 225n15, 234n8, 235n22
nusaḥ, 164

Obadia, Hakki, 5, 219n5, 225n8
"The Obvious Aspects of Ritual" (Rappaport), 154
octave, 113
octave change, 105
olam haba, 215
ornaments *(zakhārif)*, 105, 106
Ortner, Sherry B., 218
"O Tannenbaum," 49
Ottoman Empire, 23; conquering of Greater Syria and Egypt, 24; golden age of, 25; need for financial support, 27

pan-Arab folk style, 55
pan-Arab *maqām* system, 55
pan-"eastern-Arab" usage, 62
paraliturgical texts, 45–48, 210, 211
paraphrase, 17
Parashat Terumah, 144
parody, 16–17
participant observation, 4, 6, 8
passing tones, 121
pathet, 164

Zemirot, 3, 85–94, 151, 158, 201; in Ashkenazic practice, 228n5; comparison of weekday and Sabbath renderings, 85, 86–87; contrasting *maqām,* 82, 153; design of, 89–90; formulaic singing in *maqām seyga,* 74–75, 81, 82, 88, 93, 137, 152, 155, 157; Ha-Shem Melekh, 87, 89, 94; Lamnatae'ah Mizmor le-David, 89; liturgical section on Sabbath, 86–87; *maqām* of the day, 94, 101; Mizmor Shir le-Yom ha-Shabbat, 80; *murattal* style, 212; primarily biblical texts, 155; role of *ḥazzan,* 82, 92, 94; "songs," 85
Zenner, Walter Paul, 14, 21, 23, 26, 30, 32, 34, 35, 36, 218, 220n2, 221n16
zingerān, 64
Zion, Yeḥezkiel, 5–6, 56, 117, 140, 192–93, 236n6
Zionism, rise of, 28
Zohar, 143, 144, 145–46, 227n35